Not Just Batman's Butler

Not Just Batman's Butler

The Autobiography of Alan Napier

Alan Napier
with James Bigwood

McFarland & Company, Inc., Publishers
Jefferson, North Carolina

LIBRARY OF CONGRESS CATALOGUING-IN-PUBLICATION DATA

Napier, Alan, 1903–1988.
Not just Batman's butler : the autobiography of Alan Napier /
Alan Napier with James Bigwood.
    p.   cm.
Includes bibliographical references and index.

ISBN 978-1-4766-6287-9 (softcover : acid free paper) ∞
ISBN 978-1-4766-2289-7 (ebook)

1. Napier, Alan, 1903–1988. 2. Actors—Great Britain—Biography.
I. Bigwood, James. II. Title.

PN2598.N25A3 2015   791.4302'8092—dc23   [B]   2015033316

BRITISH LIBRARY CATALOGUING DATA ARE AVAILABLE

© 2015 James Bigwood and Jennifer Nichols. All rights reserved

*No part of this book may be reproduced or transmitted in any form
or by any means, electronic or mechanical, including photocopying
or recording, or by any information storage and retrieval system,
without permission in writing from the publisher.*

On the cover: Alan Napier as Alfred Pennyworth in *Batman*, 1966-1968,
(20th Century–Fox Television/ABC/Photofest)

Printed in the United States of America

McFarland & Company, Inc., Publishers
Box 611, Jefferson, North Carolina 28640
www.mcfarlandpub.com

Acknowledgments

James Bigwood

First and foremost, obviously, thanks go to Alan Napier (1) for writing his autobiography and (2) for allowing me to read it forty years ago. Second, thanks to his daughter Jennifer and her husband Bob Nichols for tracking down the manuscript and entrusting it to me. Other members of the Napier family who have been generous with their time, memories and photographs include Alan's grandchildren Christy Nichols and David Nichols as well as his brother's grandchildren, Julian Mulock and Jane Talbot-Smith and his sister's adopted son, Colin Napier. Thanks also to Alan's step-grandson, Brian Forster, Sally Boyd (Gip's niece) and her husband, Tom.

Alan's friends and acquaintances (or their descendants) who kindly participated in the project include Gary Butcher, Jenny Carver, Peter Carver, Stephanie Carver, Virginia Carver, Denny Cline, Greg Mank, Nancy Timmons, Jeffrey Vance, and Wally Wingert.

A number of Alan's professional associates were kind enough to share their memories; they include Ralph Bakshi, Don Brown, Booth Coleman, Yvonne Craig, Malcolm Davis, Gordon Davidson, Judi Davidson, Sam Denham, Leslie Easterbrook, George Englund, Joan Fontaine, Sir John Gielgud, John Gore, Rosemary Harris, David Hedison, Tippi Hedren, Linda Kay Henning, Ellen Holly, Arte Johnson, Kathy Kersh, Walter Koenig, Bernie Kopell, Fred Krug, Harvey Laidman, Angela Lansbury, Linda Lawson, Hal Lifson, Norman Lloyd, Faye Marlowe, Joe Russo, Lorenzo Semple, Jr., Christopher Severn, Winston Severn, Robert Hays Smith, Inga Swenson, Austin Trevor, Joyce Van Patten, Peggy Webber, and Jon Whiteley.

Others who never had the opportunity to meet Alan, but who kindly helped in various ways to insure the project's completion include: Danielle Bass, Peter Bigwood, Greg dePolney, Fred Guida, Bob Leszczak, Kay Chin Lim, Lars Lindgren, Charlie Morrow, Penny Peine, Vivien Straus, Jill Sullivan, Doug Youngkin and Ken Waissman.

Thanks too to the following institutions and individuals: The Victoria and Albert Theatre and Performance Archives, the late Susan Dalton and the Wisconsin Center for Film and Theatre Research, Heather Romaine at the University of Bristol Theatre Collection, Shaun Hayes at the American Heritage Center at the University of Wyoming, Jamie A. Simmons at the Texarkana Museums System Archives, Mark Eccleston at Cadbury Research Library Special Collections at the University of Birmingham, Dale Stinchcomb at the Harvard Theatre Collection at the Houghton Library at Harvard University, Annabel Valentine at the Roy Waters Theatre Collection at the Royal Holloway Archives and Special Collections at the University of London, Faye Thompson and Kristine Krueger at the Margaret

Herrick Library at the Academy of Motion Picture Arts and Sciences, David K. Frazier at the Lilly Library at Indiana University, Kathleen Dickson at the British Film Institute National Archives, Mark Quigley at the UCLA Film and Television Archive, Zoram Sinobad at the Motion Picture Broadcasting and Recorded Sound Division of the Library of Congress, Tom Lisanti at the Billy Rose Theatre Division of the New York Public Library for the Performing Arts, Philip Hallman and Kathleen Dow at the University of Michigan Special Collections Library, Pam DeTilla at the San Luis Obispo County Library, Gertrud Fischer at the Osterreichisches Theatermuseum in Vienna, Clase-Ove Standberg at the Stockholm University Library, Pernilla Karlsson at the Götesburgs Stadsmuseum, Dag Kronlund at the Royal Dramatic Theatre in Stockholm, Helen Roberts at the Huddersfield Daily Examiner, Vicky Green at the Southampton Central Library, Fiona Bridge at Packwood Hough School, and Ingemar Perup at Bonniers Förlag Publications. Thanks also to Photofest, Getty Images, Biddy Hayward at ArenaPAL and Alex Teslik at Eileen Darby Images, Inc.

The letter from Alan Napier to Reginald Tate dated November 29, 1934, is housed in the Reginald Tate Collection, University of Bristol Theatre Collection. The letter from Alan Napier to Orson Welles dated April 13, 1945, is courtesy the Lilly Library, Indiana University, Bloomington, Indiana. The letter from Alan Napier to William Dozier dated January 24, 1968, is housed in the William Dozier Papers, American Heritage Center, University of Wyoming. The *Heartbreak House* Production Essay and Program Note (Appendix B) is housed at the University of Michigan Special Collections Library, Richard Wilson-Orson Welles Collection. Dorothy Sayers' letters concerning the production of *The Zeal of Thy House* are housed at the Marion E. Wade Center at Wheaton College, Illinois, and are included in *The Letters of Dorothy L. Sayers: Volume Two: 1937–1943, From Novelist to Playwright*, chosen and edited by Barbara Reynolds. St. Martin's Press, New York. 1998.

Table of Contents

Acknowledgments (James Bigwood)   v

Introduction (James Bigwood)   1

Part One: Birmingham

Prologue: The Reason Why   6
1. Nanny and Mother Do Their Best   7
2. The Family Click   11
3. Napierolatry   15
4. Chamberlain in Excelsis   19
5. The Grove—Cast Iron   23
6. Tennal Grange—Non-Ferrous   29
7. Heritage   42
8. Trailing Clouds of Glory   48
9. Intimations of Immorality   56
10. A Talent Is Discovered   59
11. Fish Out of Water   66
12. Into the Swim   70

Part Two: London

13. A Year of Grace   74
14. Benevolent Deity   81
15. Where Is Fancy Bred?   88
16. Breakthrough   97
17. Bitter Sweet Days   107
18. Marie Tempest and Gerald du Maurier   114
19. A Lesson in Drama   129
20. Near Misses and Sweet Aloes   132
21. On the Rocks   145

22.	Ibsen, Shaw and Sayers	149
23.	Tomorrow to Fresh Woods	160
24.	Filling Quotas (James Bigwood)	167
25.	Crossing the Pond	173

Part Three: America

26.	From Sea to Shining Sea	176
27.	A Toe in the Door	181
28.	Old Friends and New Experiences	185
29.	Broadway	192
30.	Down to Earth	196
31.	Meeting Gip	199
32.	Take One (James Bigwood)	204
33.	Marrying Gip	208
34.	Take Two (James Bigwood)	217
35.	Dogs	222
36.	Take Three (James Bigwood)	224
37.	Mountains	238
38.	Take Four (James Bigwood)	241
39.	Don't Talk Politics to Adolphe Menjou	244
40.	Give My Regards to Broadway	251
41.	Take Five (James Bigwood)	265
42.	Family Affairs	273
43.	Friends	278
44.	Television (James Bigwood)	286
45.	Journey's End	294
46.	More Television (James Bigwood)	297
47.	Patriarch	306
48.	*Batman*	307
49.	Alfred the Butler (James Bigwood)	308
50.	After *Batman*	314
51.	The Vortex (James Bigwood)	320
52.	Back to Work (James Bigwood)	323
53.	Hitchcock, Hubbard and Hawkins (James Bigwood)	331
54.	Family and Friends (James Bigwood)	335

55.	One Role Too Many (James Bigwood)	339
56.	Writing (James Bigwood)	340
57.	Last Hurrah (James Bigwood)	343
58.	Playing Oneself (James Bigwood)	348
59.	*Batman* Redux (James Bigwood)	353
60.	The End (James Bigwood)	357
61.	Memorial (James Bigwood)	359

Appendix A. Acting Credits 361
    ON THE STAGE   361
    ON THE BIG SCREEN (FILMS)   368
    ON THE SMALL SCREEN (TELEVISION)   372

Appendix B. How to Approach a Production of Shaw's Heartbreak House (Alan Napier) 375

Index 379

Introduction

James Bigwood

Alan Napier had appeared in close to 100 films by the time I first became aware of him—twice a week, starting in 1966—as Alfred Pennyworth, faithful butler to millionaire Bruce Wayne in the legendary ABC television series, *Batman*. I was not alone. Despite his busy twenty-five year Hollywood screen career, this was how most Americans came to know him. Unlike many character actors who established themselves in the public's mind by playing countless variations on the same role (brilliantly, I hasten to add), Alan was a chameleon. Rarely the same in appearance from film to film, he was only occasionally requested to present his quite handsome features to the camera unadorned by wigs, prosthetics or crepe hair. As a result, unlike most of his colleagues, he was never typecast, but, conversely, he never became famous. Until *Batman*. Nearsighted all his life, Alan was allowed by producer William Dozier to wear his own very thick eyeglasses on the show, making Alfred appear almost bug-eyed and establishing his look to such an extent that all Alan had to do to become unrecognizable was remove them. This he rarely did. In addition to needing them to see, he had enough of an actor's ego to take immense pleasure in public recognition after decades of professional anonymity. In fact, while he varied his facial hair significantly in his remaining years, from mutton-chop sideburns to full beards to various sizes and types of moustaches, he kept the same style of eyeglasses until almost the end of his life.

My next encounter with Alan Napier was in 1973, while compiling program notes for a high school production of Noël Coward's musical, *Bitter Sweet*. One hundred and twenty episodes of *Batman* had firmly embedded his name—listed third in the opening credits after Adam West and Burt Ward—in my memory, so I was quick to notice him listed in the cast of the original 1929 London production of the play. Yet I was confused. He had apparently played the Marquis of Shayne, a character described in Coward's script as "a distinguished old man." In 1929? Distinguished, yes, but "old" in 1929 would have put him in his nineties in *Batman*, which Alfred definitely had not been. Perhaps I had come across Alan Napier, Sr., who had eventually produced an Alan Napier, Jr.? A reasonable assumption, but an incorrect one. Further research revealed that there was only one Alan Napier, and that he had played the sixty-five-year-old Marquis of Shayne for two and a half years on London's West End starting at the ripe old age of 26.

It would be another two years before I met Alan face-to-face. I had profiled his fellow Brit, Norma Varden, for Leonard Maltin's *Film Fan Monthly*, a magazine which specialized in articles on lesser-known Hollywood actors. She had acted with Alan in seven features (and an episode of *Batman*; although they didn't share any scenes) and was kind enough to tell me how to contact her friend, who I hoped to profile in my second article for Maltin.

Alan very graciously invited me to his home for an interview. I started by revealing how I had tracked him down. "Dear Norma!" he interjected. "You've reminded me that we were both in *Mademoiselle Fifi*!" I nodded, that film being one of the few titles from either his or Norma's *oeuvre* that I had actually seen in those pre–VCR days. "The awful thing is I don't keep very good records," he continued, "It's all in my memory. I *know* that I've been in over a hundred films, yet if I can remember fifteen of them I'm doing well. But then something crops up and it comes back into the memory." He held up a thick bound typescript and went on. "I've written an autobiographical work full of fascinating stories" (the word "fascinating" was modestly surrounded by verbal quotation marks), "but unfortunately, since I've never committed a major crime and I'm not known to have slept with any famous actresses, it's very difficult to get it published." Then, conspiratorially, "I've not tried very hard actually, but I had to do research for it so it sort of jogs my memory."

"Dear Norma! You've reminded me that we were both in *Mademoiselle Fifi*!" Alan Ward, Jason Robards, Sr., Alan Napier, Norma Varden and Fay Helm in *Mademoiselle Fifi* (RKO, 1944). Collection of James Bigwood.

Alan allowed me to borrow a copy of the full manuscript after that initial interview (there were actually three volumes in all) and my profile was completed just in time for Leonard Maltin's announcement that he was ceasing publication of *Film Fan Monthly*. This turned out to be a blessing in disguise. My article was accepted by *Films in Review* instead, but, due to a backlog of material, was not published until 1979. This required my staying in touch with Alan in order to keep the piece up to date. When the profile finally appeared, he was typically generous. "What a splendid job!" he wrote me. "Conscientiously researched, admirably composed and magnificently illustrated. I congratulate you and I thank you. I shall keep several copies on hand and when anyone asks me 'What have you done?' thrust *Films in Review* (30th anniversary edition, no less!) into his or her hand." I was grateful for his praise, of course, but couldn't help thinking that my sixteen-page article was a poor substitute for the three-volume autobiography that I had been allowed to read.

It is now more than twenty-five years since Alan's death and, thanks to the generosity of his daughter Jennifer Nichols, his autobiography is finally seeing the light. I am honored that she was willing to entrust the process to me. I have added some annotations into Alan's text (in *italics*, or occasionally brackets when needed for clarity), made minor cuts and provided chapters that fill in some gaps, most importantly the fifteen years between Alan's completion of the manuscript in 1973 and his death in 1988, but this is primarily Alan Napier's story in Alan Napier's words. And a remarkable story it is.

Part One

Birmingham

Prologue:
The Reason Why

What constitutes success for an actor must be a matter of opinion. But if playing a great number of good parts, both classical and modern, and often being generously praised by eminent critics and the public at large; if earning a good enough living to marry twice, pay alimony once, raise a family, live always in pleasant surroundings and finally own a beautiful home with no debts outstanding and money in the bank constitutes a modest level of success, then I may lay claim to it.

Above all, I had the privilege, first in the theatre in London and later in Hollywood, of playing good parts with the great players of a golden age as well as with the stars of my own generation. I imagine that a tennis player who competes at Wimbledon and Forest Hills, even if he seldom gets beyond the semi-finals, is justified in feeling that he is a top flight player.

The odds against success were staggering and it was not achieved by any particular force of character on my part. Indeed, I have always lacked drive, pertinacity and toughness. *(John Gielgud may have put it best when he called Alan "a very charming, beautifully mannered man, but much too modest for his own good.")* The success came about by the good auspices of God, Destiny, the Life Force or whatever one may care to call those evident forces for which one has no explanation.

"The fault, dear Brutus, is not in our stars,
But in ourselves, that we are underlings."

We nod our heads sagely. But maybe Cassius has not said the last word of wisdom! In my case, the merit assuredly lay largely in my stars and not in myself that I did not end up the most miserable of underlings. I had a bit of luck due me because the circumstances of my early years were not favorable; but the chain of happy accidents by which a woefully inhibited, stammering, skinny, 6 foot 5 inch, hopelessly myopic beanpole became an instantly successful actor called for the larkiest starshine, the most solicitous life force, the unlikeliest destiny or the most benevolent Deity.

I have known people—we all have—who are positively dogged by misfortune. Their stories make sad reading. I write this account of my dogging by good fortune in the hope that it will be a kind of glad tidings.

We all remember the past subjectively. I tell my story as I recall it. Others concerned will doubtless remember it differently. I ask their forgiveness for whatever may seem to them to be distortions of the truth. None are deliberate.

1

Nanny and Mother Do Their Best

My mother is going upstairs, up the broad, Morris-carpeted, oak stairs at Tennal Grange for her afternoon rest. I go up with her, holding her hand. Her dress is full and white and brushes the stairs, rustling. Four stairs, turn right; eight stairs, turn right; eight stairs and we are on the landing outside mother's room. Suddenly I cannot bear to be parted from her and hug her knees in a passion of love. "Be careful, dear! Mother must have her rest." I hug her more tightly. She takes my little hands and pulls them apart. I start to cry. "Don't be a Silly-Billy, now. Nanny will bring you down to see mother after tea." The bedroom door closes and I sit on the top stair in the bright windy landing and sob and sob.

There was the ceremonial limp kiss when we went in to see her in bed in the morning—mother always had breakfast in bed—and the ceremonial kiss when we said goodnight. There was no pleasure attached to it as my mother became older and iller, quite the contrary. Perhaps this inability to communicate love by touch of lip and hand is the saddest deprivation; and since it is, or should be, at our mothers' knee and breast that we learn the give and take of love, it is an inability that tends to be handed on from generation to generation.

The only time I remember her making a physical gesture of love was when I was recovering from a nearly fatal attack of appendicitis. I had been at boarding school in the country. I was twelve years old and my tummy ache not taken seriously for far too long. A surgeon was rushed out from the big city just in time. Drainage tubes had to be left in the incision which consequently had taken a long time to heal, eventually forming what I think is called proud flesh over the wound. My mother had not thought fit to make the journey, less than 20 miles, at the time of the operation; nor did she visit me during my two weeks of convalescence at school. One morning, however, when I was back home at Tennal Grange and the wound was being dressed, she determined to be present. Now I didn't at all mind the hospital nurse (in those days the upper classes had their births, deaths and illnesses at home) exposing my stomach or bed-washing me all over, but the idea of my mother seeing me half naked embarrassed me intensely. And when she referred to my belly as "a dear little hollow" and stretched out her hand to touch it, I nearly died of shame as I squirmed away in revulsion. She must have been suddenly moved; it had been a very close call and here was this skinny little flesh of her flesh…

I'm sure she thought that she loved us and wanted to do right by us; but I doubt if she really ever loved anyone but herself—and that in a not very demonstrative way. To be sure she loved "The Family" as people love when they say "I love God." God and "The Family" were much the same thing to mother; neither could do wrong.

Her last illness, which happened when I was married and in my thirties, was sudden. I was surprised one morning when a nurse called me on the telephone to say, "If you want to see your mother alive, you'd better hurry." I took my time shaving. I was still not equipped for the great experiences of love and death. When I reached her flat she was dead. She lay at peace. I could only think that it was a blessing for everyone that it was over.

It is my brother's story that I am the unwanted result of my father's last frustrated effort to assert his marital rights. I'm sure my mother never told him this. Did my father? It could well be true, however. My mother was never able to do more than endure the sexual act; she simply had no taste for any physical expression of love. With every advantage and the best of intentions, she failed entirely in life both as wife and mother. My conception was, *sui generis*, unwelcome; also I think the carrying, the labor and the birth. Strangely, I do remember my mother telling me once that all the pains of childbirth were rewarded when suddenly a new, little living being was lying there in mother's arm. Had she read this in a book? Had she felt it for Mark, her first born? Did she tell it to me to say obliquely "You are wanted?"

However that may be, born I was on January 7, 1903. Alan William Napier-Clavering. There was no attempt to breastfeed me, and as soon as she was well enough to travel my mother went off on a cruise to Egypt, up the Nile, for her health. Apparently, I cried with maddening persistence for five weeks until she returned, when it was discovered that my bottle formula had been inadequate. I suppose that Nanny was giving me my bottle; she was not a trained nurse and was easily overawed by professionals. Whatever instructions were given her she would carry out punctiliously. Hers not to reason why. So for the first five weeks of my life I did not have my mother's arms or breasts to comfort or warm me, nor enough nourishment to satisfy my basic needs. It would never have occurred to my parents that this constituted any particular deprivation and I am sure that nothing in particular was done to make up for it. With more to my bottle I stopped crying and became in due course a quiet, docile, rather withdrawn little boy with a permanently voracious appetite.

The story of the upper-class parent leaving her child to the care of a nurse is a familiar one. It was true of Winston Churchill, it was true of the Russian poet Pushkin, it has been true of innumerable children born to the British rulers of India. What happens to the child must depend enormously on the nature of the nurse.

Nanny, Miss Margaret Dodd, was tiny with bright pink cheeks and bright, black button eyes. I cannot remember her being anything but kind and loving; firm when necessary but never harsh. Indeed she—and to a lesser degree the other servants and a few chosen uncles, aunts and cousins—was my only source and recipient of love in my early childhood. When told that Nanny was to leave us I remember sorrow and desolation welling up in my heart like a black tide. I remember watching her from my bed in the green-linoleumed night nursery as she wrestled amicably with my elder brother Mark. She never wrestled with my sister. Though, to be sure, I do remember, also from my bed, seeing obstinate Molly, her arms glued to her sides, refusing to put on her clean Sunday combinations of prickly wool and Nanny fighting, red-faced, to force Molly's rebellious little hands into the sleeves.

Mark soon transferred his craving for physical domination onto me. As he was five years my senior, I was compelled throughout my growing years to fight an endless and eventually embittered losing battle.

Mark, Molly and Alan Napier-Clavering with their mother, the former Millicent Mary Kenrick, circa 1907. Courtesy Julian Mulock.

Molly was born halfway between us and never quite belonged in either camp. It was not her nature to belong in any camp. My father used to call her, after the Kipling story, "the cat that walks by itself." Molly and I would come close and then drift apart. At times she would feel that I was too young and enjoy promoting herself to Mark's level. But it was all very cool—I don't remember any of the three of us hugging or kissing. That sort of thing simply wasn't done in our family, though in the Family, in the larger sense—the Family that mother really loved—it sometimes was.

"The Family" was the great Kenrick-Chamberlain clan that ran the city of Birmingham for over fifty years and later sought to run the nation.

2

The Family Click

The meeting and mating of Kenricks and Chamberlains may truly be regarded as an historical chronicle of considerable consequence. It is also an entertaining tale.

Archibald Kenrick I, younger son of a Welsh landowner of some standing, came to Birmingham toward the end of the 18th century. He had been apprenticed in the iron trade and, after a false start in buckles, found his true métier in cast-iron, developing the famous Kenrick cast-iron saucepan, which was to be the family's staple product through thick and thin for a hundred and fifty years. Tenacity was perhaps the family's dominant characteristic; they were certainly not adventurous and when change in manufacturing procedure was desirable, it was from outsiders that it came. There was a Mr. Ryland for instance who brought with him a patent for stamping saucepan lids and other useful innovations. Though, to be sure, he was a cousin of sorts and later played his part in the Kenrick-Chamberlain population explosion.

By the middle of the 19th century the Kenricks were well established, citizens of consequence in the community yet socially limited by reason of their religious beliefs. All over England there tended to be a social gap between Church and Chapel; gentry were Church. But for the Kenricks there was a chasm—they were Unitarians. Conventional people did not mix with Unitarians, whom they regarded as heathen. "After all, my dear, they don't believe in the divinity of Christ, the Immaculate Conception, or the Holy Ghost!" My father affirmed that he once heard the Pastor of the Unitarian Church in Birmingham preach a sermon in which he proved to his own satisfaction that if there were a Holy Ghost it must have been a woman.

Nature abhors a vacuum, and into this social vacuum poured another Unitarian family. The Chamberlains started migrating from London to Birmingham about the time the Kenricks achieved business stability and moderate affluence. They had been only shoemakers and the Kenricks might perhaps feel themselves to be socially superior. My grandfather William, grandson of the original Archibald, certainly did. But a natural affinity, perhaps a call to destiny, would not be denied. The two families started intermarrying wholesale, with genetically propitious results. To the solid tenacity of the Kenricks, the Chamberlains brought imagination and vivacity. The blood was warm, lively and ready for anything. It also modified a taint of in-growing eccentricity which diverted your typical Kenrick from public life. In a word, Chamberlains provided the yeast that enabled the Family to rise. And rise it did with startling rapidity.

The Family's financial fortunes were secured when Joe Chamberlain and a shrewd Birmingham businessman called Nettlefold virtually cornered the English screw market by importing a patented manufacturing process from America. Hard-core Kenricks mostly stuck to their saucepans, but the Family at large spread into various branches of the metal products for which Birmingham was famous. As their wealth increased so did their prestige, their social acceptability, and their participation in public affairs.

At first the field of battle was Birmingham. The Family simply took it over with Joseph as their unquestioned leader. He municipalized everything—water, gas, light, transportation. It was the best run city in the nation and positively socialistic. As long as Joe was mayor and the Family dominated the council, no private enterprise could possibly have been better run. Unless, of course, this *was* a private enterprise… One day, at a meeting of the city fathers, a resentful councilor snarled, "Y'ere all a family click!" Thereafter, on great occasions at Highbury, Joe's stately suburban home, the Family toast, proposed with a touch of smug self-satisfaction, was carefully mispronounced as "The Click."

Then Birmingham became too small; it had to be the nation. The irresistible Joseph entered Parliament as a dangerous radical—practically a Republican. My grandfather Kenrick, an innate conservative, was swept into Parliament on Joe's coattails—almost by mistake one might say. He never uttered a word for fifteen years (Correction. On one occasion he rose to declare that, if he were not permitted to employ 13-year-old children at The Works at West Bromwich, he would either have to employ lunatics or close down!), in recognition of which he was made a Privy Councilor, which entitled him to be addressed as "The Honorable" and to attach a cockade to his coachman's top hat. Rapidly, Joseph rose to the top. Man of the people and charismatic public speaker, he became a potential successor to the great Mr. Gladstone as leader of the Liberal Party. But the indestructible Gladstone failed to make way; and in the course of time vaster fields for the exercise of power took shape before Joe's inner eye. The vision of Empire, aglitter with the gold and diamonds of South Africa, transformed Joe Chamberlain into the Great Imperialist—advocate of a United British Africa from Cape Town to Cairo and a *Pax Britannica*, supported by Imperial Tariff Protection, enveloping the world. It is easy now to see the impracticability, the immorality even, of peace built on colonial subjugation. Indeed there was always a strong body of English public opinion (contemptuously called "Little Englanders") opposed to the idea. Wilfrid Scawen Blunt, the poet rebel, denounced "that scoundrel Chamberlain!" and warned in a poem about Egypt, "Ye have sown the wind and ye shall reap the whirlwind."

But as Secretary for the Colonies at the time of Queen Victoria's Diamond Jubilee, Joe Chamberlain was a nation's hero, with leadership of the Conservative party his to assume at will. There was no hurry; he would choose the right occasion. And then a massive stroke brought his astounding career to an end. It was a terrible setback for the Family but not a knockout blow. He left a legend and two sons.

Austen was the favored one, but he missed the Premiership on a point of honor at the end of World War I. He stuck by Lloyd George, a Liberal, in whose coalition Cabinet he sat throughout the latter half of the war. I remember the snort of contempt with which my mother greeted the news that Bonar Law, "a little Scottish attorney" had "stolen" Austen's place. A year or so later, as Foreign Secretary (he looked the part par excellence) Austen became a Knight of the Garter *(as well as a Nobel Peace Prize winner)* for engineering the perfectly valueless Locarno Pact with Mussolini, and left the center of the stage open for his younger half-brother.

Joe had intended Neville to stick to the family businesses; but it was not possible to keep a true-blue Kenrick-Chamberlain out of public affairs. Neville entered Parliament late in life, yet in ten years was the Conservative Party's coming man. Needless to say he had done his qualifying tour of duty as a highly successful Lord Mayor of Birmingham.

So the Chamberlains were moving back to London whence they had come. It was as though they had used Birmingham as a breeding ground, and the Kenricks as a sustaining element in their mercurial blood. As the 20s gave way to the 30s, the Family dominance of Birmingham gradually dwindled. Uncle Byng was the only member left on the city council where, as chairman of the education committee, he painstakingly established a noble record of achievement. The name Chamberlain faded from the telephone directory. Cadbury took its place and the great chocolate family moved in. The Kenricks remained—obstinate, enduring, ingrown and immovable—still manufacturing cast-iron saucepans just as they had before the Chamberlains passed through.

Since World War II, Archibald Kenrick and Sons have experienced a period of grave trouble. Saucepans were not enough. Bathtubs were tried but proved too cumbersome and went down the drain—nearly taking Archibald Kenrick and Sons with them. But the modern Kenricks, worthy scions of a tenacious breed, clung on. In the nick of time a Mr. Shepherd, an Australian engineer whose patented zinc-alloy castors were to revolutionize the castor business, came on the scene. Kenricks, in the person of my cousin William, daringly adopted Shepherd's castor, leapt into zinc, and closed down forever the West Bromwich iron foundry that had been Kenricks' bread and butter for a century and a half. But the business was saved. Shepherd is their Lord, they shall not want.

Kenricks in Hardware, a Family Business. 1791 to 1966, by Professor R. A. Church, assigns them a place of their own in history—and hardly a mention of the Chamberlains from start to finish! But I do just wonder ... if William had not had Chamberlain blood in his veins, would he have dared to make the crucial leap? Or would he have gone down with the ship, seated on an upturned bathtub, as the dying glow of the foundry shone softly on rank after rank of saucepans fallen at last into disrepute and desuetude? (Since writing this, I have heard from William that, in fact, it was his determination to take a course in Business Management—woefully neglected by his forebears—that saved the day.)

* * *

It was a fine summer afternoon when I fell out of the Victoria onto Lordswood Road. A Victoria was a light two-seater horse carriage. Opposite the main seat, under and behind the coachman's box, was a little ledge—a folding rumble seat—which let down for emergencies. Our Victoria had no side doors. Theoretically, this made it more elegant; but I suspect that it also reduced the price—a consideration in a family where aesthetic alibis and judgments of "good taste" were often employed to justify economies.

Why I should have been sitting on this precarious ledge rather than by my mother's side I can only guess. She was dressed to the nines for an afternoon call on Mrs. Godlea and probably didn't want to be rumpled—not that I was much of a rumpler. I can't have been more than three or four; by the time I was five we could no longer afford to be carriage folk. Opposite Lordswood House, where the Pinsents lived and I was later to go to kindergarten, the carriage lurched, I lost my balance and rolled out. The carriage rolled on.

It was the dreadful forlornness of being left behind that flooded my frightened little soul as I picked myself up, quite unhurt, from the dusty road and ran sobbing after the disappearing carriage. I can still hear the relentless clop-clop of Lady Betty's hoofs. My mother must have been deep in her appointment book and my fall, so swift and soundless, passed unnoticed for a moment. It seemed an age to me before the carriage finally pulled up.

One would imagine that it must have been quite a shock to my mother when she did eventually look up and found no grave little boy sitting opposite her. But I don't remember anyone being in the least hysterical except myself. It was the terror of being abandoned. I was dusted off, my nose blown, and on we went down Harborne Park Road to Mrs. Godlea's.

Mrs. Godlea was an American, which set her apart from the other people mother called on: members of the Family, for example, or Mrs. Carver. Indeed, Mrs. Godlea was mother's tame American. Generally speaking, nothing pleased mother more than stories indicating that Americans were uncivilized. She loved repeating them in her American accent, which was high-pitched, loud, nasal and bore little resemblance to the real thing. How we used to laugh! It really was a problem for mother—this double standard for Americans. She liked her social categories to be clear-cut. The Family in toto, the aristocracy, Conservative members of Parliament and a few French families she had met while at finishing school in Paris were all right. The rest of the world one didn't know. Many years later I remember her tottering along the beach at Llwyngwril on my arm and being unable to decide whether or not to nod recognition to old Mrs. George Cadbury. Mysteriously, cast-iron saucepans were socially superior to chocolate.

It was Joe Chamberlain who introduced the double standard that so confused my mother. His third wife, after he had outlived two Miss Kenricks (the second a cousin of the first), was a Miss Endicott of Boston. And Uncle Joe could do no wrong. He was the Family's Great Man.

I saw him only once. It was during the Christmas season at a children's party at Highbury, and to me he wasn't great at all. I remember the immense Christmas tree and the green-house where the orchids were grown that became his political trademark. But he himself seemed unexpectedly little, slumped down in his invalid chair. Little but frightening, because his face had slipped sideways. He was handing out shiny five-shilling pieces as big as cartwheels to an endless line of great-nephews and nieces. Somebody—Cousin Ida, his eldest daughter at home it must have been—said, "And this is Millie's younger boy." Cousin Hilda with her faithful echo added, "Millie's younger boy," as I came up trying desperately not to look frightened or self-conscious. Uncle Joe's lips worked and out came an acknowledging grunt as he doled out the coin with a bent claw into my hot little hand.

3

Napierolatry

As the years went by, the multitudinous offspring of the Family's patriarchs married, preferably within the family group, settled into slightly less stately mansions, and produced more cousins still.

Into this enormous network of blood relationships and preferred shares my father light-heartedly married. But he was not very good at business, nor did he have much in the way of preferred shares. In time the Family came to speak of him as "poor Claude." So we Napier-Claverings had to build ourselves up with what my father did have: blue blood and famous forebears.

There was John Napier for instance, a man of towering intellect who coordinated the idea of logarithms into an exact science—an immense leap forward in mathematics—about the time that Shakespeare was writing *Hamlet*. There was Sir Charles Napier, the Conqueror of Scinde, who has a statue in Trafalgar Square "erected largely by the subscriptions of private soldiers"—a unique tribute amongst military commanders. Not to mention Admiral Napier KCB, "Black Jack," a stickler for cleanliness when men-of-war were not noted for hygienic facilities. He went to sea wearing twelve shirts so that when the top one looked dirty he could peel it off and always show "fresh" linen.

My father was the seventh and youngest child of John Warren Napier, the vicar of Stretton, a small parish in Staffordshire. He was certainly aristocratic, since his name appeared in *Debrett's Peerage* as an offshoot of the Barony of Napier and Ettrick, and certainly poor, since in order to feed his considerable family much of his time was consumed in cultivating the large fruit and vegetable garden of the vicarage, aided by any son strong enough to use a spade. This was not an uncommon situation in poorly endowed English parsonages. My grandfather's stipend was between 200 and 300 pounds a year.

Until my father ventured unsuccessfully into business in Birmingham, I doubt if any Napier had ever devoted the days of his life to any calling but that of soldier, sailor, parson, schoolmaster, lawyer, or civil servant. These, with medicine, if you stretched a point, were the only vocations appropriate to a gentleman—at least in the British Isles.

In my travels I have met many delightful Napiers, stemming doubtless from younger sons who had emigrated and taken to other ways of life. There is quite a clan of Kentucky Napiers—farmers and moonshiners maybe. The one I knew, old Elmer Napier, was a notable driver of wagon trains in Hollywood movies. *(Elmer and Alan appeared together in* Across the Wide Missouri *in 1951.)*

In this tradition my father emigrated in his late teens to Canada, nearly died of pleurisy on the prairie and returned, a trifle ignominiously, to England, home and beauty. He was by nature an artist and, though a lifelong gardener, not temperamentally fitted to taming wildernesses.

About this time his father had a surprising change of fortune; he came into an estate from a distant Clavering cousin (the family suffered under a curse as to the succession after it abandoned the Catholic faith) inheriting in his old age a considerable property in Northumberland—Axwell Park—with its attendant coal royalties. With the estate went the name of Clavering and he became John Warren Napier-Clavering.

His sons had all been educated at a minor Public School, Rossal, endowed to provide scholarships for the sons of impoverished clergy. Charlie and Lenox became soldiers, Francis a school-master, Percy a missionary, and Alan an Indian Civil Servant. Only poor Claude failed to find a career and, not daring to admit to anything so unsuitable as artistic proclivities, left early on his Canadian caper. One memory of his at Rossal that I cherish is that of his housemaster pinning to the notice board the following announcement, "Lost, stolen or strayed—The Soul of Wiggins Minor." It was a preparation for the gallery of eccentrics I was to meet later on when I went to Clifton.

What was to be done with poor Claude when he was invalided home from Canada? Academically he was not up to Oxford or Cambridge. What could he do? Well, apparently he could draw. So somehow (I never learned the full story) he ended up at the Birmingham School of Art. He was a beautiful young man, tall for those days, with a beautiful voice and way of speaking. The children of John Warren Napier had learned to speak in an English country parsonage from a Scots mother and a scholarly father whose straitened circumstances led him to lay great stress on the non-material marks of good breeding, speech and manners. They were taught the beautiful English of the north country educated upper classes and so escaped the affectations of "County," "Mayfair," or "Oxford" accents.

How my father actually met the beautiful Millicent Kenrick I don't know. If you were in any sort of society in Birmingham in those days it was hard not to meet a Kenrick or a Chamberlain, for by 1895 Joe Chamberlain's successes had made the Family respectable. The Rt. Hon. William Kenrick, P.C., young Claude's father-in-law to be, painted muddy oil landscapes and presided over the Birmingham art gallery. And some other member of the Family was undoubtedly chairman of the education committee, in the city council.

Anyhow, meet and marry they did. There must have been qualms on the Napier side on account of my mother's heathen Unitarianism, allayed perhaps by the material advantages of the match. And on my mother's side, qualms about the insubstantiality of an art student, allayed by the listing in *Debrett*.

My father's eldest brother Charlie, Lt. Col. Charles Napier-Clavering, came to Birmingham to represent his family at the wedding. My mother, very much impressed, was showing him the wedding presents. She came to a prayer-rug from Ceylon, which had been hung on the wall the better to exhibit its beauty. "And that lovely little rug," she proudly announced, "is from Percy." Uncle Charles screwed his eyeglass into his left eye, examined his younger brother's gift carefully, and declared as he did so, "Now that's a man I very much dislike!" My mother never forgot it. In the Family, presided over by the Great Man at Highbury, no one ever disliked any relation, though it was permissible to be funny about Beales. Charles Gabriel Beale, great-aunt Alice's husband, was known as "The Archangel Gabriel." At a family dinner party he was once heard to declare, "For my part, I cannot recall ever having told a lie in my life."

3. Napierolatry

To us children at Tennal Grange, the Great Men were the Napier-Clavering uncles. Maybe distance lent them enchantment, for we were hemmed in with Kenrick-Chamberlains. There they were, beyond our ken, representing the Army, the Church, India, Ceylon and all places East. There was Uncle Charlie, so splendid with his monocle and the legend of his regiment, the Somerset Light Infantry. By his humane approach he taught them to march farther in a day across the blazing deserts of Africa than any other unit in the Army. He had fought the Zulus in South Africa or the Maandi in the Sudan or something. Uncle Francis was a bit of a letdown because he was only a schoolmaster and frightfully thin. He also sniggered when he laughed. But his sons, Noel and Donald, one so immaculately pukka, and the other that choice British composite of stiff upper lip and quizzical humor, we positively worshipped.

Uncle Percy, the Reverend H. P. Napier-Clavering, was a missionary in Ceylon, remote and venerated for strange occasional gifts of coral necklaces and Rahat Lakhoum Turkish Delight. He matured splendidly, proving Charlie's early estimate of him entirely wrong. Charlie admitted it, "Greatly improved—he's seen places and people." Late in life, he married Aunt Claire, found he had made a mistake, and spent many of his latter years circling the globe in order to escape from her. He usually kept about three ships ahead; but she caught up with him in the end. On his death bed he told me in his wonderfully rich parsonical tremolo that he had been considering the exact meaning of words. "I take it that a disagreeable person is one who disagrees with you." After a meditative pause occupied by whimsical hummings and gurglings, he added with his wicked but compassionate twinkle, "Your Aunt Claire is always disagreeing with me." The old boy had a nice long respite before she followed him on his last journey.

Uncle Lenox was a dashing Army captain. He had a monocle too—right eye, I think—and was splendidly irreverent. He used to wink at us in Church at Axwell and make us laugh. And at dinner (the year we stayed at Axwell Park for Christmas) when the plum pudding came in and I wanted brandy sauce instead of lemon-for-the-children sauce, to my mother's horror he said, "Let him have it! Never too soon to have the best." He also had an eye for a pretty leg. In later life, I remember walking along the street with him in Newcastle-on-Tyne, his monocle always focused about 12 inches above ground level. "Deuced pretty girl!" he'd say without looking up.

But Uncle Alan was our real hero. He was a Commissioner in the Indian Civil Service and periodically turned up from the East, very brown and Kipling-esque, with a majestic moustache, waxed at the tips, and magnificent presents. His speech was impressively deliberate and he had a scar on his neck from a would-be Indian assassin. That he was romantically attached to my mother, who had once been out to India to stay with him (doubtless for her health) we did not realize as children. But the effect this had on Mother certainly caused her to build up his image; my mother was far from averse to arousing tender emotions provided that she was not expected to give anything substantial in return. Poor Uncle Alan! He paid and paid for his youthful deviation from the strict path of brotherly loyalty. Twenty and thirty years later, long after my mother had become a martyr to arthritis and my parents had agreed to separate, she kept my Uncle Alan, retired and unmarried, conveniently at her beck and call.

How were the mighty fallen! He took to knitting in his old age and, always a big man, became elephantine. There he would sit in his ground floor flat in Cromwell Road, that dreariest of London thoroughfares, his needles clicking, surrounded on floor and wall by the ferocious heads and spotted pelts of tigers and panthers, their amber sheen ever darkening with the long years of London soot.

Gradually the grandeur of the Napier-Clavering uncles faded and the indestructible Kenrick-Chamberlains took their place in our regard.

4

Chamberlain in Excelsis

My cousin Austen, the gartered diplomatist, I remember meeting only once. It was at my grandmother's funeral service at the Church of the Messiah in Birmingham. *(Alan's grandmother died on December 29, 1918; the funeral would have been in January 1919, when Alan was 16.)* He had evidently rushed down from London by train and, arriving a little late, slipped quietly into one of the front pews—as it happened next to me. The pungent smell of Havana cigar was heavy upon him. I looked up and encountered a glacial stare, pale and cold above the aquiline nose. He made me think of an eagle and at the idea of an eagle smoking a cigar, I quickly fell to my knees and started praying that I would not laugh out loud at Grandmama's funeral.

How different my memories of encounters with my Cousin Neville, to whom I was always attracted by the warmth and humor radiating from those brilliant black eyes. Once I remember, when we children had been nearly rained out camping at Tal-y-Bont in North Wales with my father; Neville and Cousin Annie, his beautiful wife, walked over from Bryntirion, Cousin Alice's noble country mansion facing Cader Idris and the Barmouth estuary. The Family were all great walkers, and Neville had been worried about Millie's children out there under canvas in the rain. A brilliant day had followed the great storm and he found us drying out, naked on our camp beds like lizards in the sun. We had a lovely communal luncheon, trading our fresh milk from the farm for delicacies from the Bryntirion kitchen. Then there was the time they had a children's party at their house next to the Botanical Gardens in Edgbaston. There was a conjuror, and cousin Neville asked me, as one of the older children, to help in setting the stage. To this day I remember the delight in cousin Neville's eyes at the mystification of the little children, and their shrieks of laughter at the magician's corny jokes.

My last meeting with him stays clearly in my mind. Towards the end of the 1920s my mother and father had separated. But my mother's move to London was motivated far more by the migration thither of the Chamberlains than because of friction at home. The older she grew the more she depended on the endless Family Saga to support life. Now that she was living in London her greatest joy was the occasional teatime visit of her beloved cousin Neville. However occupied he might be with the affairs of a nation staggering from a depression and hurtling towards Armageddon, he would make a point, two or three times a year, of seeing poor Millie. At the time I am thinking of, 1932, he was Chancellor of the Exchequer in a Stanley Baldwin—Ramsey McDonald coalition Cabinet.

I was then playing in *Firebird* opposite Gladys Cooper, and I was not always very dutiful in seeing my mother. To tell the truth my career was of little interest to her. I had to be in the theatre by 8:00, so on one occasion she arranged to have dinner for me at 6:30

and I promised to come early. Finding myself at a loose end I came very early in the hope of getting a cup of tea. In the hallway of her apartment house I met my Uncle Alan stepping out of the elevator—the same Uncle Alan who had been the hero of our childhood and who was still dancing attendance on my mother. He said, "If you're going up to see your mother I don't think you'll be very welcome."

"Oh? She's giving me dinner and asked me to come early."

"I don't know about that, but she's just thrown me out. The Great Man turned up for tea and she wants him to herself." And somewhat disconsolately he trundled off into the rain for a game of bridge at his club. Forty years earlier he had entertained Millie's young cousin Neville at a tiger shoot in India.

Mother took my interruption pretty well, and Cousin Neville could not have been kinder. He knew what play I was acting in and put me at ease immediately with talk about the theatre, for he had been a great student and lover of Shakespeare all his life. He remembered my performance as the dying Edward IV in a production of *Richard III* a year or so back. But my mother was not going to waste precious time on such trivialities.

"Dear boy," she broke in with her little social laugh, "Cousin Neville has been very kind, but ... Neville! More tea? You were telling me about The Beaver."

The Beaver, of course, was Lord Beaverbrook, the able and contentious owner of *The Daily Express*, and usually a great admirer and supporter of Neville Chamberlain.

In my mother's pretty drawing room in Queen's Gates Gardens, Neville revealed a humane and vibrant personality. His discussion of the problems and personalities of the day was trenchant and good-humored; and he generated a tremendous feeling of authority which I have never been able to reconcile with the popular American picture of the effete or, alternatively, Machiavellian "Umbrella Man." That he was very much aware of the subterranean rumblings that were threatening the peace of the world, and that he believed vigorous action then could and must be applied, clearly emerged. One phrase seemed to me so apt and amusing that I made a note of it when I got home.

"Poor old Ramsey and Stanley sit at the head of the Cabinet table holding hands under it and saying, 'I won't do anything if you don't.'"

This was before Mussolini's invasion of Abyssinia and Hitler's unopposed occupation of the Rhineland. Baldwin, in fact, had sold the pass to the dictators long before Neville Chamberlain came to power as Prime Minister.

For the Family, the greatest moment at last arrived—a Kenrick-Chamberlain had come out of the heart of Birmingham to become Prime Minister to the King Emperor. Yet something was missing... Had they waited too long? Or was it the country's and the empire's fault for no longer being on the up and up?

I fancy history will judge Neville Chamberlain more kindly than current fashions would suggest. Harold Nicholson, the political dilettante who wore his working class constituency like a hair shirt, detested Neville's policies and found his personality repugnant. Yet he reports that Churchill, when complimented on his noble oration on the occasion of Neville Chamberlain's death, replied that it had not been difficult. "I admired many of Neville's great qualities. But I pray to God in His infinite mercy that I shall not have to deliver a similar oration on Mr. Baldwin." This is part of what Churchill said in the House of Commons: "It fell to Neville Chamberlain, in one of the supreme crises of the world, to be contradicted by events, to be disappointed in his hopes and to be deceived and cheated by a wicked man. But what were these hopes in which he was disappointed? What was that faith that was abused? They were surely among the most noble and benevolent instincts of the human heart—the love of peace, the toil for peace, the strife for peace, the pursuit of peace, even at great peril, and certainly to the utter disdain of popularity or clamor."

As a peacetime statesman, no one can doubt that Neville would have left an illustrious name. But his innate decency and middle-class respect for established authority made it impossible for him really to believe that the head of the great German nation, the nation that had nurtured Beethoven and Goethe, could be a neurotic fiend. Hitler's monstrous perversion of all diplomatic and political usage fatally compromised Neville's image as a statesman; and the story of the great Kenrick-Chamberlain rise to the top of the ladder came to an inglorious end.

In his seventieth year, Neville Chamberlain, who had never before been in an airplane, flew to Germany as a last resort to beard Hitler in his Berchtesgarten lair and try to extract from him by sheer force of character a decent solution of Europe's problems. An immediate attack on Czechoslovakia was stalled. Later that week he flew to Godesburg, and finally to Munich for the much abused pact which is said to have sold Czechoslovakia down the river. In fact, Czechoslovakia had a far less damaging war than countries such as Poland which resisted Hitler's *Wehrmacht*—a fact overlooked by those subject to what an American historian, William Thompson, calls "Britain's guilt complex over Czechoslovakia."

Neville Chamberlain returned from Munich with a piece of paper on which Hitler had put his signature, promising to indulge in no more strong-arm tactics against his European neighbors. He was welcomed home with heartfelt acclaim by cheering multitudes—first at the airport, then outside Buckingham Palace, where he stood on a balcony flanked by his King and Queen; and finally at Number 10 Downing Street. It had been a long, tiring day at the end of a week of incredible exertion and anxiety. An old man, white and drawn with fatigue, he could only smile and wave his hand from the window. He turned away, but someone urged him back. "You'll have to say something or they'll be here all night."

Neville had reached his summit—Chamberlain *in excelsis*. If the tired heart had broken then, he would have died in triumph. Hardly able to stand, he asked, "What can I say?"

"Tell them," a loyal supporter suggested, "that for a second time a Prime Minister of England has come back from Germany bringing peace with honor."

Neville returned to the window; the crowd cheered; and he said the words that were to haunt him and subject him to ridicule when Hitler broke his promise and engulfed the civilized world in war. But that piece of paper, so mocked and reviled by his detractors, was far from valueless. It gave England a precious year to re-arm, and it convinced a world unwilling to face grim reality that only force of arms could halt the madman.

At the end, when his desperate and not un-heroic effort to save the peace had failed, when making war was thrust upon him, when his party and his country turned against him, when his health broke and all he had worked for seemed to be in ruins, what were the thoughts, one wonders, that went through his head as he lay dying of cancer. Not pride of family for sure; but love of family, I think. Memories, perhaps, of his cousin Norman, the Family's choice spirit and Neville's closest friend, who was killed in the First World War. Norman wrote from the fell trenches of Flanders of the utter immorality of war and that only tremendous efforts to improve the lot of man, in a world at peace, could wipe away the stain. Surely, surely Neville Chamberlain had tried his very best.

When I think of him, I see a man with laughing eyes, sharing his sandwiches with Millie's disheveled brood by the sand-hills in North Wales, or joking about the antics of The Beaver over a cup of tea in Queen's Gate Gardens.

5

The Grove—Cast Iron

Of all the Family's mansions, The Grove was the most familiar and important in my early life. Grandmama, stout, small and sweet as a nut, presided—a chatelaine with keys and pencils clanking at her waist—over the many delights that The Grove offered a child. In the morning room there was the cupboard containing ingenious mechanical toys and colored picture books; in the dining room the cupboard in the sideboard with Velma-Suchard chocolates and candied fruits (one each for a good grandchild after lunch); and in the drawing room—so large and full of little tables, revolving bookcases, silver and porcelain knickknacks—the cupboard with "Happy Families" and "Royal Academy" packs of cards. Grandmama understood the needs of children in an easy, quiet way. Though never demonstratively offered, her gift of love went with the toys, the chocolates and the cards; and she was charmingly greedy over buttery crumpets at tea, which helped to bring her very close.

Grandpapa, tall, handsome and white side-whiskered was cool, crotchety and emanated little affection. He was not comfortable with children. As my brother and sister and I grew older, a ritual developed of going to The Grove at the end of every holiday to receive a tip from Grandpapa to see one through the ensuing school term. A half crown, rising later to five shillings. I was always uneasy in his presence and, at a self-conscious age, suffered agonies trying to assume a demeanor appropriate to the gift to come, with its accompanying stiff catechism as to one's progress at school. As the youngest, I had to wait while Mark and Molly received theirs. And there was my stammer. On one occasion I remember Grandpapa greeted me with, "Why are you looking so hangdog?" I don't think he liked me. Molly was his favorite; she was a lovely, blue-eyed little girl with golden corkscrew curls.

The great feature of the drawing room and Grandpapa's cherished instrument of self-expression was the Pianola. How often as a child have I fallen asleep with the Beethoven sonatas distantly thumping away in the drawing room to my grandfather's relentless pedaling.

I remember the joy when I was very small of being ill at The Grove. I think I had measles there. How cozy was the children's night nursery with the gas murmuring softly in its mantle and the stained-glass figure in the window looking down on one benevolently. I don't think it was Jesus—there could have been something a little demanding, a little too "follow me" about that. No, I think it was St. Christopher, taking full responsibility. The morning would start with the noise of the front stairs being brushed down, stair by stair, with a hand-brush, by the under housemaid on her knees. Then, in she would come—an Effie, an Edna or an Ethel—with her box of paper, kindling and blacking in one hand and a scuttle of coal in the other, to do the fire. Rattle, rattle as last night's ashes are poked out and shoveled away. Then a soft susurrus of brushes as the iron grate is blacked and polished. Next the crackle of paper as yesterday's *Birmingham Post* is bunched up into a mattress and put in the bottom of the grate. Wood is neatly laid across and finally there is the creak of coal being placed on coal, with sometimes a sharp smack as a big lump is broken up to make for easy "catching." For the fire will "catch" with one match if it is properly laid. A match strikes, followed by the crackle of flames as the dry kindling catches fire on the paper. It is a success. Effie's shadow flickers for a moment, enormous on the ceiling; she has achieved another perfect fire. She sweeps the last remnants of ash and dust from the hearth, stacks her brushes in their box and rises from her knees.

"Would you like me to pull up the blinds, Master Alan? It's a lovely morning."

"Thank you, Effie, it's a lovely fire."

And indeed it is. As she goes out, the coals settle down through the collapsing kindling with a sudden bright flame and a shower of sparks. Another lovely day has begun.

I am the special charge of Grandmama's personal maid, Lucy. Hardly has Effie left than Lucy comes in with hot water in a copper jug. In no time I am sponged and brushed, and propped up with pillows and dressing-gowned for the day to come. The chamber pot from under the bed is discreetly emptied and, also from under the bed, my teddy bear restored to a place of honor by my side. I shall have all sorts of visitors. Deans, the grey-haired parlor-maid—downstairs so severe and soldier-like—brings in a lovely breakfast of scrambled eggs—for I am convalescing by now. How carefully she would arrange you in your bed before laying the tray on your lap. She stays a little, all smiles and sweetness, to make sure that you have all that you want and that your little silver hand-bell is in reach. Breakfast over, there are picture books to look at—one I remember of American trains with cow-catchers, woofing through endless prairies—or puzzles to grapple with till Lucy comes back, removes the tray and, bundling you up as if for a journey to the North Pole, conducts you to the Lavatory.

The Lavatory was a bit alarming. The door from the landing opened onto a narrow passage a dozen feet long, cold, and dark, that led to another door with a ground-glass panel, the door to the water-closet itself. This handsome artifact was up two steps and encased in polished mahogany. The china bowl, discreetly hidden under its shining lid, had a pretty design in Wedgewood blue; and when the plug was pulled the waters roared down from the cistern above with torrential determination, sweeping all before them.

Safely back in bed, the next thing to look forward to was Grandmama's visit. This morning she couldn't stay long because she was going to town in the Brougham to do some shopping. Metcalf's had sent an unripe melon and must be reproved. Was I tired of grapes and would I like a nectarine? And here was a new jigsaw puzzle of a motor car in dashing red. And so the day went on. After milk and Petit Beurre biscuits for elevenses, Damesa, the butler, with his funny, ironic smile and slow flatfooted gait would come in and have you laughing in no time. He had a very simple little puppet show—I can't for the life of me remember just how he worked it—but he was not above using it to make funny comments on his employers and the Family. Soon a sumptuous lunch would arrive followed by a sleepy afternoon and gorgeous tea. Finally a light supper of delicious bread and milk and, the gas murmuring softly in its mantle again, Grandmama would read *Uncle Remus* in her gentle, drowsy voice, St. Christopher looking down benevolently from the window. The last thing

I would hear would be the clatter of the wood-slatted Venetian blinds descending, and the gentle bubbling of the lowered gas.

Lucy, Deans, Damesa; Aunt Clara's Emma—they seemed unchanging and indestructible. I find it impossible to think of them in any other setting or to believe that they were anything but happy in their work.

Now, I have said that Damesa was not above a little ironic mockery of his employers. How was it, I wonder, that my grandfather came to engage this rather shabby-looking bachelor of Portuguese descent? Perhaps a full-blooded, haughty English butler would have seemed to him to be a little above his own station in life—or at least above his wife's. His sense of exact elevation on the English social ladder was exceptionally acute. To the world at large it would have been natural to think of my grandmother, sister of the Secretary for the Colonies of Great Britain, as socially of some account. But her husband, retired manufacturer of cast-iron saucepans, saw her in a different light. Though undoubtedly a devoted couple—they lived to celebrate their golden wedding anniversary—disagreements were frequent and, as so often happens, tended to come to a head at dinner. On one occasion my grandfather was moved to thunder down the long length of his mahogany dining room table, flanked by his favorite Pre-Raphaelites, "Mrs. Kenrick! When I married you, I raised you from the LOWER-middle classes to the UPPER-middle classes, and you've been dragging me down ever since!"

How Damesa must have winked at my father! How my father delighted in this vision of unending struggle on the middle reaches of the social ladder!

(My father and Damesa came to understand each other very well after a tricky opening when my father was first invited to stay at The Grove. Damesa would insist, when putting out my father's evening clothes for dinner, on retrieving from the dirty clothes basket the shirt my father had discarded the night before and putting back the studs and cufflinks, on the grounds that the shirt was not yet soiled enough for laundering! Once my father, a disciple of the famous Admiral, in that he liked to show clean linen, had established the idea that he alone must be the judge of this, they got along very well.)

Clearly, my grandfather must have been a queer fish to be fussing about his wife's lack of breeding—especially with all those Pre-Raphaelites on the walls and her family going great guns in Parliament. Indeed there were queer strains in the Kenricks. They were Unitarian, individualistic, conservative, conscientious, cantankerous, eccentric and mortifiers of the flesh. Austerity has always been held in high esteem by Kenricks. At the works in West Bromwich, the executive members of the firm, all Kenricks, had but one dish for luncheon. It was the same every working day of the year. Hot rice pudding. In cast-iron bowls, manufactured on the premises, with the name of each embossed around the rim— Sir George, Mr. Archibald, Mr. Arthur, Mr. Timothy, Mr. Byng, Mr. Gerald.

Sir George was a splendid Kenrick type and, since I met him only once, I shall happily rely on legend in filling out his story. Kenricks, by the way, are constitutionally spare with fine, aquiline noses. (Neville Chamberlain, whose mother was of course a Kenrick, was typical in appearance though his nature had the Chamberlain warmth.)

The single occasion when I met Cousin George was at a great evening party at Whetstone for the flower of Birmingham society, which meant 90 percent family and 10 percent outsiders. I was about seventeen and was probably only invited as escort for my mother, who was by then an invalid chair case of rheumatoid arthritis. The evening was unforgettable for me because of the entertainer who had been engaged for the occasion. She was an American. None of the Family had heard of her and there was considerable doubt in some minds as to whether an American could be relied upon not to pass the bounds of… "Well, you know what Americans are." They need not have worried; her name was Ruth Draper. As it turned out, the entire Kenrick-Chamberlain clique fell for her with a beating of saucepans and tinkling of screws, which showed their innate good taste. Ruth Draper was a great creative artist.

Cousin George received a knighthood because he happened to be Lord Mayor when King Edward VII came to Birmingham to open the new University. Knighthood was a cinch for the Family, anyhow—if it hadn't flashed a Sir George, it could have flashed a Sir Arthur, either Kenrick or Chamberlain. The Family invariably held the Mayorship. Sir George, however, was unique in one respect—he never married, not even outside the Chamberlains. On the other hand, he was a typical Kenrick in one respect—his passion for bicycling. All cast-iron Kenricks bicycled to work, and it was a long road from Harborne or Edgbaston to the works at West Bromwich. It could be said that it was speedy and convenient—but for men of means, particularly with the coming of the motor car, it was austere. It went with the rice pudding lunches—it mortified the flesh.

So year after year, Sir George would peddle away to West Bromwich in the morning and peddle his way back to Edgbaston at night. He would employ the more dignified method of mounting, raising himself from the ground by placing his left foot on the "step," a small knurled projection from the back hub, setting the bicycle in motion with a firm push of the right foot and then settling forward easily into the saddle. To mount by stepping on the left peddle and hurling the right leg over the saddle was undignified and vulgar, like a messenger boy. His arrival at the works was marked by a routine of some magnificence, and to the gateman fell a tricky duty.

Sir George's method of disengaging himself from his iron steed was even more unusual and arbitrary than his method of mounting. His left foot would reach back to the step and, letting go of the handle-bars, he would rise slightly, let the bicycle slip away from under him, land on his right foot, turn sharp right and enter the building. The bicycle would shoot forward, unattended, into the waiting hands of the gateman. And woe betide him if he let it fall! Was there a small boy, one wonders, stationed at the corner to signal the noble knight's approach? Or was the journey planned with such precision that the venerable presence infallibly arrived upon the stroke of nine?

Alas. All men are fallible, and one day when he was well up in his seventies and the world in its roaring twenties—the inevitable happened. A heavy truck failed to make way for him. Sir George was picked up unconscious in the gutter.

Back at Whetstone, doctors, nurses, and his elder sister Alice, waited anxiously at the bedside for him to regain consciousness. At last the eyelids flickered and he spoke, "What happened to the bicycle?"

"Oh, it was all smashed up."

A bushy brow shot up. "Order me another," he said, "And bring me a bottle of Bass's Ale." He made a remarkable recovery.

A year or so later, shortly before his eightieth birthday, the Family fermented with plans to pry him loose from the chairmanship of Archibald Kenrick and Sons. "After all," as my Uncle Byng, then knocking sixty, put it, "the firm could use some young blood at the helm." Sir George had been stone deaf for years and was unable to conceive that the Kenrick saucepan was susceptible of improvement. At board meetings any suggestion that it might be, fell on conveniently deaf ears. The impatient heirs, however, were spared the necessity of bawling into his ear-trumpet the claims of yeasty blood. Quite unexpectedly he resigned, as though bored with the whole business. No explanation, no sentiment. The reason became clear on his eightieth birthday. He had conceived a new project and wished to devote his entire energies to its realization.

From the heights of Harborne, which is at the western extremity of the city of Birmingham, may be seen some ten or a dozen miles to the southwest, the Clent Hills. They were our local mountains, first spurs of the undulating beauty of Worcestershire that culminates at Malverne. Great Uncle Arthur of Berrow Court, Sir George's first cousin, had celebrated his eightieth birthday by walking to Clent. There he had been picked up by his Lanchester motor car and returned to Berrow Court where, with a skull cap and cataract, he eventually fell into senescence and died. Now Arthur, as the elder of the two, had always been something of a thorn in George's side. He had launched into a wider financial world. Sat on the board of the Midland Railway. Lloyd's Bank too. Went up to London a good deal, and so on. George was set on showing who was the better Kenrick.

On *his* eightieth birthday he walked to Clent in the morning, ate the rice pudding he had carried with him, and walked back. A good twenty-four miles.

He then disappeared from view for a few years until the winter of 1939 when, one foggy morning, after reading the newspaper he went upstairs and lay down, fully dressed, on his bed. The papers were full of war news. His nephew Neville was in trouble in Parliament. The world would never be the same again.

He failed to turn up at lunch time. His housekeeper let this go. He failed to turn up at tea. The maid was sent up with a tray and was promptly told to take it away. When he failed to turn up for dinner, the housekeeper was sure something was wrong and went upstairs to make inquiries.

Sir George explained that he was tired of living and intended to die.

Did he feel ill?

Not in the least. But he would trouble her not to bother him. He intended to stay where he was. No, he would not undress. And would she be good enough to send him up a bottle of Bass's Ale.

When his attitude remained unchanged in the morning the housekeeper, deeply worried, sent for his elder sister Alice, now hale and hearty in her early nineties. Up the stairs to his bedroom she stumped, her lips pursed, her confident mind confidently made up.

"George," she said, "what's all this nonsense? Get up at once. You're being very inconsiderate."

"Alice," he replied, "you've tried to bully me all my life. But my death is my own and I shall have it as I please."

And he did. Took him six weeks. Two bottles of Bass a day. What was the point of living when the golden days of the Family in Birmingham had clearly come to an end?

* * *

Early in the 1960s, I received reassuring news that the true-blue Kendricks had not died out with Sir George. Aunt Nora, née Beale, wrote in her beautiful, neat handwriting that after a siege of rheumatism my Uncle Byng, the young blood of Sir George's time, had resumed his cold bath every morning and still, at 85, occasionally rode to the works at West Bromwich on his bicycle.

When he finally departed this life, the Grove Estate was left to the nation. Grandmama's "boudoir," a little anteroom between the hall and the drawing room, has been transferred intact to the Victoria and Albert Museum as a perfect example of a late Victorian interior. I think of it in colors of old rose and sandalwood with a great Persian vase of pampas grasses and immortelles. It was a beautiful little room to sit and dream in.

6

Tennal Grange—Non-Ferrous

My father's career as a businessman dawned brightly. The Birmingham Guild of Handicrafts was concerned with the manufacture of non-ferrous metal-work for the house and home. My father drew the designs and shared the management. I do not know where the capital to set him up in business came from, but I imagine it must have been largely from the Family. And the Family was responsible for his early success and for the building of beautiful Tennal Grange with its stables, flower gardens, walled kitchen garden, orchard and meadow; for Lady Betty, the Victoria, the pony, and the pony trap. One after another, my mother's cousins were getting married, building themselves homes and stipulating, of course, that all the metal work should come from the Birmingham Guild.

Beautiful work it was too. My father was very much influenced by the progressive ideas of William Morris. His designs were simple, light, functional and handcrafted. I have recently recovered the silver napkin ring made for me by the Birmingham Guild over sixty years ago. It bears the hammer marks of the craftsman who fashioned it; hammer marks which were virtually my father's trademark on silver, copper, brass and bronze. Electric light fittings, fire-screens and fire irons, door handles and locks, silver vases, napkin rings and christening mugs—any non-ferrous metal thing that could be decoratively useful in the house. And all expensive because they were custom designed and handmade.

To cut a sad story short, when my poor father ran out of his wife's relatives the business began to falter. Lady Betty and the Victoria departed; then the pony and the trap. Woolridge, our gardener, moved into the stable yard cottage to compensate for a cut in his pay.

When competitors with machine-made hammer marks undercut the Guild prices by fifty percent, the handwriting was on the wall. In a desperate salvage operation my father went to America in 1911, hoping to find a new market in the New World. And find a new market he did—but not for the Birmingham Guild. Indeed he very nearly never returned. The ladies of New York were so much more appreciative of his masculine charms and unassuming, aristocratic manner than his frigid wife had ever been. He stopped writing home and my mother was panic-stricken. Though she may well have been happy to be spared the horrors of the marriage bed, the loss of status as an abandoned wife would have been intolerable. The Family deputed Cousin Donald—a favorite grownup of my childhood, so generous with tips when he turned up unexpectedly at Tennal Grange in magnificent motor cars—to reason with my father on one of his own business trips to the New World.

Cousin Donald had married Cousin Bertha, so splendid at children's parties, and was the manufacturer of the casement windows at Tennal Grange which obstinately refused to keep out our windswept rain. His sudden visits were often in answer to mother's protests. A better man to bring my father home could not have been selected; for Donald too had a roving eye and being, like my father, an outsider to the Family, shared with him a certain irritation at the inevitable touch of smugness in so successful a clique as the Family Click.

Return poor Claude eventually did, defeated and diminished. Soon after, he sold out of the Birmingham Guild of Handicrafts for a song. His successor made a fortune, manufacturing the weapons of World War I.

The summer of my father's defection was notable to us children because, for the first time, our August holiday at the seaside was not spent with the Family. How could my mother face the unspoken thoughts of a dozen or so beloved uncles, aunts, cousins, nephews and nieces? So we were packed off to Frinton-on-Sea to stay with Uncle Percy, my father's clerical elder brother. My mother wished to be alone for the return of the prodigal so that she might establish a *modus vivendi* which would not reveal anything unsuitable to us innocent children; for my father had undoubtedly been sowing some belated wild oats in New York—and enjoying it. The older I get the more I wonder why he ever did come back.

Actually Uncle Percy rather spoiled my mother's plan of pretending nothing untoward had happened. At family prayers in the morning he would insist on praying for my father. This naturally aroused our curiosity. Though the terminology was obscure to us, evidently Dad had been a bad boy.

Uncle Percy was home from Ceylon on leave, having recently married a female missionary far too late in life. As I have said, he lived to regret this and spent the last years of his life sailing round and round the world, visiting young men he was fond of with Aunt Claire a ship or two behind him. At Frinton, in the little seaside house rented for the August holiday, the full horror of this predicament had not made itself felt. All was benevolent sweetness; he even had Aunt Claire's sister, a Miss Gedge, staying with them. And best of all there was Uncle Percy's dog, Bruce.

Family prayers in the morning were new to us and terribly boring and embarrassing—Unitarians did not pray *en famille*. They took place around the breakfast table after breakfast. Uncle Percy was evangelical and the phrase "prayer and fasting" would have smacked of Rome to him. Years later, when I found myself out of my depth one day in a discussion with Aunt Claire as to the suitability of breakfasting before taking Holy Communion, a subject on which I was both ignorant and indifferent, Uncle Percy rescued me with his usual excellent good sense. "I agree with the fellow," he intoned, "who said he couldn't see the difference between laying the Divine Body on an egg and bacon, or laying an egg and bacon on the Divine Body."

Anyhow, at Frinton, with our tummies comfortably lined with poached eggs and tea, we went down on our knees, eyes at table level or lower, while Uncle Percy would pray for practically anything that came into his head. When Mark swallowed a plum stone he was prayed for; I was very careful to be a good boy at Frinton so that it would not happen to me. There was one glorious morning when Bruce jumped through the wide open window behind Uncle Percy's back, landed on his master's shoulders and bowled him over. Uncle Percy collected himself, perched his pince-nez glasses back on his nose and, with his own engaging dirty-little-boy snigger, prayed for Bruce, who was happily taking advantage of our kneeling posture to lick our faces.

I was always fond of Uncle Percy. His initials were H. P. and at about the age of sixty, he wrote a round-robin letter to all his relatives saying that he had always detested the name Percy and in future wished to be known by his first name, Henry. At the same time he sent each of his nephews and nieces a check for 300 pounds saying, "This is some of my ill-gotten gains from tea." (He had once invested a small sum to encourage the cultivation of this, for Ceylon, new crop, with no expectation of it proving a bonanza.) "I feel that it will give you more pleasure now while you are young than at the unpredictable time of my demise."

* * *

Judy, our first, our very own dog, came from the Grove coachman, Hicks. Little old Hicks, who drove the Brougham, sitting high up on the box, with a cockade on his top hat because grandpapa was a Privy Counselor. Hicks lived in the lodge at the entrance to the Grove drive. Its rooms, a parlor-kitchen downstairs and bedroom up, were tiny. So were Hicks and Mrs. Hicks, tiny and agreeably simian.

On this spring afternoon, suddenly far too warm for our winter combinations, the little parlor with its coal fire was stifling. On the floor were five enchanting objects, gamboling together, falling over their own feet, yapping, squealing, and nuzzling their mother, who lay comatose, panting and happy, on the hearth rug in front of the fire. And one of them was to be ours. I think I was five years old. The happiness was almost too much to be borne.

I don't remember how we made a choice, but I do remember the loving kindness of the Hicks's—the wreathed smiles with which they deferentially presided over our ecstatic excitement. What we received from them was sandy, soft and flop-eared—reputedly the offspring of an Aberdeen and a wirehaired Terrier. She developed a constitution of iron and unquenchable vitality, but remained small and low to the ground, short-haired, and to other eyes than ours, unremarkable for her looks. Later, it was her exploits that attracted attention; sometimes, alas, far from favorable. Now, she was being adored; handed from one child to another, licking our faces, yapping, struggling to get away, and then settling in our arms as if she had found the perfect place for a nice sleep. Suddenly the Hicks's parlor became unendurably suffocating. "Oh, thank you, Hicks. Thank you so much. Goodbye, Mrs. Hicks. Goodbye!" And we were gone.

So there we were on that fine spring afternoon, Mark, Molly and I, ten, seven and five with a pup to take home. And we didn't really know how to handle the situation. I think Hicks must have got her a little collar and I remember he gave us a piece of string for a lead. We supposed that Judy would walk at the end of her lead as we had seen other dogs walk. And so she did for the first few yards, after we had carried her to the sidewalk outside the Grove gates. Then, suddenly, she panicked and wanted to go back. Oh bitter moment; she didn't love us anymore! She pulled one way, we pulled the other. Then she sat down on her little, fat backside and cried. Mark, never a patient soul, started yanking her by main force along the pavement, the collar forcing up her ears. I couldn't stand it. "No, no, please! You're hurting her." I ran to pick her up and she struggled out of my arms and fell, not safely onto her feet, but with a sickening thud. Had I hurt her? Had I killed her? Not a bit of it—Mark had let go and she was hightailing it back to The Grove. Someone stepped on the trailing end of the string and she was jerked to a stop. We picked her up again and started on our long walk home.

Judy grew into the perfect dog for three reasonably irresponsible children. To her, we were the Trinity; one yet three and equally worshipped. She was also indestructible, inexhaustible and un-losable. One trick that my father insisted on—at meals she must instantly,

Alan, Molly and Mark at Tennal Grange with Judy the dog, 1912. Courtesy Julian Mulock.

on the word of command, retire to her basket and stay there silently until released. I have firmly intended to instill this admirable ordinance with each new dog I've owned, but have met with less and less success as the years have gone by. My present little darling sits at my feet all through dinner making endearing little noises until, when I think the family won't notice, I surreptitiously sneak her a morsel from my plate.

As we grew into the bicycling age Judy would accompany us on long trips through the country lanes of the Warwickshire-Staffordshire borderland where we lived, dashing up banks, forcing her way through hedgerows, digging at rabbit holes, chasing hens. But it was in North Wales, the Family's choice for summer holidays, that Judy discovered her desperate addiction—sheep.

How many sheep Judy actually ran to death I do not know. But one was very nearly the death of *her*. The Grove was set in ten or a dozen acres of park land. In one field some cows were kept to provide fresh milk and cream, and in another, at certain times of year, a choice young sheep would be imported, to be fattened for Grandpapa's table. Nowadays we talk only of lamb, no matter at what age the animal we are eating may have been slaughtered. Then, lamb was lamb, and choice mutton was the greater delicacy. The whole point was that it had to have a privileged upbringing for privileged tables—no undue exertion to toughen the muscle fibers, and a plentiful supply of luscious grass. I remember saddle of mutton at The Grove; it melted in your mouth.

One fatal day such a privileged paragon was run to death (heart presumably) by Judy a week or so before it was due to grace the Grove table at a great Family dinner party. Grandpapa was furious. We were rightly held responsible since we had brought Judy over from Tennal Grange. While we were playing Pirates on the lake, which had a rowboat and an island, we had forgotten all about her. Why hadn't we heard her yapping? It probably came in one ear and went out the other. At one moment Judy was sentenced to death by Grandpapa, who had summoned us to his sanctuary, the library. Molly and I instantly burst into tears and Mark put on his obstinate look. There was a ghastly silence. Finally, as Grandpapa couldn't stand sniveling children, the sentence was commuted. But if ever again...

I imagine they ate the sheep eventually. Though I do have a vague memory that Judy was said to have started work on one hind quarter of her fallen prey, when discovered by Mr. Eeds and chased off with vengeful hoe. But I'm afraid all that exercise may have toughened the muscle fibers of an otherwise choice saddle of mutton.

* * *

Apart from the Family, our constant playmates were the Carvers, who lived in Wentworth Road. Mrs. Carver was mother's prime feminine admirer. Originally a Miss Creswell from Gibraltar, she was married to a taciturn, deaf, retired brewer. Gibraltar is a little world, nostalgic always to its natives, but also evidently a prison, in that emergence into the great world goes to the heads of its more adventurous children. So it was naturally agreeable for Mrs. Carver to know the daughter of the local ruling caste Kenrick-Chamberlains, a daughter, furthermore, married into Debrett. Besides, they had cultural tastes in common and I imagine originally met in mother's play-reading society, "Caliope."

I don't remember much about Caliope except that when it met at Tennal Grange it pre-empted all else in importance and that mother's voice dominated the airwaves from the open drawing room windows. I have no doubt that mother was the group's star and Mrs. Carver, who had a lovely sense of the ridiculous, its leading character woman.

Mother had the gift of inspiring devotion in other women. I imagine she was what one casually describes nowadays as "a latent homosexual"; which is a convenient thing to be if one finds the hetero-physical equipment in any way distasteful. As the years went by, Mrs. Carver never failed. When needed she would come and sit with my mother in our garden whatever the temperature might be. Mother was a fresh air addict and, furthermore, she was equipped with a variety of thermal devices. She would brave almost any weather condition. But poor Mrs. Carver's Gibraltarian background caused her to feel the cold. We did our best to wrap her well for the long mornings of chitter-chatter she put in with mother. I never heard them call each other by their first names; indeed I have no idea what Mrs. Carver's first name was.

There were four Carver boys. The whole family longed for a daughter and sister, so Molly became very special to them. Christian, the eldest, nobly and aptly named, and a little older than Mark, was destined for early death in the abysmal horror of World War I. (One of those pathetically un-heroic little facts that sticks in my mind—it was reported that he suffered terribly in the trenches from indigestion—the sort of thing from which heroes, one felt, should be exempt.) Maurice, the second brother, was Molly's contemporary and later, a brief, insubstantial idyll, her betrothed. Humphrey, my age exactly and close to me also in extravagant height, followed. Then, after an interval, Francis—young enough to make him a misfit in our games. That is, we Napiers thought him a misfit—but the loyal, loving Carvers always brought him along once he had emerged from babyhood. I think my father named him "The Inevitable." The other Carver boys he liked—they were well disciplined by their father from whom they inherited a very decent taciturnity. "Little boys should be seen and not heard." But Francis took after his mother, and was exuberantly garrulous.

Other constant playmates were the Harborne House Kenricks—Tim, Joan, Frances, Wynn, Barbara, Becky and Peter. Day after day, through all the holidays, we played in each other's gardens, but mostly at Harborne House and Tennal Grange. The Carvers' was a neat little suburban house in a row, with a neat little back garden, only suitable really for Grandmother's Steps or Cockup, whereas we and the Kenricks had big, rambling gardens where everything was possible—Tin in the Ring, Robbers and Travelers, even Prisoner's Base. And of course French Cricket, Colors, French and English, and Beckon.

Humphrey Carver, Alan's contemporary, set down a remarkably similar version of these events in a family memoir written for his grandchildren: "The core members of this group of Harborne children were the Carvers, the Kenricks and the Napier Claverings. For each Carver boy there was a Kenrick and a Napier Clavering of about the same age: Christian and Mark and Tim, Maurice and Molly and Joan, and so on. The ultimate significance of this core group was not that we knew one another between the ages of 6 and 9, but that we continued to be devoted friends through the subsequent school years. When we came back home for the holidays, from Naish or from Rugby, the first priority was to get together with the Napier Claverings (always known as the NCs) and the Kenricks.

"Our lives in Harborne would have been very different if it hadn't been for the big houses and spacious gardens in which the Kenricks and NCs lived. Those gardens were our playgrounds all through the year and those houses were the setting for nursery gatherings and games in the winter holidays, for the many versions of hide-and-seek and for our evolving talents for acting charades.

"As I look back on this aspect of our childhood I marvel at the skill of my mother in setting up this social situation for her children. She was relatively a newcomer in Harborne and had no previous connection with that whole network of Birmingham's first-families, the Chamberlains, Kenricks and Nettlefolds who were the founding generation of Midland industrialists and who became wealthy in making the pots and pans and tools, the bicycles and motors, that were the basis of British Empire trade. The Kenrick and Napier Clavering children we knew were grandchildren of the patriarchal William Kenrick who lived at 'The Grove,' the most stately home in Harborne; it was surrounded by a large landscape park and contained 'art nouveau' and William Morris decorations that are now in the collection of the Victoria and Albert Museum. The young Kenricks lived at 'Harborne House,' a pleasant Regency house and garden near 'The Grove.' The NCs lived at 'Tennal Grange,' a house and garden designed and built in the early Lutyens period. How lucky we were, in the enjoyment of these beautiful places! How profoundly they affected my own future life and career! And what a genius my mother was to put us into this kind of childhood environment!"

Where "Cockup" came from I don't know. I never met anyone else who played it. The players' business was to avoid being hit by the tennis ball carried and thrown by the "he." When hit, you became "he" but you were first subject to a penalty. You had to bend over up against a wall, your little bottom exposed to the rest of the players, each of whom at the distance of a dozen paces had the delicious privilege of throwing the ball with whatever savage force he could muster at this tempting target. It proved a release for aggression with almost no possibility of inflicting pain. Mark and I always thought that Molly's skirts gave her an unfair advantage. However, as we all grew older and she ceased to be a totally sexless little object, the Carver boys began to let up on Molly. This seemed to me idiotically spoilsport; play the game for all its worth or the fun goes out of it! As she moved towards puberty, they would deliberately throw wide, and finally, blushing and inarticulate, refuse to play Cockup at all. Mr. Carver, who so longed for a daughter, must have witnessed our innocent gambols and communicated his deep disapproval. His sons, throwing a ball at those parts of an innocent maiden! So Maurice eventually became engaged to the innocent maiden. Alas, the parts remained inviolate.

Humphrey Carver again: "When Maurice was back in Harborne, his opposite number, Molly Napier Clavering (we called her 'Wog') was no longer the lovely child with long pigtails who had been chased along the garden-paths of Tennal Grange. I feel that, from Maurice's side, it was more a matter of honour than of love, that they became engaged. But from the outset one could sense that there was an awkwardness about it; the magic wasn't there. This was the one distressing episode of the Oxford years, except that it sharpened Maurice's decision that his next step must be to leave England."

* * *

The watershed between being, perhaps, quite an engaging little boy—with memories of Uncle Joe, mother's skirts, and bringing Judy home—and being a sad and awkward little boy with a stammer, was my pneumonia.

This happened when I was five years old. Both lungs were eventually affected and, in those days long before antibiotics, such an illness was inevitably serious, had its "crisis," so beloved by Victorian authors, and couldn't fail to make one the center of attention. The whole household revolved around one's needs and waited hushed and anxious for a happy outcome. Mark and Molly were sent away with Nanny, and Nurse Broadbent, a professional, moved in to care for me.

My father was always a great one for nicknames—he couldn't call a spade a spade, it had to be a bloody shovel. Mark was Mark most of the time—but when occasion served he could be Pigdog. Molly, whose real name was Mary, to my father become Wog; and I, Mungo, or Puppy Dog. He wanted me to be christened Mungo, having found in some old family papers a character entered as, "Kentigern or Mungo." *(Kentigern, also known as Mungo, is the patron saint of Glasgow.)* Had I had a son, I would certainly have called him Kentigern—a noble name. A favorite dog—at whose birth I assisted one stormy night in California—finally inherited it. *(While Humphrey Carver's granddaughter's dog became Mungo.)*

So when my hospital nurse first came into the night nursery at Tennal Grange to introduce herself to her feverish little charge she briskly announced:

"I am Nurse Broadbent, come to look after you. And what's your name, my little man?"

It is reported that I replied after a reflective pause, "My weal name is Alan William Napier-Clavering: but if you can't wemember that you may call me Puppy Dog."

Dr. Huxley, the Family's G.P., was a homeopath, wore a top hat and made house calls in a Hansom cab. He called twice a day. As the crisis approached he made up a special prescription. Grandmama had come over from The Grove to be in charge that day. She gave me twice the prescribed dose, legend records (what was Nurse Broadbent doing?) and when Dr. Huxley called back in the evening and heard what had happened he ran up all thirty-six stairs to my third floor sickroom two at a time. I was sleeping peacefully. The crisis had passed.

I now suddenly think, "Where was mother on that momentous day?" In fact, she plays no part whatever in any memory of illness. Not hers to soothe the fevered brow.

I enjoyed my convalescence enormously. Every morning I would get a funny postcard or a little gift from Nanny Dodd—an eggcup perhaps with "a present from Clevedon" painted under the glaze. Everybody spoiled me—our spirited cook Eliza, Martha the Parlor-maid, and whoever happened to be housemaid at the time. At last the day came when Mark and Molly returned and everything went back to normal. I was no longer the center of attention and I developed a catastrophic stammer.

In our childhood there were many great trees; and boldness in climbing carried status. In this I was not at a disadvantage; I had a good head for heights, good judgment and strength enough in hand and wrist and skinny arm. Being lighter than Mark and Molly I could sometimes trust myself to boughs that would not carry them. The great tree in our lives was the magnificent Cedar of Lebanon at the Grove, which rose serenely from the eastern edge of the lawn opposite the morning-room veranda.

It was so regularly and symmetrically formed that climbing it was almost too easy. But you could go out on a long sweeping limb and use it as a swing; or pursue your destiny up and up to the very topmost tip. I do not know its height in feet, but up in your lofty, swaying crow's nest it was possible to view the varied and extensive territory of the roofs of the house, where different pitches of slate came together at the great hall skylight, then down to the dining room skylight, and on and up over the rambling kitchen and servants' quarters. Looking down, there, far away, was the bald top of Mr. Eeds' head as he rebuked the gardener's boy (who also cleaned the knives and boots) for failing to roll the gravel of the terrace in perfectly straight lines. The pleasant garden sound of cast iron on moist gravel would drift up and counterpoint the soughing of the breeze in a million cedar fronds.

After a stay at The Grove I remember my mother giving me a half crown, or maybe only a measly one and six, to tip the gardener's boy for services rendered to our boots. I was dreadfully embarrassed and remain embarrassed by tipping to this day.

In our own garden there was the famous oak. This was very much more difficult than The Grove's cedar. It stood in the hedge dividing our property from Tennal House next door. We always assumed it was ours, yet the barbed wire that supplemented the hedge certainly came on our side of the tree. This was forcibly impressed on me when I fell out of the oak. I think a rotten branch gave way, perhaps ten or twelve feet up. In falling, however, the inside of the little finger of my right hand caught on a barb of wire and tore the flesh clean to the bone. The fall knocked all the wind out of me. I came to, only to find a precious flap of flesh hanging loose, and my blood pouring down in a red stream. How I howled!

They got me to bed and the finger bandaged; but when Dr. Huxley arrived, with his mottled purple face and humorous grey eyes, it had to be opened up, carefully disinfected because of the rust on the wire, and sewn up. No local anesthetic in those days. It was the first experience of great pain in my life. When my finger healed it provided an invaluable guide as to left and right; I knew my right finger had the scar and only had to feel it with my thumb to be free of the panic moment—which way? Which way?

Our right to climb trees was never questioned. Nor to climb cliffs for that matter when we were at the seaside. How often was one within an inch of death! I suppose children who are denied this freedom to risk their lives are not total losers. One may say that their parents are overanxious or one may say that they love their children too well to be able to endure the anxiety. Of our parents it could be said either that they were wisely careful not to be overprotective or, alternatively, that they did not care urgently enough to bother. Anyhow, survive we did. Taking risks has been so much a part of my life that I must believe one's survival is a matter not of wisdom but of destiny.

A year or so ago I heard of some reasonably un-overprotected children (were they my grandchildren?) who were invited, by an aberration of our democratic class structure, to a party of privileged upper echelon movie producers' children. My grandchildren—I'll call them that—spotting an alluring tree on the lawn of the half-timbered, half-provençal chateau in Beverly Hills to which they had been invited, were very soon halfway up and calling to the others "C'mon up. It's easy! We can see a lady sunbathing with nothing on!" Nobody followed. When they finally came down, a little chip of Zanuck, Goetz, or Selznick stock, full of admiration, asked, "Who is your tree-climbing coach?"

* * *

In the winter there were the rounds of Christmas parties to look forward to. One was rather overdressed it was true; my portrait, age five, water-color on vellum by Charles Gere, shows me in purple velvet with a Little Lord Fauntleroy collar. But the games were madly exciting—Turn the Trencher to break the ice, General Post, Hunt the Slipper, Russian Candles, Blowing the Feather, and Musical Chairs.

Alan Napier-Clavering painted by Charles Gere, 1908. Courtesy Julian Mulock.

As we grew older these lovely parties tended to give way to children's dances. These seemed to me infinitely boring and embarrassing. Those silly little cards with tasseled pencils. Having to ask some simpering girl to dance with one—the easy, comfortable girls were always booked up. Being prodded by a grownup to approach a fat, unknown wallflower. Oh, it was unendurable! To be so close, so hot, so tongue-tied! Games were fun and made sense—you competed and had your moments of failure and your moments of triumph. And when they played games, girls were virtually the same as boys. But dances! How could you win? You just hoped you wouldn't get stuck with anyone too awful for supper.

Fortunately at our house and at the Carver's we never went in for dances. We played charades instead. It was the playing of charades that foreshadowed my eventual choice of a career. The form of charades we used to play was not "the game" as played today in America by the "beautiful people," but a form requiring the improvisation of little stories into which clues were inserted. "You be the father and Molly the mother, and I'll be the professor who comes to tell them their son has blown himself up!" Endless invention of character

Alan's father, Claude Gerald Napier-Clavering, 1913. Courtesy Jennifer Nichols.

was necessary. I could do it, and I loved to do it—because when I was being someone else I did not stammer. And I could make the grownups laugh. It filled me with a sense of power. It was better even than being ill.

Just as Christmas marked the high point of the winter season, so did our August seaside holiday mark the high point of the summer. And both provided happy reunions with those misguided members of the Family who were condemned to live in London, like our Debenham cousins.

Nineteen-twelve was the year of our first visit to North Wales. The place selected was Nefyn, on the north of the Lleyn Peninsolar of Caernarvon. For some reason there was no Family presence. Did my father protest that he was sick and tired of playing second fiddle to my mother's relatives? Or had the Family not yet forgiven Claude for his defection in America?

Somehow my father was coming closer to me. I remember his stern face when he took us out in a rowboat—we were to go around the headland for a picnic—and a current carried us out to sea. The wind rose putting a chop on the waves and he had quite a fight getting us back to shore. Mark was sick over the side disturbing the trim of the boat and an envious wavelet splashed over the stern. I could see that my mother was frightened. But my father's powerful arms kept pulling and suddenly, in the lea of the headland, the wind dropped, the broken waves gave way to a gentle learwater swell and we were saved.

My father had taken up painting again. Delicate water-color landscapes. One thinks immediately of Dylan Thomas' hilarious, "pale, lady watercolors, like lettuce salad dying," from *Under Milk Wood*. But no, in anything he did, my father had the professional touch. Though his watercolors were pale, they were also masculine and living.

At Nefyn I started a long history of sun worship. It must have been a fine August. I clearly remember the hypnotic drowsy ecstasy of lying on hot sand and, after braving the sea's chill embrace, feeling through skin and skeletal rib the sun's strong rays invade and penetrate one's entire being. On the beach at Nefyn I underwent my initiation torment; for one long afternoon, lying on my front near my father as he painted, I went to sleep. When I woke up I had sunstroke. I rode back to our lodgings in the village standing on the step of my father's bicycle, my hands on his shoulders. The calf muscles of the supporting leg cramped, my head swam, and I wanted to throw up.

"Dadn, I can't ... I can't any more..."

"What's the matter?"

"My leg ... I think I'm going..."

"Hang on a minute. We're nearly there."

I hung on.

* * *

Next summer it was Dyffryn and the grandparents' golden wedding. We stayed at a farm house at nearby Tal-y-bont, owned by a charming family of very Welsh Williamses.

Two things I remember about my parents at this time, things so disparate and so hard to accommodate side by side. How impenetrable and difficult to assess or explain are human relationships. One's own are hard enough—other people's impossible. For at Tal-y-bont I remember my father telling his American jokes and even singing in approximation to the tune and lyric,

"But if you meet a girl like mother
Get married like your dear old Dad,"

in a sentimental mocking voice to be sure, but with no bitterness. Side by side with this I also remember Molly desperately concerned and convoking Mark and me to ask us if we didn't think Uncle Alan should have been our father, because she had heard mother and Dadn having a row last night ... and...

I suppose they often had rows after the children had gone to bed. They must have forgotten there was only a thin, ill-fitting door at the farmhouse between them and Molly's sleeping quarters. The significant thing is that Uncle Alan's name had cropped up. Years later, I learned that my mother had, in fact, carried on a considerable flirtation with Uncle

Summer holidays in Tal-y-bont. Mark, Alan and Molly with Judy, 1913. Courtesy Jennifer Nichols.

Alan—begun I suppose when she went out to India "for her health." Indeed, my brother tells me, that on one occasion quite early in their marriage, my father walked into the drawing roam at Tennal Grange to find his frigid wife in the arms of his frightfully pukka elder brother. Were there agonizing reappraisals? Or was it merely a matter of social embarrassment? Since Uncle Alan regularly visited us whenever he was in England one must presume the latter. Yet, on Uncle Alan's side, I imagine the feeling was deep and steadfast. It is likely that mother justified the failure of her marriage to my father with the thought, "If only I had met Alan first," the excuse of many who attribute repugnance for the marriage bed to the one who shares it with them, rather than to their own distaste for it.

* * *

I have written that my childhood was overcast by the unending series of physical combats promoted by my brother. I had independent testimony of this from my sister a year or so ago. She had kept up over the years with the Williams' family at Tal-y-bont, and told me how "young Mr. Williams"—now a white-haired old man—recalled to her the terrible fight Mark and I had that first year we spent at Tal-y-bont.

"They was going at it so fierce I was afraid for the little one and had to go in and part them."

I have no recollection of this whatever; but I'm glad I put up a good fight. What I do remember is the kind of provocation. In the sand hills behind the beach at Tal-y-bont there grew great clumps of a type of reed, the tips of which hardened into brown spiny points like porcupine quills. Mark had an endearing habit of selecting a good long one, say three or four feet, and, walking behind me as we came up from the beach, jabbing at the bare calves of my legs. The reed was not rigid enough to inflict injury, indeed he'd have been lucky to draw blood, but ... oh, so infuriating! What was one to do? Snatch at it? He would whisk it away. Snatch at it again? Seize it? He would pick another. Try to get behind him and jab at his calves? Yes, you could try that. Maybe that's how the fight started that young Mr. Williams had to stop.

Many years later, Mark Napier, in an audio cassette recorded for his grandson Julian, touched briefly on his relationship with his younger brother. "My brother Alan William, known as Mungo, was five years my junior with a temperament which would go to considerable lengths to avoid trouble. Since we've all grown up, he's accused me of bullying him, something I indignantly deny, but secretly suppose had some truth."

7

Heritage

Only sunny days. Yes, that's how I remember my childhood. But an adult acquaintance with the facts of the English weather convinces me that my memory must be at fault. Is this convenient forgetfulness part of a personal survival kit? "Tennal," by the way, means "In the sun."

Well, if I force myself, I can remember playing shop in the green linoleumed playroom upstairs on wet days; and once running down in a passion of rage-at-injustice, pursued by Mark, the unjust, to lay my complaint at my parents' feet. Only to be told not to bother them—we must settle our own disputes.

Then there were our knee-caps. Where mother dredged up this particular misery from, I don't know. Knee-caps were an ingenious economy device to save our knickerbockers. When I was young, shorts were not correct wear for little gentlemen. No, we wore knickerbockers, buttoning just below the knee, in stout worsted cloth. Now, any little boy is liable to fall and scrape his knees from time to time; and skin grows back. But worsted doesn't. Mark preferred to be on his knees to standing; so, apart from involuntary falling, he was constantly throwing himself on his knees in order to do what he had in mind to do—whether it was to read a book or to "mend" his bicycle by knocking off with a stone any part that didn't work. The wear and tear on his knickerbockers must have been considerable. And then someone told mother about knee-caps. They were pieces of leather about six inches square with straps attached that buckled behind the knee. Our shoemaker in Harborne, Mr. Healey, made them to order, and whenever we went outdoors to play we had to wear them.

Oh, how I hated them! If you strapped them too loose they slipped down around your ankles. If you strapped them too tight they hurt the tendons behind your knees. In any case the edges stuck out and at every step rubbed together. Flap, flap. Flap, flap. Flap, flap as you ran. (To this day I cannot bear the sound, attractively suggestive to many men, of well-stockinged thighs rubbing together as a woman walks.) And above all, nobody else wore them. The Carvers didn't wear them, the Harborne House Kenricks didn't wear them. Nobody wore them. Only us, because mother said we couldn't afford to go through our knickerbockers at that pace; But I didn't go through my knickerbockers! I didn't fall down much! It was all Mark's fault. And it was the mark of the beast.

Then there was the fatal day with the pony. Molly was good on a pony—it was her thing. Mark does not come into this memory. It was on a day when an older cousin was staying with us and it happened in the mouth of a shady lane. I was persuaded to sit on the pony. I was very frightened but I let myself be placed astride this giant beast because I had faith in my cousin. Reins were put in my hands. And then someone gave the pony a smack on its rump and it took off. I was soaked to the depths of my being in black terror. I don't know how far or how fast the pony went. Somehow I hung onto its mane. Oh, the awful jolting, the sight of earth flying by below me and the whipping branches from the hedgerows that lashed at me from the side and from above. We came out into the open and eventually the pony stopped. I fell off shaken with silent sobbing. It was the birth of a phobia.

From that day I never went near a horse if I could help it until I came to Hollywood some thirty years later and found that I'd better get over this phobia if I wanted to survive in motion pictures. Just as other phobias had to be overcome to survive as a human being.

Lordswood House was where the Pinsents lived. It was like one of the big houses the great-uncles lived in. Mrs. Pinsent was a distinguished nonconformist of some kind—women's rights I think. The Family only knew nonconformists. And at her house a little kindergarten class convened supervised by a Miss Collinson.

Humphrey Carver: "We all went through the same succession of schools, with minor variations in the early stages.... The first stage took place in the School Room at the Pinsents,' only five minutes walk from Weatherbury. The Pinsents had an only child, Hester, clearly destined to be a 'blue-stocking' like her mother. Next door to the Pinsents lived Dr. Auden, Birmingham's Medical officer of Health and the father of W. H. Auden, the poet, who was about the same age as Francis. Christian and Maurice were taught by Miss Lotka who became an Anglican nun. My teacher was Miss Collinson who had a professional skill and was an excellent and patient teacher."

Poor Miss Collinson! Early on she suffered devaluation in our eyes because, reading *The Lady of Shallot*, she pronounced casement "cazement."

"Mother, Miss Collywobbles said cazement...."

"Miss Collinson, Molly. What did she say?"

"Cazement in *The Lady of Shallot*."

"*Cazement*? How ridiculous! Casement of course."

"That's what I told her. I said we have casement windows here."

While I have always thought a teacher's authority precarious enough without being undermined by the pupil's parents, it is really for the child's sake that one should endeavor to sustain it. Devalued, the teacher may lose face; but the child will lose faith and with it the desire to learn. However, there have been times when child or grandchild have sought self-vindication with a rather smug, "Well, Miss Snodgrass says ..." and one has had the greatest difficulty in not replying, "Your Miss Snodgrass is talking through her hat!"

For us young Napier-Claverings there was only one way to pronounce any word, and that was the way mother and Dadn pronounced it—because that was the way people out of the top drawer spoke. All other ways were cause for contempt or merriment.

Apart from *The Lady of Shallot*, Miss Collinson taught us penmanship—she was on safe ground here, as mother's was appalling—and making little conical receptacles for hair ends and nail clippings out of strips of colored paper. I suppose Mark and Molly received these valuable preparations for life's journey before me.

Indeed it must have been while my siblings were at Lordswood House that mother started teaching me poetry, long before I could read. She was clever and patient at this—it was an act of love and I responded by learning easily and well. There was Shelly's "I bring fresh showers to the thirsting flowers!" and Kipling's "Excellent herbs had our fathers of old," and Stevenson's, "Up into the cherry tree who should climb but little me," and many others—all while I was three years old. And hot on their heels Matthew Arnold's "Come dear children let us away, down and away below." Oh, how I loved "The Forsaken Merman"! I used to say it over to myself night after night from beginning to end and see "great whales come sailing by" and all the other submerged marvels Matthew Arnold imagined before aqualung photography proved him to be right. As a special event for both of us I sometimes said it aloud for Molly. And there was Henry Newbolt's "Admirals all for England's sake," which I was called upon to recite to grandpapa and grandmama in the morning room at The Grove. But when I came to the bit about Nelson that says, "and he clapped his glass to his sightless eye and 'I'm damned if I see it,' he said," I pretended I had forgotten (and hated having to pretend because it was my pride not to forget) because I didn't dare to say "damned" in front of grandpapa.

The sound of poetry was my mother's great gift to me. It has stood by me all my life. When you learn poetry by ear, as the great legendary poems of history were learned and handed down, its necessary shapes are as clear and inviolable to you as a tune is to a child brought up on music. You would think the two went naturally together, but this is not necessarily the case. My mother was totally unmusical—she really could not tell the difference between the Marseillaise and the Star Spangled Banner. I consequently had no music in my childhood which has left me musically illiterate and insecure with any but the most familiar tunes. My singing causes the musical to shudder. Conversely, I've heard musicians quite unable to recognize their own horrific manglings of the obligatory rhythms of say, the Limerick, or the simple, noble march of the iambic pentameter. And I'm amazed at the audacity of composers whose settings violate essential rhythms of the poems that inspire them. How did they come to be inspired, one wonders, if they misread the poem's rhythms?

When you start riffling through the attic of memory, it is amazing how many incidents come to light from earliest childhood. Because they are at the bottom of the pile—well covered by a conglomeration of more recent happenings which, through exposure to light and the incessant fall of dusty trivia have lost both shape and hue—the early memories come up sharp-edged and brightly colored.

This is a spring morning on the terrace at Tennal Grange. My father is digging a few yards away. It is the wallflower border under the pantry window. There is a keen little wind but, when the sun cleaves through the clouds it is hot on my back, and the dark crimson wallflowers give forth their wonderful dark crimson scent. A centipede runs out as I lift a piece of edging sandstone that has come adrift. I head him off with my bit of stone, this way and that. My father's spade makes a pleasant sound as it drives through earth and pebble. The centipede climbs on my little rock and comes dangerously near my finger. I shake it off onto a flat surface of sandstone. I grind it out of existence.

This became a family story but the wallflowers and the sun on my back and the amazing articulation of the centipede are as vivid as the moment. The story: "Dadn." "Yes?" "I found a dear little crawl." He turns over half a dozen spadefuls of earth. "Dadn." "Yes?" "I've killed my dear little crawl." The thing that comes over to me now is the evidence of easy communication with my father. Again, a hot summer morning and an aching void in my middle that says lunchtime. But no—I want to bring another load of earth to my father in my little child's wheelbarrow. I load up at the potting shed, come round the path by the servant's hall, all along the terrace at a run, and onto the grass walk that separates the long, east border from the rose garden. There is a little brick edging where the grass meets the terrace. I'm getting tired and manipulate this hazard carelessly so that one handle of the barrow jerks out of my hand and goes straight into the pit of my empty stomach. I'm winded. Sudden pain and gasping for breath. My father quickly picks me up in strong arms, laying me on the grass walk, rubbing my hollow midriff and saying words of reassurance.

So I begin to wonder whether the memory—"my father was cold and not at ease with children" was not a later impression put forth by my mother and overlaying the real truth. For there was also the delicious ritual at lunch on Saturdays. My father would come home from business in time for lunch that day—Parliament had decreed a half day off for every British worker. A bottle of Whitbreads India Pale Ale would stand on the table, and after pudding there was cheese and cream crackers and crisp celery from the garden. But Dadn liked toast instead of crackers and if he was in a good mood he would carve a little horse out of the piece of toast and a little man out of the piece of cheese and stick the man on the horse's back with a dab of butter. And then it would happen—the horse would come, gallop, gallop, across the white tablecloth; gallop, gallop up your arm, into your mouth and gallop, gallop down the red lane.

"Again, Dadn, please. Oh, again."

It doesn't suggest a cold and distant figure now that I come to think about it.

* * *

Looking back on this somewhat chaotic account of my early childhood I think that the desire to point a moral and adorn the tale may have led me to distort the picture. For instance, whatever hindsight may imply it never occurred to me at the time that I was being in any way short-changed by my parents. The lesson that we were a superior family automatically carried the corollary that they were superior parents. The fact that my Aunt Cecily warmed my cold little heart because she happened to be a very outgoing, loving and maternal woman, in no way affected my acceptance of my mother. Years later, when I wrote to tell Aunt Cecily of my impending divorce from my first wife, in her letter lamenting this development, I was amazed to read, "You were always such a loving little boy." I suppose that in her presence this solemn child's eyes must have come to life. They certainly followed her with spaniel adoration.

Nor did I have a permanent sense of injury as far as Mark was concerned. I accepted the idea that it was part of life for older brothers to impose their wills by force if necessary on younger brothers. And I certainly don't blame him now. Neither of us had received, by precept or example from our parents, any effective instruction in the art of love. It was not just that they did not envelop us in any show of love—they never even demonstrated affection for each other, at least in my time. Whether there was an ambience of love between them in Mark's infancy I cannot say; though his closer contact with my mother suggests to me that, as a baby, he may have been warmed by the dying glow of our parents' love. Naturally he would resent a newcomer when the demand for love already exceeded the supply.

That my background could be regarded as in any way over-privileged would never have occurred to me either. On the contrary I felt positively underprivileged in comparison with our richer relatives who evidently had more of the things that money can buy. It was because of this that one secretly prized so highly those gifts of lineage and class which my parents did provide.

I do hope, by the way, that these constant references to blue blood have not led the gentle reader to misjudge us as being then or, heaven forbid, now a pack of effete snobs. In fact, these gifts of dubious value were my parents' substitute for love and true concern. Similarly, elaborate and costly gifts of toys and jewelry are often the love substitutes of wealthy parents whose deepest concern is for material possessions and the status they confer. In both cases the parent, unable or unwilling to pour forth the balm of natural love, gives instead a symbol of what is important for his own self-esteem—in the case of my parents: class, in that of the rich man: money.

So all the teaching I had that I was "out of the top drawer," and the implication that the world was the oyster of the British ruling class, provided me with little assurance of personal validity when I moved out of the family cocoon into the competitive world of my peers. Indeed it took me half a lifetime to have any faith in my essential manhood.

The Concise Oxford Dictionary defines "snob" thus—"person with exaggerated respect for social position or wealth and a disposition to be ashamed of socially inferior connections." I don't think we were snobs; I think my brother and sister and I were led to overvalue—as had our father before us—certain rather trivial aspects of life. For my father this "gift" was natural. But for my mother, with her wealthy middle-class background, to glorify blue blood was indeed a trifle snobbish.

My Uncle Henry, with his innate humanity and good sense, contributed an interesting definition in this tormenting field. We were mowing the vicarage lawn one hot afternoon at Tetbury, a small cure of souls he once ministered to in Oxfordshire. Suddenly, out of the blue, he observed,

"A gentleman, I take it, is one who knows how to behave himself and be at ease with his superiors, his equals and his inferiors."

"Very nice," I said, and added as an amusing thought, "But where will he find superiors if he's a king?" Uncle Henry thought for a moment, looked up at a sky rapidly being overcast with thunderclouds, and said,

"If the King is a gentleman he'll be perfectly at ease up above." A few heavy drops of rain plopped down on our bare heads and thunder rumbled in the distance. Uncle Henry sniggered,

"Oh, dear, I'm afraid the King must have just misbehaved."

His definition would of course make no sense in a classless society—but I have yet to find that utopia. It would be very naive to imagine it exists in the United States. My friend Brian Aherne used occasionally to throw some very grand dinner parties at his house on the beach at Santa Monica, for the big-wigs of the movie business. The night after, my wife and I would be invited, as cozy old friends, to sup on the leftovers. (*"Oh he was family, sure,"* laughs Joan Fontaine [*then Mrs. Brian Aherne*]. *"Family gets leftovers!"*) I was not invited to the grand affair because, as Brian explained, not being in the same economic bracket as the other guests "I would feel uncomfortable and not know how to behave." I entirely agreed with him, which, if one accepts Uncle Henry's definition, makes me (like Mr. Salteena in *The Young Visiters*) not quite a gentleman—at least in Hollywood. Now Uncle Henry—he'd have had no difficulty in holding his own with any Mayer or Cohn.

The heritage my parents gave me—the pearls they scattered on my lawn—let us call this "family pride." One little pearl, so exquisitely nonsensical, should not blush, I feel, unseen. It is the story of my great-aunt, Augusta Napier. She was tall, thin as a rail, with an ingenious system of whalebone and elastic carrying a covering of the finest black lace high up around her swanlike neck.

Once, on being asked if she was related to Lord Napier of Magdala (who has a nice equestrian statue in Kensington) she replied with a withering little smile, "Oh dear, no." The point is that the Napiers of Magdala had, a couple of generations before, adopted the name Napier because the famous Peninsula War Napier brothers had given it a very good standing in the army. But to Aunt Augusta the occasion was rather as if a lady of the well-known Agnew family were to be asked if she was related to *Spiro* Agnew! And the lavender charm of the story lay in Aunt Augusta's inflection of amused surprise that anyone could possibly make so ridiculous a mistake.

Such were the tales on which I was fortified for the battle of life.

8

Trailing Clouds of Glory

For the next ten years of my life, I would be at boarding school for three quarters of the year. Nanny had done her best and departed; mother was to be with me for some time, still doing her best; and there was always Mark.

Indeed, Mother's best was a very good best—a gift of love and, like many such gifts, also an expression of self-love. Reading aloud was mother's forte and she gloried in it. The world of romantic fiction was her natural element—far more congenial to her spirit than the world of flesh and blood. After all, we never hear of Sir Walter Scott's heroes and heroines actually going to bed together, nor does he tell of little lordlings sucking the breast or nuzzling in their mother's laps. It is all on a higher plane with frequent renunciations of things carnal, and much solitary self-denial.

Every day of the holidays she read aloud to us after dinner summer and winter; and in the dark months often between tea and dinner; yes, and sometimes even in the morning before lunch. Richardson, Scott, Jane Austin, Thackery, Dickens, the Brontës (all of them), George Elliot, Trollope, Conrad, Kipling, Stevenson, John Buchan, and Galsworthy—she read them all to us. What a gift of literature enjoyed! One of her great triumphs was Shaw's *Candida*. I must have heard her read it half a dozen times. Politically, Shaw was, of course, not to be taken seriously; but his dispassionate approach to passion suited mother down to the ground. She also made many a noble stab at Shakespeare, leaving out the awkward bits. As the years went by and she became totally crippled, she would come down to tea from her afternoon rest exhausted by the constant battle with pain, unable to speak above a whisper. I can hear the sound of her disconsolately munching, with dry tired chops, a piece of thin brown bread and butter. Tea over, would she read to us? Yes, dear. No, she did not feel like starting on a new novel. How about a Shakespeare? She suddenly brightens. "Yes. Let me see now, I don't think we've read *Lear*." And ten minutes later, my father, halfway across the garden, would hear her voice ringing out clear as a bell.

I've seen the same triumph of mind over matter with professional actors. When I was studying at the Royal Academy of Dramatic Art, I had the privilege of being taught by a wonderful old war horse, Rosina Filippi. She too was arthritic, but, since her livelihood depended on it, remained ambulatory with the help of crutches. In class somebody up on the stage would fail to bring a scene to life, "No child, no, no, no." And she would hoist herself painfully up the four steps onto the stage. "You're running away, child. This is your field of battle. Command it. Like this." And she would throw down her crutches and sweep across the stage like a queen. Then she would grip the arm of the nearest male student. "Bring me my crutches, boy," she'd say to another, and laboriously ease herself back down the steps and into the seat from which she had started.

8. Trailing Clouds of Glory

As a reader, my mother was a real pro. Indeed, she was a different person—warm, generous and with great charm. As a young woman she must have been quite beautiful, with her abundant auburn hair and milk-white skin. She dutifully followed her father's taste in Pre-Raphaelites, and succeeded in looking as if she had been started by Sir John Millais and kindly finished off by Edward Burne-Jones.

It must have been the year after I was packed off to boarding school that mother went up to London and stayed with Aunt Cecily in the great Debenham mansion at 8 Addison Road, in order to undergo the Schroth-Ebardt treatment for arthritis. This was a drastic regime, devised by a couple of German theoreticians of dictatorial bent, involving a period of starvation followed by a meticulously nonsensical diet. My mother never recovered from it. I say nonsensical advisedly since, with another fifty years study of arthritis, the medical profession is still unable to come up with a cure. Cortisone has been tried, oil and vinegar to lubricate the joints, and even gold; but aspirin remains the best bet. The one thing all the experts agree on is that a normally varied diet is to be preferred. At home all our vegetables and fruits were organically grown in the kitchen garden at Tennal Grange, our bread was home-made from stone-ground flour by a little woman who delivered it on a bicycle twice a week; our fish was sent by mail, unfrozen but fresh, by the Live Fish Company of Grimsby; our milk and butter came from the farm down the road and our meat was butchered locally. Any change dictated by Drs. Schroth and Ebardt must necessarily have been for the worse.

Before the treatment my mother could get about on her own quite tolerably; after it, she was dependent on wheelchairs, sticks and supporting arms for the rest of her life, though sometimes there might be a period of slight improvement. When Dr. Coué, apostle of autosuggestion, came to visit Birmingham, there was talk of mother going to him to learn his secret, "Day by day in every way I get better and better." Our Dr. Huxley, who had borne the brunt of ministering to this incurable disease for many long years, confided to my father that, while it would do no harm, he was rather afraid that Dr. Coué would come away from the encounter with a pain in his knee.

The period of the Schroth-Ebardt treatment was remarkable for me because, for a week during our spring holidays, Mark and I went up to London to stay at The Debs' green and blue tile palace. The magnificence of the life led by a merchant prince and the vastness of London made a deep impression on me. Also the grapefruit which were part of mother's diet—a new fruit which had not yet permeated into the suburbs of Birmingham.

Back at Tennal Grange there was the joy of finding Mable, eldest of our Ryland cousins, in residence to take care of us. I wonder now how she got on with my father, for it was one of the Ryland girls who had seen him at a restaurant in London a year or so before with "another woman," probably an actress. The family must indeed have felt poor Millie's marriage to be a *mésalliance*. No Chamberlain was ever faithless to a Kenrick or vice versa—though Uncle Gerald was, alas, impotent with poor Aunt Ruth. Of course there was cousin Donald Hope … but then he was immensely successful in business, even though his windows mysteriously failed to keep out the rain at Tennal Grange.

A curious thing occurs to me—that my mother never spoke to us of her childhood. Apparently her life began when she and her elder sister Cecily went to finishing school in Paris. Was she then unhappy at the Grove? And what happened to my grandmother, so comfortably affectionate with us? Did W.K. succeed in imposing his superior class and Victorian "governor the father" dominion over her to such a degree that the Grove became a chilling monument to rectitude? Had he not, by nobly foregoing the siren voice of Art for the respectable summons of profitable Commerce, somehow earned the right to see that no one else had any fun?

If one can blame others for being ill-equipped for life, in our family the blame must evidently lie with my mother. My poor mother who knew no better and sincerely did her best. How far must you go back? My grandparents raised four children. Darling Aunt Cecily, who had eight children of her own and love enough left over for a timid nephew; Uncle Byng, a cool shy man who led a long and successful life in public affairs as well as in business and in marriage. And then my mother and Uncle Gerald—both virtually impotent. Why? "The sins of the fathers shall be visited on the children to the third and fourth generation." The famous biblical curse holds a terrible psychological truth. For how shall children, never blessed by the tender arts of mother-love communicate these arts to their own children?

Knowing that I have not been the best of fathers and that my daughter had a deplorable mother, I am so grateful and deeply relieved to see my grandchildren growing in the light: talented, uninhibited yet responsible, loving and, thank the Lord, with a sense of humor even about themselves.

* * *

Going to one's first boarding school clearly marks the end of childhood and for many the end of innocence. But not for me. Packwood Haugh, fifteen miles to the south of Birmingham, was situated halfway up a gently rising hill in the flat, lush Warwickshire countryside.

It was a school for forty boys from the age of eight or nine to thirteen. It was owned and presided over by the Bradshaw family, Mr., Mrs. and Miss; and in my day it was of a purity unmatched.

The Bradshaws were the nicest people in the world. Old Miss Bradshaw, the Matron, was a trained hospital nurse, and responsible for our health. Her face was in that early stage of mottled purple, which had overrun all of her brother's that was not concealed by beard. Indeed, she had a suspicion of beard herself, which was no handicap to one whose job it was firmly to administer licorice, cascara, Gregory's powder and quinine and see to the health and cleanliness of forty obstreperous boys. We were well looked after—as soon as the first sniffle and sneeze signaled the end of summer holiday immunity to lurking germs, it was sniff and gargle and temperature taking morning and evening for the whole school.

"Laddie, laddie, my arms are achin' with pain, laddie, achin' with pain," Miss Bradshaw would lament as she shook down the thermometer for the hundredth time that day.

Mr. Bradshaw was a good mathematician and a good classical cricketer—or as good as an elderly man wearing pince-nez spectacles could hope to be—and at heart a gentle humanist. Mrs. Bradshaw was a beautiful and loving human being. They had three daughters and a little boy; but we were all Mrs. Bradshaw's children.

I did not make a very auspicious start at Packwood. For one thing, Mark, who had preceded me there, had not been popular; so that, far from a bonus of good will to greet me he left a legacy of prejudice.

As time went on, things improved. I took happily to cricket and "soccer" and suffered less from my stammer than might have been expected. Mr. Podmore, the senior assistant master, a stern disciplinarian and an ex–Blue footballer, also had a stammer—so imitating stammering for fun was not done at Packwood. Instead, we imitated Jordan's Brummagem accent about which Mr. Ebden, second assistant, was pleased to be very funny. I remember him chalking up on the board "IGHPNY" and saying, "That is not, Jordan, the correct pronunciation for the word ha'penny."

Mrs. Bradshaw, who I am sure instinctively reacted to my need for love, conducted a weekly Sunday school class. I endeared myself to her by composing a deeply religious and technically expert poem in my ninth year. Because of the variety of poetry my mother had taught me from infancy I had rhyme and rhythm in my bones. The second verse describing a sunset went:

> On one side dark grey clouds were hanging o'er
> A mighty temple made of flaming gold
> Portrayed so finely that me-thought I saw
> A Picture of our Lord, and to the fold
> He welcomed back the lost sheep that had strayed:
> I fell upon my knees and, wondering, prayed.

However sickening the sentiment, this was quite an achievement for a child of nine. I remember it to this day because I composed my poems in my head at night, without pen, paper or light and had to memorize them lest they be lost to the world by morning. I had no doubt but that I was a genius. The main trouble with this poem was that I never believed in that sort of God nor said an honest prayer in my life. However, dear Mrs. Bradshaw gave me her Sunday school prize that term, a Common Prayer Book in limp brown calf, even though I wasn't very good at learning my catechism.

Certain subjects that appealed to me, English Composition, History and Geometry—those squares and triangles made visual sense—I was good at. But things like Arithmetic and Latin, that needed close concentration, I found hard to master.

It was at Packwood that music came into my life. It came with the Church of England services every Sunday—at Lapworth in the morning, where the Rector was Mrs. Bradshaw's brother, and at Packwood Church for Evensong, where stern Mr. Couchman spoke dry good sense from the pulpit. It was said that one year, when Christmas day fell on a Sunday, he cut his sermon to the bone. "I am sure you are all as anxious as I am to get home to your Christmas dinners. God be with you. In the name of the Father, the Son, and the Holy Ghost. Amen." No nonsense about Mr. Couchman. Then I remember the passing bell tolling from Packwood Church, when Mrs. Couchman died. The evening services, dimly lit by flickering candles in the winter months, always had a dreamy, mystic quality; and the Sunday after her death when Mr. Couchman's steady voice broke on "lighten our darkness, oh Lord," was flooded with a pure emotion that echoes in my heart today.

The morning service at Lapworth was more fancy. It was a bigger church, and I imagine either that it was a well endowed living or that Mr. Bell had means of his own. Anyhow, a curate did the singing bits of the service in a fine tenor voice and the responses came back true and strong from the choir. But it was the *Hymns Ancient and Modern*, that I looked forward to, especially "Holy, Holy, Holy," "Lead Kindly Light," "All Things Bright and Beautiful," and "Onward Christian Soldiers." I had a rather somber favorite, "When I Survey the Wondrous Cross" which I used to sing to myself in a dirge-like chant with indescribable feelings of sweet sadness ... "See from his head, His hands, His feet, Sorrow and love flow mingling down...."

Never for a moment, try as I may, have I achieved any positive belief in a God or the life everlasting. But the beauty of the Anglican service, which I encountered at this impressionable age, later made the mystical experience and a belief in Christ as inspired ethical teacher, acceptable ideas.

During my school days, I must have listened to well over 400 sermons. I don't believe a single one made any serious impact on my consciousness, though two I remember well for their comic value—both of them at Clifton, my future public school. On one occasion a visiting missionary from China, anxious that we should participate in the reality of his experience, began: "This afternoon I shall take you in my wheelbarrow …" and lost all 600 of us in a hurricane of suppressed laughter. The other was when the Archdeacon of Bristol, the Venerable Dr. So-and-so, a dear old gentleman with tremulous voice, jowls and belly, told us the tale of a youth who, finding himself left alone in his employer's pastry shop, began pocketing a few goodies… Little did the wretched youth surmise that, by an ingenious system of reflective mirrors, his every act was being scrutinized. The moral of this tale evidently was that we wretched youths were also being scrutinized by God—with or without the benefit of reflective mirrors.

* * *

It must have been in September 1911 that I went to Packwood, because I remember Mr. Bradshaw telling us of the sinking of the *Titanic*, which was in April 1912. World War I broke out in 1914 during the summer holidays. I will tell of that in another place. But I remember taking part in hay-making at Packwood, as one contribution to the war effort, and how delicious was the farm workers' cold tea in the heat of the day. Another contribution was knitting. Yes—the need for wool scarves and head covers, or Balaklava helmets, was apparently so great in the endless bitter trench warfare that even little boys were roped in to knit. As far as I remember we knitted mostly when we were sick in bed with feverish colds. Apart from scarves, I contributed three mittens.

In addition to the food getting worse (and one hadn't thought there was much room for decline), Mr. Smith, the third assistant master, left to fight for King and Country and lost a bony leg, formally much admired on the soccer field. A Miss Potter moved in to teach English and History. I got on very well with Miss Potter and under her enlightened rule, in the Autumn term of 1915, there was a school production of *Macbeth*, in which I played the lead.

Apart from Parents' Day in the summer term, when there would be a sumptuous spread of cold salmon and strawberries for lunch and which my parents dutifully attended—my father embarrassing me by playing cricket and not keeping a straight bat—my mother and father never came over to Packwood to see me. Other parents did; there was Miller for instance. When his parents came he rushed up to them in wild excitement and, climbing up his father like a little monkey, exchanged passionate kisses with both Dad and Mama. This struck me then as terribly embarrassing and bad form; now I think—"how right, how uninhibited, how beautiful." Yet Miller committed suicide at Oxford over some sexual tangle before his thirtieth year. God moves in mysterious ways.

For this performance of *Macbeth*, however, my mother did appear; it was her field. In the interests of realism she insisted that a long, Celtic mustache be stuck to my long upper lip, much to the grief of dear Mrs. Bradshaw, who thought my innocent face, as I piped

"Pity, like a naked newborn babe, striding the blast; or heaven's cherubim, horsed upon the sightless couriers of the air ..." was inexpressibly beautiful. I really didn't mind one way or the other; I knew I was going to be great in the part anyhow. In fact, I did have a precocious talent. *Remarkably for productions in boarding schools at the time, the major female roles, which ordinarily would have been played by boys, were cast with girls—specifically two of the three Bradshaw daughters. Playing opposite Alan as Lady Macbeth was 12-year-old Christine Bradshaw. Lady Macduff and the First Witch were played by her older sister Ursula.*

This high level of achievement continued into the so-called Spring term. I was just thirteen years old. It was a bitter February and the ground was too hard for soccer so we played Prisoner's Base instead. My knowledge of the game, from playing it at home, made me a superior strategist and I shone. Later, I did well in the cross-country paper chase, hitting, to my own surprise, a tireless lope that brought me to the front and filled me with a sense of indestructible power.

And then I got a pain in my tummy, attributed to green apples by Miss Bradshaw and ignored too long. Just in time, Mrs. Bradshaw had a hunch, confirmed by the school doctor, that it might be appendicitis. A surgeon was sent for from Birmingham and I was operated on, pretty well *in extremis*, on a kitchen table by acetylene lamp light.

My undetected appendicitis had been a very near thing. Whether it burst during the operation I don't know, but drainage tubes were left in the wound and the walls of the cavity packed with yard upon yard of Dr. Gamgee's iodoform gauze. I remember being encouraged to drink a lot and feeling strangely perforated when liquid poured out of the wound into the bandage. Taking the tubes out was nothing; but removing the gauze which had adhered to the walls of the wound was a traumatic experience. Hearty, enormous Dr. Hollick, who went his rounds on a Budge Whitworth motor bicycle, said in his stentorian voice, "You'd better hold on to the bars above your head, boy, because this is going to hurt. And we don't want the whole school to know, do we?" Half of the school must have heard him.

Many years later at the Oxford Playhouse I acted in Strindberg's play *Creditors*, in which there is a vivid description of a medieval torture. Through a gash in the belly of the victim, the end of his gut is pulled forth and attached to a windlass which remorselessly winds out the full length of the intestine, turn after turn. At the first rehearsal I nearly fainted; it brought back so vividly the pain and fear of that morning in the sick room at Packwood when Dr. Hollick burrowed in with his forceps to pull the idoform gauze out of my abdominal cavity yard by adhering yard. Maybe they have a different technique for packing wounds today. I hope so.

Eventually I recovered. They kept me in bed for five weeks—two of them back at Tennal Grange—since the wound, only stitched at either end, had to heal slowly from inside. When I did get up I had to wear a surgical belt with a pad over the scar. I say I recovered; at times I have wondered if I ever did quite recover. As a schoolboy I was never again to feel as assured and successful in work or in sports. I started to grow enormously tall for one thing—what is called outgrowing one's strength—but in my mind, and surely in my subconscious, a feeling of no longer being on top of the world is associated with this disembowelment trauma. Was it a symbol of castration? Did it tie up with some "thou shalt not" implanted years before by Nanny? Many people seem to take pride in their surgical scars and, like Lyndon Johnson, cannot restrain themselves from showing them off. I have

Packwood Haugh. Summer Term, 1916. Alan is in the front row at the far right. The girl in the white dress two rows behind him is Christine Bradshaw, Lady Macbeth to his Macbeth and Portia to his Shylock. Courtesy Packwood Haugh School.

always hated my appendix scar and felt ashamed and degraded by it. The other day I read an article in the daily paper on the importance of furnishing a great show of love and support to children after major surgery. One would think there was little need to urge such a course; yet my mother, who was able three months before to come down to Packwood to see me play Macbeth, never made the fifteen-mile journey to my sick bed. I was just thirteen years old.

I returned to Packwood towards the middle of the summer term. Mr. Bradshaw had made me "captain" of the school, that is to say head prefect, over the heads of many boys—Brooke, Kempson, Miller, Barlow—who outshone me scholastically. I think he was impressed by my ability to meet changed, more arduous, war-time conditions during the icy February and March of the preceding term. Maybe, too, there was a desire to make up for the failure to recognize earlier the serious nature of my bellyache. All through my life people have tried to foist the role of leader on me; a role that I can play on the stage but I have no will to assume in life. I certainly failed on this occasion. My cricket had gone off for one thing—I was not seeing the ball so well. Later it was discovered I needed a new prescription for my glasses; I had entered a period of galloping myopia. *None of this prevented Alan from undertaking a second major Shakespearean role for Miss Potter, however. In July 1916 he appeared as Shylock in* The Merchant of Venice *with Christine Bradshaw again playing opposite him in the role of Portia.*

* * *

One of the great joys of youth is that feeling of absolutely inexhaustible energy and spirit—a sort of intimation of immortality. I remember being caught up in this divine ecstasy on warm summer evenings at Packwood when, through the long twilight in a period of drought, we would water the cricket pitch. The cricket field, a lovely meadow surrounded by tall elms, lay below the kitchen garden. We would fill the watering cart, a tank on two uncertain wheels, from a hand pump by the greenhouse and trundle it down to the parched cricket pitch. I remember the God-like feeling as I took the handles of the heavy tank and, with others pushing and pulling, steered and balanced my juggernaut left and right through the winding paths of the kitchen garden, past the hazelnut tree at the corner and on down the field at a run. And then, empty, how we rattled it back up to the pump and I, none other, indefatigably worked the handle, the heavy suck of the water testing the strength of my tireless thin arms. "That's enough, boys. High time you were in bed." "Oh, just one more, Sir! Please! One more for the match tomorrow!"

When I returned to school after my operation I seemed to be unable to recapture this sense of mastery and felt for the first time the mortal intimation of being submerged by life.

9

Intimations of Immorality

By 1916 the German U-boat campaign to starve Britain into subjection was alarmingly near to succeeding. And, since this was a predicament without precedent, the British government of Mr. Asquith was far less successful in its efforts to ration what food there was equitably than were the World War II counterparts of Chamberlain and Churchill.

Having put Packwood behind me, I had now moved on to Clifton College, Bristol, ninety miles southwest of Birmingham. Now, the owners of private boarding schools and the housemasters at Public schools were essentially in the hotel business. (This is no longer true of Clifton, where teaching and catering are totally divorced.) They engaged to provide bed, board and education to forty or fifty boys for nine months in the year for so many pounds, shillings and pence. If they were to make a decent living, let alone put something by for their old age, it could only be done by the ingenious economy of their catering. Mr. Bradshaw had little talent for hotel-keeping and my housemaster at Clifton, Mr. Mayor, had absolutely none. It was a cruel strain to put on men of academic bent and neither Bradshaw nor Mayor retired wealthy, despite thirty years and more of distinguished work as educators. The food provided for the boys in their care during the conditions of universal shortage in World War I was inevitably poor in quality, with little protein content. At Mr. Mayor's house it was abominably cooked. There was enough to fill the belly if your gorge did not rise, as mine rises now at the memory of fish pie at Clifton. This concoction was a kind of marine disaster: streamers of black skin like old bicycle tires drifted on a tide of greasy water against chunks of grey potato impaled on glutinous fish-head bones. Stir it at your peril; a cold fish eye might return your gaze. Ersatz sausages at breakfast come to mind; tough skins enclosing some nameless fat and cereal that wearied the jaws and adhered to the teeth. Mussratt, a fat rich boy from Lancashire, won the sausage eating competition one morning with twenty-one of these grizzly bolognas discarded by weaker brothers.

Dormitories were of course entirely unheated since coal and oil were hard to come by. So, to a considerable extent, were classrooms. Our "studies," little living closets for two, which were theoretically heated by hot water pipes, were seldom even warm. But the worst misery was the lack of hot water for bathing. 1917 was a bitterly hard winter and I remember lying in bed at Clifton, shivering under a pile of dayclothes added to the bedclothes, and hearing the lions roaring in the zoo across the road from the school. Poor beasts, they were cold too.

The autumn of 1916, then, was not a good time for anything, certainly not for starting a new life at a big boarding school. Mark and I overlapped for one term. Theoretically this should have been a help. But Mark was not popular at Clifton either. He had a study to himself.

9. Intimations of Immorality

During my first term I experienced the first official beating of my life. It was for forgetting three times to take Siepmann's pajamas up from the washhouse to the dormitory. He was Head of the House—just and strong. Three slashes on the bottom with a cane. It was quite unbelievably painful. I bore him no grudge.

Mr. Mayor, my housemaster, who was so incompetent a hotel-keeper, was a splendid classical scholar and an unconsciously comic character. He was also a human being of great integrity. He had a dog, an extraordinarily untidy Aberdeenish terrier, called Murdock. Never can the theory that master and dog come to resemble each other have been more perfectly illustrated than in the case of Henry Bickersteth Mayor and his dog Murdock. They were indistinguishable. Eyes obscured by falling grey hair, a waddling walk accompanied by grunts. It was even said that they smelt alike. But the remarkable nature of this family resemblance did not stop there. To aid him in his catering responsibilities, Mr. Mayor called in alternately his two spinster sisters Flora and Alice. Of course we called them Flora and Fauna. They were dear, wonderful women—but totally incompetent as housekeepers. Twins, they were indistinguishable from each other, from their brother, and from Murdock.

Mr. Mayor was never quite at ease with boys. He was a bachelor and seemed to have somehow sublimated all those problems of sex that distract the rest of us. Then, quite suddenly, he got married during one long summer vacation. Our excitement and hilarity at this, to us, most improbable eventuality, can be imagined. At the first lunch of the autumn term, Mrs. Mayor made her official appearance.

It was more than one could have hoped for—she too was indistinguishable from Murdock! I can see her as clear as can be, her eyes shining benignly through a fringe of grey hair, standing there by the Mayor's side, smiling endearingly. She was a dear soul and the food improved immediately. Mr. Mayor also spruced up considerably.

This happy union was, alas, childless. We horrid boys were deeply disappointed for it was confidently anticipated that any litter would be born with grey hair falling over its eyes.

* * *

During my five years at Clifton, I received altogether about 50 or 60 lashes with the cane—four or five at a time usually and usually for being late. I felt no resentment: merely fear of the inevitable and very considerable pain. They did me no harm and they did me no good. I continued to be pathologically unpunctual until, twenty-five years later, I found it distressed my darling second wife so much that I was cured by love.

One caning I did resent and I consider wrong and cowardly today. Because my form master in Four Alpha, Mr. Charles Russell, thought I was not working hard enough he reported me to Mr. Mayor and recommended a caning. This Mr. Mayor administered. There had been no warning; there was no specific charge of inattention or insubordination. It was cowardly of Charles R. as we called him, to pass the buck to the Mayor and wrong of the Mayor to beat me without trying to find out if I was up against any particular difficulty. I suspect neither of them wanted to get into an inquisition of a boy who would inevitably, under strain, get agonizingly stuck in the toils of his stammer, which was at that time at its worst. Terrible grimacing, terrible guttural stops and clicks; sometimes no words would come at all. The anxiety associated with being asked to construe a phrase in Latin did, I think, make it harder for me to concentrate fully.

I have to admit that, as time went on at Clifton and I began to feel less of a total failure, I learned to use my stammer. It seemed only fair to me that, since it stood in my way with some questions the answers to which I really knew, when asked something I ought to know but didn't, an insuperable convulsion might overcome me. The innocent or merely weary master would say, "you mean '*pluribus in unum*.'" or whatever it was. I would nod my head, blushing shamefully, and the class would proceed.

The worst beating I ever had—six strokes raised to eight because it was detected that I had put on three pairs of football shorts under my trousers to lessen the impact—was administered by the House Sixth, the prefects. This was for carrying the baiting of Mr. Ronnfelt, our house tutor, to outrageous public lengths. Boiled rice, with a meager spoonful of jam of no identifiable fruit origin, was one of our frequent desserts. We found that by rolling a few grains into a little ball and holding it to the tip of the blade of a table knife pulled back like a catapult, one could playfully project a small rice missile at a friend or enemy across the table. Mr. Ronnfelt sat at the head of one table, I at the bottom. Ronnfelt baiting was a very popular sport. What I did on this occasion I did to achieve acclaim and popularity. One day the boiled rice was stickier than usual and I had a very springy knife. I rolled a large ball of jammy rice and held it to my knife's end. It was Mr. Ronnfelt's turn to say grace at the end of the meal. As he rose I let fly. Down the fifteen foot length of the table my missile flew and burst like shrapnel all over the target. I was an instant folk hero. But inquisition and punishment inevitably followed. I remember thinking as I let fly, "I must be out of my mind!"

Poor Ronnfelt! A war-time replacement (why isn't he fighting? Because he's a dirty, rotten German, of course!), he had some skin trouble which resulted in stains on his underpants. This we learned from the Matron. After that, he never had a chance. He once approached me, humanly—as one suffering creature to another—and I knew then that he was not the monster we had invented to justify our vendetta. But I did not dare to go over to the enemy. I didn't seem able to afford that much moral courage.

10

A Talent Is Discovered

I remember well Armistice Day at Clifton—the end of the war. The news came through during a Latin verse class with the Mayor just before noon. We were given a holiday for the rest of the day to celebrate. It was raining hard and I felt a cold coming on. I went to the Matron hoping to be allowed to retire to bed in the sick room. But I did not have the temperature necessary for this blessed relief from my chilly study and the obligations of school routine. It was one of the less joyous days of my life. Next day the cold had developed into influenza and my temperature was over 100°. Hurray! Oh lovely day! Oh merciful surcease!

I suffered a great deal from feverish colds while I was at Clifton and had two severe attacks of the Asiatic influenza which is said to have claimed more lives than the terrible war it succeeded. How I enjoyed my illnesses! To be in a warm bed, in a warm room, looked after with loving care by our dear Matron. To have special food and lots of time to read for pleasure instead of instruction. No rugger practice in the rain. No miserable showering in the dank washhouse with the water running cold. The only times when I would not have happily protracted my illnesses forever was when they threatened to interfere with theatrical performances.

How it was discovered at Clifton that this stammering nonentity could act I do not remember. A feat of clairvoyance by Flora Mayor, perhaps. But it was in acting that I found myself.

Every Saturday night at Mr. Mayor's house there was communal entertainment, or at least activity, in the big dining hall. It could take the form of House Boxing, House Debates, or even Alice Mayor singing Scottish folksongs. Boxing, for me at least, was agony and participation was compulsory. When you are so short-sighted that you cannot see the look in your opponent's eye, you are a sitting duck, for it is the eye that flashes advance information. Debating was little better because of the terror of becoming idiotically tongue-tied; and Miss Mayor's singing many found excruciating. Then someone had the bright idea of celebrating the last Saturday of the term with a theatrical performance. An extraordinarily silly little farce was chosen (I don't even remember its name), and Flora Mayor (who had been a professional actress for a brief spell and played third witch in *Macbeth* with Sir Frank Benson) directed it and cast me as a lovesick housemaid. Everyone thought she was mad. I was sixteen, tall and skinny; yet I instantly got into the skin of the part. Three days before the performance I came down with one of my feverish colds and on the great day my temperature was still over 100°. Conclave in the sick room—Mr. Mayor, Miss Mayor, the Matron and Murdock. Also Webster, the head of the house, who was no actor but was playing the lead. Should Napier be permitted to appear?

I felt my whole future hung on the decision—and perhaps it did. I, who usually tried to wring every drop of invalid privilege out of the least tremor of fever, swore that I had never felt better in my life. Mr. Mayor was torn. On the one hand, he had a strong feeling that exceptional circumstances did not justify the breaking of sound rules; on the other he always suspected me of being a bit of a malingerer and perhaps I should be encouraged not to nurse my petty illnesses. Permission was finally given and I played my part in a light-headed sweat. Yet, from the moment of my first entrance, though my head was swimming, I knew I held the house in the hollow of my hand. It was a *succès fou*; I stole the show and immediately became a personality in the House.

Next year the school did a play down at St. Agnes' Parish Hall in Bristol, where we had a mission to the under-privileged. *Dearest Mama* by Gertrude Jennings, a writer of popular farcical comedies in those days, was the chosen play. I played Dearest Mama. My daughter in the play, a part taken by a pretty little blond boy named Manderville, had to be saved from a fatal indiscretion.

This was a period when Irene Vanbrugh was starring in A.A. Milne comedies at the Haymarket theater, and I remember Flora Mayor showing me how Miss Vanbrugh would doodle on the floor with the tip of her parasol to produce an effect of humorous uncertainty. Nearly twenty years later when I was in a play with her in London I told her of this. She said, "Did it work?" "Yes," I replied, "I got a big laugh." "It sounds very old-fashioned, doesn't it?" she mused. "And of course no one uses parasols nowadays." A year or so ago, playing in *Affairs of State* in Chicago, with Celeste Holm I did the business with an umbrella for fun. It still works.

My favorite line in *Dearest Mama* was, "My child, you are tottering to an abyss; your mother must save you." A wave of delighted laughter enveloped me; they loved it.

How did I know how to play this ancient battle-axe so convincingly? Next day Mr. Muirhead, one of the science masters, who had never said a word to me before, came up to me in the quad to tell me, with that touch of sycophancy in his voice so often used when congratulating actors, that I'd been "really quite professional." I was a school character now.

During the following holidays my godmother, Great Aunt Agnes, invited me up to London for the night to go to the theater with her. Aunt Agnes was the widow of Walter Chamberlain of Harborne Hall, who abandoned Birmingham and the Family zoo in his early Rolls Royce for the joys of his own private zoo in Surrey. I think Aunt Agnes had always been a secret city-lover, and when he died she moved to a handsome house in Hyde Park Gate.

She was a very gentle old lady with a soft billowy face and figure. I can't imagine why she determined to issue this invitation to me unless it was the thought that she had not done very much about the somewhat vague and unspecified duties of a godmother. She took me to see Gerald du Maurier in *Bulldog Drummond* at Wyndham's theater.

The whole evening was pure enchantment—driving to the theater in Aunt Agnes' Rolls Royce, the splendid commissionaire who held the door for us when we arrived and directed us to the appropriate stairway for our seats, the gilded decoration of that beautiful small theater, the elegance of the occupants of the stalls and the gaiety of the five-piece orchestra playing selections before the curtain rose.

Eventually the house lights begin to dim, the orchestra concludes, and mounting excitement suffuses my whole being. Amber light, like a sudden dawn, bathes the red and gold curtain, a hush falls in the audience and, my heart beating with exquisite anticipation, the curtain rises and the play begins.

Instantly, I forget it is a play. It is a happening of unquestionable reality in a world populated with people of extraordinary vividness and beauty caught up in an adventure of almost unbearable excitement. And at the center, the heartbeat and radiant source of this unmatched magic, Gerald du Maurier.

There has never been anyone like him. That is what the theatergoing public said of him during his thirty fabulous years in management. That is what every actor said of him who ever had the fun of working with him, as I was later lucky enough to have. The critics grew tired of singing the praises of his unique accomplishment and tried to earn their living by saying he should put on better plays. I shall touch on this as I try to evoke something of his unique quality when I come to that period of my life when I met and worked with him. At the time when I saw him in *Bulldog Drummond* he was at the top of his powers and, on the stage, the man above all others you would want by your side in this tightest corner of a desperate situation. Cool-headed, quick-acting, of steely courage; yet with a touch so light, a humor so nonchalant and a charm so irresistible because of its gay insolence. He was not good-looking, he was not conspicuously tall or well-built. He was Gerald. I fell under his spell that night. I worshipped him until the day of his death. I shall revere his memory to the day of mine.

But I cannot say about this evening, "From that moment I knew I was going to be an actor." In fact, I had no sense at all of what my future would be—I was a schoolboy and never thought of myself in terms of being adult and earning a living, nor did anyone confront me with this impending necessity. When I could shut my eyes to it no longer, acting seemed quite impossibly difficult—not difficult to perform, but difficult to sell to my parents as a possible career. It simply was not done in my family. As Uncle Alan said when I was finally driven to take the momentous step, "I cannot understand any man wanting to spend his life pretending to be other people." It was no good trying to explain to him that I found myself so unsatisfactory that to pretend to be other people was the only way I could survive.

At the end of that school year, summer 1921, I had every hope of leaving Clifton in a blaze of glory. A group of us, masters and boys, founded a school dramatic society and chose "The School for Scandal" as our opening play. Lady Sneerwell was assigned to me and I was confidently anticipating a personal triumph in the role when a ridiculous accident befell me. I contracted severe water on the knee while practicing my curtsies and was unable to perform.

It would not be true to say my school days were the happiest in my life; yet my last two years at Clifton were not unhappy. The war was over, the food improved. Though still undistinguished in school work and in games, I had achieved a certain standing. I could act, and I could write. In my enjoyable literary commando raids against the Establishment, I first came close to John Houseman, my oldest surviving friend—as I would have called him until I ran into Francis, the inevitable Carver, not long ago, who antedates him by five years. Our careers and our mutual affection have brought Jack and me together off and on for more than half a century.

Much has been written about the horrors of the public school system by sensitive souls embittered for life by savage beatings, subjected to the horrors of homosexual assault, or, alternatively, denied the pleasures of romantic pederasty. As for those who complained of being seduced by the housemaster's young wife they simply didn't know when they were lucky. Any system concerned with the education and supervision of young males entering the age of puberty and subject to the pricks and pimples, the energy and impotence, the achievements and frustrations of that difficult period must register a percentage of failure. In fact, the English public school has consistently shown a decent level of success.

In the free and liberated atmosphere of co-educational day schools in America in 1970, half the kids are taking drugs in preparation for anarchical protests when they get to college; and those who graduate reasonably uncontaminated are certainly no better equipped to cope with real life than the average public school man; nor have their brains been better exercised.

One of the tremendous values of the public school system is that, through discipline, it does teach a necessary modicum of self-discipline. Another is that it exposes the young to the delights of eccentricity. I would say that at least half the teaching staff at Clifton in my day were in some degree eccentric. This may have been due to the wartime necessity of retaining men who had passed the age of retirement or had simply had more boy-in-the-rough than they could take. I can only count this my good fortune.

Many schoolmasters deliberately put on a gaudy robe of eccentricity when in contact with their pupils in order to ensnare attention and protect their sensitive private selves from the abrasive wear and tear of daily contact with anarchic boys. As the years go by the robe may become the man. Others, like the Mayor, are natural eccentrics—that is to say the traits we found so hilarious were innately part of their personalities. The value to the young, apart from the fact that cleverly employed eccentricity helps to rivet attention, is that it also helps to breed a spirit of tolerant acceptance and makes nonconformity, when accompanied by excellence, seem admirable.

The sort of behavior I'm thinking of could not long endure in a compulsory state-controlled school. Kenny Fisher, a science teacher, in his high pitched ringing voice to my brother—"Napier-Clavering, you egregious mountain goat, your only convenient resting place is a sewer!" What magnificent invective! What a splendid use of words for a science teacher!

But the greatest eccentric of them all was Daddy Milne. Mr. Milne, a Scotsman, was a brilliant mathematician who, after many years at Clifton, went on to a professorship of higher mathematics at a leading university. Early in his career he probably learned that English boys found a Scot's accent laughable; and dinning vulgar fractions into the unreceptive heads of spotty boys was no part of his genius. So he invented a persona which properly belonged in an asylum, and we loved him for it. He would enter the classroom with his books balanced on his mortar-board hat. Any sound from the class was greeted with a sibilant "Hushie, hushie," as though the least vibration of noise might upset his balance and precipitate a catastrophe. When he reached his desk in safety mild applause was allowed. His books, removed from his head and neatly laid on the desk, a ceremonial sneeze would follow. Leaning forward on the desk with firmly placed hands, he would kick up his heels high in the air as the sneeze erupted. This only occurred if the air was impregnated with chalk dust; we did our best before his entrance to disseminate chalk dust.

Then he would look us over with sour disfavor, his hot grey eyes flickering. He was lean, mouse-haired, of middle height, wearing always the same light grey suit with a stiff

10. A Talent Is Discovered

collar straight up and down in front, from which a wisp of grey chest-hair emerged. Sometimes a dissertation on current events, in his trenchant Edinburgh accent, might follow. I remember for instance some very amusing observations on "Comrade Kair-r-r-r-ensky," and the early days of the Russian revolution. Then, suddenly, to our mathematics! The problem was demonstrated with tremendous verve upon the blackboard and we were ordered to try our luck on the examples in our textbooks. "Peeege two three fooor! Peege two three fooor! And stick in!" Anything louder than the scratch of pens was instantly greeted with "Hushie," followed by anything picturesque that came into his head, such as "Hushie hotfoot," "hushie buthblepuppie," "hushie rumblebelly," and so on. Lists were kept by ardent "hushie" collectors and 137 original varieties recorded. A good new hushie was greeted with hoots of delight. Sometimes this would provoke no more than a sour "Stick in, stick in!" and sometimes an armed onslaught. This was the greatest fun. With a rolled-up newspaper in his hand he would leap, Dracula-like, his black gown flying in the air, from desk top to desk top flailing away at the heads of his rebellious pupils. Order of a sort restored, he would go his rounds with an enormous red pencil. Looking over your shoulder he would assess your work. If the answer to a problem was wrong, he would shout, "Pigsmeat!" and write a large red P.M. across the page and, as he moved on to the next boy, chant: "In thunder-r-r lightning or in r-e-e-en, tur-r-r-n it over-r-r and do it age-e-en!"

The Daddy Milne I knew would not have lasted a week in the Los Angeles School District. But when he hissed "Hushie handsaw!" he may well have been giving a sardonic word to the wise that he was but mad north-north-west.

He was indeed the Koh-i-noor diamond in the crown of Clifton eccentricity. But how clearly I remember the pearls that surrounded him. Stumpy Smith, whistling through his teeth with every sibilant. Three-quarters-of-an-inch-margin R.C. Carter entering a classroom vacated by the Rev. Mr. Philips—"Open the window, Ullathorne! This room has a strong odor of sanctity and unwashed boy." One's-daughter-Gwen Charlie Russell, whose preference for the impersonal "one" over any personal pronoun led him, when taking a poll on masturbation at his house, to ask the boys, "Does one touch oneself?" Did any hardy boy ever reply "One does," one wonders? Josh Polack—"Oh my God, my God, what have I done to deserve this?" when a boy threw an inkpot at him. Young M.R. Ridley—"I don't mind 'damn' and 'bloody' but 'bugger' and 'fuck' I bar!" And A.D. Imlay, a beautiful cricketer, who had had a tracheotomy which fascinated us with the thought that he breathed through a hole in his neck, and who made Milton come alive to us as he reveled in the verbal pictures—"Then wander forth the sons of Belial, flown with insolence and wine!"

And there was a noteworthy saying of the great J. E. King himself, the Headmaster. He had a splendidly dry way of speaking, the consonants of his words etched deep into a rasping nasal resonance. In the corner of his eye a twinkle lurked. But on this particular occasion there was no twinkle. There had been questionable goings on between some of the boys in his own house—the School House—and he was going to see to it that the heresy did not spread. He summed the matter up, to the whole student body collected in Big Hall, with admirable realism and precision.

"You may waste yourselves beneath your blankets; but interbuggery I will not have!"

This story must have been legendary at Clifton, for Alan's older brother also passed it on to his grandson: "The Head Master, John Edward King, was the first layman to hold the post at Clifton, and a man I liked and admired. After a particularly juicy scandal of the kind inevitable in monastically run institutions had erupted in his school house, he preached a sermon in chapel (where masters' wives and day boys' mothers were admitted to a section behind the altar) in the course of which he produced the historic phrase 'I know I can't stop you boys wasting yourselves beneath the sheets, but interbuggery I will not have!'"

One can only imagine how many versions of this story were passed down through the years.

Our school anthem at Clifton, "Let Us Now Praise Famous Men," was performed in chapel at the annual Commemoration Service. The singer of the alto solo part, "And some there be that have left a name behind them," became a unique school hero just as long as his voice did not break. Unique because, as in most schools, heroism was generally only recognized on the playing field.

It is a beautiful anthem and goes on to consider the lot of those who have left no memorial. I'm sure that there have been memorials to J. E. King—indeed he is praised for his fairness as head master of Bedford-Grammar School in Hesketh Pearson's autobiography. I would like to add my appreciation of his work at Clifton. To supervise the mental, moral and physical development of 600 young males from the ages of "puberty to adultery" seems to me to be an alarming responsibility under favorable conditions. But to do it in wartime in a country fighting for its life and near to being starved into surrender, a country scraping the bottom of the barrel for any man who could fight—this must have been a nightmare. Where was he to turn for replacement teachers? Somehow the quality of a civilized seat of learning was maintained and somehow J. E. King maintained his own quality of brisk and humorous good sense.

When I paid Clifton a visit while I was studying at the Royal Academy of Dramatic Art, J. E. King came up to me in the Quad to ask me what I was doing. I was surprised that he even knew my name. He wanted to know what my curriculum was. When I told him Voice Production, Elocution, Fencing, Dancing, and Stage Falls his eyes twinkled and he broke in, "Splendid, splendid! M'yes. Just the place for the clergy. Oh, except for the Stage Falls." Then, after a chuckle, he added, "Not that an occasional fall from grace wouldn't do some of them a world of good."

As for J. E. King's permission "to waste ourselves beneath our blankets"—this pastime came to me late, not until I was sixteen, and was not of obsessive concern while I was still at Clifton. I have no doubt that "interbuggery" took place elsewhere, but there was none in the dormitories of Mr. Mayor's house.

The only other thing about my time at Clifton that I remember as significant was my insane passion for motor bicycles. For my last two years I was obsessed. Every week I bought two magazines devoted to them which I studied from cover to cover. I knew the exact price and track record of every motorcycle manufactured in England. I watched them so avidly on the roads that I could identify by the sound of the motor with my eyes shut a BSA, a Douglas, a Triumph, an Ariel, a Norton, or an AJS and even an occasional water-cooled, tow-cylinder Scott. They were my passion and my greatest desire was to ride one.

One day when I was seventeen or eighteen I accompanied my mother over to a place named Barnt Green on a visit to cousin Nelly. There my cousin Spencer let me ride his AJS motor bicycle—an act of amazing generosity that leaves me overwhelmed with gratitude to this day. I remember the ecstatic excitement as the pulsating and impatient machine leapt away with me into the delirious world of speed on wheels. The power that I barely controlled was terrifying and intoxicating. I felt like Mr. Toad in *The Wind in the Willows*. For a first time out, I drove much too fast along the country lanes that surrounded this pretty southern suburb of the city of Birmingham. But destiny, as usual, was good to me. Some children ran out from a roadside cottage; I could have killed them, but I missed them by inches. Sobered, I returned and delivered back to Spencer his beautiful machine unscratched. I had had one of the best quarter hours of my life.

I never attained to the Sixth Form at Clifton but I did pass the Higher Certificate examination, which qualified me for the Universities. I have always been able to pass as a well-educated man, knowing enough of life and literature to converse intelligently on any but highly technical subjects. This, not so much because of what I learned at Clifton, but because the training in learning enabled me to profit from a natural spirit of curiosity. Also, to give credit where it is due, because my parents were in the habit of speaking well about politics, literature, and the events of the day.

Somewhere I came across a quotation—or did I write it myself for a play?—to the effect that the purpose of education is to enable one to distinguish that which is first rate from that which is not first rate. This is far removed from the popular view today, which might be formulated thus—the purpose of education is to enable one to get by in life with a better job than the other fellow. The truth, perhaps, is that education has many benefits to bestow and each man will grasp for the benefit his soul craves.

11

Fish Out of Water

I left Clifton at the age of eighteen in a state of arrested development—intellectually, emotionally and, conditioning all else, sexually. I was to enter upon a very cock-eyed period of my life, the first year being particularly hideous. The event which ushered in this epoch was in itself sufficiently bizarre. I was best man at my brother Mark's wedding to Elizabeth Sprigge, a ceremony at which the bride was in love not with her husband to be, but with his father, who was himself deeply in love with her. *Mark's grandson Julian has more to add about his strikingly unconventional grandmother. "That marriage only lasted for two years. Just long enough for them to have two daughters. They separated. Mark went to Sweden and Elizabeth stayed in England. And if she shacked up with Claude at that point, well, good for her! She was certainly a hottie, and she certainly did have an affair with my father before my father married my mother, Elizabeth's daughter. Of that I have no doubt. So she worked her way through three generations!"*

I suppose my parents were exercised about what to do with Alan. Mark, soon after his wartime service in the army was over, had spent a year at the University of Grenoble, because he was supposed to have a talent for languages which might aid him in the overseas branch of Debenham's Limited, where a berth had been reserved for him. Molly, who had done well academically at the Edgbaston High School for Girls, was allowed to go on to Oxford. She may have had a scholarship; or perhaps a fond Uncle Alan put up the money. But there was certainly no question of my going to Oxford or Cambridge.

I had not distinguished myself academically at Clifton or shown any aptitude for a reputable career. The army, the navy, the civil services, the church, education, medicine and the law all seemed to be beyond my grasp, nor did I feel an avocation for any of them. So, though heaven knows I had shown no aptitude for business either, a little scheme was eventually cooked up to dump me into Elliott's Metal Works. This was a Family subsidiary in which cousin Archibald Kenrick of Harborne House held a position of importance.

Elliott's Metal Works manufactured brass tubes, so I was sent to Birmingham University to study metallurgy. The prospects of my distinguishing myself in this science were not very good since a firm grasp of mathematics had always eluded me. I would think I understood a principle, but then, when putting it into practice with the manipulation of figures, a fog would rise from the floor of my brain and I would lose my way. Before going to the University, I studied with a coach, halfway across Birmingham, to master Trigonometry and Quadratic Equations. Today I have no ideas what these words mean.

When I explored the University I found the red brick buildings ugly and, when I became a student, my fellow students incompatible. For the most part, they came from a class going up in the world and they were there to improve themselves. I came from a class

"What to do about Alan?" Posing with his Oxford scholar sister and showing no hint of the elegant persona to come, 1920. Courtesy Julian Mulock.

rapidly going down and I was there out of desperation. I did not do too badly in the lab work because I have always possessed manual dexterity and a sense of what makes wheels go round; but all I remember of my two terms at this unloved and unlovely Mater is that when you bend a rod of tin it gives out a little piteous sound called "the Cry of Tin." I was a fish out of water and my struggles, as I flapped despairingly in an uncongenial element, were miserable.

To have no life goal at the period of maximum sexual energy is a dangerous thing. If a goal-less youth is "normal" the pursuit of outlets for this tremendous head of steam may become obsessive. Unwanted pregnancies, broken hearts, impractical early marriages, even venereal disease may result. Oh, it's not the end of the world—indeed, for the young man it can be very enjoyable—but for parents or guardians it may be a harrowing time; their darling little boy may suddenly turn into a ravening wolf, a bad lot, fit only for export to the colonies. (I have often wondered whether the "remittance man" is not responsible for much of the vital energy of our colonial cousins.)

But what if a youth, entering into manhood without a goal, happens also to be so hideously inhibited that he has no dreams of lovely women—no, nor even dreams of lovely boys. The head of steam is still there. It cannot be totally bottled either by noble aspirations or by fear of dreadful consequences. Sublimated it can be, to a degree, through the safety valve of an inspirational vocation—I imagine divinity students manage to get by with only a modicum of masturbation. I know that a year later, during my first six months as a drama student in London my very soul and all my energies were so occupied with my work that I never gave the problem of sexual outlet a thought—and this after being hideously hag-ridden for the ten months after I left Clifton.

When I look back I am surprised that my motorcycle did not supply more of a sublimatory activity. The first thing I did on leaving Clifton was to invest my life savings, for the most part tips from uncles at Christmas, in a second-hand Douglas motorcycle. I had never fancied Douglasses but this seemed to be the best I could get for my money—thirty pounds. It was a lemon. Now, in the psychological mystique, these roaring mechanical steeds are supposed to be phallic substitutes. I guess my motorcycle was a very poor substitute—no power and more of a whimper than a roar. Once, when I journeyed on it to North Wales, I used a cheap map that did not show mountain ranges or gradients. The road I chose went straight up a mountain side. My wretched machine could not make it—not with me on board. I had to run by its side, all the way up the hill, steering it and supporting it as it chattered and coughed—just able to drag its miserable self painfully, yard by yard, to the top. We were both utterly exhausted when we got there. I remember coasting down the other side at breakneck speed in the gloaming, hoping to find, before dark, a repair shop for the bike and a place to lay my head in Blainau-Festiniog.

Of course, it is highly probable that if it had been the powerful swift monster of my secret dreams I would have killed myself. As it was, I did succeed in running head first into a large truck which was delivering chemicals to Birmingham University. I lost half a front tooth and gouged a hole in my leg just below the knee. Worse, although I did not discover this until the time came for me to sell it, the cycle sustained a crack in the forward diagonal tube of the frame. Now, this machine was my only capital—all that I possessed of value. I was then about to go to London to become an actor and needed clothes, the sort of clothes my parents did not supply. So I did a tremendous cleanup and paint job on the motorcycle hoping to get a good price for it. I reckoned on twenty to twenty-five pounds. And then I came on this crack, a little rusted at the edges.

If I admitted its existence my capital went down the drain. So I put a clip over it, to hold a Bowden cable, and concealed it. I sold the bike for twenty pounds. It was a terrible thing to do and no matter what I told myself—that I had driven the bike safely in this condition for a year—sometimes, in the watches of the night, I would sweat with fear that the buyer might be killed. I would plan to seek him out and warn him.

I had sold the machine through our village bicycle shop in Harborne, J.W. Dingley's. One day, passing by, I looked in on some pretext and asked enormous, stentorious Mr. Dingley if the buyer had been satisfied.

"Oh, yes." he wheezed. "'E liked it all right. Till it fell in 'alf."

"What?" I cried in terrible apprehension.

"Comin' up 'Arborne 'ill, 'e was—quite slow. Didn't 'urt 'isself at all. Seems the frame was rusted through. Lucky it didn't 'appen while you 'ad it, wasn't it?"

"Yes." I said and made a quick exit. I did not really feel bad about cheating the poor man, so long as I had not killed him.

* * *

For a boy with ingrained feelings of fear, distaste and guilt over the physical manifestation of sex, a boy only too ready to believe that sickness, demoralization, perhaps even insanity lie inevitably in wait for the committed masturbator, what misery and ultimate despair the late, implacable onslaught of adolescence can bring! From seventeen to twenty-five the biologists tell us the male is "enjoying the period of his most eruptive sexual potency." If such a boy looks in the mirror and hates the image he sees, masturbation become a punishment on himself for not being physically acceptable. He becomes involved in a love-hate struggle with his own body.

Perhaps "before" and "after" pictures in an advertisement for a mail-order physical culture course may strike his eye. There were many such when I was young. There he sees himself—thin-armed, flat-chested, his little belly protruding through bad posture. That's the him he hates. But then, behold, six months later—there is a young Greek God, his splendid chest swelling over the smallest belly, molded into a muscular concavity. Physical culture promises a solution of his problems; he will sublimate sex by making his own body worthy of love.

In my case it was a course called "Maxalding." Mr. Max Saldow, rather in advance of his time, had devised a course of isometric exercises copiously illustrated by splendid pictures of his own remarkable physique. Maxalding became my religion—a religion in which the holy of holies was the concave muscular abdomen. Work away as I would—and did—my smooth-boned type of physique simply would not assume any mass of muscle. But the greater failure lay in the fact that sex cannot be sublimated by an obsessive interest in one's own body.

12

Into the Swim

For a young man to waste his energies in masturbation instead of making love is sad enough but not uncommon—but to be caught up in a vortex of guilty self-destruction with no help at hand and no saving goal in sight is something else.

This was my condition from the time I left Clifton till the abrupt end of my student days at Birmingham University. No one suspected anything was wrong; there was surely no one to whom I could confide or go to for help and counsel. Indeed, the idea of turning to a parent for help was not part of my childhood training. I had never heard of psychotherapy.

I lived at home, ate three meals a day and drearily made the five mile journey to and from the University on my decrepit motorcycle. I took to playing Rugby football for the University on Saturday afternoons—not in the first team since I was too tall for a forward and too slow to play three-quarter. We were a scratch collection to put it mildly, and I had never really enjoyed the game. My height was supposed to give me an advantage at line-outs, but as often as not I would get some tough little brute's elbow in my gut or groin and be rendered helpless. But it was another way of mortifying the flesh, and, hopefully, would leave me too tired for other secret activities over the weekend. However, it was Rugby football that saved me.

One cold and misty afternoon at Smethwick, I tore the tendons of my right ankle stumbling at speed over the leg of a prostrate opponent. The pain was momentarily acute—but in Rugger there are, of course, no substitutes. I hobbled on as best I could until the end of the game.

Then I had a good look at my ankle, and observed that the swelling was tremendous, pressing hard against the lacing of the boot. I was about to untie the lace when our Captain came up and said, "Wait a mo! How are you going home?"

"On the old motor bike."

"Well, I wouldn't take your boot off, if I were you. You'll never get it on again. That looks pretty bad to me."

So I left the boot on and chugged home through the slippery tram-lined suburbs of Greater Birmingham. Back at Tennal Grange I had to cut the boot to take it off—the whole foot and ankle were monstrously swollen and painful. I looked at this deformed extremity as I lay in a hot bath and thought, not unhappily, "This is it. I can retire from life." I hopped downstairs and showed my father. "You had better go to bed. I'll call the doctor."

Doctor Huxley was by now dead or retired and our family physician was Dr. Farncombe—busy, little, red-haired and coming up in the world fast. He had moved into the Pinsent's old house, Lordswood, where I had gone to kindergarten. He prescribed complete bed-rest for at least two weeks.

12. Into The Swim

"You mean I can't go to the University?"

"Not unless you want to be a cripple for life. I've never seen an ankle in worse shape. Why didn't you stop playing as soon as it happened?"

"Oh, well," I said. "It was thirteen all and I didn't want to…"

"You didn't want to let the side down, you silly fellow," he interrupted, making an instant hero of me. He was very good at buttering up his patients. I smiled modestly but already my mind was working furiously. Two weeks. Then I could not take the upcoming exams which I had to pass if I was to prove myself worthy of Elliott's Metal Works. I didn't expect to pass them anyhow, but this would let me out! I stretched my good leg luxuriously and looked forward to the delicious privileges of being an invalid without feeling ill.

Very soon the great design began to formulate. Fate had stepped in and removed me from the brass-tube stakes. I would tell them. I would say that I had considered everything very carefully and, since it was the only thing in life that I excelled at and wanted to do, I would like to become an actor.

Fortunately, at that moment, "they" were my father and my sister-in-law Elizabeth. My mother was away on holiday for her health, somewhere on the south coast with Uncle Alan. Elizabeth was very strong for the arts; she was herself a commencing author. *Elizabeth Sprigge, in addition to translating works from Swedish, French and German, wrote biographies of August Strindberg, Jean Cocteau, Sybil Thorndyke, Ivy Compton-Burnett and Gertrude Stein, among others. She was also the author of several children's books.* She was also tremendously influential with my father. So, instead of the opposition I anticipated, it was instantly agreed that I could have a shot at it. By the time my mother returned, the momentum of events had carried me to a position where, whatever her misgivings, a grudging acceptance of a *fait accompli* was inevitable.

I am very conscious of the hand of Destiny, for if this accident had not befallen me, I'm sure I would have done some last minute "swotting" for my basic science tests and maybe even passed—or at least been shown willing enough to be quietly dropped into an inferior niche at Elliott's. And I doubt if my decision to ask to be allowed to try to be an actor—which is not a very robust stance—would have stood up to strong parental opposition. It was the happy accident of Elizabeth rather than my mother being in residence that did the trick for me.

I had performed with local amateurs in Ian Hay's *Tilly of Bloomsbury* with great success, and encountered some of the members of "The Pilgrim Players" who developed later into Barry Jackson's celebrated Birmingham Repertory Company. Seeking advice from these semi-professionals as to how to get started I was greeted with a fervent, universal "DON'T!" Surprised, rather than discouraged, I pursued a plan of Elizabeth's to go up to London and see a couple of actors her family knew, one of whom was the well-known Shakespearean, Godfrey Tearle. He was starring in a one-act play about Francois Villon in a variety program at the Coliseum. I attended a matinee and went round afterwards with my letter of introduction to see the great man in his dressing-room.

When I think how often the same sort of thing has been done to me and how one dreads having to try, as kindly as possible, to discourage these sometimes woefully unsuitable aspirants, I am amazed at how much time and trouble Godfrey devoted to me. Indeed, he was a very kind and delightful man. No one could have seemed less suited to a stage career than myself. Godfrey was exceptionally tall for an actor in those days, being well over six feet. Yet, stooping apologetically, I topped him easily. And the momentous importance of the occasion brought my stammer into flower. So that I had to explain, again apologetically, that I didn't do it when I was actually acting. His advice was that the best way to get started was to go to the Royal Academy of Dramatic Art. He did not tell me that my aspirations were ridiculous—wisely he must have decided that I must find that out for myself. When I talked to him about it many years later he said, "Oh, I never tell strangers that they haven't hope. To begin with they won't believe you, and to go on with, you can be so wrong. Well, look at you, for instance."

I had never before been in a professional actor's dressing room. That was in the days of Leichner greasepaint and it did have its own intoxicating musty smell. Once my first nervousness had been put to rest by Godfrey's kindness, I felt utterly at home in that atmosphere of spirit-gum, greasepaint and cocoa butter.

PART TWO

London

13

A Year of Grace

My parents agreed to stake me in London for a year, on an allowance of three pounds a week, if I could get into the Royal Academy of Dramatic Art.

For the audition I chose the speech from *The Importance of Being Earnest* in which Jack Worthing complains of Algernon drinking his Perrier Jouet and eating his cucumber sandwiches. When I stepped out on the little stage to face my judges, suddenly the capacity to get out of my own skin and into Jack's—escape, through acting, from my stammer—started to desert me and I felt my vocal organs locking up. I was about to panic when Kenneth Barnes, the Principal, called out, "Just a moment, Mr ... er ... um" and then, in a loud whisper to the secretary, Dora Sevening, "Who is it?" By the time he looked up from his whispered colloquy and said "All right, go on," I had succeeded in imagining myself back into Jack Worthing and went through without a hitch.

I was accepted.

If ever there was a case of a round peg finding its appropriate round hole it was the case of Kenneth Barnes and the R.A.D.A. In those days, before the arts were subsidized, the first essential for the Principal of that teeming womb of notable actors was that he should insure its survival; and by hook and by crook, by flattery, influence, effrontery, humility, courage, and perseverance; through times of indifference, times of depression, times of war, and times of social change, Kenneth Barnes kept the flag flying and left the R.A.D.A. a well-endowed, well-equipped national institution.

As a brother of the famous Vanbrugh sisters, Violet and Irene (whose parasol technique Miss Mayor had imparted to me at Clifton) he knew everyone who was anyone in the theater world. As the son of a distinguished cleric he also stood high with the Church of England; and he established valuable ties with Buckingham Palace. He used every resource he could muster to win friends and influence people for the financial support and social prestige of the Academy. Instruction in the theater arts was fortunately largely left to his talented staff.

It has been suggested that he was an unmitigated snob; if he was, it was for the greater glory of the Academy rather than to glorify himself, and the knighthood that crowned his career was well earned. He did indeed have a Restoration character—his ruddy complexion and brown bright eyes, twinkling but somewhat shifty would have looked thoroughly at home under a periwig.

A dozen years after I left the Academy, being then a successful West End actor, I was invited to be one of a panel of judges at the annual graduation performances of the advanced students. Athene Seyler and J.H. Roberts were the other judges. During one long afternoon, we watched and judged and awarded marks. Next day we lunched with Kenneth before completing our task during another long afternoon. As we were drinking coffee before resuming our duties, Kenneth ran through the list of pupils and the achievement scores we had awarded to them the day before, nodding approval here, indicating admiration for our judgment there. Suddenly he stopped, frowned, took a sly glance at us and said, "Dear me ... that won't do at all. You've given Pansy X only fifteen points!"

"Pansy X...?" we reflected, "Oh, she was the blond girl who ... yes, we didn't think she was very good."

"Really!" said Kenneth. "Well, I'm afraid we can't have that. I shall give her twenty-five. She's the niece of the Bishop of London."

We protested. But undoubtedly he saw to it that twenty-five points stood to Pansy's credit. So I imagine that the little pause that saved me at my audition was occupied by Kenneth asking his secretary if I was related to anyone important.

In fact no one in my family was ever connected in any way with the theater, and it certainly wouldn't have entered my head to let it be known I was related to a Chamberlain. Anyhow I don't think they were in office at that time—Cousin Austen had just been supplanted by Bonar Law.

My first room was a grubby little attic with a gas ring near Mornington Crescent. It had the advantage of proximity to the R.A.D.A.; one could walk there in ten minutes or go by underground to Goodge Street, also in ten minutes. In spite of the excitement and satisfaction of my new life, I felt great loneliness—as anyone who has always lived *en famille* must—on pigging it in rooms for the first time. Pigging it at school is a very different thing, since one is a member of a communal pig-sty where the swill is fed to one. Having to get one's own solitary meals on a lean budget—that is a very lonely thing.

It was not easy for me to make friends rapidly, and, at first, I found my new life a good deal less satisfying than I had expected. Schools cannot teach people how to act. The functions they serve are to correct bad speech, tell you what you must not do on the stage, give you a fitted gymnasium, so to speak, where you can develop your acting muscles, and finally arrange a show-case for you to exhibit your wares to anyone looking for young talent. The most valuable experience for an aspiring young actor is to work with and watch a first-rate experienced professional. If one's membranes are sufficiently permeable, one absorbs something by osmosis. Perhaps nowadays an exceptional school like LAMDA does more—but in my day, the R.A.D.A. under Kenneth Barnes was having a hard time surviving and, as I have indicated, the Principal's doughty talents were engaged on that front rather than in providing inspirational instruction.

I was one of a very unpromising class. Apart from myself, none of the members achieved any success in the theater except for a pretty boy who went into the management side, and a talented but undisciplined girl whose career was sporadic, stormy and not up to the promise she had shown. A degree of self-discipline is essential for durable success in the theater.

The considerable time taken up with voice projection and elocution was largely wasted on me. It did not touch my stammer problem, which, being essentially psychological, was curing itself as my confidence grew. My parents had brought me up to speak immaculate English, and I had naturally an agreeable voice. A Mrs. MacKern gave us all sorts of exercises to do as homework—holding our diaphragms and shouting Boo, Bow, Bah at ourselves in the mirror—which I very soon abandoned as idiotic. Classes in fencing and period dancing provided valuable training in physical coordination and elegance of posture and movement; and instruction in make-up was invaluable to one who was going to make his living out of portraying a wide range of eccentric old gentlemen.

But, for me at least, the principal value to be gained at the R.A.D.A., was from contact with three exceptional personalities who rehearsed us in plays. In the beginners' class, unfortunately, I saw little of them. They were Claude Rains, Helen Haye (not to be confused with Helen Hayes the American star) and Rosina Filippi, of whom I have already written.

From Claude I may have acquired a sense of panache and the value of using to advantage one's position on the stage. During a dress rehearsal, I remember him leaping onto the stage, pushing me two feet to the left and shouting, as he pointed up to a batten of lights, "D'you see that light, boy? Well, what the hell d'you think I put it there for? Get into it!" On another occasion when he must have felt in no mood to watch our feeble efforts, he simply started reading *Hamlet* and kept right on till the hour was over. Riveted by his rich husky voice and bright mischievous eye, I think I absorbed more sense of how to bring the printed word to life in that hour than from anything else I experienced during my year of training at the R.A.D.A.

At our first class with him, as he took the roll-call, he asked each of us whether we wanted to become "straight" actors or "character" actors. The answers were pretty evenly divided, I, of course, answering "character." He looked down the list and he looked us over. Then he said, "Every part is a character part. It takes many years for a personality to become interesting enough to stand on its own. Fit yourselves to the character created by the playwright. That is what acting is."

This dogma, with which I heartily agree, opens interesting fields for speculation. There have been great stars, particularly in motion pictures, who seemed always to be themselves—Clark Gable, Gary Cooper, Ronald Colman—whatever they played. They were symbols of male attractiveness and their fans wanted no disguises. In the theater Gerald du Maurier seemed always to be his irresistible self—although he was, in fact, capable of entering the skin of a thousand other characters, as he would demonstrate when directing a play. On the other hand the greatest actor of our day, Laurence Olivier, chooses to amaze us with an astonishingly varied gallery of totally dissimilar characterizations. Yet we always know it is Olivier—no one else can etch so deep, no one else holds us in so firm a grasp by sheer force of personality, on stage or in camera. How an actor achieves this remains a mystery. I have known stellar personalities who were quite unimpressive in private life and remarkable private personalities who cut very little ice on the stage.

The second remarkable teacher, some of whose qualities I like to think rubbed off on me, was Helen Haye. Incisiveness, the need to give value to each new thought instead of dribbling out one's lines incontinently, respect for crisp craftsmanship—these were her valuable contributions. She had a crisp impatience with students who were sloppy in their work. Her toe would start tapping the floor and out it would come "Darling child!" When Helen Haye started "Darling child," it meant trouble. As—"Darling child! Christ almighty himself could not make love to you if you insist on standing like a sack of potatoes with the lumps in the wrong places!"

The third of my inspirational teachers, dear Rosina Filippi was a wonderful old warhorse with a rich and generous nature. From her I think I gathered a little courage and the idea that an actor should laugh at trouble and never say, "I can't." I knew that she, with her high, high standards, saw that I had talent. Her regard for me stiffened my backbone and her great brave laughter warmed my heart.

I remember her talking to the class one day and saying, "An actor must have charm, you know. Oh, that long lanky thing over there has it, if only he wasn't so tall." Funny to think of a Method instructor of today telling his students that the *sine qua non* for an actor was charm! Yet I would take Miss Filippi, an actress of total integrity and an inspiring teacher, over any doctrinaire of the American Method.

The truth of the matter, perhaps, is this. Sincerity of emotion and the capacity to think and feel oneself into another's skin must be inherent in the makeup of a would-be actor, just as physical coordination must be inherent in the makeup of a would-be tennis player. A teacher of either acting or tennis is wasting his time, and the student's money, unless these capacities are at least latent. Surely the teacher's business in both cases is to show the student the techniques whereby his natural gifts may be put to most effective use. There are general rules that all must observe; and there are particular skills to be learned which will help the student to make the best use of his natural strengths and to disguise or compensate for his natural weaknesses. It is in this field that the teacher shows his quality.

"Method" tennis lessons would presumably consist of endless exercises in physical coordination and watching the ball. Showing the student the proper grip for forehand, the change of grip for backhand, the follow through, the positioning of the feet—all this would be downgraded as old-fashioned technical trickery. Now, while it is true that painstaking work on coordination and watching the ball might produce some remarkable playing— particularly from natural athletes who would instinctively hold the racket efficiently and play well anyhow—which would one expect to win the match, the "natural" player or the one trained in technique? And which would be the pleasantest to watch? The one trained to a graceful, flowing style or the one snatching temporary victory from defeat by a quick eye and improvised flick of the racket?

And is there not an indefinable charm in the performance of a master technician on the tennis court, arising from the ease, the assurance and grace which he brings to every shot? There is a similar quality in acting, springing from ease, assurance, and grace. This, I imagine, is what my Miss Filippi meant by charm. Today, we do not set much store by charm, not in acting nor in tennis; the powerhouse service followed by the killing smash is much admired, and similar violence in acting. When I think of Gerald du Maurier or Jean Borotra I doubt if the modern manner marks an advance in civilization.

Genius, I suspect, is largely an outpouring of creative energy, channeled by an exacting personal technique; without which all is but water poured on sand.

One of the men in my class was a little fellow called Sam Pickles. He was older than the rest of us, maybe in his early thirties. He was a pixie with more attractiveness than positive talent. But the other two men were so incompetent that Sam and I naturally gravitated together. It was not long before he told me that there was a nice attic room next to his, at number 37 Belgrave Road in Pimlico. The room was bigger, cleaner and airier than the one I was in, so I moved. One did not feel so lonely in the evenings. Sam and I could eat our kippers together and rehearse for the next day's work. There was something funny about him because he had a wife, older than himself, who looked in from time to time but did not live with him. If he had any designs on me they were certainly blunted by my armor of asexuality.

During my second term, however, a crack in the armor, small but significant, developed. I was possessed by what I can only describe as a schoolboy crush (better late than never) on a typical dizzy blond flapper of the period, Molly McSomething. She was in a senior class and I had no idea of how to approach her. Why should she look at me when she was so beautiful that she could obviously pick and choose anyone she pleased? So I wrote poems to her. I showed them to another student, an elderly matron taking up acting far too late in life, who was deeply touched and flattered by my confidence. She urged me not to give up hope. Spurred on by my elderly confidante, I eventually asked dizzy Molly to go to the movies with me and, to my surprise (I might almost say consternation) she accepted. It was my first date; but at nineteen I couldn't possibly admit this. I must be a polished man of the world. From what I had read and heard, I thought that I ought to hold her hand. But the right moment never seemed to arrive. Then I got interested in the movie and forgot she was there. After it was over I saw her home. Again, from what I'd read, I thought I would be expected to kiss her when I said goodnight, and I had never kissed a girl in my life. Panic seized me as the obligatory scene approached, and all capacity for conversation vanished. What had I had for dinner? Were there onions? Had I brushed my teeth? Should I start on her cheek and work sideways to the mouth, or, since I was so tall, start on the forehead and work down? I remember delivering her to a rather shabby little semi-detached front door. She must have had a very dull evening, poor girl; so, with practiced skill, she dodged my clumsy effort at an embrace and shut the door in my face.

Yet next morning, playing a love scene in the R.A.D.A. theater, I knew I was attractive and perfectly convincing. The stage directions told me what to do and I had become someone else. Nevertheless, Molly McSomething was a beginning. I had at last been stirred by the bittersweet pangs of love for another human being.

One day at the R.A.D.A. an interesting event took place in our Common Room in the basement, where we could buy cheap lunches and cups of coffee. A steep flight of stairs led down to it from street level at one end, and, at the other end, there was an open fireplace with a club fender. On this occasion reclining on the fender with her top, or business end fondly supported by Reggie Gardiner and her ankles at the other end tentatively supported by me, was a very pretty girl. Reggie had just observed, looking at me, "Now, that's what I call calf love," when the girl espied, coming down the stairs, a fat and not very prepossessing young man. "Look! Look at that." She said. "If it's a new student, it's a shame to take the money!" We made inquiries and found that his name was Charles Laughton. In the world of the theater, where appearance would seem to count for so much, it is never safe to judge by appearances.

For me the main significance of this recollection is that I had at least got as far as holding a girl's ankles. I still had a long way to go.

* * *

During my time at the R.A.D.A., I retained a sort of vicarious umbilical cord with my mother. I was on very good terms with her indispensable maid, Florence. From time to time, Florence would give notice and then be talked into staying on. I remember saying to her once, "Florence, you are going to stay, aren't you?" "Yes," she said grimly. "Yes, I'm staying. But oh, your poor father! At least I'm not married to her."

Since there were no laundromats in those days, for reasons of economy I had a conspiracy with Florence to send my laundry home by parcel post for inclusion with the family wash performed weekly by old Mrs. Bragg, who lived down Tennal Road in Camomile Cottages and collected and delivered it in a wheel-barrow. The redoubtable Florence would then pack my things up and post them back to me. But when I moved to Belgrave Road something funny happened—a week passed and there was no laundry. Then another week. I began to get desperate and my remaining shirts pretty gray around the collar. At last it transpired that my mother, with her sure instinct for the aristocracy, had given Florence my address as 37 Belgrave Square. I was new in London and ignorant of the significance of Belgrave Square as an address. So next Sunday morning I set out to track down my errant laundry. It was a longer walk than I had imagined—one had expected Belgrave Road and Belgrave Square to be adjacent.

Eventually I found the Square and thought the houses looked rather grand. Then I identified No. 37 and my heart quailed. It was an immense edifice occupying an entire corner. A wide flight of stone steps led up to magnificent double doors. I took a deep breath and rang the bell. Almost at once the double doors were flung open by two footmen—two, not one—uniformed in wasp-striped waistcoats, who stood at attention flanking the entrance. It was like something out of a multi-million dollar period movie. Not a word was spoken and I was wondering what the hell to do next when a most superb figure came through an inner door and walked towards me. When he was suitably flanked by his satellites, he spoke. "Sir?"

"Um … my … my name is Napier-Clavering and I'm afraid there's been a mix-up. I think you've got my laundry."

A look of utter disbelief froze his bland expression for a moment and I was on the point of turning tail. Then, like the sun breaking through clouds, a smile of comprehension dawned.

"Ah! The packages! Yes, indeed Sir." Without so much as looking to left or right he continued, "James. You will bring Mr. Napier-Clavering's parcels."

Off went James and the butler smiled at me serenely. I suddenly became garrulous.

"I'm afraid my mother's maid got the address mixed up…"

"Think nothing of it, Sir."

"You see, I have rooms at number 37 Belgrave Road and…"

"A very natural error, Sir, if I may say so. A beautiful day, is it not?"

You would have thought he handed out parcels of laundry to strange young men every day. James appeared bearing two rather tattered brown paper parcels in his arms. The butler took them from him and held them out to me rather as the Archbishop of Canterbury holds the cushion on which the crown rests at a coronation.

"Thank you," I said.

"Would you like John to get you a cab, Sir?"

"Er … no … no thank you. I think I'll walk."

Sensing perhaps, that I did not have the price of a cab on me he beamed his approval. "Yes, indeed, Sir. It is a beautiful morning."

His hands clasped over his belly, he waited till I was safely down the steps, smiling benevolently. Then, as he turned into the house, the great doors closed quietly behind him.

I discovered that this house belonged to Lord Howard de Walden, one of the wealthier members of the peerage, and that many years before, my father had stayed there in connection with designs for Birmingham Guild metal fixtures for the noble Lord's yacht. Whether this had any bearing on the extraordinarily dignified courtesy with which his butler handled the matter of two tattered brown paper parcels I really do not know. But it was butlering at its immaculate best. There was no attempt to patronize or intimidate me. Visitors at the front door of the Master's house were always to be put at ease.

14

Benevolent Deity

My year at the R.A.D.A., in which I was to prove myself, was drawing to a close. I felt that I had proved something—my three best teachers had shown belief in me by giving me leading parts to play. I could create on the stage an instant reality in my person by the power of imagination. I knew that I belonged—that I was born to be an actor. But how was I to convince anyone that I was employable? How was I to convince my parents that I could ever earn a living? In fact I did not worry about this; I lived for the moment, and the extreme improbability of my ever getting a job simply did not occur to me.

And then began an extraordinary sequence of lucky breaks and improbable coincidences. It was as though some benevolent Deity took me by the hand and, with no plan on my part, no indomitable determination to overcome obstacles, led me round these obstacles, picked me up when I stumbled, pushed me forward when I hesitated, compensated for my errors of judgment when I did try to guide myself and finally led me, through a series of successes, to a position where no one could say I did not belong in the world of the theater. I even achieved, with the aid of a minute private income I inherited at the age of twenty-one, financial independence.

At the end of each Spring term, the R.A.D.A. put on a Public Show at a West End Theater. It was the great event of our year and the cream of the crop of second year students had a chance to show what they could do. Every manager was invited. Prizes and medals were awarded and a few lucky stars of the R.A.D.A. firmament got jobs. I, of course, was not supposed to be eligible because I had only put in one year at the Academy.

But it so happened that Mlle. Gachet, the remarkable lady who conducted the French Class at the Academy, needed someone to play the High Priest of Baal in *Athalie*, by Jean Racine, and no one in the class seemed suitable for the role. She needed someone with presence, dignity and authority. The French Class was an extra I could not afford, but, when she threw the part open to the rest of the Academy, I volunteered. This was my doing, my moment of courage. (Indeed, I have always believed that I could play any part written, with the possible exception of Tiny Tim.) It may have been this belief in myself that led my kind Deity to take me by the hand. My school French was a little rusty for I had taken German during my last year at Clifton, but I had a good ear from my mother, who spoke excellent French. So, though at first I had very little idea of the significance of what I was saying, Mlle. Gachet sensed some quality in me that she needed, and gave me the part. She was a splendid director.

This then is how it came about that, with a white beard down to my navel, on an afternoon in March 1923 at the Queens Theater in Shaftesbury Avenue, I declaimed the High Priest's warning:

> *Grande Reine, ne croyez pas que le nuage crève!*
> *Abner, chez le grand prêtre, a devancé le jour,*
> *Pour le sang de son fils vous savez son amour.*
> *Mais qui sait si Joad ne veut pas en leur place*
> *Substituer l'enfant dont le ciel vous menace....*

or words to that effect.

In the audience, separated because of the heavy demand for seats, sat James Bernard Fagan and his wife, Mary Grey. Fagan had just started a professional repertory theater at Oxford with a company of young actors. He had an extraordinary eye for talent, and the company, called The Oxford Players, was soon to achieve astonishing success, and a great number of its players' lasting fame. Among the young unknowns who worked for Fagan in the Oxford Players—many of them starting their careers there— were John Gielgud, Flora Robson, Margaret Webster, Tyrone Guthrie, Robert Morley, Emlyn Williams, Glen Byam Shaw, Alan Webb, Richard Goolden (the perennial Mr. Mole in *The Wind in the Willows*), and James Whale, who became the dean of early horror movie directors in Hollywood.

Fagan did not actually found the Oxford Players. He was recruited to run it by Jane Ellis, a not very successful London actress, who had managed to find the financial backing and an appropriate performance space for a professional repertory company in Oxford. The power behind the organization, she performed as a member of the company starting with its inaugural production of Shaw's Heartbreak House *in October 1923 and made her last appearance there in 1925. She retired from acting in 1926.*

Jim Fagan must have been in his fifties at this time. He had been a successful playwright and producer and had recently done a season of Shakespeare at the Court Theater in Sloane Square in the wake of Granville Barker's notable occupancy of that theater. This had not been a great success, partly because he insisted on putting his wife, Mary Grey, into the leading parts. Mary was his second wife and a very beautiful woman—that is to say she had a face of classic perfection surmounted by ash blond hair. But she was not young and below the chiseled perfection of her face she was very amply proportioned. She was more than a little deaf, had a lovely sense of humor, and a bell-like laugh. She used to tell, against herself, the story of Mrs. Patrick Campbell meeting her in Sloane Street and saying, "I hear Jim's putting on *The Dream*. What are you playing? Bottom?" Mary dearly wanted to be a great actress and played many of the leading parts at Oxford. Jim worshipped her and she could twist him round her little finger.

On this particular afternoon, Jim and Mary were looking for a replacement for young Tyrone Guthrie, who had not worked out very well as an actor. As the Fagans told it to me later, the moment my scene came to an end Mary turned to catch Jim's eye and he nodded "Yes."

One of the problems of making up a stock company of young actors is to find someone to play the old men. A real old man, if he is any good, will want too much money; and an indifferent old ham will have difficulty with his lines and be out of key with the young enthusiasts who cheerfully embrace the grueling work of doing a new play every week. Furthermore, he will not be able to play a younger role if a play should come up with only young men in it. So you look for a young actor who happens to have a real talent and the right face and physique for playing older men.

The Fagans already had one such actor—Richard Goolden. But Richard was small and at his best in fantastic parts, so they needed in addition someone taller and with a wider range. It was my staggering good fortune that amongst *all* the legitimate finalists at the R.A.D.A. show—and many played older parts—they sensed from my performance in French as the High Priest of Baal that I could be their man.

In due course they made inquiries for me at the R.A.D.A. Again it was my good luck that it was Dora Sevening, the secretary, to whom they spoke, not Kenneth Barnes. According to the rules, she should have said that I was a first year student and thus not available. However, as she told me later, the thought came to her, "That poor lanky boy! He'll never get an offer like this again," and sent me a telegram to Tennal Grange, where I had retired, broke and with no proof of success to offer my parents and no clear plans for the future.

At my interview with Fagan at his house in St. John's Wood my luck held. I am ushered into his room by a maid and stand uncertainly in the shadow by the door. He is busy at his desk by the window and, hardly looking up, waves me to a chair. Eventually he comes over to me, book in hand. I start to rise. "No, no. Sit down." He looks at me quizzically for a moment. He finds a place in the book and continues, "My wife and I saw you the other day at the R.A.D.A. show. Would you like to join my company at Oxford?"

I could hardly speak. "Oh ... oh yes, Mr. Fagan!"

"Well, it seems you can play old men. Let's see what you can do with a younger part." My heart sinks. "We'll be doing *The School for Scandal* next season. Here's a scene with Benjamin Backbite." My heart rises. Luck again! From working in the play at Clifton as Lady Sneerwell, I knew Benjamin Backbite backwards and was able to get into his skin and give a full-blown characterization. I wish I had had the flair to say, "I'd much rather play Lady Sneerwell." Jim would have been delighted; but I was much too overcome with awe and anxiety to try to be funny.

"Very good," he said. "I think you'll do. Your salary will be three pounds a week and you will also be assistant stage manager."

"You mean I ... you..."

"Yes. It's a deal. You're engaged."

I got up to go and, tall though Jim was, I towered over him. "Christ Almighty!" he said, "I've just fired Tony Guthrie for being too tall and clumsy and I believe you're taller than he is. Oh well, I said I'd have you and I will."

In fact Sir Tyrone and I are exactly the same height; but I have always had the faculty of moving tidily and not appearing to be as tall as I am—unless I wish to.

That first season at Oxford, where we did a new play every week—and before that critical audience had to do it well—I started indifferently as a bearded constable (the beard to give me weight) in Pinero's farce *Dandy Dick*. But the next week was a different affair. In Ibsen's *Lady from the Sea*, I played Arnholm, the bumbling, aging school-master who proposes marriage to Boletta, the daughter of the house. Here I was in my element. With Mr. Mayor as a model, and my capacity to imagine and make real the eccentricities of age, I achieved something the Fagans thought quite remarkable.

A friend of theirs, a successful literary agent, happened to come down to Oxford to see the production. And he happened to represent C.K. Munro, the playwright whose *At Mrs. Beam's* had been one of the outstanding successes of the previous years. On the strength of this man's urgent recommendation after he had seen me in *The Lady from the Sea*, I was engaged by the actor-manager Dennis Eadie to play a very good character part of an old Cambridge professor in Munro's new play *Storm*, which was due for production soon after the Oxford Player's Summer season finished!

The impossible had happened. By a series of extraordinarily lucky breaks, here I was, the unemployable freak, going into a new play by a much admired playwright in the West End of London not six months after leaving Drama School!

The part was a bearded academic in his sixties. When I arrived—my callow twenty-year-old self—and met at the first rehearsal all these famous and assured West End actors, my courage wilted and I started stammering. For some reason the stage manager, Herbert Chown, a man at the top of his profession, seemed to understand, took me aside and said, "Don't worry. Nobody's going to judge you yet. Learn your lines and we'll see what you can do."

I did all right. In fact I made a notable success.

In the course of the run David Garnet, the author of *Lady into Fox* and many other wonderful books, came round to see me after a performance to congratulate me. I still had my make-up on. Introducing himself, he said, "You must have lived in Cambridge all your life. How is it we've never met?" I started to take off my wig and beard and said I'd never been to Cambridge. I did not add that my only knowledge of Oxford was six weeks at the Playhouse.

How does an actor accurately portray something of which he has no direct knowledge? Charles Laughton had a theory that good character acting came out of one's memory bank—that the born actor subconsciously stores away everything and everyone he sees for future use. I'm sure this is true. But it does not cover portrayal of the unknown. At this time I had absolutely no personal knowledge of Cambridge or Oxford professors. Again, at a later date, I played a sculptor and was praised by someone in that field for what I did with my hands and, particularly, a shaping gesture I made with my thumb. I had never seen a sculptor at work. Another time I played a drug addict with no experience of addicts or addiction. How is it done? Certainly not by cleverness. I think most of it comes from the truthfulness of the dramatist's writing. He has created the reality and the actor, holding up the mirror of his imagination, reflects this. Also a good education in classic fiction is a tremendous help. When I played Professor Bolland so convincingly in C. K. Munro's *Storm*, I suspect that professorial characters out of the immense richness of literature read to me by my mother rose out of my subconscious, or memory bank, and, blending with a knowledge of eccentric scholarly types at Clifton, clothed Mr. Munro's truly observed character with flesh.

In the matter of the sculptor I fall back on the theory of divine inspiration. Joan heard her voices; I was guided to make motions with my thumb. And the older I get the less of such talents for divination do I possess. Perhaps they are granted to the young in lieu of experience and, as experience encrusts us, our antennae become desensitized.

It was understood by the Fagans and the Eadie management, from whom I was earning five pounds a week that I would rejoin the Oxford Players for their Autumn season. But I had lost contact with Fagan and felt unwilling to give up the glory of playing in the West End and the slightly better salary which I felt I might even improve. So I went to Mr. Gibbons, Eadie's manager and stated that I was prepared to stay on in *Storm* if they would raise my salary. After much haggling he agreed. Eight pounds a week. The Fagans were outraged and I was told never to darken their door again. In fact *Storm* did not run much longer. I had made the wrong choice; money and status instead of the opportunity to develop my talents by playing greater parts. I was to make the same mistake again. Not, I think, because I am really avaricious but because in childhood one was always short of money as well as of love.

My luck however still held. Fagan needed someone for the last play of the autumn season and I think he was unwilling to let go his "find." So, after a suitable ritual of penitence with Mary Grey—"How could you be so disloyal to Jim?"—I was received with an ample embrace back into the fold.

The last play of the next season was Richard Hughes' *Comedy of Good and Evil* in which I played the male lead, an old Welsh clergyman, Mr. Williams. It happened that a big producing company in London had the little Ambassador's Theater on their hands, empty after an unexpected failure. A representative came down to Oxford and decided to transfer us for a run. So here I was for a second time within my first year as an actor, playing in the West End. And this time it was the male lead, a part for which I was singularly well-suited. I knew the Welsh accent and people from all those summer holidays in North Wales. And the mixture in Mr. Williams of obstinacy and gentleness, operating from a background of extreme poverty, in a field of supernatural happenings (the devil in the guise of a beautiful little girl visits Mr. Williams to test him) suited me perfectly. I got extremely good reviews.

James Whale, who was to became rich and famous as the director of the 1931 *Frankenstein*, was assistant director and set designer for the company. He also played small parts. I can see him looking up from the *New Statesman*, in which Desmond McCarthy, dean of London theatre critics, had written extraordinarily flattering things about my voice and persuasive charm.

"Well, Alan," said James, "you'll never look back."

On the contrary, I have spent my whole life looking back to this extraordinary start to my career.

The Comedy of Good and Evil proved too philosophical to be popular and only ran three weeks. However, even more fantastic fortune was around the corner.

* * *

We opened our summer season at Oxford with *The Cherry Orchard*. Nowadays this sounds a routine thing to do. But in 1924 it was extraordinary. Until this production, Chekhov had never been successfully produced in the whole of the English speaking world. The few single performances, put on by *avant garde* enthusiasts, had been laughed or booed off the stage by the audiences and ridiculed as dramatically unacceptable. I think these earlier productions, by straining to make the Chekhov structure conform to that of the "well made play," had merely made him appear ridiculously incompetent.

Jim Fagan directed the play with a completely open mind. As it was the first play of the season we had more than a week to work on it and we were fresh from our vacation and not acting at night. I was cast as Leonid Gayef, Mme. Ranevsky's elderly brother—Stanislavsky's part. I had never heard of Stanislavsky; I just knew it was a damn good part and right up my alley. And the fact that one existed in a tragicomic field, where the audience might legitimately laugh or weep or do both at once, seemed totally acceptable. I recall one member of the cast saying to Fagan, "But is this supposed to be funny—should I get a laugh or try to kill it?" and Fagan answering, "Just try to be real and I think it'll work."

Fagan was clever in establishing a wonderful atmosphere; the feel of a great country estate disintegrating was familiar to the Irishman in him. And James Whale did a brilliant job evoking a tender visual beauty out of almost nothing.

The first night was memorable. After my last exit as Gayef, it was my job to hurry out to a little shed—the theater's sole lavatory—where wood and a hatchet waited for me to make the sound of the cherry orchard being cut down, bringing the play to a close. I had very little time to get back into the theatre for the curtain call. Breathless, I rushed on stage. Dead silence from in front. The sickening thought, "We're a flop: it didn't work" was just curdling one's stomach when something started out in front. A wild storm of applause. The curtains parted and the audience stood up and cheered. We turned to each other, fell on each other's necks laughing and weeping. It was an historic evening marking the first total acceptance of a Chekhov play by an English-speaking audience. Eva le Gallienne's successful production in New York followed a few years later, showing that change was in the air and acceptance overdue.

Nigel Playfair, famous tenant of the Lyric Theatre, Hammersmith, came down from London and booked our production for the month of August. We played to full houses and transferred to the Royalty Theater in the West End, where the run had to be cut short because of Fagan's commitment for the autumn season at Oxford.

Again, now twenty-one years old, I won extraordinary praise from the critics, having mastered in ten days of rehearsal a part Stanislavsky took seven months to rehearse. Now, I write these apparently arrogant words to reflect how one felt at the time—absolutely on top of the theatrical world. It's true that the great George Bernard Shaw took me down a peg. Shaw had been an admirer of Chekhov for a long time; he was also an old friend of Fagan's, so when he saw our production he had plenty to say, most of it favorable. But he also said that I was playing Gayef much too old and shabby. Fagan called a rehearsal and tried to rejuvenate me. I was furious; I knew that what I did worked. Who the hell was GBS to find fault when all the critics had praised me? The fact of the matter is that when one is twenty-one it is much easier to play seventy than fifty, and I had to play him skinny rather than eupeptic because I was skinny. And, indeed, it did work: for the next fifteen years I would run into people who would say, "I shall never forget you in *The Cherry Orchard*."

A visiting American academic, Clarence DeWitt Thorpe of the University of Michigan, was invited by Fagan to attend the 100th performance of the play at the Royalty Theatre. Thorpe wrote about the show and the company in an article for the Quarterly Journal of Speech *where, after summarizing Fagan's Oxford vision (from which Jane Ellis was conveniently omitted), he described a backstage visit with R.S. Smith, who was playing the role of Simeonof-Pishtchik: "I talked to Mr. Smith, a big, fine affable fellow, and found him, along with Mr. Fagan and others, expressing a wish I had already found myself fervently uttering—that the Company might come to America and play before our university students. Mr. Alan Napier, who, as Leonid Gayef, should share with Mr. Smith honors as stars in this really all-star cast, was in the dressing room when I was talking to Mr. Smith, and he most earnestly seconded the suggestion of an American engagement. I left the theatre with the firm resolve to do all in my power to make such an engagement possible." Unfortunately, he was ultimately unsuccessful.*

The point that I really want to make from this glowing account of my early successes is that I could never have survived as an actor or as a human being without them. I was still too tall and, though the stammering hazard had grown less, a hazard it remained with occasional frightening lapses into aphasia. But my good fortune in having the chance to play these splendid parts and receive splendid reviews insured me a place in the English theater. Though theoretically unemployable, I could not now be ruled out.

15

Where Is Fancy Bred?

Behind this shield of outward success which brought its own happiness and sense of validity, and indeed kept my head above water, my development as a human being was depressingly crab-like—a scuttle to the left, a scuttle to the right, but very little forward movement.

What I see through a glass now is not altogether dark, though it had its murky moments. I see myself walking back from rehearsal at the playhouse to my digs (board and lodging, but no bath, thirty shillings and sixpence per week) and thinking, "It's Spring in Oxford and the May trees are in bloom. I've got a job. I'm doing all right in it. What's wrong? Why aren't I happier? Why don't I love anyone? Why doesn't anyone love me?" I liked the other Oxford Players; they seemed to like me. But I was lonely; I was outside the stream of warm life that surrounded me but into which I could not, or was afraid to plunge. I was playing at life on a stage but not living.

Between seasons at the Playhouse I would return home. My family accepted the fact that I was now an actor but there was a curious lack of interest or belief in my success. None of them had come to see me in *Storm*. When I was preparing at home for the next season in which I was to play crafty old Clive Champion-Cheyney in Somerset Maugham's wonderful comedy of manners *The Circle*, I remember my mother, with an incredulous little laugh, saying, "Dear boy, how can you possibly know how to act a man of the world like that?" The fact was that, somehow, I did.

Vacations, after doing a new play every week for a season of eight weeks, were really necessary. Sometimes when I have felt almost ashamed of the easy way I have earned money in Hollywood I would say to myself, "I earned it at Oxford." Every play we did was a classic of its kind and the text and the audience both demanded brave effort at perfection. Our weekly schedule was consequently killing. We rehearsed for next week's play from ten-thirty to one and from two to four-thirty. Then one learned one's lines and had the evening meal. Back to the theater for a performance of the current play. Then home to work on one's lines again, maybe 'till one or two in the morning. Dress rehearsals were on Sunday after two performances on Saturday. Monday morning, our only free period in the week, was usually devoted to having a bath at the Randolph Hotel since most of our digs, necessarily the cheapest to be found, did not have bathrooms. When one had two big parts running, mastering the lines was like trying to climb Mount Everest in five days. It is amazing how one managed.

During one vacation I stayed with my mother at Burford, where she was having one of her periodic changes of air. I took with me a copy of *The Brothers Karamazov* and for three days I was completely out of this world. No book ever stirred and possessed me as did the first reading of that extraordinary work. It was part of my growing up. I grew a beard and went on long walks through the Cotswold lanes as it churned inside my head and vitals. There was a road (sign-posted to "Lechlade and Filkins," suggestive of unmentionable country goings-on) down which I remember passing a little local school one afternoon just as the children were coming out. They all started jeering as they gathered round me screaming "You oughter shive! Why don't you shive yourself!" It wasn't much of a beard and I was evidently before my time—no one would think anything of it in 1972—but suddenly to be screamed at by a hostile horde of brats gave me a chilling sense of being an outcast.

Then, before another season began at Oxford, one of the company, Glen Byam Shaw, asked me if I would like to share rooms with him. I was touched that he should want to do this and immediately accepted. He was two years younger than I—a boy of nineteen with an enchanting uninhibited gaiety of spirit. Our first afternoon together—a Sunday before starting in on rehearsals the next day—we went for a walk in the mellow autumn sunshine before returning to our new digs for tea. Oxford seemed particularly beautiful and we laughed and chattered nonsense arm in arm through ancient twisting streets. And then we fell silent, under the spell of golden light on spire an old quadrangle.

Back in our digs I was standing by the mantle-piece waiting for our landlady, who had just brought in the tea, to leave. It was a tiny room. As I turned from the fireplace Glen stretched up his hand, gently pulled down my head and kissed me. I was utterly amazed. A great wave of emotion filled me, and I could feel tears in my eyes. All I could say was "You ... you mean you like me?"

He roared with laughter and said, "Of course I like you, you silly old thing. I think you're terribly attractive."

"Me?" I said.

"Yes. You." and he kissed me again and added, "Come on. Let's have tea. I'm hungry."

I remember the deep blue of the sky and the image of a tree and the house opposite reflected in the landlady's best silver teapot.

I was filled with a passion of grateful love for my friend. It was not devoid of sex since I cherished the idea of lying with this beautiful creature in my arms—but I was quite unprepared to translate this romantic feeling of adoration into anything so unthinkable as a homosexual affair.

Nevertheless a great tenderness survived. His affection was real and lasting. As for me, I shall always love him for his charm and sense of fun and warmth of heart. But he had given me much more than friendship—he had shown me that I could be loved. I no longer felt totally excluded from the warm waters of desire. I could paddle happily in them even if I was not ready to plunge right in.

It is my belief that a great proportion of mankind—male and female—are naturally capable of feeling love for members of their own sex. But our culture, for reasons of expediency and social convenience, tries to polarize the sexual drive and insists that everyone must be either hetero which is "normal" or homo which is not. Indeed, in our world it is more convenient to be hetero, so we try to forget the total acceptance of bisexuality by the ancient Greeks, whose culture we otherwise revere.

It has always seemed strange to me that a career or a marriage can be ruined if it should transpire that a man once felt love and expressed it sexually with another man;

whereas the knowledge that he used unlovingly to unload his desire in whore-houses or in casual loveless encounters with nymphomaniac amateurs, is happily accepted as an indication that he is a real he-man.

I have maintained contact with Glen, the early recipient of my grateful love, though years by the dozen may go by without our meeting. In 1947, with my dear second wife, Gip, I went back to England for my first visit in nine years. Glen had been happily married to that lovely actress, Angela Baddeley, for over twenty years and knew all about the inevitable failure of my first marriage. I was very anxious to see him again and to bring him and Gip together. As I knew it would be, our encounter was a great success. He and Gip took to each other at once and I could see he was happy that his old friend had finally achieved the happiness in marriage that he knew so well himself. He was now a father of two, and established as an outstanding director in the English theatre.

The years go by and Gip dies of cancer.

I go back to England uncertain of where I want to live, sometimes even uncertain if I want to live, existing for the moment only, unwilling to think of the past. Then, one day, I remember this old friend. I call up and he asks me to dinner. Angela is in a play so she cannot be with us. Glen and I have a wonderful evening talking about old times, for I cannot easily speak of the present emptiness and of my sense of irreparable loss. We pick up Angela at the theatre and go back to their apartment for more talk and a final drink.

"I must go," I say and kiss Angela goodnight. Glen is standing there, very little changed from the days at Oxford forty years ago except that his hair, like mine, is now white. He reaches up a hand, gently pulls my head down and kisses me. I have no words to express what comfort this gesture of love, echoing down the years, conferred on me.

I see a turn of the wheel less happily remembered. I am sitting at my make-up table in the long men's dressing roan at the Lyric, Hammersmith, taking off my beard after a matinee of *The Cherry Orchard*. It is very hot and I am stripped to the waist. James Whale comes up behind me and looks at me in the mirror with his sardonic, calculating smile. "I know someone who would be nuts about you," he says. "Me?" I ask incredulously. "Oh yes. That broad chest. And these." Gentle finger tips define my shoulders.

I really am puzzled. I've been far too busy with our heavy acting schedule to devote more than spasmodic attention to my former compulsive exercising, and still regard my body with dissatisfaction. A few days later James asks me if I would like to go to a party. What sort of party? "Oh … all men. Four or five couples." Now, though I was innocent of actual experience I was not so naive as to misunderstand the drift of what he was proposing. I still had not had the initiative to plunge into the waters of sex and here the initiative was not demanded of me. My curiosity was aroused and I thought, "If I don't like it I can always get out at the last moment." "Bring your pajamas," said James, "it'll start with dancing."

I have never felt more of a fool than I did solemnly fox-trotting round a room with this man who was the putative admirer of my broad shoulders. There were four other couples and the room was not large. I have never been a good dancer and my "date" was supposed to be leading me, even though he only came up to my shoulders. After treading on his toes a few times I said, "I'm not very good at this, I'm afraid." "No," he said, "Let's have a drink and get to know each other." I found he was gentle, amusing, well-read and not at all effeminate. He had a job at the foreign office. He was older than I but still quite young. I liked him. After a time he said, "It's a bit crowded here. Why don't we go back to my flat."

I was a little drunk and I wanted to get away from all these rather queer young men who eyed each other knowingly and giggled. "All right," I said.

However, when I found myself lying naked on a bed with this hairy-chested man bouncing about on top of me I knew beyond all doubt that this was not my idea of togetherness, nor where my inhibited sexual drive should be taking me. "What am I doing?" I thought as I looked up at the molded plaster ceiling above me—not so much revolted as painfully embarrassed.

Afterwards, in the bathroom, I sat on the john and looked dispassionately at poor Ned, soaping himself in the tub and looking vulnerable, as short-sighted people do without their glasses. "I'm sorry," I said. "I should never have got into this. I'm afraid I disappointed you."

"Oh no! You're so beautiful and masculine. I just hope you don't hate yourself. Tell me though, why did you come to the party?"

I could not explain my long hang-up of inhibition (although John Fowles has since expressed it beautifully in *The French Lieutenant's Woman*: "… in such wells of loneliness, is not any coming together closer to humanity than to perversity?") so I said, "When I left home to make my fortune on the stage my father said to me 'try everything once.' But I don't think he meant this," and we both laughed. Then he added, "Look, I hope we can meet again, just as friends. I promise I'll not bother you."

We did meet. One day he drove me down to his special little beach on the South Coast, past Alfriston and to the west of Eastbourne. It is probably a Butlin's Camp now or a housing development. Then, you could only get to it through a wide meadow. You parked your car by the roadside, climbed over a style and walked. He told me that in the spring the meadow was full of cowslips. Long after we had ceased to meet—Ned wanted more than friendship, though he never did "bother" me—I used to go there in the late spring. And it was true; the field was a carpet of cowslips and the warm honey-sweet scent of them hung in the air.

The last time I saw Ned I was in a box at the Chelsea Arts Ball with my first wife. He was down on the floor with a tall slender youth who had come to the ball in a helmet and a fig leaf as Apollo. I did not think that Ned was going to be disappointed. I hoped not.

Not long after my failure as a homosexual I see a surprisingly different picture. In a corner of the stage at the Oxford Playhouse, after the afternoon rehearsal was over and everyone else has left, there I am in the arms of a tall handsome young woman being almost suffocated with passionate kisses. I don't remember how it started, but I have a sort of idea that she was lurking in the shadows and leapt out on me as I headed for the exit. My first reaction was one of alarm and claustrophobia. Then a strange excitement began to take possession of me and I became aware that, taken off guard by the sudden assault, I had risen manfully to the occasion and was pressing into her soft belly. M, as I will call her, uttering little cries of ecstasy, was going limp and acquiescent in my arms. She was no lightweight and in another moment we would have been on the floor if the stage manager had not come back to set the stage for the evening performance.

M was a local amateur who sometimes joined the company for crowd scenes or a small part. When I spoke of my experience—because of the stage manager's return, it was certainly no secret—a seasoned Oxonian of the company laughed and said, "You too? Didn't you know? She's our local nymphomaniac. Can't keep her hands off any man."

Though my dreams of a passionate romance were somewhat dashed by this cynical observation, I nevertheless accepted with alacrity when invited to tea to meet her mother. Alas, that finished it. Mama was evidently on the lookout for a husband for her profligate girl, and I certainly was not ready for that. I also found that M was not really my cup of tea. I have always preferred slender, delicately built women with lively minds, and she was rather coarsely Amazonian and intellectually void behind her amorous propensities.

The French have a delightful phrase, *"reculer pour mieux sauter,"* which describes my next three and a half years. I withdrew from further assault on the fortress of the West End Theater, also on the female of the species, in order to make a better jump when the time came.

However employment was constant. If one was not at Oxford where I played more of the leading roles as John Gielgud and others moved on—one was doing a season of classics at Huddersfield, perhaps, or playing bit roles for Jim Fagan in his great West End success *And So to Bed*, a delightful period comedy about Samuel Pepys and Charles II. The Huddersfield season was put on at the Theater Royal during the August "dark" period between ordinary touring attractions. We were to do Chekhov, Ibsen, Gogol and Pirandello; and the local textile workers would be able to see these masterpieces for threepence in the gallery, and two shillings and sixpence in the stalls. I thought they might throw eggs at us. In fact, they were a wonderful audience—more attentive and enthusiastic than the Oxford audiences I was used to. I was playing younger parts and managed very well. We had an old actor, John Burton, playing "my" parts—that is to say the old men.

In the train going to Huddersfield this remarkable old man, touching my arm, pointed to the sulfurous sky and endless rows of wretched little sooty hovels that housed the industrial workers of the North and confided, "Dear Boy, when I see a sight like that and reflect on the lives those poor people live, I thank God I am an actor!" What courage! He was eighty-two years old and earning six pounds a week in a stock company producing a new play every week. As a boy he had played with the great McCready. *(William McCready gave his farewell performance at Drury Lane in 1851, playing the role of Macbeth. Burton would have been seven then, so his claim is certainly plausible, especially considering that the murder of Macduff's young sons is an important element in the play.)* Ten years later when I was playing a leading part at the Westminster Theater, he came round to see me, frail but in possession of his faculties, and said, "I knew you would make it, my dear boy. You have the voice."

There were a lot of small parts in *And So to Bed* and Jim Fagan kept them open for his Playhouse players between the Oxford seasons. I originated the part of the pickpocket who knocks Pepys on the head, precipitating his romantic involvement with one of Charles' mistresses. I also understudied Charles and, one foggy afternoon, had to go on for my principal. I had not been properly rehearsed and I did not really know my lines. It was a lamentably poor performance. In fact, one would hardly expect a virtual virgin of twenty-three to have the weight to play that sardonic saturnine lecher, Charles II. So, when my telephone rang in Hollywood many, many years later and a very Russian voice said "Thees ees Eugenie Leontovich. Vill you play Charles II in *And So to Bed*?" I leapt at it in the hope of wiping out my shame.

Miss Leontovich had played the part of Mistress Pepys in the original New York production. *(Actually, Yvonne Arnaud, who played Mistress Pepys in London, went to America with Fagan in 1927 to recreate the role in New York. Eugenie Leontovich toured the United*

States and Canada in the part starting in 1928.) This second time around I was in my forties and sufficiently pickled in the ways of the world. I think that the ghosts of Charles and Jim Fagan were content.

During the Oxford Players seasons there were many highlights—Captain Shotover in *Heartbreak House*, Dr. Knock, Malvolio—and a low-light in a new play, which has an ironic story. In Emlyn Williams' fascinating memoir of his early life, *George*, there comes a sad climax to the start of his career as a playwright when he sells his first play, *Full Moon*, to Fagan for production by the Oxford Players. He is unable to attend the first night because he is tied to his mother's bedside in North Wales where she is desperately ill. But, he writes, at least he could see and imagine every moment of the play in his mind's eye because he knew exactly what Alan Napier and Glen Byan Shaw would be doing with the leading parts. Now, I do not say that he wrote the parts for us—but his familiarity with the work of the company meant that, when Fagan accepted the play, Emlyn knew very well who would be playing them, and he felt every confidence in us. But the sad fact of the matter was that *Full Moon* was the last play of the season and I was utterly worn out.

Great playwrights, such as Shakespeare and Shaw, develop a mastery that gives their dialogue a flow—the way one thought follows another appears to be inevitably right—making the lines easy to learn. A beginner's dialogue will often exhibit a certain tentativeness and, if the actor is tired, be dreadfully difficult to memorize. With Emlyn's play I had this difficulty and on that first night, while he was serenely trusting us to bring his creation to life, I was in fact fluffing and fiddling and losing my grip—indeed, giving a very poor performance. (*However, Williams goes on to describe his being back in Oxford in time to see the Saturday evening performance "well directed and well acted" and recalls the joy of walking with Glen Byam Shaw, Alan Webb and Alan Napier back to their "digs," for "a theatrical supper which fitted me like a glove, kippers and chips and tea and beer and 'shop.'"*)

I have a delightful memory of Emlyn which does not appear in his book. Shortly after this production of *Full Moon*, I was back in *And So to Bed* at the Savoy Theatre and one afternoon Emlyn suddenly burst into my dressing room.

"Hello Emlyn," I said. "What on earth are you doing here?"

He was bubbling over with high spirits and answered, "I've come to London to make my fortune on the stage." In moments of excitement he still had the charming lilt and pure vowel sounds of the Welsh. I said, "I thought you were stuck in the depths of Wales having trouble with your family." (One had heard that his father wanted him to go into the Church.)

"I was," he said. "Oh, I had a terrible row with my father. So I hit him on the head with a frying pan. And here I am!" Fagan found him a part in *And So to Bed* to tide him over and a brilliant career in the theater was inaugurated.

Emlyn Williams' second volume of autobiography, Emlyn, *had not appeared in time for Alan to reference it in his own book. In it, Williams recalls Alan trying to broaden the younger man's unadventurous taste in theatre ("What about that play next Sunday from the Finnish, with new techniques and masks—symbolism, expressionism, don't they fascinate you?") as well as helping with his old age makeup when he played the Burglar ("an old and villainous man") in Shaw's* Heartbreak House.

The Oxford Players also went to Glasgow for a season which opened with *Dear Brutus* and *Heartbreak House*, in both of which I played the leads—Dearth and Captain Shotover. The plays and the actors won enthusiastic reviews and excellent houses. Soon after *Heart-*

break House opened, I received a message from a local parson inviting me to preach in his church next Sunday on Church and Stage! I was petrified at the prospect as I had never spoken in public except on the stage. I was also the victim of a lot of teasing from the company. At the time I was sharing rooms with Glen Byam Shaw and Alan Webb in Renfrew Street up above Sauchiehall Street. And I remember both of them, with wicked mockery in their eyes, saying "Go on, old boy! Of course you must do it—think of the publicity for the company! You can't let us down."

So I spent a sleepless night trying to compose a suitable sermon. What I didn't realize was that the parson was under the impression that I was an elderly leading man whose fame he had somehow failed to catch up with. My gift of being convincing as an old man had completely deceived him. Next morning he came to the theater to have a chat with me and when, instead of a grey-haired dignified man of authority, he found a nervous rather callow young fellow of twenty-four, he was extremely embarrassed. I hurriedly said I really didn't think, with our heavy schedule of rehearsal, that I would have time…

"No, no," he said. "Indeed indeed. I had no idea… Another time perhaps…" and we called the whole thing off with mutual satisfaction.

Some months later a sad loss befell the Fagan entourage. Jim had gone to New York to launch a successful production there of *And So to Bed*. This was at the time when sound was being added to movies and English actors, stories and writers were all the rage in Hollywood. Jim was signed to a long term contract as a writer at a fabulous salary. He fell in love with the wonderful climate, as sun-loving refugees from the grey skies of England do, and experienced a happy feeling of rejuvenation. It has always been possible to be funny about the movie business; but in those days Southern California was a smog-free paradise of endless sunny days. Jim started playing tennis again and, careless of that cold little breeze that so often blows in from the ocean about five o'clock in the evening, caught a chill that turned into pneumonia. That was before penicillin and he did not have the constitutional strength to survive. He was a splendid man of the theater and indeed my first discoverer and supporter and the architect of that premature blaze of success which, I reiterate, was necessary for my survival.

With Jim's death the original Oxford Players Company disintegrated. Later, an effort to revive it somehow resulted in my returning to London in a terrible play called *Out of the Sea*. I only remember that I played a Cornish coastguard and had to enter singing a sea chantey about blowing a man down—agony for me and the audience, since I have trouble holding a tune or maintaining a key. The whole venture was ignored rather than condemned; and when *Out of the Sea* was replaced by *Dr. Knock*, though we earned some good reviews, they did not bring in an audience. After the play's success at Oxford it was a chilling experience to play in a vast empty London theater where an occasional guffaw of laughter would echo emptily and shame the laugher. *Alan has compressed history here. The New York production of* And So to Bed *was in 1927. In Fagan's absence, Alan's final season with the Oxford Players was supervised by Claud Gurney, previously Fagan's assistant. Fagan did indeed wind up in Hollywood, where he died, but that was not until 1931.*

During this year, 1928, I was also again engaged by Dennis Eadie for a detective thriller by A.E.W. Mason. In it Eadie played the famous French detective Hanaud and I an eccentric Russian villain. I also understudied Eadie who, a few weeks after we had opened, suddenly collapsed and died in Brighton one weekend. It was decided to continue the run, bringing in another star. For two weeks, while he was preparing for it, I played the lead. This time I knew my lines and had a very good opinion of myself since, to tell the truth, Eadie had not been very good. He had taken to hating audiences and did not bother to characterize Hanaud. Though we did not know it, he had been a sick man all the time. *(The star who eventually took over the lead from Alan was Edmund Gwenn.)*

It happened, though, that just about this time Charles Laughton burst upon the West End, making his first big commercial success at the Haymarket Theatre playing Agatha Christie's famous Belgian detective, Poirot. I went to see him, as one up-and-coming actor to another. I had a wonderful afternoon and, I have to say for myself, felt not one pang of jealousy as I freely accepted the truth that my Hanaud was not in the same class as the brilliant Poirot of Charles Laughton. It is true that he had had the advantage of being directed by Gerald du Maurier who was matchless in this field; nevertheless, I knew that he made me look like a talented young character actor from the provinces pretending to be a Frenchman, whereas he was M. Poirot, flawlessly dominating a production of polished elegance.

Nineteen twenty-nine was a crucial year for me. It began with my being engaged by a remarkable little actor-manager called Leon M. Lion to play in a tour of Galsworthy's *Loyalties* and *Justice*. Lion had his own rather peculiar system of making a good living out of producing failures; but he also dearly loved the theater and, as a gesture to Art (which also stood a sporting chance of realizing a profit) periodically revived what he called "My Galsworthy Cycle." I learned a great deal from him and, in particular, the importance of not being embarrassed about my height.

In *Loyalties*, I played that splendid old bastion of the establishment, General Canynge. Lion, of course, played the lead, De Levis, the upstart Jew who accuses Dancy, an "officer and a gentleman," of stealing.

Now, instead of casting all the English club types with small actors to make his own lack of stature less noticeable, Lion did the exact opposite. He cast the tallest actors he could find, so that when he swept out of the club with the line, "My race was old when you were all savages!" the audience reaction was tremendously sympathetic to the little fellow who came out on top of all those snotty great aristocrats.

At rehearsal, feeling terribly embarrassed to be towering so greatly over the leading actor who was also my employer, I stooped and tried to make the least of my height.

"Dear boy," said Lion, "stand up, for Heaven's sake! If you apologize for your height the audience will notice it and worry about it all evening and not pay attention to the play. But if you came on with your shoulders back looking your best, they'll think 'what a fine looking man' and then forget all about it." He was perfectly right. People who have only seen me on the stage or screen are always surprised, when they meet me, that I am so tall. And I can remember only one occasion when a critic has referred to my height, although for twenty-five years—until James Arness came to light—I must have been the tallest actor in the world of any standing.

It was my good fortune that little Lion took to me. He enjoyed formulating rather elaborately complicated sentences which would get hung up in mid-stream for lack of the right word. At this point, waving his cigar in circles in the air he would embark on a series of humming noises like a kettle about to boil over, "Hmm-er ... hmm-er ... hmm-er...." I was very good at finding the right word and popping it into his mouth. "Exactly, dear boy! Exactly!—Counterpoint is the very word," and he would beam at me, chuckling with delight, as off he went again to bring his storm tossed sentence into port. It was also possible to pop the wrong word into his mouth, whereupon with the same, "Exactly, exactly—the very word," he would go off on a new tangent and end up, if he ever did reach port, in a totally unexpected haven. But this was a naughty game and I only played it later on in the many years of our acquaintance.

He also had a jackdaw passion for collecting—his collection consisting of rare words and phrases. I imagine that his formal education had been negligible, though one would not have guessed it from the florid exuberance of his speech as an elderly man. One Sunday on this tour of *Loyalties* and *Justice* he invited me to accompany him from Manchester to Edinburg in his ancient, spacious, chauffeur-driven Minerva motor car, instead of going by train with the rest of the company. In the hideous outskirts of Manchester conversing on the horrors of industrialized suburbs, I found myself—as it seems to me now rather affectedly—using the phrase "*Lacrimae rerum*": the tears of things. In self-defense I can only say that Lion liked his conversation well spiced with exotic plums. He rose to this one beautifully.

"What is that, dear boy? Lacrimae, I know. What is rerum?"

I explained. And sure enough nine months later in a letter to the *Times* on the state of The Theatre, *Lacrimae rerum* brought his argument to a close with an air of well-digested scholarship.

It was a recommendation by Leon M. Lion that gave me my chance of finally storming the fortress of the West End.

16

Breakthrough

During these years of busy and successful apprenticeship in the theatre I lived, when I was in London, in rooms in Ebury Street with my old Clifton friend, John Houseman. At that time the name was spelt Haussman, for his father was a French speculator in the grain business with interests in Rumania and the Argentine. His mother, an English lady, insisted that her boy receive an English Public School education. When Jack left Clifton, instead of taking up a scholarship at Cambridge he chose to spend a year in the Argentine learning the grain business; and when he returned to London pursued this avocation there. (I have since learned that it was not a matter of choice, but of economic pressure. *Run Through*, John Houseman's book of memoirs, tells the true story.)

Another Cliftonian friend and I welcomed him back with enthusiasm and, shortly after his return, he suggested that I should leave my Belgrave Road attic and take a room in the Mary Street House where he was comfortably ensconced. Jack also had literary ambitions and had brought back with him some very evocative stories, remarkable for atmosphere rather than plot, about life on the Pampas, which I remember chiefly by the haunting refrain that ran through them, "*Povre chicito, povre chicito.*"

When an actor is in a London run he has plenty of spare time and I spent many pleasant hours punctuating Jack's often elliptical prose. The question whether to be a writer or a businessman—his father, a millionaire one year and broke the next, had regrettably died broke—exercised Jack considerably. Finally, having met Desmond McCarthy, the distinguished critic who wrote so kindly of my performance in *The Comedy of Good and Evil*, Jack submitted his Argentine stories to the great man for an opinion. The verdict was, "If you are content to starve in a garret you may eventually became a writer of some standing," or words to that effect. So Jack determined to pursue a career in grain.

He had many connections through his father, and after a year or so in London moved on to the United States. We carried on a splendid correspondence in rich biblical English as each of us advanced in his respective calling. I remember particularly the final letter from Jack (shortly before the stock-market crash wiped him out), which concluded, "Now indeed am I the meteor of the West; verily I pull the strings of the Pacific. Riches are mine and power and the glittering prizes of Ashtaroth."

We had a very pleasant times together while he was living at No. 145 Ebury Street, ministered to by the landlady's daughter, Olga Titoff, a name which led to a good deal of juvenile mirth. We went together to see Pauline Lord in *Anna Christie* at The Strand Theatre. We saw Claude Rains and Edith Evans in *Getting Married* at the Everyman Theatre, and a splendid production there of *Major Barbara* with Felix Aylmer as Cousins. And on Sundays I took him to 8 Addison Road to play tennis with the Debenhams. It was an easy undemanding friendship and it meant that one was not living entirely alone. We were compatible since Jack was also a late developer in the realm of sex; yet he was more the man of the world than I and helped me to emerge from my shell. On the other hand he was totally devoid of any family background or relatives of his own age in England and enjoyed being accepted into my vast family connection.

When I eventually followed him to the United States, where he had abandoned grain and found his place in the Arts as Orson Welles' right-hand man in the Mercury Theater, our reunion was joyous and of great value to me in my endeavor to start a new life in a new country.

* * *

A pleasant aspect of my private life at this time was my happy relationship with my brother. From the time he returned from his World War I army service, his attitude to me entirely changed. He became an affectionate elder brother and, when I began to achieve my early success in the theater—a period when he was having a bad time—far from showing any envy of my success, he was more interested and encouraging than other members of my family. I remember once when he took me out to his favorite little restaurant in Soho— in those days we all had our favorite little Soho discoveries—I was able to talk about sex to him very comfortably and to ask him what one did with a girl if the necessary erection for final union did not at first present itself. "Oh, don't bother. Just play around for a bit and before you realize what's happening, everything will be all right." This trivial little recollection I revive because it indicates a warmth and closeness that my picture of Mark during our childhood would hardly lead one to expect.

The inquiry into the mysteries of passion that I posed to Mark recalls a relationship I enjoyed at this time with a delightful Irish girl, Joyce, which, if I had had a little more assurance, might have developed very agreeably instead of petering out into nothing.

One summer night I really believed the, moment of revelation was at hand. We decided—it was actually Midsummer Night—to celebrate the occasion by swimming in the Serpentine. In those days Hyde Park, surrounded by spiked iron railings ten feet high, was closed to the public at sundown. We approached from the Bayswater Road side at twenty minutes to midnight and, choosing a moment when no pedestrians were about, somehow managed to clamber over the high palings. Joyce, who was light as a feather, mounted my shoulders, gave me a hand up from the perilous top, and we both landed safely on the other side.

It was a moonlit night, warm and still, and the empty park, as we quickly ran into the shadow of the great trees, seemed mysterious and remote. Suddenly we were not in seething London anymore; we were in a great medieval chase with avenues of majestic trees stretching as far as eye could see. Holding hands we made our way down to the edge of the lake, on the Kensington Gardens side near the north end of the bridge over the Serpentine. Quickly we undressed—Joyce quicker than I—and there she stood, white and slender, naked in the moonlight. With the shedding of my undershorts I suddenly felt liberated—a very satyr and, leaping to my feet, took her warm body in my arms. "Come on," she whispered, "give me your hand," and we plunged into the cold, black waters of The Serpentine.

Immediately a tremendous noise arose. The whole duck and water fowl population of the lake burst into a noisy protest at this disturbance of their rest. It was rather alarming after the total midnight silence. The water seemed very cold and the footing disgustingly muddy, so that when we got out, goose-pimpled, dirty-footed and with nothing to dry off with, any passionate inclination gave way at first to laughter and then, when we heard heavy footsteps, to alarm.

We had forgotten that close at hand was the Ordnance Repository, guarded day and night by a sentry. I suppose the quacking of the geese had aroused his curiosity. Quickly we grabbed our clothes and tiptoed from our exposed position into the cover of a clump of bushes. With wet hair dangling down our faces and the smell of mud on our feet, we alternately giggled and held our breath. When the footsteps came no nearer, we dressed and made our way back to the Bayswater Road. Waiting until we saw a taxi approaching from Marble Arch, we once more scaled the lofty palings and landed on the sidewalk just in time to call "Taxi" and leap into the cab as it drew to the curb. I remember the look on the driver's face, "I know what you've been up to!" and my regret that his conclusion was not justified.

* * *

And now my Uncle Henry comes back into my story. Uncle Henry, by the way, was the only member of my family I remember coming to see me perform at the Oxford Playhouse. For him it was quite an event. Strictly evangelical, he had been brought up to regard the theatre as a sinful institution and, until he saw me in Elmer Rice's *The Adding Machine*, he had never seen a play in his life. By this time, he had long ceased to hold such narrow views and was very tolerant of the human condition; but theatre was just not part of his life. The old boy had come home from Ceylon, had taken on a temporary cure of souls at Tetbury near Oxford, and expressed a desire to see what I was up to. So I got him a seat for a matinée. What made the situation all the more intriguing was the fact that in this curious impressionistic play his nephew was playing the part of God. He took it very well and I had a lovely day with him at Tetbury the next Sunday.

The Adding Machine *was the sixth show of an extremely grueling season for Alan. Preceded by Shaw's* Heartbreak House, *Georg Kaiser's* Morn to Midnight, *Strindberg's* Easter, *Alfred de Musset's* Fantasio *and Jules Romain's* Dr. Knock; *it was followed by J.M. Barrie's* What Every Woman Knows *and Sheriden's* The Rivals. *Eight plays in eight weeks. Scheduled to return a month later for another six plays, Alan was overwhelmed. On January 20, 1928, the* Oxford Chronicle *reported: "It will be learned with regret that Mr. Alan Napier will not be able to join the Oxford Players this term. He had a bad breakdown in December, after a particularly strenuous session. His many Oxford admirers will wish him a speedy restoration to health."*

The 1928 spring season proceeded without him, but following its official close in February, there was a special one week revival and the Oxford Mail *welcomed back its star. "Alan Napier's return after his illness would be welcome in any case, but it is doubly so in view of his brilliant performance as Dr. Knock. In this role he scores a real triumph, for the part 'fits him like a glove.' 'Dr. Knock' is practically a 'one man show,' but with Mr. Napier as that one man nothing more could be desired." The* Chronicle *was no less effusive: "The cast is a powerful one. The name part is played by Alan Napier. In every particular he is an artist, and keeps the play going with a swing, for there is scarcely a moment when he is not the leading character." It was this production that was brought to London later that year in an attempt to salvage the disastrous reception of* Out of the Sea. Dr. Knock *was Alan's Oxford Playhouse farewell, and he went out on top.*

It was shortly after this that Uncle Henry sent all his nephews and nieces the generous check for three hundred pounds which I have already referred to. I determined to blow mine on a trip abroad.

Richard Goolden, of the Oxford Players, had often regaled us with tales of his friends in Austria, a country to which I have always felt strangely drawn. As soon as my tour with Leon M. Lion was over, I contacted Richard and worked out a plan with him. I would go to Munich and on to the Bavarian Alps where he would join me later with a platonic girlfriend. Journeying to strange lands is always exciting—more so perhaps in the days of boats and trains—but this journey was to be very special. I was determined that I would not return a virgin. Somehow, I felt the momentous step would be easier to take abroad, in that cradle of romantic love, Vienna.

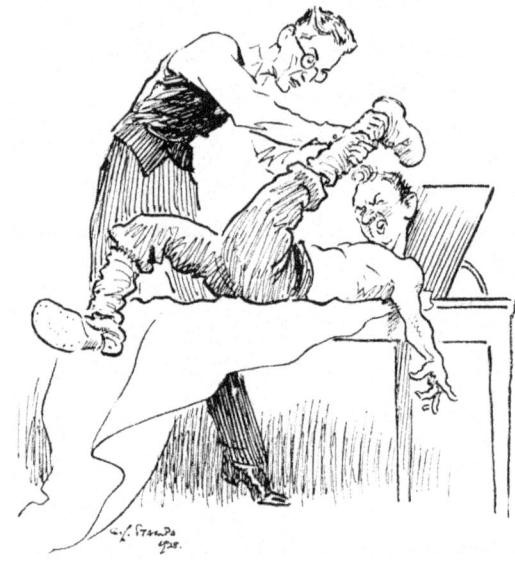

"Punch" caricature of Alan as the title character in Jules Romains' *Dr. Knock* and Harry V. Pease as his patient. Strand Theatre, 1928. © Punch Limited.

Munich before Hitler was an enchanting city. I went to the theatre and to art galleries and museums. Inadvertently I got drunk on the famous export beer at the Bierhall that Hitler subsequently used as his headquarters. And I was very lonely. Then I went on to Garmisch-Partenkirchen, a dear little place before winter sports blew it up into a world renowned resort. I climbed the Zugspitze, bought myself lederhosen, boated on the Eibsee and discovered a secret island where I could swim and sunbathe naked. It was all very beautiful. I loved being greeted with "Grüss Gott" by everyone I met as I rambled through woods and meadows. And I was very lonely. Then Richard arrived with his repertoire of old English music hall songs, a suitcase adrift with Torbet's Lactic Oats, and Penelope. And I wasn't lonely anymore.

We soon moved on to Innsbruck and then to Salzburg where, at The Golden Horn, there were bugs in the beds and Penelope's bed collapsed. Summoning the manager, Richard, who was the German expert, explained, "We have broken the bed!" The manager roared with laughter and said we had ordered for the Gnädiges Fräulein a bed for one only.

All this time I was thinking, "It's lovely to have Richard and Penelope here, but how am I to achieve my de-virgination with them about?" Later Richard told me that nothing could have been easier—Penelope was very much taken with me. I think back and see that I was twenty-six years old, tanned, tall, in lederhosen and not bad looking. I just had a mental block about myself and sex. And it wasn't that I was unaware that Penelope was a very attractive woman.

We had a very fascinating time in Vienna staying with an acquaintance of Richard's, an English ex-diplomat who, at the time of the terrible post-war inflation, had bought for

16. Breakthrough

a song, a small palace, where Mozart had once taught young countesses to play the piano. But my quest was still unrealized so I stayed on after Richard and Penelope had gone home. I saw *Rosenkavalier* at the Burgtheatre with the great cast that included Lehmann, Schumann, Olszewska and Mayr. I saw everything that a tourist should see and my last day dawned. It was now or never.

Sitting in a cafe in the shadow of the Stefansturm, I saw a pretty blonde girl, alone at a table nearby. She had a frail, pale, ingenuous look that attracted me. I caught her eye. She smiled. With my heart in my mouth I went over and, in my halting German, stammered the request that I might sit at her table. How I got around to the vital question, "Would she?" I have no idea. I expect she made it easy for me, though she was very insistent that it was only possible (a) because her mother had been ruined by the inflation and (b) because she liked me very much. She took me to a sleazy hotel nearby and, as I hadn't much money left and wanted to know where I stood, I asked if she would allow me to make a small contribution towards the upkeep of her ruined mother. Graciously she accepted, naming a reasonable sum.

So we got into bed together and I found that it wasn't difficult at all. I kept telling her, apologetically, that it was my first attempt, which she refused to believe, saying only that I was so brown and so tall. We had a very nice time. Finally she got out of bed, did peepee in a chamber pot, and quickly put on her little panties saying it would be extra if I wanted to do it again. That was when I had to admit to myself that she was probably a professional and not a romantic conquest who allowed me to help her mother. I made a quick calculation that I really couldn't afford any more, thanked her very much, took a taxi to my hotel, picked up my suitcase, and went on to the Bahnhof in nice time to catch the train home. I was terribly pleased with myself.

One fortress taken. There remained the West End.

Generally speaking, you can safely question a man's intelligence, his honesty, even his courage; but question his sense of humor or virility and you are in deep trouble.

I must claim to be an exception to this generalization for, while I have an unshakable confidence in a sense of humor which has stood by me through thick and thin, I am quite prepared to admit that I have never been very good at sex. I have never been very good at tennis either, though I've played off and on all my life. On good days, in my prime, I've pulled off some remarkably good shots, while on bad days I have sometimes hardly been able to get the ball over the net. Yet I've never had difficulty finding partners. People expect me to be better than I am, and then go along with me for the pleasure of my company. And so with sex.

Having described my late entry into the sex sweepstakes and, so to speak, established my preference, I shall spare the reader any further details of my playing. Love is something else. Though it may be conditioned by it, it is not totally dependent on prodigious sexual performance.

Storming the fortress of the West End may sound a little melodramatic in these days of a much more fluid theatrical structure. But in the 20s and the 30s actors who regularly played in the smart London commercial theatre belonged to a comparatively small élite. The touring theatre provided a much larger field of employment than it does today. There were Number One Tours that only visited the best theatres of the major cities, and there were Number Two Tours that visited a hundred towns that now have only movie houses.

Finally there were Number Three Tours—God knows where they went, though sometimes it might be to play a Welsh village at crack of dawn for the entertainment of the night shift miners.

Many excellent Number One Tour actors earned a good living yet never made the West End. Perhaps their accents were not quite up to the comedies and dramas of this period, which were concerned almost exclusively with the privileged classes. Oh, there was always a comic maid or charlady or postman or policeman; and a select group of dearly beloved character actors played them. But it is true to say that, up to a point, the West End elite was a class affair, occasionally brushed with snobbery.

Of course the attraction of belonging was tremendous. You could live in London; you "created" new roles, whereas a touring actor was usually expected to imitate his London prototype. You were at the top of your profession. Not that some of the foremost actors did not, for one reason and another, prefer to tour. Martin Harvey, one of the most sublime actors of the English theatre, rarely visited the West End. But he did not so much tour as conduct a royal progress through the cities of Britain from one end to the other.

But when you were young and in the modern movement of brittle realism or the dawning Chekhovian theatre, London—the West End—was, as we say if we are young and in the idiom of today, "where it was at."

By 1929 I had served an honest apprenticeship. I had appeared in I don't know how many dozen plays of all styles and periods in Rep at Oxford, Huddersfield and Glasgow, and I had done a Number One Tour with Leon M. Lion. I was totally confident of my talent and beginning to have some confidence in myself. In those days, before movies had made agents indispensable, out of work actors used to take out little advertisements in the personal column of the *Daily Telegraph* on Wednesdays ... or was it Thursdays? They were called theatrical cards. One might read—

>Percy Mainwaring.
>At Liberty.
>Just finished thirty-two weeks with
>Matheson Lang.
>Chinese parts a specialty.

After a season at Oxford in which I had played Old Blayds in *The Truth About Blayds* and a youth in some other play, I invested in a theatrical card that read—

>Alan Napier
>Anything from nineteen to ninety.

With such a range how could they deny me?

Alan's "theatrical card" story was one of his favorites. I know of at least four instances of him telling it, although sometimes it was, "Anything from eighteen to eighty." It's a slight disappointment to discover that the theatrical card in the June 10, 1926, edition of the Daily Telegraph *actually reads, "Alan Napier. Shortly at Liberty. Tall men of any age." But, still. How indeed could they deny him?*

For all sorts of reasons they could still try to deny me very well. I once went to see a leading agent in April, when the longest running Christmas pantomimes had just closed. He was very civil to me because Fagan had sent me. But, after a few pleasantries, he said, "Well, Mr. Napier, who knows? We might be able to get you something in Panto next Christ-

16. Breakthrough

mas!" In other words he did not see me as a potential legitimate actor at all, he saw me as a freak.

But my kind Deity was looking out for me. When Noël Coward was preparing *Bitter Sweet*, which was to be the outstanding success of the 1929 season, he had a problem in casting. The story kills off the hero at the end of Act II. In Act III the heroine must find a happiness that satisfies the audience's feeling for romance without reducing the validity of her deathless love for the hero, Carl Linden. So Noël invented the Marquis of Shayne, in his sixties yet wonderfully charming, understanding, handsome and her passionate admirer for many years. In a short scene Lord Shayne has to convince her (and the audience) that he is speaking the truth when he says, "I think perhaps I can make you happy—anyhow, happier."

It was a problem. This actor had to be tall; Peggy Wood, who was to play Sara Linden, the heroine, was not a small woman. He had to be elderly: yet devoid of such unromantic things as a paunch, flat feet or bad teeth. He had to be patently, and to the manner born, of noble birth. And he had to have presence; he had only a one page love scene in which to sell himself as a happy prospect for the rest of Sara's life. It was a beautifully written scene but the impact must be instant.

C.B. Cochran, the great impresario who was putting the play on, happened to have dealings at this time with Leon M. Lion over another venture, and casually referred to this casting problem for *Bitter Sweet*. Lion told him about me; General Canynge had been just that age and I had made a very handsome figure. *Austin Trevor, who was cast in* Bitter Sweet *as Captain Lutte, the officer who kills Carl Linden in Act II's climactic duel, remembers it slightly differently: "Do you know, I was responsible for Alan getting* Bitter Sweet*?" he said in 1976. "Cochran came to me and said, 'Do you know of an actor who could play Lord Shayne?' I said 'Get Napier.' He said 'I don't know him.' I said, 'He's a very young man, he's about twenty-four years of age, but he'll make up old.' And he engaged him!" Trevor had played General Canynge in Leon M. Lion's 1928 London production of* Loyalties *before Alan took the role on the tour, so whether it was Lion or Trevor who passed his name on to Cochran, it was certainly due to his performance as Canynge.*

So, soon after I returned from Austria, I received a call to go to Cochran's office in Picadilly. Now, the deluxe presentations of C. B. Cochran were far above anything with which I had so far been associated, so I entered his rather grubby little outer office with my heart beating madly. At first I did not even get to see Cochran; I talked to his manager, Frank Collins, a lean, saturnine man with black beetle brows (as I discovered later, also with a heart of gold) who looked at me with a chilling lack of enthusiasm—I was twenty-six and the Marquis had to be in his sixties—and said he did not think Mr. Coward would like anyone who looked "made-up." He was practically showing me the door when I said, "Oh, but I *wouldn't* look made-up. That's the point! Let me do a demonstration make-up for you." Just then Cochran came in, looked at me with no more enthusiasm than his manager but, after a muttered exchange with Frank and some shrugging of shoulders, agreed to let me appear at an audition. I was given no script or description of the character.

For this crucial test I managed to secure my wonderfully unwiggy General Canynge wig from Willie Clarkson's—the legendary theatrical costumier of that era. This, I felt, was half the battle.

In the dressing room assigned to me at the Pavilion Theatre where the auditions were being held, the lights were not good and I had trouble with my make-up—my hand would not keep steady. Down in the wings of the stage dozens of chorus girls in all sorts of outlandish get-ups were waiting for their turn. I got more and more nervous wondering if my wig-join would show, if my suit looked good enough. Suddenly a stage manager came up to me and said, "All right, Mr. Napier. They're ready for you now." I walked out onto the stage and was almost blinded by the brilliant concentration of light, but also excited by it. This was my element. The part was a distinguished elderly peer; I would be distinguished, elderly and an aristocrat. From the dark pit of the auditorium Noël Coward's unmistakable voice said, "Very nice. Will you say something, Mr. Napier?"

I had prepared a scene from Maugham's play *The Circle* that would bowl them over with my brilliant acting. But suddenly my mind went blank. "I'm terribly sorry" I said, "I … I've forgotten…" "Thank you." interrupted Noël, "that's fine. Will you come through to the auditorium." At the pass door Frank Collins met me and asked how much money I wanted; I had apparently got the job! (I settled for far too little.) When he asked me to say something, Coward merely wanted to be sure that I had the aristocratic accent and tone of voice to go with the aristocratic appearance which fully realized his concept of the Marquis of Shayne.

At my first rehearsal—I was not called till ten days after the rest of the company since I only appeared in the last act—a disaster similar to that of my first approach to Professor Bolland in *Storm* beset me. I was unfamiliar with the ways of big musicals. The stage of His Majesty's Theatre was packed with hostile natives, as they seemed to me, in the form of chorus girls and boys who I was sure, were all thinking, "What on earth is this young man doing here?" Peggy Wood, with whom I was to play the scene, naturally a shy person, was not feeling too comfortable as an American playing an English girl in a very English cast. Perhaps to seem more English she was wearing a Harris Tweed skirt, heavy brogues and a stand-offish manner. It was just before the lunch break when my scene was called. I had still not been given the script in advance and so had no opportunity to imagine the Marquis and invent his reality. Nor was I called on to do the preliminary scene in which Lord Shayne establishes himself with the other guests at the great evening party he is giving for Sara Linden the heroine—the scene on which I had been feverishly working in a dark corner of the stage. No, Coward decided to do the crucial proposal scene. I stuttered and stumbled my way through, establishing no valid character and no rapport with Peggy Wood. My hand was trembling so violently I could hardly see to read the lines.

"I'm sorry," I said, "I … I…"

"Let's try it again." Coward crisply interrupted.

I was no better.

"Thank you. All right, we'll break for lunch and then start with Act I."

I wandered off into my dark corner to pick up my umbrella and go home. I had failed. They would call me and say I wasn't quite what they were looking for. I'd missed my great opportunity.

Coward was in the middle of the stage surrounded by a mass of experts—set designers, dance directors, orchestrators, stage managers and so on, all seeking his attention. He happened to look up over their heads and he saw me. With a flash of actor's intuition he guessed what I was feeling. Pushing through his entourage he walked over to me and said, "Look,

I'm always terribly nervous at first rehearsals myself. But never quite as nervous as you. Don't worry! I'm not worrying—I'm sure it's going to be all right."

That sort of imaginative sympathy is something one never forgets. And it did turn out all right. I was to make a very great success in the part. If the director of *Bitter Sweet* had been one of the new breed of non-actor directors, who rarely have any understanding of the terrible vulnerability of the sensitive actor until he has found the truth in himself that matches the truth in his role, I doubt if I could have made it or if he would have bothered with me. It would have been so easy for a less perceptive man to say, "I don't think we can take a chance. Better get so-and-so. At least he'll be safe."

* * *

The rehearsing of *Bitter Sweet* was a revelation to me. It was all Coward's creation—the book, written with his particular quality of crispness, tenderness and humor; the lyrics, whether humorous, poignant, heroic, or romantic—all so deft and literate; and above all the music, so overwhelmingly evocative of the mood of the scenes it illumined. To watch Noël developing all the elements of this elaborate work and bringing them together into a whole of compelling theatrical validity, filled me with wonder and a deep inner joy. A magical brotherhood enveloped the entire cast as we fell in love with *Bitter Sweet* and this amazing man, who tirelessly controlled and guided and prodded until everything fell into place. One day, a whole expository scene was suddenly cut and, lo and behold, the play leapt forward, spectacular action making the excised words unnecessary. Noël had a wonderful cast. He used every ounce of their talents and his grip on the final shape of the play never relaxed.

As soon as the awkwardness of my first rehearsal was over, Peggy Wood and I got on together splendidly. I admired the complete integrity of her work and she saw at once that, despite my youth, deep inside me I knew and could realize the essential quality of Lord Shayne. So indeed did Noël. He never had to tell me what he wanted; only to find the two of us the most effective positions possible on the stage. One move he gave put me well upstage of Peggy. Feeling a little uncomfortable I instinctively started edging down, so as to play the scene fifty-fifty.

"No," said Peggy, "what are you doing? I ought to like it, I suppose, but it isn't right for the scene. This is your moment—stay where you were. Oh dear, I shall never be a real star!"

She was a lovely actress to work with; we reacted to each other in perfect tune. But it was not till the dress-rehearsal that I really made a deep impression on the Cochrans and Collinses and dress designers and all the other big-wigs of the production. Then, in my beautifully tailored period evening clothes, with silver hair and moustache, subtle make-up and sure assumption of elderly dignity and charm—then the love scene with Peggy took wings. It was brilliantly written and, in four words exactly, Noël revealed the heartbreak of two delightful human beings. The Marquis is trying to persuade the opera singer, now middle-aged, to settle in London for the Autumn. She says, no, no—it's cold and grey and foggy.

"But fogs can be delightful. You can sit on a rickety iron fence and watch the children picking up horse-chestnuts."

Sara has been softly fingering the piano. She stops and looks up.

"Whose children?" she asks—thinking of the children she never had by Carl Linden. The thought hangs in the air for a second and Lord Shayne, accepting it, replies, "Just anybody's."—thinking of the children he will never have by her.

"Whose children?"

"Just anybody's."

At the dress rehearsal the whole theatre went still and you knew that tears were filling every eye. It was the same throughout the run of the play. It was brilliant playwriting and Peggy and I did not, I think, fail our playwright.

The production was a huge success, running two and a half years, and the whole company remained in love with it. It was a genre operetta, romantic and sentimental; the message being that love is the only thing that matters. Don't play at love and fritter away your capacity to feel. Wait for the real thing and give it your whole heart.

It has never, I believe, been successfully revived despite the popularity of many of its songs. Why, I wonder? Perhaps because it is a difficult play to bring off, demanding perfect casting in *all* the major roles. There will never be another Peggy Wood to span the ages from eighteen to eighty as she did. Nor another Ivy St. Helier to make us laugh and shed a

Alan as the Marquis of Shayne in Noël Coward's *Bitter Sweet* at His Majesty's Theatre, 1929. In a 1976 letter he commented, "I'm staggered at how beautiful I am in the picture of Lord Shayne. If only I'd realized it at the time...." Collection of James Bigwood.

tear with her picture of the little, ugly, comic, heart-broken chanteuse. The tenor? Well I think a tenor can always be found—though George Metaxa was not easily duplicated in the New York production. As for myself, I was very touched, years later, when I ran into Noël in a dark nightclub in New York and said, "Alan Napier—d'you remember?" and he answered, "My Marquis of Shane. How could I forget?"

17

Bitter Sweet Days

After the first night of *Bitter Sweet*, there was no official party given by the management. But a girl called Nancy Bevill, who played one of the sextet of bridesmaids in the play, gave a party for a select few—some twenty, of which I was one—in her charming semi-basement flat in South Kensington. She had been on tour with Noël many years before (which probably accounted for her being in the play) and Noël was there. He played the *Bitter Sweet* tunes on the piano and it was a very gay affair ending appropriately with "I'll See You Again." I did not then realize how much I was destined to see of Nancy Bevill.

In fact, with my new found assurance, I was soon having an affair with a glamorous lady, a good deal older than myself, who had taken an important part in the production. To tell the truth, I was flattered by her regard and enchanted by her delightful companionship rather than overwhelmed by passion. When she had to go to America on a professional assignment, the affair petered out. *Could this have been Gladys Calthrop, the designer of the scenery and costumes for* Bitter Sweet? *She was nine years Alan's senior, and went to New York as the designer of the Broadway production of* Bitter Sweet, *which opened on November 5, 1929, four months after the London premiere. Although widowed, her emotional attachments tended to be lesbian, but, as we will see, this would not have been a unique pattern for Alan.*

Another involvement resulting from my new found affluence was my first car, a second-hand Austin. Though not quite such a lemon as my motor cycle, it left much to be desired. It had a malign tendency to skid and a maximum speed of about fifty miles per hour—the latter shortcoming somewhat mitigating the former. At least it enabled me to make trips into the country, an aid to romance, and to stay late into the night when invited to a party after public transportation had ceased.

It was not long before Nancy Bevill began asking me to go home with her after the show to her flat at 24 Roland Gardens. She had a spare room which she sub-let to a woman friend and, as time went on and I was spending so many nights at Roland Gardens, the idea came to both of us that it would be nice if the woman friend moved out and I took her place. In fact Nan and I were becoming very much attached to each other. She had tremendous charm—that sympathetic warmth that makes one feel that everything one says is interesting and amusing. Not classically beautiful, she had lovely eyes, green and sparkling; a happy spontaneous laugh and a slight, rather boyish figure. It was not love at first sight for me, but a growing feeling that this was someone with whom I could share my life. I could tell her of my inhibitions and backwardness in sexual development and encounter understanding and acceptance. Indeed, even a feeling that this made me all the more attractive to her.

So I moved into Roland Gardens and a happy period of my life began. At first there were reservations about the idea of marriage. She did not hide from me that, after her first unhappy marriage, she had become involved emotionally with women and had left America with a broken heart when she had been supplanted in a homosexual affair by a female rival. But it seemed that I was all she wanted now, and I was innocent enough to think that I could "cure her" of something that had been a passing weakness, brought on by the aggressive masculinity of her first husband.

When, in the course of time, she told me that she was pregnant I was filled with happiness and pride and a great surge of tender love. I begged her to marry me at once and have the baby. I knew that, not very long before, she had prevailed on her old family doctor, Joe Brown, to relieve her of someone else's embryonic child; so, when she happily agreed to have our child, I felt secure and looked confidently to the future. I know now that I was somewhat disingenuous. But, at the time, I think Nan may very well have believed that all would be well between us. She was very feminine and wanted to complete her cycle as a woman: to have the full experience of birth and motherhood. I think, in fact, that she chose me to be the father of her child partly because I was gentle and loving in an undemanding way and partly because we had the same sort of background. Of good Devonshire stock, her mother, the dominant figure in her family, had not filled Nan's childhood with tenderness or love. When Nan expressed antipathy for her mother to match the indifference I felt for mine, we were in tune. We knew that we had lost out in childhood; but we could joke about it, sharing the loss, and feel no bitterness.

Nancy Bevill in *Bitter Sweet*, when she and Alan first met. Sasha/Hulton Archive/Getty Images.

Neither of us could know that, once our child was born, I would, in effect, have served my purpose and that her basic preference would prove to be for her own sex. That was not to manifest itself for some time or be finally accepted by me until long after the fact was evident.

For a time we were tremendously happy and in every way compatible. We were married and the baby, born within the run of *Bitter Sweet*, was known as "the bittersweet baby." We christened her Jennifer Mary—Jennifer after a favorite cow Nan had had when she was a little girl (I thought it a pretty name nonetheless) and Mary after my sister Molly.

Before I became involved with Nan I had the good fortune to be accepted into a very special and delightful coterie. It was a girl called Audrey Cameron who introduced me to Ian and Muriel Rankine. She had been the stage manager of R.A.D.A. Players shows in which I had been involved, and she must have been very fond of me to feel I was worthy to be brought into the world of Ian and Muriel. *(Audrey Cameron became a producer at the BBC, and in 1966, was awarded an MBE for her services to the theatre.)*

Muriel had been an actress in the famous Horniman Repertory Company in Manchester, and was devoted to the theatre and the bright young people of the theatre world. She married a wealthy man, Ian Rankine, who had worked at the Foreign Office during World War I and, when the war was over, retired to Bletchingley in Surrey to live the life of a country gentleman—or rather the life of a gentleman living in the country—while dabbling in finance in the city and pursuing the literary way of life. Eventually he produced a charmingly amusing novel (Goodbye to the Lady, *which was published in 1937*).

Muriel was pert and dark and a rock of integrity. The phony, the pretentious and the cheap had no place in her philosophy. Ian was sandy, a little bald, with kind and humorous blue eyes and a slightly spreading figure. His philosophy was more flexible than Muriel's. It was their practice to invite for most weekends in the year a group of congenial people from the theatrical, the legal and the diplomatic worlds. The food and wine were superlative and the house and garden at The Old Rectory beautiful and handsomely maintained.

The parlor-maid, MacDonald, was an old family retainer of Ian's. One sunny noon, as we sit sipping sherry in the garden, I see her bringing out an old panama hat and plopping it onto her master's head unbidden.

"The thatch is getting a wee bit thin, Mr. Ian."

"Go away, you old fusser!" Ian growls, taking off the hat.

"I'll go. But ye'll do best to keep that hat on your head, if ye don't want to addle your brains!"

Dutifully Ian puts it back.

Only twenty miles south of London, lying between two main arteries to the coast, Bletchingley was happily untouched at that time by the ribbon development stretching its tentacles out of London. It constituted an island of unspoiled English countryside. You came to the Old Rectory, a lovely Georgian stuccoed house painted a soft primrose, by a maze of little lanes. It was backed by a spinney of birch and alder and looked out on rolling parkland. In the spring you could walk to a wooded hillside carpeted with bluebells.

The Rankines were my friends and generous benefactors for ten years. Why they were so kind to me I shall never know; my gratitude was all I had to offer in return. At the house I met Nicholas Hannen and Athene Seyler, May Whitty and Ben Webster, John van Druten, Auriol Lee, Leslie Banks, Kate Cutler (for whom Noël Coward wrote *The Vortex*, though Lilian Braithwaite reaped the fame of playing it), brilliant young lawyers and witty retired diplomatists.

When I told the Rankines I was getting married they welcomed Nan and, later, our child with open arms. And when the prospect of divorce eventually arose they stood by me in that difficult time. My innumerable visits to the Old Rectory shine in my memory like a string of stars in a firmament of truly gracious living. The phrase has become debased by vulgar usage: I use it to describe an unpretentious, lively elegance of life that would be hard to match anywhere in the world today. I remember the excitement of driving down after the show—first *Bitter Sweet* then all the other London plays I worked in—finding my special way through South London, striking off into the country lanes and arriving in the crescent driveway of that lovely house to be greeted by the excited barking and friendly paws and tongues of the Rankine's Airedales. Then—a room full of friends behind him—Ian standing in the spacious hall, his hand outstretched in welcome.

There was a sad end to this tale of open-handed hospitality. It was Ian's weakness that he had to maintain the pose of the grand seigneur and, hoping to fortify his financial position, he speculated with his inherited capital. Shortly after I came to America I heard the sad news that he had died suddenly of a heart attack. He was penniless. Muriel had to move into cheap lodgings in London where she eked out a living working for the BBC *(due perhaps to her friendship with Audrey Cameron?)* till she too died in an air raid in World War II. We had been corresponding fondly and she enjoyed enormously the stories I used to tell her of my dogs in California. She had been deeply devoted to hers and the idea of her having to live in a London room without her beloved Airedales pierced my heart.

Dogs had come back into my life—vicariously at Bletchingley and actually with Nan, who was a confirmed dog lover. During our time together we were never without dogs, nor have I been without them since, whenever I have had a settled abode.

Bitter Sweet was a long play. The final curtain fell at 11:15 and I did not make my entrance until ten minutes to eleven. This had many advantages; one of them being that, during the run, I was able to appear at different times in three other productions in which my roles terminated early. Apart from adding to my weekly earnings this made for a full and exciting evening.

Incidentally my earnings from *Bitter Sweet* hardly warranted the phrase "my new found affluence." The sudden question of salary, raised by Frank Collins at the pass-door of the Pavillion Theatre at my audition, when I had no idea that I had actually been accepted for the part, caught me off guard. I gulped and said, "Would fifteen pounds be all right?" Thirty would have been agreed to happily and a good agent would have got me forty-five. But it was only when the play ran on and on and I calculated that I had thrown away thousands of pounds that I had any regrets.

The first of these supplementary activities was a production of *Little Lord Fauntleroy* at the Gate Theater. Somewhat cut, and acted with deliberate gravity, it was a hilarious success. I played the venerable Earl of Dorincourt and Elsa Lanchester was exquisitely revolting as the little Lord. It led to an amusing event.

I had only just time after the final curtain at the Gate to make my way to His Majesty's theater and get on the stage for *Bitter Sweet*. Indeed this was only possible because, for the ancient Earl, I used the same wig and makeup that served me so well for the noble Marquis. The only difference in appearance was that I added long trailing ends to my white moustaches and brushed my white hair forward in a Gladstonian hair-do. My period clothes were appropriately antique.

In this egregious disguise I would leap into my car at the Gate and drive hell-for-leather to His Majesty's. One wet and foggy night, as I was circling Trafalgar Square, a woman stepped off a traffic island right in front of me. Jamming on my brakes and turning the wheel sharply, I avoided her but skidded smack into the pillar defending the island. The immediate effect of the impact was two-fold. It jammed my electric horn so that it brayed forth incontinently, and it shot my pince-nez eyeglasses off my nose.

As the Earl of Dorincourt in Frances Hodgson Burnett's *Little Lord Fauntleroy* at the Gate Theatre Studio, 1931. Elsa Lanchester is Fauntleroy. Courtesy Gary Butcher.

The braying of the horn instantly collected a small crowd. What they saw appeared to be a very old and decrepit gentleman in sponge-bag trousers, a Gladstone collar and a long frock coat, clambering woozily out of the car. Instantly he appeared to fall back, his hand on the seat. Perhaps he was feeling faint? Someone patted him solicitously on the bottom and asked if he was feeling all right. Would he like a nice lay down? A stream of filthy language, as I searched for my missing glasses, was the only reply—fortunately drowned by the insistent horn.

All I was concerned with was getting to His Majesty's in time for *Bitter Sweet*. At last I found my glasses and emerged, every ancient inch of me, as a constable came up. The woman who had precipitated the event had disappeared; but the crowd was on my side.

"It wasn't the old gentleman's fault. It's lucky she wasn't killed. She stepped right out in front of him."

"'Oo stepped out?" asked the Constable.

"Officer," I said, hoping to clarify the situation. "I'm not what I appear."

"Arf a mo,'" said the constable, more confused than ever.

"That's just it—I can't wait! I'm an actor. I have to get to His Majesty's Theater." And without more ado I took off. To the amazement of the onlookers the ancient gentleman was suddenly running like a young stag due west towards the Haymarket.

I made it to His Majesty's in time. After the show I found my car parked neatly by the curb under the eagle eye of Sir Charles Napier, aloft in bronze on his honorable plinth. There was even enough juice left in the battery to start the motor; and a dent in the bumper proved to be the only damage. I drove home and never heard a word from the police. I had left the scene of the crime before the constable had had time to pull out his little notebook and he probably thought it wiser not to attempt a report.

Another play I incorporated in my *Bitter Sweet* evenings was a dramatization of Aldous Huxley's *Point Counterpoint*, produced by my loyal supporter Leon M. Lion. It was not a good play and he did not improve its chances by casting me as Everard Webley, the fascist man of iron. I was not comfortable in the role and had a guilty feeling that I was letting the author down which alienated me from Huxley at this first encounter. (Again, as with Charles II in *And So to Bed*, I was able, years later in Hollywood, to make amends when I directed and played in a revival of Huxley's *Giaconda Smile*, earning his approval and lasting friendship.)

In *Point Counterpoint* it became an even closer thing getting to His Majesty's in time. Lion relished his role so much that, between the opening night and the final performance five weeks later he put ten minutes onto the playing time! He was a great one for squeezing the last drop out of a dry lemon.

A production of *Richard III* was the last of these twice nightly ventures. I played the dying Edward IV; and it was this performance that Neville Chamberlain praised the last time I saw him, at my mother's flat in Queen's Gate Gardens. Baliol Holloway played Richard. Baliol Holloway, that splendid Shakespearian who did so much to keep the bard alive and well in this period when he was out of fashion, and when going to the Old Vic was a sort of theatrical slumming.

The idea of playing for two and a half years would fill me with consternation today. But in those days before movies and television, theater was one's livelihood and the long run much to be desired. I would still have found it a test of endurance had it not been for constant activity in other theatrical ventures. Apart from the three productions I have referred to, there were also many experimental "Sunday night shows." In one, a drama in which I played the leading role of the great Russian writer Turgenev I earned, in one of the evening papers, an extraordinarily gratifying review which I shall quote. It will be the only occasion for such self-congratulation, justified I hope by an amusing twist.

> If it were but for one individual performance alone, that of Mr. Alan Napier, the Stage Society's production at the Prince of Wales's last night of *The Borrowed Life*, by Gladys Parrish, must be counted an occasion of distinction ... he presented a portrait so masterly, so exquisitely toned and balanced as to assure him definitely a place among the aristocracy of acting, for which he has for some time indicated his potential merit.

This appeared in the first edition, read largely by racing addicts wanting to know who won the first race; in all later editions, owing to an unfortunate slip by the type-setter, the words "that of Mr. Alan Napier" were omitted and the hero of the evening became anonymous.

When asked if I collected newspaper clippings of my career I always used to answer, "Good heavens, no!" till one day I found these yellowing but still flattering reviews of *The Borrowed Life* and others of Fauntleroy in the bottom of an old trunk, yes, in an attic. I see why I kept them: I was young, on a wave of success, and dreaming of stardom. To even the score (and it is honest of me to have preserved this review also), Mr. Ivor Brown, one of the leading critics of the day, wrote of *The Borrowed Life* "...Mr. Alan Napier stared into vacancy as one exalted in spirit but low in vitality, but he did not seem to find very much. I shared his plight, finding in this play only an outline...."

Well, you can't win 'em all.

18

Marie Tempest and Gerald du Maurier

Some weeks before *Bitter Sweet* closed, Frank Vosper visited me in my dressing room at His Majesty's to tell me that a light comedy he had written for Marie Tempest, called *Marry at Leisure*, was soon to be produced at the Haymarket Theatre across the road. There was a part in it for me. Marie Tempest! The greatest name in English comedy for half a century. To go straight from *Bitter Sweet* into a play with her was almost unbelievable good fortune.

Vosper was a strange man and mine was an odd role for which he may well have had Ernest Thesiger in mind when he was writing it. He had actually cooked up an old auntie character with typical homosexual jokes and turns of speech. He was looking for an actor to masculinize this creature without losing the campy fun. I imagine his choice fell on me for the reason I got many of my parts—because no typed actor was suitable and it was felt that I would come up with something that worked. I was duly engaged at a pleasant increase of salary and the day of the first rehearsal arrived.

I have referred to the disease of unpunctuality, something akin to a fatal addiction, from which I suffered at this time. Now, Marie Tempest was known as a martinet in the theater and a stickler for manners and form in her companies. When touring the colonies, the arrival of her company at a new city was an event; all the ladies were required to wear long white kid gloves for it. There must be nothing slipshod about Miss Tempest's entourage.

Imagine, then, the dread and horror with which I realized as I rushed up to the stage door for my first encounter with this formidable figure, that I was thirty-five minutes late. "I'm stark staring mad," I thought. "What can I do? What can I say?"

I tiptoed onto the stage, where a scene was already being rehearsed. In mid-sentence Miss Tempest, in long white kid gloves, broke off. There was total silence and she stared at me with that basilisk eye I was to know so well when it was used to chill a tea-cup rattler at one of our matinées. I stuttered out some feeble explanation. She never said a word but turned to her husband W. Graham-Browne, who was directing, and articulated icily,

"Shall we continue, Willie?"

I stood frozen to the spot, unable even to remove myself from The Presence.

This was when my very kind Deity pulled another of his fabulous tricks on my behalf. The very next line Miss Tempest spoke contained the word "heinous," which she pronounced HAY-nous. Her husband was an Irishman and corrected her,

"Not HAY-nous, Mary, HEE-nous!"

Now, they had a good humored habit of bickering—it was a running gag with her that

Willie was an old fool who didn't know what he was talking about, and with him, that Mary made preposterous pronunciamentos. But this! To correct her, Marie Tempest, in front of the whole company, on the pronunciation of the English language—that was going too far! I was known to her only as the Marquis of Shayne in *Bitter Sweet* who had been so impeccably Eton, Oxford, and Belgravia that everyone assumed I had in fact been to Eton and Oxford and hailed from Belgravia. So Miss Tempest, forgetting all else, flashed "Nonsense, Willie!" to her husband and, turning to me as one patrician to another, asked—

"How is that word pronounced, Mr. Napier?"

"Of course you're right, Miss Tempest. HAY-nous."

"Ah ha! D'you hear, Willie? HAY-nous!"

I was in. My late arrival was forgiven and forgotten. Indeed I had arrived just in time. I had vindicated her; and from that moment we were friends. I never encountered anything but kindness, understanding and indeed a very warm affection all the years I knew her. As for me, I adored her. And when I hear people criticize her as a woman or as an actress, I will have none of it. She was a remarkable human being and the greatest mistress of the stage I have ever known.

When I came to know her, Marie Tempest was no longer beautiful, but she had the tremendous attraction of vivacity and piquancy—"a rogue in porcelain" was the classic description. Above all, she had the most wonderful sparkling eyes that could change in an instant from kittenish mischief to that basilisk stare of disapproval. She wore clothes beautifully and had an unusually long, elegant stride for so small a woman, and a truly regal bearing. She knew and used every trick to make up for any flawing by time of her youthful prettiness.

I have to confess to a passion for craftsmanship. To see a master carpenter lay his hand to a piece of wood—the confident boldness with which he puts saw and chisel to work, using the nature of the wood not fighting it—that is beautiful and satisfying. He does not set out to be an artist. He sets out to do the job right. Marie Tempest was a master craftsman of theater; and for nearly sixty years, from the age of twenty to seventy-eight, it was superb craftsmanship that kept her at the top of her profession. "Marie Tempest In …" was an almost infallible guarantee of success in entertainment. Whether or not she was a great artist has been debated; but her mastery of the stage is beyond question. In regard to this I would paraphrase Captain Shotover in *Heartbreak House*, "Your craft sticks to you if you stick to it but art has a way of slipping through your fingers."

Sometimes, to tell the truth, she had to be told that a line was funny, but once the fact was revealed she would get her laugh with that easy assurance that makes an audience love the source of their entertainment. Confidence, skill, charm and energy she possessed in abundance—the energy unimpaired by the years.

To renew her vital forces, one of her rules of life was to have a complete rest in bed every afternoon. This led to an amusing situation at matinees, which she liked to play at a rousing clip so that she could get home for her rest. Willie, her husband in the play as in life, tended, on the other hand, to be a little lethargic after lunch. This led to the performance being conducted on two planes—there was the play (and she never short-changed the audience) and then there was the sub-play in which she kept a running *sotto voce* assault on Willie.

"Wake up Willie!"

"Get on or I'll say your line for you." (And she did!) Then to me,

"The man's a fool!" followed by her line to the audience; and during the laugh, "Damn bad actor too!"

There was even a third plane on which, with eagle eye, she would quell a tea-cup rattler in the fourteenth row.

On top of all this was Willie's habit of thinking up things to make Mary laugh, which they both could incorporate into the performance without the audience having any idea that an irrelevance had been added. To me, a newcomer to the Tempest three-ring circus, not to laugh out of character became almost impossible. I finally begged Willie to desist.

"Oh my dear fellow," he said, "Marie has a silly idea that she has cancer of the womb and if I can give her a good laugh she forgets all about it." One could but bow to this. I pictured Willie sitting on the toilet in the morning thinking up mischief to make his Mary laugh and I had to love him for it.

During rehearsals of *Marry at Leisure* there was a memorable moment. The play included a scene in which Mary had to pretend to be drunk. She made a great fuss about this. It was unbecoming for her, the *doyenne* of the English stage, to do such a vulgar thing. (When she came to perform the scene, I may say, she played the hell out of it.) One day, when she was raising her usual protest, Willie cut her short with, "Well, if we're going to put the play on at all, you're just going to have to do it." At which Mary, who was sixty-six, observed, "Ha! In another ten years, I suppose, one will be playing character parts."

On the occasion of the dress rehearsal she produced for me a remarkable *obiter dictum*. We were playing contemporaries, Mary and I—say forty-five years old. At sixty-six, this did not faze her in the least; but I, at twenty-nine, felt that a little aging was the least I could do to even things up. Besides, I was very good at painting the lines and hollows of age on my face. So I walked proudly onto the stage a ravaged forty-fiver. Mary took one look at me.

"Dear boy, what's all that mess on your face?"

"Oh, well, Miss Tempest, I thought a little age would be appropriate."

"Nonsense, dear boy. Take it off, take it off! Remember this—whatever you play you must always look your best."

Well, it's not "method"; but it certainly helped to keep Marie Tempest a top flight star for sixty years. She was very kind and helpful to me in many ways; she would tell me quietly of bad little habits I had—doing too much with my face, swaying when I should be standing still—things of which one is unconscious that mar that technical perfection which she had disciplined herself to achieve.

She was one of the most delightful hostesses imaginable. I shall never forget an enchanting lunch at her house in St. John's Wood. "A picnic in the garden" she called it; and we were to bring the baby. I don't know whether she really loved babies, but she certainly held our child in her arms and cooed to her like a devoted grandmother. Nan, of course, adored her and Nan's natural facility for expressing admiration was not unappreciated. For some reason Willie was not there and another young actor (Mary liked young men) had been invited to make up a four. The food and wine were exquisite and the time went gaily by until the other young man went just a little too far in telling a *risqué* story in which he used a certain word. Marie was far too good a hostess to do more than suggest, "We are not amused"; but that evening a note was delivered to my house by hand apologizing for the fact that a guest in her house had used an unforgivable expression in the presence of my wife. Mary's start in life had been humble and she enjoyed playing the great lady.

But she could also unbend. One of Willie's jokes—she had stolen one of his lines earlier, so he spoke her curtain line in revenge—made her laugh so much that, in a moment of double weakness, she confessed to a supporting actress in the play, Mignon O'Doherty, as we took our curtain calls, "Migs, I've laughed so much I peed my pants!" This was at the matinée; at the evening performance she was articulately frosty to Migs, as an indication that confession in a moment of weakness was not to be presumed on.

In the years to come I never missed a Marie Tempest play if I could help it. Later that year she appeared in a play about Catherine the Great in which she played the Old Empress, Elizabeth. Madeleine Carroll played Catherine and there was a ticklish situation as to which lady should occupy the star dressing room. I feel sure that Mary won! She certainly stole the play.

Historically the Old Empress died of dropsy at the age of fifty-three. Marie Tempest was now sixty-seven. When I went round to see her after the performance she stretched out her hands to me and said,

"Look, Alan—I made up my hands to be old."

Instead of laughing I felt tears in my eyes and said, "Oh Mary, your beautiful hands!"

She put them around my waist and looked up at me, her eyes twinkling with mischief; and, by God, I felt her attraction as a woman.

The last time I saw her was in *Dear Octopus* and I shall never forget the moment when the children and grandchildren who have strayed from her loving tentacles came together again and ask her to sing to them as she used to do when they were children. "What shall I sing?" "Sing the Kerry Dancers." And she did. The voice was gone; but the song's aching remembrance of things past filled one's heart as that indomitable little figure at the piano faced and revealed the heartbreak of "gone, alas, like our life, too soon." It was a moment of profound emotion. Later, when she took her solo curtain call and, at seventy-four, curtsied to the ground, it was a moment of fabulous showmanship.

Marie Tempest, 1864 to 1942. It was my privilege to know you, to work with you and to enjoy your friendship. It was also my good fortune to believe that heinous is pronounced HAY-nous by the best people.

On reflection, I believe that I have done my family an injustice; for my mother certainly came to see *Bitter Sweet*. It was a noble effort because of her crippling arthritis; and, because of her crippling lack of musical sensibility, the impact of the production was lost on her. She had never seen a musical before and, for her, all that singing just confused the issue. She said mine wasn't a very big part, was it?

And my father certainly saw *Marry at Leisure*. He was living on the Island at Thames Ditton at the time, for he and my mother had been separated for many years. His bungalow house faced on the backwater and, when paying him a visit, rather than using the ferry at the end of the island, one approached the house from the boat-yard opposite, where one hailed him across the water. Eventually someone would hear and pole across in a punt to pick one up. On the occasion I am thinking of, knowing he had been to see *Marry at Leisure* (although of course he had not come round to see me after it) I called out as, Charon-like, he poled towards me, "How did you like the play?"

From midstream he shouted back, "I never saw you worse!" which effectually ended that topic of conversation. But it also shows that he had seen me in other plays in which he did not think much of me either.

* * *

After the selling of Tennal Grange and the Family exodus from Birmingham, for a time my father, Mark and Elizabeth had maintained an interesting *ménage à trois* at Pottingdean. Mark had parted company with Debenhams Limited and was looking for a new career.

At one time he flirted with the promotion of an amusingly bogus product called Billowzone—a green crystalline salt you put in a saucer by your bedside at night in order to breathe sea air. In the morning you gargled it, added it to your bath water and, if you were ingenious enough to effect a means of transportation, poured your bath water onto the asparagus bed if you had one. Despite the variety of its therapeutic and horticultural uses it failed to find a market. However Mark's ingenious mind devised this advertising jingle for it which today, when sex sells everything, might have saved Billowzone from oblivion. It was before its time, however, and could not be used.

> Uncle Bert and Auntie Mable
> Fainted at the breakfast table,
> Let this be a serious warning
> Not to do it in the morning.
> Now Billowzone has put them right,
> They do it morning, noon and night;
> And Uncle Bert is hoping soon
> To do it in the afternoon.

Advertising however was clearly Mark's forte and he joined the staff of the great J. Edward Thompson advertising empire. In due course he was assigned to Canada, where he made a new life for himself.

My father, Elizabeth and her two daughters moved to Thames Ditton. During the years Mark and Elizabeth had lived in Sweden when he was with Debenhams Ltd., they had picked up enough Swedish for Elizabeth to add translations from the Scandinavian languages to her other literary activities. She would came to my father and ask, "How shall I put this in English?" He would say, "Bring me the Swedish dictionary and let's see exactly what it means." From this, he gradually became her collaborator and finally took over the translation jobs entirely.

So much translation, particularly from the French, is bad because the translator knows the language so well that he thinks in it and becomes unable to escape from the innately French constructions which are innately un-English. Because he never knew the Scandinavian languages well enough to think in them, my father's translations into English were superior. There is objective proof of this; he came to command a higher rate of pay than the standard translator's fee. He would slowly work out, the dictionary ever at his side, the exact meaning of the sentence and then recast it into English usage. This work became his second, entirely congenial career. He and Elizabeth gathered around them a delightful literary coterie.

Nearly every Sunday there would be a gathering of choice spirits at "Rivernook," his house on the island, to which Nan and I were invited. The drinks, the Fortnum and Mason ham, and above all the coffee were always superb. In the summer, camp beds were erected on the porch and we would often stay for the weekend, swimming and boating and lying in the sun. He created a way of life that was Bohemian without squalor. He had rebuilt the house so that it looked and was run rather like a ship. In the midst of suburbia there bloomed an oasis where essential values were cultivated, free from bourgeois prejudice and vulgarity. The man who delivered the kegs of beer always referred to my father as "The Captain." He was the captain of his soul at last.

During the time of the *ménage à trois* at Rottingdean a strange situation arose. My mother determined to visit the trio for one of the changes of air that were a part of her life. What she made of Elizabeth's relationship with my father—what rationalization or, alternatively, what dark images floated through her mind—heaven only knows. But down to the sea at Rottingdean she went and, incontinently caught, instead of sea air or Billowzone, typhoid fever. The crisis developed suddenly and it was Elizabeth who, intuitively doing the right thing (whatever that happened to be) saved her life.

When she was convalescing I went down for a visit to cheer her up and be of what service I could in the house. One morning I was sitting in my mother's room. She appeared to be sleeping, but suddenly came out of a daydream and with some excitement announced,

"I've been having a wonderful idea for populating the Empire!"

She did not offer any elaboration and I was too dumbfounded to ask. One thinks one knows the confines of one's family's inner thoughts and suddenly whole fields of unsuspected territory reveal themselves.

She made a good recovery but the illness must have weakened her system and when, a year or so later, influenza struck, she succumbed very quickly. One could say it was a merciful release; she had lived with pain and the exhaustion of pain for many years and she must have been lonely. Indeed, she was essentially lonely all her life since she never had the taste or aptitude for physical human contact—the lovely surcease from aloneness to be found in pressure of hand to hand and warm body to body. It is amazing, lacking this, how well her interest in literature and politics maintained in her a sort of joy of life.

When I started writing this book, a sense, engendered by what I have learned since childhood, of deprivation of all that is meant by mother love informed my subjective picture of my mother. It had to be said to explain the sort of youth that I became. Now that no bitterness remains, I would say that her limitations were her misfortune and that she supported her disabilities with admirable vivacity and courage.

* * *

The arrival of our child stirred in Nan and me thoughts of leaving the flat in Roland Gardens. It was a treasure among basement flats by reason of a beautiful large studio room at the far end, built out into what had been the garden of the house. This was a bright sunny room with a great round skylight in the domed ceiling. The rest of the apartment was short of sunlight, however, and I longed for a garden of my own, a garden the baby could play in. St. John's Wood seemed the ideal neighborhood, but St. John's Wood was expensive. We kept looking.

One day, out of the blue, a bargain fell into our laps; at least, it seemed to be a bargain. For five hundred pounds we could buy the end of the lease of a handsome medium-sized house with quite a large garden in Springfield Road—just north of Lord's Cricket Ground. It was the last five years of a ninety-nine year lease. Somebody said something about "dilapidations." Dilapi ... what? I'd cross that bridge when I came to it. The house was just what we wanted and we came to terms with the owner.

We might as well pursue the matter of "dilapidations." I was to learn that, when a lease runs out, the holder at that time is liable for the cost of restoring the premises to the pristine perfection they are presumed to have been in when erected. This house would have ninety-nine years of degeneration to be made good, which explained why the former owner was happy to unload on us for so little. I had an estimate made as my five years drew to an end—an unhappy time from every point of view—and it was frightening. I don't remember how many hundreds of pounds, but far beyond my means.

And then my kind Deity, who has never quite abandoned me, led me to a solicitor who had an agreeable mania—a mania for doing the Eyre Estate in the eye (the Eyre Estate owned large chunks of St. John's Wood, including my house). He took on my case without a fee for the sheer fun of it, discovered that the Eyre Estate had committed itself to a rebuilding plan that would involve pulling down my house and the house next door, and on these grounds got me clear out of the obligation to pay any dilapidations at all. In effect, I lived in this charming house for a rental of one hundred pounds a year.

And we did enjoy it for the first few years. I loved to putter in the garden and found that I had my father's green thumb. I remember having a great success with outdoor tomatoes ripening into October against the sheltered, sunny, rear wall of the house. Nan had a great time redecorating the interior. She was a splendid house painter with a passion for soft greens, and she was very good with curtains. Our drawing room overlooked the garden and she would lean out of the window and ask me what 18 times 6½ was, and laugh happily when I answered, "I'm busy planting bulbs! Don't be stingy. Try 18 times 7."

It was not long after *Marry at Leisure* closed that I received a call from Leon M. Lion offering me a part in a new play by Clifford Sax, with Jean Forbes-Robertson playing the lead. It was an extremely literate piece, delightful to play in but apparently caviar to the general, since it did not run long. Nor was Mr. Lion an easy man to get a good salary from. So, when the weeks went by and Christmas hove in sight and disappeared I was beginning to worry about money. When would I get another good job?

Not that I hadn't been working—I had. I was in great demand for special Sunday night performances of new plays put on by The Stage Society or The Repertory Players as showcases for the West End managers.

Then, one bright January morning in 1932, my telephone rang.

"Hello, this is Gerald du Maurier."

I couldn't believe it. The great Gerald du Maurier, from his unapproachable pinnacle of fame, calling me! Someone was playing a practical joke. But no, there was no mistaking that voice.

"I'm doing a new play by Edgar Wallace called *The Green Pack,* and we thought, Mrs. Wallace and I, that we would rather like you to play one of the parts. Pretty good part as a matter of fact." *(At this point, Edgar Wallace was in Hollywood, working on the screenplay for* King Kong, *probably his best known credit today. Victoria Wallace, his second wife, had started as his secretary and was a key figure in the production of all of his plays.)*

I suppose I said something and he concluded, "Look, you live in St. John's Wood don't you? I'm just next door to you in Hampstead. Why don't I pick you up in twenty minutes and take you down to Wyndham's?"

Gerald du Maurier himself! Actually coming to my house to pick me up—like a God descending from Olympus. By what miracle had he come to think of me for a part in his production? Ever since I had seen him in *Bulldog Drummond*, I had had fantasies of standing on a stage, to tumultuous applause, with Gerald du Maurier. It was a dream come true.

The drive to the theatre through Regents Park in an elegant open car—January or no January—was a breathtaking exhibition of nonchalant disregard for the rules of the road. I even dared to ask him if he had much trouble with the police.

"No," he said. "I've discovered a wonderful trick. When they stop me and say 'Wots yer name?' I suddenly develop the most appalling stammer. 'Uhge … Uhge …' I say, 'Uhge … Uhge … Uhge …' and by this time there are half a dozen cars stacked up behind me. So, in desperation, they let me go."

I didn't believe a word of it because there weren't many policemen in London who would not have recognized Gerald du Maurier; but, as he dashed in and out among the traffic islands, it sounded amusing and even plausible. And it came rather near the bone because, in a similar situation, my own "Uhge … Uhge … Uhge …" might not have been simulated.

That a reference to stammering should occur at our first meeting was strangely significant, for I would not now be writing this story if du Maurier had not stood by me when my stammer overcame me at a crucial moment on the stage. For that support I owe him my survival as an actor. In gratitude I should like to recall, as best I may, something of his matchless quality.

* * *

A few years ago when I was staying with my niece in Cornwall, she took me over to have tea with Gerald du Maurier's daughter, Angela, at the house in Fowey his family loved so well and which, in part, is carved out of the living rock of the cliff that overlooks the river harbor. As I walked into the long living room, there, right in front of me, hung a full-length portrait of Gerald. It was so amazingly alive that my heart turned over and tears came to my eyes. I expected to see him step forward with his quick light tread and to hear the beautiful, totally unaffected voice say, "Hello, old fellow. Got something in your eye? Have a drink."

When I moved nearer to the painting I saw, of course that it was much more than a painted photograph. It was a brilliant technical organization of brush strokes to give the *impression* of vibrant reality—just as the kind of acting of which Gerald du Maurier was the past master, gave the *impression* of the very breath of life. A whole generation imitated him but none could touch him. People who were envious or ignorant would say, "That isn't acting, it's just behaving—or misbehaving—on the stage." What nonsense! Gerald, to my knowledge, put more energy and technical expertise into appearing not to act than a Donald Wolfit puts into playing *Lear*. It was known in those days as "The art that conceals art." It involved technical skills such as appearing to throw away lines while making sure that every syllable was heard by every person in the audience; and a thousand apparent understatements that, through a miracle of exact timing and calculated cadence of voice, communicated to every head and heart. And then there was the charm. Daphne du Maurier wrote a fascinating book about him called *Gerald*. I enjoyed it enormously; but felt that she had perhaps left something out—the quality of charm. Being his daughter, she may have taken it for granted. Anyhow, it was matchless.

The flavor was dry. The light quick step and deft movements contributed. The crisp caress of the beautiful voice was a vital part. But the main ingredient was the sudden raffish smile that creased the worn, unhandsome, boxer's beautiful face and brought the eyes in whose depths lay the knowledge of grief, to a life of dancing, daring impudence. That was the outward manifestation; behind it lay intimations of a sensitive and generous soul, shielded by a show of mockery without malice and insolence without arrogance. It was a cool wine of tremendous class, potent and exhilarating.

Nowadays, his kind of acting and the plays that demand it are out of fashion. We admire non-realism; and very nice it is to see actors free to use every extravagant resource of voice and gesticulation. But it must not be supposed that what they are doing is harder or more demanding or even more revealing than the exquisitely polished realistic acting of the school of du Maurier.

Gerald was often chided for not playing the classics or "worthwhile" modern plays. I know very well why he didn't—it would have bored him. In a first-class play, all you have to do for success is to say the lines intelligently—provided you have a good actor's endowment of presence and magnetism. Gerald's genius lay in his capacity to create entertainment out of nothing.

All he required was a framework of plot and a group of varied characters. Then, at rehearsal, he would go to work—creating, improvising, clothing the bare bones with flesh and blood from his artist's instinctive knowledge of human nature and his actor's imagination that turned this knowledge to theatrical effect. I think he was quite opposed to the idea that the Theatre's business is to educate. He believed that its business was to entertain and to enable its successful practitioners to live like gentlemen. In this he was at one with Shakespeare, whose ambition was to retire to Stratford in genteel affluence and who never wrote a line with the idea of educating us or improving our social consciousness.

Du Maurier could also see no reason why we entertainers should not have fun providing entertainment. And indeed, guided by his sure hand, we did. He was the least pompous, least self-important, and most generous of that reviled race of men, the actor-manager. At the time I worked for him he never took a solo curtain call. We were his company, who had spent the evening with him dispensing magic. We would all share in the applause.

Gerald appeared in only a few movies before his death in 1934. Driving with him through Leicester Square one evening, I remember him saying, "Look! In two theatres at once!" and, sure enough, it happened that Herbert Marshall's name was glittering in electric lights over the two movie houses then open on the Square. "That's what I should have done. Gone to Hollywood. Think of the money! Bart could buy me out twice over." It had never occurred to me that the great Sir Gerald du Maurier could possibly have any financial difficulties living *en prince*, at Cannon Hall, the Hampstead mansion, set in a large walled garden, which was for many years his home.

One of the movies he eventually appeared in was directed by Alfred Hitchcock *(the film,* Lord Camber's Ladies, *was actually produced by Hitchcock, but directed by Benn Levy)*, and evidently the two men recognized each other's outstanding quality. They also discovered a mutual taste in practical joking. Soon after their encounter, when Gerald went into a new play at the St. James' Theater, Hitch determined to pull the joke of all time on him. In those days, milk was still delivered from house to house all over London in rattling carts drawn by ponies. Hitch rented a pony for the evening, bribed the stage doorkeeper, and introduced it into Gerald's dressing room just before the second interval. It was not a large room and the pony seemed to fill it. Gerald came off stage and went to his room. He never batted an eye. Patting the pony's head affectionately, he said, "Hello, old fellow," then, turning to Hitchcock, added, "Really, Hitch, you are enormous. With you in here there simply isn't room to turn round."

In *The Green Pack*, in which I appeared with him at Wyndham's, he played a little joke on me. I was playing a character called Mark, and on my first entrance I had the business of going to a window at the back of the set and looking down into the street below where I "see" Gerald. I shout to him, and he shouts back that he is coming right up. One night, soon after we opened, Gerald hid himself behind a lamp where I could not see him and, as he called out his line fired a water pistol into my eye. Anything unexpected paralyzes one on the stage but in this case no harm was done; the play could go on without my full attention. As I turned back into the room mopping my face in puzzled confusion Gerald entered, and, during the round of applause, gave me a wicked grin and dropped a casual, "Got something in your eye, Mark?" It dawned on me that Gerald had fired the fatal shot, and that I had been accepted.

My favorite tale of Gerald concerns his fabulous theatrical inventiveness and gaiety. It was told to me by Gladys Cooper. They often played opposite each other and she admired him tremendously—so that it was natural for her to ask Gerald to direct a new play she was doing, even though there was no part in it for him.

"Love to. When do you start?"

"We're having a reading at The Playhouse next Tuesday at two-thirty. Will that give you time?"

"Fine. Fine. I'll be there. What? Oh, yes, the script. Thanks. What's happened to your hair? It's lovely."

On the Tuesday, after a pleasant lunch at his club, the Garrick, with maybe half a bottle of Hock, Gerald arrived.

"What ... what's the great table doing in the middle of the stage?"

"Oh," said Gladys. "I thought we'd just sit around and read the play. People seem to like that nowadays."

"Oh, no, no, no, no," said Gerald. "That's a terrible bore. Let's pitch right in and do it."

In no time he had taken hold, and the first act was assuming the most amazing life. The cast were all delighted—Gerald found so much more in their roles than they had been able to see for themselves. Variety, humor and excitement were bursting the seams of what at first had appeared to be a rather long, dull exposition.

Slowly an uncomfortable thought began to take form in the back of Gladys' mind.

"Gerald," she said. "It's terribly exciting what you're doing but ... but how will it tie in with the end of the play?"

"I haven't the least idea," Gerald replied. "I haven't read it."

"Oh," said Gladys. "Well, wouldn't it be a good idea if you did?"

"If you say so, yes."

So the rehearsal was called off until ten-thirty the next morning and Gerald went back to Cannon Hall and read the play. Next day he started in on the first act quite differently—but with equal invention.

How did Gerald's magic work? To begin with, every du Maurier production had a quicksilver lightness of touch and an appearance of inevitability. Even if it was all made-up moonshine, one's heart was in one's mouth while it was happening. Laughter was never far away and, to one's amazement, there would be a prickle of tears in one's eyes that such an enchanting fellow should run such danger and, in the end, win such devotion from some headstrong girl—for he preferred his beloved to be a conquest rather than a pushover.

"That's not life as I see it," a Seeker after Significance in Drama would say. Well … there was once a lady who watched Turner painting a sunset and said, "That is not how I see it, Mr. Turner." "Don't you wish it was, Madame?" the great painter answered. Gerald du Maurier brought his own sense of the color of life to what might have been trivial anecdotes and raised them to the dimension of superb entertainment. (I must not leave an impression that Gerald du Maurier never appeared in a good play. In fact he starred in many plays by Sir James Barrie.)

There were those, for the most part actors who failed to gain employment from him, who accused Gerald of being a snob. I would say rather that he was selective as to the people he chose to associate with, which seems to me to be anybody's unquestionable right. I like very much, in this connection, the story of how Gerald put Tallulah Bankhead in her place. Her first great success in the theatre was playing opposite Gerald du Maurier in *The Dancers* in 1923. When he engaged her she was a comparatively unknown American girl who had come to London looking for a more congenial climate for her many talents—London has always been such a tolerant city. At the end of the first day of rehearsal, most of the other members of the company having gone, she called across the stage in her powerful spoiled-Southern-Belle accent, "Hey there! Gerald!" He looked up, walked lightly over to her and, with a bright smile, said, "Miss Bankhead, only my intimate friends and the stagehands call me Gerald."

It was not long before she became an intimate friend.

* * *

Since writing this appreciation of Gerald du Maurier I received resounding confirmation from an exacting and knowledgeable source. Alfred Hitchcock was at a party I attended for my friend John Houseman and his book *Run Through*. Hitch was naturally a center of attention, but at last I got a chance to ask him if the story of Gerald and the milk-cart pony had been previously published.

I have known Hitch for thirty years—I played a part for him in *Marnie*—but we've somehow never been close. Yet as soon as I said "Gerald" his blue eyes warmed and we were drawn together. He gave his blessing to the story and told me others involving Gerald and practical jokes. Then, tapping my arm he said,

"There was never anyone could touch him. He could stand on the stage and do nothing! Nothing! That's the test, you know."

I did know. Wearing this ultimate power to fascinate with such nonchalance was the gift which made Gerald unique.

* * *

For the first two days of rehearsal of *The Green Pack*, I was perfectly miserable because I could find no way of bringing my part to life. I played one of a trio of adventurers seeking gold or diamonds or something in Portuguese West Africa. Gerald, obviously, was the nonchalant leader, the heart and soul of the expedition. Then there was a comic character modeled maliciously by Edgar Wallace after his friend, Nigel Bruce. The third man, tagging along for no very good reason, and apparently devoid of any point of view or character, was the role assigned to me.

Another "Punch" caricature, this one of *The Green Pack*. Alan Napier, David Hawthorne and Gerald du Maurier. Wyndham's Theatre, 1932. © Punch Limited.

Gerald left me alone for a time to see if I could come up with any creative ideas for this unpromising material. When I failed to do so, he came over to me during a lull in rehearsal and said, "Look I've got an idea about you. I think you're the kind of fellow who is too bloody lazy to shave and swears horribly under his breath."

That was all I needed. Mentally I added "Fuck you" to everything I said, and immediately a sardonic laconic, mocking, lazy but alert, scrubby-bearded gentleman adventurer evolved—a perfect foil to that suburban stickler for cleanliness and etiquette, the Nigel Bruce character. That is what I call good directing—putting an idea into an actor's mind which instantly triggers his creative imagination. From then on, I had no trouble; I had been given a shield of character to protect me from "just being myself."

Once Gerald had provided me with a character to portray, the rehearsals of *The Green Pack* became a fascinating experience. Edgar Wallace's first act proved to be a very lame affair until Gerald recreated it extemporarily. He would suddenly say, "How would it be if …" and off he'd go creating a whole scene. You had to be quick-witted to hang on to what he had invented for you. I have always had a capacity for instant absorption of direction (particularly if it is good) so, since I was able to keep up with Gerald, my part improved by leaps and bounds. And I reveled in the approval my quickness earned. Swiftly and surely, what had been leaden exposition turned into exciting revelation laced with a dry ironic humor. I faced the first night with happy anticipation.

For those who knew Edgar Wallace the occasion was overshadowed by news of his death in Hollywood. However, the play was well received and I looked forward to a long and delightful run working with and learning from this brilliant and attractive man. It was a wonderful time.

One day Gerald invited me to Cannon Hall to tennis the next Sunday. Because Nan did not play and disliked the role of tennis wall-flower—also because I was afraid my tennis might not be up to Cannon Hall standards—I invented a prior engagement. Another invitation a week or so later I treated the same way; I was not asked again. I have always bitterly regretted my stupid lack of self-confidence. It lost me the chance really to get to know du Maurier and his delightful family. But then, at that time, I was still only valid in my roles as actor.

In fact, in *The Green Pack*, I very nearly lost that validity. As the run continued I contracted an appalling cold which lead to copious and unpredictable attacks of nose-bleeding. There is nothing more disconcerting on the stage than the fear of being suddenly distracted from the proper performance of one's role by a physical irrelevance. When making up before a performance—and I never left myself any margin of time—an attack might come on and I would lie on my back on the dressing room floor praying for it to stop. Improperly bearded, perhaps, I would get on the stage only just in time; fear of a recurrence of bleeding preventing me from assuming Mark's character. Suddenly I was not Mark—I was Alan, with a bloody nose; and Alan was liable to stammer. The whole performance became a nightmare. And worst of all the final line of the play which explained the mystery and tied the strands together was mine—I had to say, "The green pack!"

Now the hard "g" in green was the most difficult sound for me to articulate. Night after night I approached that moment in a sweat of terror. I invented tricks to get me by, such as an indeterminate "uh" or "mm" sound, sliding into the "g" of green, so that it sounded a little like "The … uh … reen pack." It was not very good, but by forcing an air of nonchalance, a thousand miles from my actual state of terror, I managed to get by.

Then one night I had a total collapse. I simply could not utter. There in Wyndham's theatre, in one of the smart successes of the London season, an actor at a crucial moment was reduced to grimacing ridiculously as he produced nothing but meaningless grunts. It seemed to me to be an eternity of shameful horror.

Gerald saved the situation by saying the line for me. I expect he came in pretty quickly—he must have sensed my predicament—and the audience probably never realized that anything was wrong. But to me it was the end. How to explain to the rest of the cast? *They* knew all right. "What on earth happened, Alan?" I brushed them aside, dashed up to my dressing room, tore off my beard and went down to see du Maurier.

"I'm terribly sorry," I said. "I've got kind of run down or something with all this nose-bleeding. I don't know what to do. I don't think I can go on. I must ask you to accept my resignation."

He looked me full in the eye, quite sternly though not unsympathetically, and said, "No. No, I won't accept your resignation. If you give up now, you're finished. You'll never come back. Go home have a good drink, get your nose fixed and don't fuss." I couldn't speak. I made a sound like a sigh, or a sob.

He got up, put a hand on my arm and smiled. "Alan," he said, "I promise you that you'll manage."

And manage I did. But I was never free from fear for the rest of the run, even after I had my nose cauterized. Indeed, I'm quite sure that, but for du Maurier's moral support at that moment, my career would have been finished and with it all hope of my leading a decent life. I would inevitably have disintegrated into one of life's most miserable casualties.

18. Marie Tempest and Gerald du Maurier

* * *

The existence of stammerers in the world of the theatre is interesting and more widespread than people imagine. We recognize each other by a kind of free-masonry. I prefer to think of us as people with occasional difficulty in uttering. There are so many variations of stammering, a childish complaint which we have to overcome, or disguise, if we are to survive. Of course it is a formidable addition to the nervous strain to which any sensitive person is subjected in the business of appearing before an audience or a camera.

In looking for an explanation of my early success in the theatre, despite the fact that I never played a part for which a man of less excessive height would not have seemed preferable, I wonder if the quality that led to my employment may not have been, in part, a vividness of performance produced unconsciously by the necessity of transcending difficulties in uttering. Robert Farquarson, a well-known actor in the 20's, who was also a stammerer, had this quality of extreme intensity. I remember him giving a heart-breaking performance as Uncle Vanya. And it is my belief that Gerald du Maurer himself may have had, in some measure, the same problem; and that some of his extraordinary magnetism may have sprung from it.

I suspect that for some reason, just as G's were a hazard for me, L's were uncomfortable for him. The villain in *The Green Pack* was called Louie. Gerald had a delightful habit of belittling him by apparently having difficulty in remembering the name. He would say, "Our friend ... er ... what's his name ... Louie is probably doing so and so." But he did not always put in the "what's his name." I think it was a bridge to uttering Louie if that should suddenly become a hazard. These are the tricks one uses to surmount hurdles in uttering.

And there was an occasion—Miles Mander, another actor with a problem in uttering reminded me of it years after the event—when du Maurier was unable to continue in the middle of a first night. The curtain was lowered, Gerald came before it with an explanation that he had been the victim of a *"crise de nerfs,"* begged the audience's indulgence and, after a brief pause, successfully continued the play.

The idea that this could happen to so great a performer and be transcended—for when he looked at me in the eye at the time of my collapse he seemed to say "I know, I know."— has given me the courage never to give in when the black terror of inability to utter has climbed on my back.

In my old age, because I really don't give a damn; I am no longer hag-ridden by this fear. I say to myself, "It will be all the same a hundred years hence" and scramble over the hurdle, or by-pass it; with no great difficulty. Maybe I am consequently a duller actor than I used to be.

* * *

Towards the end of the run of *The Green Pack* my customary luck in landing one good part after another deserted me.

Robert Nichols (not to be confused with Robert Nichols, the American actor who subsequently became my son-in-law), was an English poet, a less well-known member of that notable band of World War I poets headed by Wilfred Owen and Siegfried Sassoon. In association with a strange little man of the theatre, Maurice Brown, he had written a remarkable play called *Wings over Europe*. It calls to mind Oscar Wilde's theory of Art anticipating Nature, for in this play Nichols anticipated atomic fission. His young scientist realizes the enormous geo-political significance of his discovery and brings it before the British Cabinet. The play is concerned with their momentous deliberations on the subject of how this frightening power should or should not be used. The play did very well in New York and Maurice Brown had every hope of repeating this success in London.

I was offered the major role of the British Prime Minister, a character modeled on Arthur Balfour, for many years the brilliant leader of the Conservative Party. *The Green Pack* was due to close soon and I accepted. I rehearsed several days and Nichols and Brown were very happy with what I was doing with the role. Then Mrs. Wallace determined to extend the run of *The Green Pack* since word that it was closing had stimulated business. I asked to be released and du Maurier said he would raise no objection. Mrs. Wallace however, refused to let me go.

The part I had been rehearsing was given to an excellent actor (he had taught me elocution at R.A.D.A.) who justly became famous as he grew older. But for this role he was too dry and pedantic. *(H.R. Hignett, Alan's replacement, born in 1870, was more than twice Alan's age!)* The cabinet discussions were deprived of an aura of aristocratic charm and a certain philosophical elegance. The play failed. *(It managed twenty-one performances compared to ninety performances in its original 1928 Broadway run.)* Robert Nichols, who became a close friend of mine, always maintained that if I had been able to play the part the result would have been different.

The "if onlys" of an actor's career—every actor has a dozen—are not interesting or important. I only refer to these happenings because they show my benevolent Deity at last faltering. And I think it is interesting that a poet—a man of insatiable curiosity and unexpected areas of knowledge—did, in the early thirties, imagine the enormous power and significance latent in atomic physics. Indeed, Robert Nichols was touched with genius. He was also a tortured soul and collaborating with him on a play, as I did later, was a very exacting experience. The play, alas, was never satisfactorily completed.

However, I did not have to wait long for another magnificent role in the West End. I was engaged that summer to play Gladys Cooper's husband in *Firebird*, her autumn production at the Playhouse Theatre. Gladys must often have met Gerald at this period and I'm sure discussed with him my suitability for this role. He evidently spoke well of me since I was engaged—her first choice—some weeks before rehearsals started.

19

A Lesson in Drama

Gladys Cooper, that great actress to be and most wonderful human being, whom it was my good fortune to know and increasingly revere for nearly forty years, was coming to the end of her reign at the Playhouse Theatre when I played her elderly husband in *Firebird* by Lajos Zilahy.

I say "great actress to be" because one of the wonderful things about Gladys was that, starting young in the theatre as a great beauty, she never fussed about her looks but steadily learned and improved in her vocation until ultimately, in her old age, she achieved greatness.

In 1932, after being a reigning beauty for twenty years, she was indeed a very good actress. I also found her rather cool and intimidating. Oh, I was overawed by her reputation and, as usual at early rehearsals, felt an obligation to try and justify my having been chosen to play a man so much older than myself. I was not aided in this by Mr. Gilbert Miller. He was co-producer with Gladys having discovered *Firebird* in Vienna on one of his European fishing trips for ready-made successes. Auriol Lee, whom I had met at Bletchingley, was supposed to be directing us; but, through bad timing, she was still working on another play—the one with Gerald du Maurier at the St. James, where Hitchcock staged his practical joke with the milk-cart pony.

In the interim Gilbert Miller took over. His methods did not impress me any more than mine apparently impressed him. Until he was told I was hired I am sure he had never heard of me and he liked his productions to be star-studded. The play was conventionally carpentered with a big scene to end the second act. I, the Prime Minister of Hungary, through a scene of mounting suspicion and revelation discover, as I cross-question my wife, that she has not only been unfaithful to me but has also murdered her lover! In the last act it turns out that the mother was covering up in order to save her daughter.

On the afternoon of the third day of rehearsal, Gladys and I had our first shot at this scene. London was having one of its rare, intolerable heat waves; 90 degrees were registered that day. By 4:30 Gladys had had enough and rehearsal was called off for the day. As I was about to go Mr. Miller called out,

"Just a moment, Mr. Napeer!"

"Yes, Mr. Miller?"

"I got to have a little talk with you."

"Oh dear," I thought, "what now?" He beckoned me to him in the middle of the stage and came very close, his belly arching towards me—too close for such a hot day, too close for Gilbert Miller.

"Mr. Napeer," he said, "you English are very good at light comedy, but you don't unnerstand Drama."

"Oh? What's the difference?"

"There you go!" he yelled triumphantly. "I said you didn't unnerstand. Now I'll tell you. In Drama you can't use any upward inflections."

I was dumbfounded. I had played in at least fifty plays of every kind—ancient and modern, stylized and realistic, comedy and tragedy, farce and drama. I had played by instinct and by ear—finding the truth in my roles and, from that base, presenting performances which were, to say the least, true to life and theatrically acceptable. If this had not been so I could not conceivably have been standing on the Playhouse stage that afternoon. I was not only dumbfounded at what appeared to me to be crass idiocy, I was also panic-stricken. All the more so when Mr. Miller continued.

Gladys Cooper, Frank Harvey and Alan Napier in *Firebird*. The Playhouse, 1932. University of Bristol Theatre Collection/ArenaPAL.

"Now Mr. Napeer, we will take this scene through, you and I, and I don't want to hear one upward inflection from start to finish.

"What you're saying doesn't make any sense to me," I feebly protested.

"It'll make sense, all right. And that's the way it's going to be."

For a quarter of an hour, with Mr. Miller giving a very unlikely showing as Gladys Cooper, I stuttered my lines in a flat monotone. Then, my actor's instinct outraged, I finally broke out,

"I can't go on with this. It's too hot and I'm tired. You'll have to excuse me."

"O.K. But remember what I just told you, and you may make out in this role, Mr. Napeer."

"The name is Napier." I said and left.

Next morning I went straight to Gladys Cooper and said: "I'm afraid I shan't be able to play the part, Miss Cooper."

"Why? What's the matter?"

"Well, Mr. Miller doesn't think … that is, he says I can't have any upward inflections…"

"Gilbert?" she said with amused contempt. "Good Heavens, you don't have to listen to Gilbert! He doesn't know what he is talking about."

"But he said…"

"I've never heard such nonsense! Play it just as you want to—you're going to be fine. And don't listen to Gilbert—Auriol is directing the play."

A huge wave of relief washed over me and a sudden warmth for Gladys. Gilbert started rehearsals saying, "We'll begin with the big scene in the second act." And he gave me a knowing nod as he went out front to listen to us. Gladys patted my hand and we started. I played the scene exactly as my instinct told me it should be played. It was a splendid piece of theatrical writing and I forgot all about Gilbert Miller. At the end I was amazed to hear him say,

"There you are, Mr. Napeer or whatever your name is. What did I tell you?"

I turned to Gladys, open mouthed. In that lovely clear voice of hers she said, "What did *I* tell you?"

Auriol Lee soon took over and, as was her custom, slept through most of the afternoon rehearsals. The actors, who were all first rate, would work out their problems for themselves. A very happy arrangement.

In those days Gladys relied confidently on her excellent capacity for total recall and never put her book down until the dress rehearsal, when she appeared not to remember one line. Since we were opening cold at the Playhouse with no out of town try-out, this was a somewhat alarming experience. As a result, I was dreadfully nervous on the first night, which Gladys sailed through without a single moment of uncertainty.

The play was a big success. Mr. Miller said he thought I had quite a future. Years later I met him at a party in New York for Lewis Milestone.

"Don't tell me," he said, "I know you—Allen Napeer! I put you in a play with Gladys Cooper."

"Napier," I said. But he had already moved on. *(Gilbert Miller directed the New York production of* Firebird *himself, with Judith Anderson in the lead. It closed after 42 performances.)*

20

Near Misses and Sweet Aloes

From the point of view of status in the profession, *Firebird* marked the highest point in my career in the theatre. I was playing "opposite" to Gladys Cooper. (Though, in fact, I shared billing with Hugh Williams who played the lover, and the detective in the story, Frank Harvey.)

From now on I could stay where I was—a supporting actor—or go up to the position of having someone play opposite to me—that is, become what we call a star. I never made it, though I have come very near. True, I have played many leading roles in what we now call in America "Off Broadway" productions. But it is one's salary that tells the tale; I was never to earn, in England, a higher salary than the one I received for *Firebird*, miserable though it would seem by present day standards and only a quarter of what I made in New York for parts of equivalent value.

The kind Deity who had so far held my hand, opened doors for me, pulled me out of quicksands, won friends and engineered favorable circumstances for me, seemed now, with a friendly pat on the back, to say, "You're on your own, fellow, no more special favors. I've seen you through the worst of it and now it's up to you to make a go of your life."

Looking through my record in *Who's Who in the Theatre*, I see that I was seldom out of work for more than a week or so, but only here and there do I come upon anything worth recording because of the people involved or some amusing contretemps.

In a production of *The Witch*, for example, for all its short and inconspicuous run, I encountered two of the nightmare hazards an actor can be faced with on the stage. This very Scandinavian piece—the author's name was Wiers Jenssen—tells of witchcraft in a little Norwegian town. The old pastor (my part naturally) has a new young wife, and when his good-looking son returns from college at Uppsala, the predictable occurs. But the pastor's old mother puts it down to witchcraft rather than sex. In the first act an old witch is pursued by a lynching mob into the pastor's garden, where she seeks sanctuary from the kind old man.

The old witch was played by that remarkably potent little actress Haidee Wright—she was indeed tiny—and my young wife by that beautiful leopard of a woman, Leonora Corbett—she of the wicked and seductive eyes and irrepressible sense of humor.

What are these two nightmare hazards? One is to be indecently exposed before an audience; and the other to invert a piece of dialogue so that it takes on a horribly inappropriate significance.

On the first night of *The Witch*, Haidee Wright is on her knees pleading for sanctuary—a moving moment if ever there was one. She had been used to hanging on the lapels of my coat since to save her poor old knees, she had rehearsed the scene standing up. But this is the first night. She is giving her all. Instead of tugging at my lapels which are out of her reach, she tugs at my flies and tears them wide apart.

"Have mercy on me!" she cried. "Have mercy on *me*," I thought.

That was bad enough. But worse was in store. It would be good for this story to say that the second disaster was also on the first night. But it was not. I know, because I can see a couple of tea-cups on the front of the stage. It was at the first matinée and we were playing at the Little Theatre, rightly named since it was so small that the ladies in the front row only had to stretch forward to put their empty intermission tea-cups on the edge of the stage. Being a matinee, the audience was almost entirely composed of old ladies.

Within spitting distance of the old ladies, I am sitting at a long refectory table in my garden with my young wife by my side, my handsome son at the head of the table. His recent return from college prompts me to some pretty boring reminiscences of when I was a young dog at Uppsala. I sigh and conclude "and here I sit, shut up in Bergen, for all the world as if I had never been young." On this inauspicious afternoon, patting my young wife's hand and unaware of any lurking danger, I say:

"And here I shit, sut up ..." and I know something is wrong. But the full horror of what I have said has not dawned. I go back to correct the error and painstakingly repeat it "And here I shit..." With a little whoop of joy, Leonora collapses forward onto the table, shaking with laughter. Geoffrey Gamer, my son, never had much control; as soon as he sees Leonora, he is gone too. I look wildly out over the audience (thank God I'm too blind to decipher any expressions on those ancient faces in the front row), catch a wicked glimpse from the corner of Leonora's eye and that does it. Howling with hysterical laughter I collapse too.

How we continued the play at all I don't know. But that, of course was not the end of it. I could protect myself from Haidee by having my flies sewn up, but there was no protection from the memory of this shameful moment with my nearest and dearest. Every night I approach the scene in terror, not daring so much as to glance at Leonora, whose eyes I knew would be saying, "Go on. Do it again."

At the dress rehearsal of *The Witch* an ominous event occurred—an intimation of the coming decline of the actor *vis-à-vis* the set designer and lighting expert. The director, Frank Birch, had come into theatre from Cambridge: he was a professor, not an actor. Until then, the only other alleged director I had encountered who had not also been an actor, was Gilbert Miller.

Nancy Price, the producer, who was also playing my old mother, had a big scene in the third act, sitting behind that ubiquitous refectory table. Halfway through it she breaks off and says,

"Frank, this won't do, you know."

"What won't do, Nancy?"

"Well, I've got to have more light. I can't play this scene with no light on my face."

"Oh? I'd love to give you more light, Nancy, if I could. But it would spoil the beautiful shadow I have on the leg of the dresser."

Those were his words. I thought it ridiculous then—I did not know it was the shape of things to come. Of course Nancy got more light. She was the producer.

* * *

The year 1933, which brought me such horrendous comic catastrophes in *The Witch*, had better things in store for me. Tyrone Guthrie (whose shortcomings as an actor had provided me with a matchless start to my career) came back into my life; his brilliant talent as a director providing me with a new image that very nearly raised me to the top of the ladder.

The Lake by Dorothy Massingham, was an awkward, rather unattractive play. But Guthrie, like du Maurier, had the gift of making dull exposition seem exciting, and awkward incidents inevitable. Without his sure hand and inventive humor I doubt if *The Lake* would have succeeded. Indeed, when Jed Harris gave it a far more pretentious production in America with Katherine Hepburn and Colin Clive, it was a sad failure. *(It was of this production that Dorothy Parker famously reported that Hepburn ran the gamut of emotions from A to B.)* What the play did have, as often happens when the dramatist has been an actor, was magnificent acting opportunities, particularly for a grief-stricken young wife and her understanding aunt. Marie Ney gave an outstanding performance as the wife and Esme Church supported her with quiet integrity of exquisite quality. To justify the harrowing grief of the last act it was obviously necessary that the young husband, whose sudden death motivates that grief, should be a man of unusual quality and attraction, and the bond of love between them passionately felt. When I was asked to play the husband I knew it was a challenge; but it was also a chance to show that I was not just a clever character actor of old men parts. John Clayne must provide the vital love interest.

In the first act we learn that the girl has been having an affair with an unprincipled married man. Also that her mother is a social climber, pushing her daughter at John Clayne, a Guards' officer of means as well as principle, for the wrong reasons. These were the circumstances that set the play in motion, but were incidental to the tragedy of an unstable girl finding at last a deep and steadfast love; then having this snatched from her by death, before she can even taste it, when her husband dies in an accident—drowned in the mother's artificial lake—as they drive off for their honeymoon.

The faithful lover (a romantic concept of a dramatist who had perhaps herself failed to find happiness with the common sensual man) fitted me very well. Marie Ney and I took to each other at once and the one passionate embrace allowed us lacked nothing in conviction. It was in the scene that preceded this (as in the scene I have described in *Bitter Sweet*) that I had to reveal a quality that would justify what was to come. It was a long scene but it, too, had its moment of emotion revealed in simple sentences. She says,

"John, I do love you." He answers,

"It's been a long time."

Out of context, trite. But it told of a girl finding a glory in life she had not thought possible, and a man's reward for patiently believing that she would.

One of the pleasantest things that ever happened to me was when, years later, Trevor Howard walked up to me on a movie set in Hollywood and introduced himself, saying, "I know you. When I was at the R.A.D.A. one of my teachers was trying to make some point to me and said "go and see Alan Napier in *The Lake* and you'll see what I mean."

The play was originally produced at the Arts Theatre Club for a few performances. It was so successful, however, that a transfer to the Westminster Theatre was arranged. In the meantime I had been approached by Basil Dean to play General Canynge in his film production of *Loyalties*.

I had done a few films and felt uncomfortable in the medium—my natural gift for projection, invaluable in the theatre, was a positive disadvantage in front of a camera. Trying to hold myself back and do less for the camera I had fallen between two stools, being neither easily natural nor theatrically effective. The films I had done so far had seemed to me to be pretty trashy stuff in any case. In one, entitled *In a Monastery Garden*, I played "Count Romano of Rome," and was somewhat surprised when I walked out onto the balcony of my villa in Rome to see a wide bay painted on the backcloth with "the beautiful Isle of Capri" rising, rock-bound, on the horizon. When I pointed out that Capri lay off Naples several hundred miles to the south, the scene designer was somewhat miffed. What was I, an actor or troublemaker? A hurried conference was held and a cypress tree painted over Capri.

The filming of *Loyalties* was a very different matter. With General Canynge, whom I knew so well from my tour with little Lion, I felt I might be able to forget the camera and present a portrait that would stand up on film. It amazes me that I had achieved such a reputation for impersonating the elderly English aristocrat at his best, that I was chosen, despite the obvious problem of making a man of thirty believably old to the searching eye of the camera. The job was so important, financially as well as because of Basil Dean's dominant position in the English Theatre, that I had no choice but to relinquish my part in *The Lake*.

I will return to the filming of *Loyalties* later, for my association with *The Lake* was not over. Another actor took my place at the Westminster Theatre opening, but the moment *Loyalties* was over I was asked to resume the part of John Clayne. We transferred to the new Piccadilly Theatre for an extended run. It was always a woman's play, but there were indications that I had made an impression as a young leading man. A New York producer wrote that he would like me to keep in touch with him as he would be looking for the right vehicle with which to launch me in America. This came to nothing (I think he went broke) but, more importantly, as the run came to a close I received a script from Basil Dean of a new play by the successful author of *Autumn Crocus*, Dodie Smith. The male lead was a married man who inspires a romantic passion in a seventeen-year-old girl. Mr. Dean wanted to know if I would be available for this part. The play was to open at the Haymarket Theatre in the autumn.

"This is it," I thought, "it's dead right for me. This will take me to the top." I wrote saying that I would indeed be available. A week went by with no further word. And then a brief note came asking me to return the script—I had already learned most of the part—as Mr. Dean had engaged Miss So-and-So to play the girl, and since she was so very small, he felt he must look for a shorter actor to play the man. Ian Hunter, who later became my very good friend, was engaged.

This was the first time I had been told I had lost a part because I was too tall. I think now how lucky I was to get all those other good parts in spite of being too tall. At the time, it seemed a cruel and arbitrary decision. *(All the more so as the actress in question was in fact Marie Ney, opposite whom Alan had just played in* The Lake!*)*

* * *

The filming of *Loyalties* turned out to be an unexpectedly pleasant experience. Basil Dean had the reputation of being a terror as a director. He could reduce strong men to tears with his bullying sarcastic manner. I was not accustomed to being bullied and my self-confidence could very easily be shattered. I need not have worried, for Basil Dean was very effectively taken care of. The part of Dancy—the "officer and gentleman" who in fact has committed the crime of which De Levis has accused him—was played by Miles Mander and Miles, who had the advantage of having considerably more experience in film than Dean, was not a man who accepted bullying lying down. He had a very effective method of coping with bullies, which was demonstrated during the week of rehearsal that preceded the shooting of the film.

Dean would tell him to make a certain move. Looking Dean straight in the eye, Miles would say, "You want me to do that?" Dean would shout back,

"Of course I want you to do it! I wouldn't tell you to do it if I didn't."

"Very well," said Miles and, with painstaking lack of conviction, he would make the move. "Is that what you mean?"

"Yes … if you…"

"All right" and Miles makes the slightest suggestion of a weary shrug. He never refused to "follow direction"; he tacitly questioned it. And if ever Dean showed signs of fury Miles would quietly ask "Where exactly is the camera now?"—a blow below the belt to a dyed-in-the-wool theatre man.

At the end of the week, he had effectively broken Dean's aggressive spirit and the rest of us had no trouble at all.

Laurence Hanray, Algernon West, Philip Strange, Alan Napier, Miles Mander and Heather Thatcher in *Loyalties* (Associated Talking Pictures, 1933). Collection of James Bigwood.

20. Near Misses and Sweet Aloes

Basil Rathbone, who played De Levis, brought with him an air of Hollywood glamour and his own light-hearted fun, and the shooting of the film turned out to be a delightful experience. The second assistant who gave us our calls for the morning and collected us from our dressing rooms for the upcoming scene was a young fellow called Carol Reed. In the light of his brilliant subsequent career I can only think it was a pity he didn't direct *Loyalties*, which turned out to be a dull and stagey affair under Dean.

* * *

At the end of the run of *The Lake* I must have been "hot," for I was immediately able to assuage my disappointment at losing the Dodie Smith play with the balm of being simultaneously sought for a new play by the great George Bernard Shaw and a revival of *Hay Fever* by Noël Coward.

I hate making decisions and in this case made the wrong one. But while I was still dickering I was able to go to the first reading of *On the Rocks* and meet Shaw in person. He was in his late seventies and stalked onto the stage saying that he had just been knocked down by a car backing out of a show-room in the Great Portland Street. Great solicitude by the Cassons, who were putting the play on. *(The Cassons were Lewis Casson, who was also starring, and his wife, Sybil Thorndike.)*

"It was nothing," said Shaw, "the young fellow in the motor was more upset by half than I."

That night I had to make my decision. Shaw was rather out of fashion just then and *On the Rocks* had not seemed to be Shaw at his best. *Hay Fever* I had adored with Marie Tempest in the lead; and, even though I could not understand why Noël had engaged Constance Collier for the revival, I felt sure it would be a success. Besides, I saw myself as being very effective as the diplomatist.

Next morning I went down to the rehearsal of *On the Rocks* to report my regretful decision. Shaw could not have been kinder.

"You're perfectly right," he said. "You're much too young and handsome to be playing this old fellow in my play. You run along to Mr. Coward—you'll make much more money with him."

In fact *Hay Fever* failed and *On the Rocks* ran for five months.

The failure of *Hay Fever* was interesting as a vindication of Marie Tempest. Noël describes his leading lady as a retired actress going to seed in the country; I imagine that is why he cast Constance Collier for the revival. And that is exactly how she played the part—very funny she was too. But she was in no way glamorous and the play took on the sad hue of retirement. Marie Tempest on the other hand never for one instant suggested a woman going to seed. "Whatever you play you must always look your best." She sparkled throughout the play, filling the stage with her robust self-confidence. It may not have been what Coward had imagined but, by God, it worked! Two years the original production ran; three weeks the revival.

But it was as stimulating as ever to be rehearsed by Noël. The assurance of his approach, the complete knowledge of the actor's craft, the infallible instinctive stage-sense never failed. He would raise the pitch of a scene by split-second timing, add point by an unexpected inflection, encourage always intensification of attack while curbing self-indulgent exaggeration.

It was not as exciting as working with du Maurier since the play had already been neatly constructed by the director. Rehearsing it was like fitting together a carefully prefabricated structure. With du Maurier the work was more creative, since he chose to build with ill-prepared lumber, often worm-eaten and shoddy, designing the house as he went along. A charming rambling, yet elegant structure would miraculously arise—apparently viable in all respects, yet owing its durability, in fact, to Gerald himself. He was the king pin. Remove him and the entire edifice would collapse. Noël's plays can always be revived with other actors; Gerald's improvisations are unthinkable without his matchless presence.

Du Maurier, Coward and Guthrie—I have never met any director who could touch them for inventiveness and the instinct for using their material, actors and script, so that the finished product had an appearance of effortlessness in achieving theatrical conviction.

* * *

The year 1934 began with another leading man role which one hoped might lead to the top of the ladder. *Private Room* was produced at the Westminster which ranked as an "Off Broadway" theatre. That is to say, it did not carry West End salaries, but, if successful there, one hoped to be transferred to the real West End.

Private Room was a nice little play about a man who, seeking an arranged divorce, hires a professional co-respondent in order to go through the obligatory charade of committing adultery. Unknown to him, an innocent young girl is substituted at the last moment for the anticipated old professional. In a long scene of mingled comedy, sentiment and

With Thea Holme in *Private Room*. Westminster Theatre, 1934. Courtesy Gary Butcher.

drama, the hero finds himself so enchanted by the girl, and she by him, that he is tempted to turn charade into reality.

The production was notable for me because of an unexpected hazard. I collected a fan, a lady who was obsessed with a mad passion for me. She was also an alcoholic. For one thing, she kept stealing my picture from outside the theatre. (Finally the commissionaire, responsible for looking after the front of the house, gave up and made a deal with her: she could have the picture for the week-end as long as she returned it on Monday morning.) This did not worry me. My trouble with her derived from her habit of sitting in the bar during the first act—she bought a seat in the front row for every performance—and getting happily pickled there. Then she would assume her seat for my big scene in the second act. Very soon she got to know all the jokes by heart. She would savor them in anticipation and burst into raucous laughter even before I had made my points. This was no help for me or for the rest of the audience.

But worse was to befall. On the last night of the run she had a dilly up her gin-soaked sleeve. There was a dramatic moment when I go to the door, center back stage, and turn the key. Am I going to insist on my rights and disport or am I going to be a gentleman and send her home unsullied? A pregnant pause ensues. I forget what the line was for which the audience was waiting with baited breath; I only know that my admirer, with a terrible drunken imitation of my voice and manner, said the line for me.

* * *

One likes to think of an audience as a docile instrument one coaxes into attention and then beguiles, controls and finally enslaves. That is what it usually appears to be. But the whole relationship can very easily be blown apart by one rotten apple in the house, one breakdown in the smooth performance of the play. Yet the will of the audience to be entertained, to go along with the make-believe, I have found to be very endearing—particularly if one puts a brave face on adversity.

The most interesting example of this I encountered many years later, in 1968 to be precise, when playing in *Affairs of State* with Celeste Holm in Chicago. It was theatre in the round where one's proximity to the audience is maximum and one's control, in a sense, minimum, since at any given moment a third of the audience is behind one's back. In the middle of the play one night, owing to a terrific thunderstorm, the lights suddenly failed. Total blackness resulted; and then one feeble spotlight glimmered from the lighting booth operated by some subsidiary system. It happened that at the moment of failure I had a plate of candies in my hand, part of the stage business. While we were wondering what to do— asking the audience if they would like us to continue by candlelight—I handed the plate of candies to the front row people next to me. This gesture of including them in our predicament they much enjoyed. Candles were brought on stage, the candies were returned to me and we continued.

Never had the ensuing scenes gone so well. The audience was busting itself to show appreciation of our effort to entertain them in adversity. When the lights came on again the whole performance suddenly went flat. The audience had exhausted itself on our behalf and the fun had gone out of the evening.

This production in the round brings to mind the interesting thought of how an audience will accept and go along with any convention on the stage which is boldly established from the start. A performance is never real life; it is always "let's pretend." People in real life never communicate in iambic pentameters—yet let the director establish a sense of communicating reality in blank verse, and the audience will believe that Hamlet is more real than their own lives.

Shakespeare is played in one convention, Coward in another, Shaw and Chekhov each in different conventions, Sheriden in his, *Oklahoma* in yet another—there is no end to it. "Let's pretend this is real"—believe it and the audience believes with you.

Coming to central staging for the first time, with members of the audience sitting all around you within a few feet, I thought "Oh, this will be like movie acting." But no, as the director pointed out to me, "in this big central stage theatre you must remember that all the time there will be two or three hundred people behind your back. They must hear you. You must get to them." In other words, however intimate and naturalistic the play might seem to be, vocal projection was absolutely necessary. And in whatever convention a play is to be played, that convention must be established in the very first moments. Then the audience tunes in and adjusts. If the play is begun on the wrong wave length and the audience has to re-tune later, there will be a period of disbelief from which the performance may never quite recover.

I had to begin this modern, realistic play looking up from my newspaper and telling the butler I did not wish to speak on the telephone to anybody. In real life one would hardly raise ones voice, and that is how I spoke at early rehearsals. When it came to the performance, however, I bellowed it. Then, when told it was the President speaking, I took the call and spoke on the telephone with the same volume. Every word was heard and the audience was happy. Another actor enters and takes my level. It has become real to the audience. After a matinee I was walking my dog in the car park and ran into some delighted old ladies. "Oh, it was wonderful!" they said. "You could hear every word for once. And it was so natural—just like it was happening in your own living room." I thanked them and thought, "In your own living rooms you would have been positively deafened."

After *Private Room* I see from *Who's Who in the Theatre* that from various suburban theatres I tried, unsuccessfully, to impose myself on the West End as a leading man. At the Fulham Grand I remember, in midwinter, opening twice nightly with a 103 degree fever and water trickling down my dressing-room walls from burst water pipes. I had taken the job because the leading lady was the mistress of a West End producer. The play was called *Forsaking All Other*; I was sorely tempted to forsake the Fulham Grand after the first performance.

What *Who's Who* does not tell me are the dates of my appearances at the Old Vic. I can only presume that the feeling that it was a kind of slumming for a West End actor to play at the Old Vic induced me to forget to list them.

In 1934, however, play at the Old Vic I did in a revival of the Vic's production of *The Cherry Orchard* with Charles Laughton playing Lopakhin. Leon Quartermaine, who had been with them for the season, had played "my" part of Gayef, but was no longer available for the revival and I was asked to take his place. It is always uncomfortable to move into a production already set, particularly if one has played the part in another production. *(Not to mention the fact that the 1925 production featured a different translation than the 1934 version. Having to relearn the lines with slight variations cannot have been easy.)* They have their pattern, you have yours and I was conscious of having been the original English Gayef.

However, Tyrone Guthrie was the director and his fluid and tactful approach allowed me to adjust without too much difficulty. Besides, there was the joy of watching Laughton at work. His Lopakhin was superb.

Two years running I was invited to be a member of the Old Vic Company and each time I turned down the offer because I knew I could make more money in the West End. I believe now that I made a great mistake. My voice and impressive bearing made me a natural for Shakespeare and, though the parts offered me—the supporting old men—did not seem alluring, I believe that I might have well have proved my metal and been promoted to some of the great roles. The Old Vic has been the field on which many a stellar reputation has been made. Maurice Evans was engaged for a season of supporting roles; but when the audience rose to cheer him as Octavius in *Antony and Cleopatra*, Lillian Bayliss promoted him over Alan Webb's head to play *Richard II*. This performance led to his becoming one of the outstanding figures in the theatre, both in England and America, for the next twenty years.

Richard II, in fact, was the other production in which I appeared at the Old Vic. For the life of me I cannot recall where it fit into my schedule, but play old John of Gaunt with Maurice I assuredly did. *It was a two-week revival in April 1935 of a 1934 production in which Alan's role had been played by Alfred Sangster. The press welcomed the new addition to the cast, with the* Times *noting that "the part of Gaunt is given by Mr. Alan Napier more sensitiveness and humanity than are often enabled to appear through its rhetoric," and the* Daily Telegraph *adding that "Alan Napier now plays John of Gaunt and gives the old man dignity and strength. There is a finer lyric quality in the England speech than he succeeded in finding last night, but his death warning to Richard held the house." Another paper pointed out—somewhat more prosaically—that "by a coincidence the parts of the brothers John of Gaunt and the Duke of York are played by Mr. Alan Napier and Mr. Frank Napier, who, however, are not related."* Maurice's performance was breathtakingly good, and to this day I can hear the beautiful tenor voice ring out with affronted majesty, "Northumberland, thou haught insulting man!"

I was a good John of Gaunt; at least Miss Bayliss, that extraordinary woman, certainly thought so, expressing her opinion in her very strange way. On the first night, after old Gaunt had breathed his last, I met Lillian back stage. She patted me on the chest and said "My dear, you looked lovely!"—just that, nothing more. As I was a very grey old man in very grey old robes I was somewhat puzzled and reported the encounter to my fellow actors in our dressing room.

"Oh, that's the highest praise she ever gives," they said.

Miss Bayliss had been brought up on opera (under Emma Cons, her aunt, the Old Vic had been an opera house and Lillian took to Shakespeare *faute de mieux* when opera failed) and apparently the aging opera stars only wanted to know how they looked. To tell them they looked lovely was to confer the ultimate praise. Lillian carried the habit over into Shakespeare.

I will resist the temptation to retell the well-known stories of Lillian Bayliss—from me they would be second hand. I only know that, try as I would, at our two encounters as actor and manager, though she was generous in appreciation of my talent, in the matter of salary I was unable to screw her up to more than thirteen pounds a week. That is the reason why I missed my chance of winning, if not fortune, at least a little fame as a Shakespearean actor.

A notable result of the success of *Richard II* was an invitation by the BBC to broadcast it with the Old Vic company. I had never worked in radio before; possibly, I imagined, because there were those in the drama department of the BBC who had known me at the Oxford Playhouse and were not unreasonably apprehensive of the stammer which in those days was liable to overcome me at rehearsals. *(Alan is certainly referring here to Val Gielgud, John's elder brother, who had stage managed and played small roles at Oxford and, as the BBC Head of Productions since 1929, was in charge of all radio dramas.)* In *Richard II*, I came with the package. I must confess that I was full of fears in face of this new medium. However, all went well. Indeed I found the microphone wonderfully congenial for Gaunt's dying "royal throne of Kings" speech. To whisper it with love and indignation contending, as the spark of life flickers and flares up before it dies, allowed one more subtlety than one had in the theatre where the need to be heard was at war with the realistic presentation of physical weakness.

I was not to work on radio again until I was employed by Orson Welles some years later in America. Part of my new life there was to have no history of stammering, so no-one knew with what agony of nerves I faced that first American broadcast to sixty million

With Diana Wynyard in *Sweet Aloes* at Wyndham's Theatre, 1934. Collection of James Bigwood.

listeners. In the event, Orson's majestic trick of bringing order out of chaos at the eleventh hour, of riding the air waves like a triumphant Viking, filled me with such wonder, admiration and excitement that all nervousness was lost in the joy of battle. *Alan's first radio show for Welles, a one-hour adaptation of Agatha Christie's* The Murder of Roger Ackroyd, *in which he played the title character, had the added delicious chaos of Welles playing scenes with himself, in the roles of both Hercule Poirot and Dr. Sheppard.*

In the late summer of 1934, low in funds and no longer so high in hopes, I accepted thankfully but hardly with enthusiasm an engagement in *Sweet Aloes* by Joyce Carey. This was to be a major West End production and my role was once again a benevolent elderly peer—a Lord Farringdon.

Joyce tells an amusing tale of how the play came to be written. She had taken a job as play-reader in New York for a leading producer there. After reading a few hundred terrible scripts she thought, "Heavens above—if one can't write something better than this garbage!" On a dare to herself she determined to concoct a script out of all the old clichés, a script which would at least be worthy of being submitted to a producer. In fact Joyce's fastidious good taste saw to it that the result, *Sweet Aloes*, was a perfectly acceptable little play, in the sweet and sour taste of the period. It ran for eighteen months at Wyndham's Theatre, London. I doubt if this would have been the outcome had not clever Binkie Beaumont, of the producing firm of Howard and Wyndham, engaged Tyrone Guthrie to direct it. Tony worked his magic of investing what was basically a soap opera with humor and plausibility. The play was also graced by a beautiful performance by Diana Wynward in the leading role, which she endowed with her charm, beauty and gift of making the commonplace seem profound.

Although Lord Farringdon was a come-down from what I had hoped lay before me, at least he was moderately well paid and, since he only appeared in the first act, I was able, towards the end of the run, to repeat my *Bitter Sweet* trick of playing in two plays at once and earning two salaries. But before I come to this I must tell of yet another hazard that can confront an actor.

Lord Farringdon was one of those fine old English gentlemen who know and love their glass of port. His daughter invites him to dinner to meet her young man, and in order to impress her father with her suitor's suitability, purloins a bottle of the old man's own port. There is a big moment while he tastes, assesses and approves the wine. I did not give any great thought to this; I just did what my memory bank told me was right. One evening Laurence Olivier was in the audience. He came round afterwards, very kindly looked in to see me, and said, "Alan, there's something quite wonderful about your business with the port—you know, tremendously fine old English gentleman, and all that." I was very flattered.

And then I began to think, "What do I do that's so wonderful?" I really hadn't thought of it as anything particular. I began to analyze and fuss about it. Next night I felt self-conscious, and the indications of crusty connoisseurship I had produced instinctively seemed now affected and pretentious. I doubt if I was ever again able to do the scene as well as I had on the night when I impressed Olivier. Since then I have tried to avoid ever praising an actor for any specific moment in his performance.

I imagine that this visit by Olivier took place after I had been engaged to appear, contemporaneously, in the notable production of *Romeo and Juliet* in which he and John Gielgud were to play Romeo and Mercutio, swapping roles in the middle of the run. John, an old friend from the Oxford Players, was directing and wanted me for the Prince of Verona. Since *Romeo and Juliet* was to start at 8:00 p.m. it was found that I could combine the Prince with my role in *Sweet Aloes*. As in the case of *Little Lord Fauntleroy* and *Bitter Sweet* I could use the same basic old man make-up; and the fact that Wyndham's and the New Theatre, where *Romeo* was produced, stand back to back with their stage doors opening on the same alley, facilitated matters. I made up at Wyndham's, stuck on a beard for the Prince of Verona, went over to the New Theatre, dressed and played my opening scene—"Rebellious subjects, enemies to peace!"—dashed back to Wyndham's, took off the beard, played Lord Farringdon, put back my beard and dashed back to the New Theatre just in time for "Where are the vile beginners of this fray?" and the rest of *Romeo*. There was no real problem; but one evening I did cause a slight sensation by entering to castigate the citizens of Verona with pince-nez glasses jiggling on my nose. I realized something was wrong when I found myself seeing the other actors' faces so clearly—I was used to seeing them in a comfortably myopic blur.

What a cast that was! Olivier, Gielgud, Peggy Ashcroft as Juliet, Edith Evans as the nurse (there could never be a nurse to touch her), Alec Guinness as a Capulet hanger-on and the apothecary (no one guessed his brilliant future), Harry Andrews as the troublemaker who says "shall I bite my thumb at him," Glen Byam Shaw as Benvolio, and other wonderful actors now dead and forgotten.

The production was a tremendous success and eventually outran *Sweet Aloes*. I found it very dull spending the whole evening in one theatre with the long waits between the Prince of Verona's three scenes; I used to spend the evening in Freddy Lloyd's dressing room (he was a delightful Capulet, finding much welcome comedy in the part), doing *The Times* cross-word with him; or, alone in my own room, tormented with hideous suspicion as to what might be going on in Nan's bedroom at Springfield Road.

21

On the Rocks

By the time *Sweet Aloes* opened, my marriage was already on the rocks. Ladies from Nan's American past kept turning up at Springfield Road. They were all very pleasant to me, finding me "so sensitive," which I suppose meant that I did not throw them out of the house.

In fact, the marriage had been on the wrong foot from the start. Nan had insisted on separate rooms on some health pretext; but the idea was also postulated that it was so much more civilized for me to visit her in answer to the call of love rather than to fall into a habit of casual copulation. Used to bachelor ways and living with my inhibitions, I fell for this specious argument, but the call of love was frequently not returned and visits to her bed became rarer and rarer. One of the many attractions of going down to Bletchingley lay in the fact that we were always given a double bed there, which made our visits little honeymoons for me.

Soon after *Sweet Aloes* opened, Nan told me that she wanted to go to Paris for a few weeks with the current favorite. Let us call her Gwen. Gwen said it was a crime that Nan, with such a beautiful voice, had given up her singing. Gwen knew a wonderful voice teacher in Paris with whom Nan could work for nothing.

I found it hard to say no; furthermore it seemed to me that anyone was bound to get pretty tired of Gwen, cooped up with her for any length of time. Indeed, I was getting tired to death of Gwen's constant presence at Springfield Road, justified ostensibly by the fact that she was painting Nan's portrait. So I agreed to their going. She wrote to me from Paris that she and Gwen were going on together to the South of France to stay with Gwen's father. In all, she was away for over six months.

Something had to happen to me in this interim. It is hard after so much bitterness and more indifference to recall one's feeling; but I do know that I wrote loving letters all the time, free of reproach, always believing Nan would come back to me and always keeping the door wide open since, apart from sex, our tastes and habits were so comfortably compatible.

But nature, abhorring vacuums, chose to play a strange trick on me. A few weeks after Nan had gone to France I went down to Bletchingley for the weekend. As usual, on my arrival in the hall of the house, there was Ian standing in a doorway to welcome me. Over his shoulder I saw a face. If it is possible to fall in love in a split second, then I fell in love with this face. It seemed to me to be unbelievably beautiful and a warmth came out to me from the depths of the smiling brown eyes. Ian moved and I was amazed to see that the face belonged to a boy in his late teens.

"That's that," I thought. I even laughed a little grimly at the idea that I was so conditioned at Springfield Road to see women with boys' haircuts that it did not occur to me that this face might not be a woman's. But when I went to bed I could not get it out of my mind's eye, nor the idea that its owner was looking for some sort of help or guidance. The next day I found the boy as charming and intelligent as he was beautiful. He wanted to be an actor and was instantly attracted to me as one is to a successful adult in the profession one wishes to adopt. On Monday I drove him up to town, told him of my marriage predicament which had made me vulnerable to a sudden vision of physical beauty. "I thought I'd fallen in love with you last night, but, as I'm married and want to get my marriage back on its feet again, I am not going to make the sort of advances that I am sure you must be used to." He nodded ruefully and added that at the moment he was having hectic affairs with two girls in Chelsea. But I could see that he was flattered by my admiration and touched by my forbearance.

In ancient Greece, we could well have become lovers; there was a strong mutual attraction compounded of a desire to protect and guide on one hand and to admire and serve on the other. In twentieth century England we did not become lovers. But a warm friendship resulted which was to last many years and to play a strange part in my life. At the time … it at least kept me from any heterosexual activity that might have proved a more obvious threat to my marriage. *This new acquaintance was John Justinian de Ledesma, better known under his stage name of John Justin. Best remembered today for his breakthrough role as Ahmad in Alexander Korda's 1939 fantasy,* The Thief of Bagdad, *he had a long and varied career on both stage and screen.*

* * *

I was right about Gwen. The time came when Nan wrote that she had become impossible to live with. Nan wanted to come home. I wrote her a long letter—as it seemed to me then generous and sensible but in fact entirely naive—to the effect that we had learned our lessons and could now settle down into a renewed state of married bliss, sharing a bedroom as husband and wife should.

It did not work out that way. Nan's girl friends still invaded the house and feeling unwanted and outnumbered I invited my young friend constantly as a kind of a counterweight. I could rationalize a humane justification; he was broke and not, I felt, getting enough proper food, so I invited him to dinner two or three times a week. I, of course, had to leave immediately after for the theatre. Sometimes he would stay on and I liked to think of him enjoying the phonograph, the books, the warmth and comfort of my house. So it went through the winter of 1935.

One Saturday night when we were to go down to Bletchingley, Nan was inexplicably late in picking me up—I had gone to the theatre by bus and underground, leaving her the car. There was something fishy about her explanations and something hostile about her behavior when we eventually reached the haven of our double bed. A hateful suspicion began to worm its way into my mind. The current ladies in attendance I knew were not Nan's cup of tea, but what if John …? I fought the idea down as a monstrous and unworthy jealous imagining.

Then came the night of our great party. Nan was very good at giving parties. She prepared the most delicious American style hors d'oeuvres, then unfamiliar in England, and we bottled in advance—icing as needed—a potent rum and lime cocktail. This particular party was ostensibly important because Nan had persuaded me to let her invite Gwen. All

21. On the Rocks

that was over, she said, and an attitude of let bygones be bygones would show the generosity of my nature and my faith in the validity of our marriage. Because my whole being was disturbed by a deeper anxiety, I had agreed to let Gwen return to the fold.

John was invaluable at these parties. He helped prepare everything and was assiduous at handing round hors d'oeuvres and refilling glasses. In fact he stayed with us, sleeping on the drawing-room sofa, for a day or so in advance. On the great day a shattering revelation was made manifest shortly before the party began. In the process of getting ourselves spruced up for the evening, I went into the bathroom to shave at the basin while John was still in the bath.

I saw it first in the mirror. My heart missed a beat and I turned. There it was, quite unmistakable—the mark of a bite on the shoulder. A human bite. Nan's particular trick that I knew so well in moments of erotic ecstasy. I knew the very spot, the very feel of it.

Of course there were denials and explanations and no time, nor preparedness on my part, for a showdown. For me the party became a grotesque nightmare; and Gwen's protestations that I was a noble sensitive and civilized human being, idiotically irrelevant. I went up to my room before the last guest left so that I would not be alone with the two I suspected until I could decide what I must do. I lay in the dark trying to subdue the waves of anger, self-pity and grief that made it so hard to find the real truth. Not whether Nan had been sleeping with another man—in the pit of my stomach I knew that—but whether there was any hope, any sense, in trying to preserve a relationship threatened from all sides. One thing that made this development particularly hard to bear was the fact that Nan had been going to some kind of psychotherapist (at considerable expense to me) who had sent me a message to the effect that, in seeking to enjoy my marital rights with Nan, I was merely unloading on her my hidden desires for John Justin. That was evidently the story Nan had told the psychotherapist at the very time she herself was engaged in encouraging the advances of this highly sexed youth nearly twenty years her junior.

At 5:00 in the morning I went down to the drawing room where John was sleeping and the truth came out. His grief was that he had hurt me so much. "I'm much fonder of you than Nan. What can I do?"

I told him he could give me a divorce by making full confession. In those days adultery was the prime ground for divorce. (His family insisted that he should leave the country before the case came up; but he made a deposition, fully admitting adultery, before he departed.)

In effect I had a watertight case which, uncontested, would have given me the custody of our child, and Nan no alimony. I was sitting pretty. But I was also desperately lonely and unsure of my capacity to cope with the raising of a child by myself. The idea that I might marry again never occurred to me. Despite all that had happened, I see now that I still really loved Nan. I could not have been such an idiot if this were not the case.

Five days before the case was to come to trial—Nan had found 24 Roland Gardens once more available and I was back at Springfield Road—Nan sent me a record of the tremendously successful and nostalgic song "These Foolish Things (Remind Me of You)."

I fell for it. I called her up to thank her. She suggested we should meet at a movie theatre. We saw the picture, holding hands. She asked me to dinner at Roland Gardens the next evening. I arrived. I took her in my arms. Reverting to my tennis metaphor, I never played better or, hit the ball so hard.

So I called off the divorce and lived to regret it for the next thirty-five years. I still was not really grown up.

My "tennis playing" deteriorated very rapidly and I used to think that this is what brought about the failure of my second attempt to salvage my marriage. Having had a true marriage since, I know that this was not the reason. The reason was put to me with crystal clarity when my final separation from Nan became inevitable two years later. A leathery lesbian (and a very decent chap) put it to me succinctly. "My dear Alan, if you haven't got a clitoris, you haven't got a hope."

22

Ibsen, Shaw and Sayers

My immediate failure at tennis was brought about by a surgical operation and a tremendously exacting schedule of work. I had been engaged to play the lead—and again I thought "This is it!"—in a play called *Gentle Rain* at the Vaudeville Theatre co-starring with Viola Keats as my wife and Haidee Wright as my mother. Real West End, this, with my name in electric lights. I was to be an air pilot who crashes. At the end of the second act he is given a merciful release from his suffering by a compassionate wife. The curtain falls as he holds her hand and says the Lord's Prayer. I wept when I read the play and I was sure it would be a huge success.

But in the middle of rehearsals I had to have growth removed from the neighborhood of my Adam's apple. It turned out to be a benign cyst but the operation was long and tricky since the damned thing was nestling in a nexus of vital plumbing and wiring—all sorts of arteries, nerves, and windpipes being intertwined around it. I started to work again too soon and I don't think I was at my best. In any case it was a silly little play. An eminent surgeon I knew came to the first night and rather dashed my hopes when he said,

"I don't know what all the fuss was about. I put people in that condition out of their troubles all the time." The critics agreed, and the play failed.

Without a break I went straight into a season at the Westminster Theatre, where my great friend Michael MacOwan was directing, to play the lead, Hjalmar Ekdal in the *The Wild Duck* by Ibsen. This was eventually followed by a play at Wyndham's (a failure) and then back to the Westminster for Shaw's *Heartbreak House*. In fact I was rehearsing and playing continuously for the eight months succeeding my operation and the initial attempt to re-cement my marriage. The lease of Springfield Road expired at this time and I returned to Roland Gardens and a separate bedroom, where I climbed into bed every night too tired to attempt any unwelcome lovemaking.

Playing in *The Wild Duck*, Ibsen's greatest play in my opinion, led to a very humbling experience for me. Rehearsals seemed to go swimmingly, and I fully anticipated the kind of success to which I was becoming accustomed. At the first night, indeed, the audience applauded with enthusiasm when the curtain fell. I had ordered copies of all the papers published in London—some eight or nine in those days—to be delivered the next morning, and looked forward to a chorus of praise to enliven my breakfast.

I opened the *Times* and could not believe my eyes. Quickly I pushed it aside and sought the entertainment page of the *Daily Telegraph*. Another bad review for me. There must be some mistake! But no, in every single paper I was harshly condemned with words like: "but for Mr. Napier's disastrous performance…." What had happened? How could the critics, up until then always so kind to me, be so cruel? Worse—how was I to face the rest of the company (who had been generously praised) and the second night audience? Above all, where had I gone wrong?

When I arrived at the Westminster for the second performance, shaken and discouraged, Michael MacOwan met me at the stage door with words of comfort and reassurance. Generously he took the blame himself.

"It was my fault. I should have seen what was happening. What you are doing works very well for most of the audience, but it annoys the critics because I let you, so to speak, editorialize what Ibsen is saying. You caricature Hjalmar instead of playing him straight—saying between the lines, 'Look what a monster of selfishness I am' instead of just being selfish and letting the audience draw their own conclusions."

I could not see what was wrong with this and protested, "But the play went very well and I got all my laughs, didn't I?"

"Oh yes. But the critics must have felt insulted by your practically saying, 'This is funny. See how ironic that is!'"

It was hard to assimilate this idea and to change what had been so carefully planned at rehearsal. I know now that the analysis was correct, for I have seen other actors, particularly when playing Shaw, do the same thing. The actor's "cleverness" comes between the audience and the playwright's words, which are quite capable of making their effect without being underlined by the actor. This trick insults the intelligence of the audience and destroys the reality of the scene. I have never been guilty of it again. The reason I fell into it in *The Wild Duck* was because I felt I was miscast. When Michael asked me to play the part, I said:

"Oh but Hjalmar's a self-indulgent little chap. He should be soft and fat."

"Not necessarily," said Michael. "It'll be a challenge. I'm sure you can do it."

But I still felt physically wrong and started underlining Hjalmar's self-indulgent characteristics to counteract the impressions of my rather austere appearance. I remember Tony Guthrie saying to me once, "You know, *inside*, I'm really a fat little man"—and my immediate reaction, "Not me, never."

It was a lesson learned. But I have always regretted that, given the chance to play one of the great parts in dramatic literature, I muffed it.

I went straight from the Westminster back to Wyndham's for a short-lived play in which I was referred to before my first entrance as "the most eligible bachelor in Sussex," played a love scene with Vivian Leigh, and ran onto the stage in the last act in white flannels and a tennis racquet. "Tennis anybody?"— I'm glad not to have missed that cliché of the period. Then to the Westminster again for a memorable experience—indeed, one of the most memorable experiences of my career.

The Westminster management had secured permission from George Bernard Shaw to put on a revival of *Heartbreak House*; and the great man consented to supervise rehearsals himself. Indeed, he insisted. Of course, when Michael told me of this I wanted to play the 88-year-old Captain Shotover again. But no—he thought I should play Hector Hushabye. He had a good Shotover available, but Hector was the difficult role and I was the man for it. It was a new direction. Shotover for me was easy, and I happily agreed to play Hector.

For the first few days of rehearsals Shaw was busy elsewhere. I shall never forget his first appearance. The call was for ten o'clock and Shaw had sent a message that he would be a little late, so Michael decided not to waste time and we started the first act. It had been assumed that Shaw would come in by the front of the house. In fact he came in by the stage door, and, hidden in the wings, listened to us unobserved. Suddenly he strode onto the stage, his long mackintosh crackling and flapping as his arms flailed, and exclaimed,

"Stop! Stop! This won't do at all. You're playing my play much too fast! If the audience can't hear or understand what you say at the beginning, how are they to know what sort of people you are, or why you do what you do later on? If a playwright is worth his salt, every word is important; and I'll not have you rattling my words like so many Hail Mary's. We'll take it again from the start."

Words of wisdom indeed. I have seen play after play ruined because the director gets bored with the opening and, forgetting that the audience will be hearing it for the first time, berates his actors for dragging that long boring exposition. A.B. Walkley, the dramatic critic of *The Times* at the period when Shaw was writing his famous dramatic criticisms, wrote a charming description of the joy of watching a play slowly unfold. The hush in the audience as the houselights dim. The tingle of expectation as the curtain rises, preferably on an empty stage. A little world is revealed. What will transpire there? From what quarter will the wind blow? He goes on to describe how the clever playwright will, by dropping a hint here and a hint there, stimulate your curiosity and gradually involve you in the destinies of the characters revealed upon the stage.

Shaw was a born man of the theatre and understood actors. Because he could always be one jump ahead of them, instead of fearing and hating them (as those who come into the theatre without technical stage sense so often do) he was at ease with them in the most patient and friendly way.

"No, my dear," he says to the girl playing Ellie Dunn, "you haven't quite got the hang of it," and he plays a whole scene for her. Then, returning her book to her, he says, "That's the idea. But because you're a beautiful young woman and I'm an ugly old man you'll do it much better than I."

From the beginning he liked my Hector. Indeed, he said to Michael: "It was clever of you to get Napier. Leo Quartermaine made quite a good shot at the part, but this man *is* Hector." This was the time when Shaw had been persuaded by Gabriel Pascal to let him make a film of *Pygmalion*. Shaw told Pascal to come and see me in *Heartbreak House*. I was his first choice for Higgins.

For nearly a year Pascal dickered with the idea while he was raising the capital for making the film. I used to visit him in his flat in Mayfair where he plied me with Hungarian peach brandy and we talked about the Master—for Pascal's admiration for Shaw, like mine, was boundless. But the backers very naturally insisted on an established star, since Wendy Hiller, who played Eliza so beautifully, was then unknown in the film world. To tell the truth I don't think I was equipped with enough camera-confidence at that time; though in the theatre I could have given a Higgins of whom Shaw would have heartily approved. *The closest Alan ever got to a production of* Pygmalion *was on the* Lux Radio Theater *in 1939, when, playing Colonel Pickering to Brian Aherne's Higgins, he created—with just his voice—a tubby, jolly character completely at odds with his actual physical appearance.* So my sorrow at being finally turned down was tempered by relief at not being called upon to do something I felt to be beyond me. I did, in fact, take part in a test with Phillip Merrivale as Pickering and Wilfred Lawson as Doolittle. The test was really for Lawson; and one knew at once that he *had* to play the part. He was superb. I felt that I had muffed my opportunity, though I don't imagine I would have been chosen even if I had done a better job. It has taken me nearly thirty years to be at ease in front of a camera.

One typical Shavian comment I recall from rehearsals of *Heartbreak House*. It is a very long play and Michael MacOwan had the temerity to ask Shaw if we could make some cuts in the last act.

Alan Napier and Mary Grey in *Heartbreak House*. Westminster Theatre, 1937. Angus McBean Photograph. © Harvard Theatre Collection, Houghton Library, Harvard University.

"No. No," said Shaw, "they've just played *Hamlet* in its entirety at the Old Vic, and it's never been more successful." (This was Olivier's first *Hamlet*.) "If the public can stand Shakespeare in his entirety, they can stand Shaw. You'll do it the way I wrote it."

And we did. And the public loved it. Every word.

Mary Grey, the Oxford Players mother of my career, came out of retirement, as beautiful as ever, to play Hesione—she had been the original Hesione of Shaw's choice. *(Although* Heartbreak House *had its world premiere in New York, Mary Grey played Hesione in the original 1921 London production under the direction of J.B. Fagan.)* It was her great part, for she embodied perfectly that wonderful Shavian concept of the mature woman who is wife, mother, lover, friend, and intellectual equal of man. When I think of reviving *Heartbreak House*—and I know I can play Shotover as Shaw meant him to be played—the stumbling block is to find someone to play Hesione. Actresses no longer grow in the Shavian mold.

Of Shaw I must say that I owe him an immense debt of gratitude. Reading his plays, seeing them, and acting in them has given me more pleasure than I have derived from any other writer. His thinking about life has been the strongest influence in forming my own views and tastes. One of my favorite quotations comes from his *Intelligent Woman's Guide to Socialism and Capitalism*. After a ten-page dissertation on political economy he starts the next chapter as follows: "Now that you know more about political economy than the average Prime Minister of England…"

No one intending to direct a play should embark on this difficult field of endeavor without reading a little pamphlet by Shaw entitled "How to Rehearse a Play." It is filled with wisdom and understanding and it makes it quite clear that the director's job is to co-ordinate the actors' talents into the most exact interpretation of the playwright's intentions. That and nothing more. The pamphlet, be it noted, is called "How to *Rehearse* a Play"—which implies that it should be a work of co-operation rather than of dictation.

To have been rehearsed by G.B.S. and to have earned his approbation I count the highest point of my career as an actor.

* * *

It was now 1937 and Fascism and Nazism were casting their ominous shadows over the English scene. Even the world of the theatre, so happily engaged for twenty years in escaping from life into teacup comedies and detective thrillers, began to reflect the threat to life and liberty spreading like a cancer over Europe.

Soon after the run of *Heartbreak House* was over I was engaged to play the Nazi prototype, General Rakovsky, in Elmer Rice's prophetic melodrama *Judgment Day*. We opened at the little Embassy Theatre in Hampstead and soon transferred to the Strand Theatre for an extended run. One of the pleasures of this production was Glynis John's performance—I think it was her first professional appearance—as a heartbroken child of twelve. I remember thinking "this child will be a great actress" and later watching her swift rise to stardom. When we next played together in New York, though the production was a misery for me, and a theatrical miscarriage, Glynis' presence was the one thing that made it endurable.

Judgment Day also, I forget how, brought me into contact with Princess Bibesco, who delighted me with her definition of a bore. "A bore," she said, "is someone who won't listen to you." So true—you think you're having a conversation with someone and then you notice that, while you are talking, he is looking over your left shoulder with dead eyes waiting for you to stop interrupting him.

A few months later I played in the first play to be done in England realistically showing the destruction of human decency in Germany by Nazi anti-Semitism [*Take Head!* by Leslie Reade]. It was a complete switch from General Rekovsky, for I played a dear old professor whose wife was "a Jewess." When I read the play I remember thinking that it seemed very melodramatic and being amazed when the director, George Owen, assured me that it was a realistic tragedy and no whit exaggerated what was taking place in Germany every day. But England was not ready to face such barbarity and the trial run at the Arts Theatre led only to a single subscription performance at the Piccadilly before an all Jewish audience. The impact was profound and memorable. Rather ungallantly I have to add that lifting my dead wife from the floor, after she had been shot by storm troopers, a poignant moment in the play, initiated twenty years of recurrent back trouble for me. However I got a wonderful review in *The Jewish Chronicle*.

As General Michael Rakovski in Elmer Rice's *Judgment Day*. Strand Theatre, 1937. Angus McBean Photograph. © Harvard Theatre Collection, Houghton Library, Harvard University.

It is interesting to note that the producers were in considerable doubt as to whether the Lord Chamberlain would license the play for public performance (the Arts Theatre, being technically a club, did not require his license). Whereas *Judgment Day* had been placed in a mythical Central European country, this play was quite specific in naming and condemning Hitler, the head of a "friendly" nation. If the German Embassy had protested, the Lord Chamberlain might well have withdrawn his license. His office was concerned with seeing that the theatre did not affront sensibilities, political as well as moral.

From *Judgment Day* I returned to the Westminster and Michael MacOwan to play opposite Cathleen Nesbitt in a play called *Land's End*, by F.L. Lucas. Why is it that when highbrow writers descend to melodrama they are always drawn to Cornwall? What is there about those rocky cliffs that invites bloodshed and disaster?

Cecil Trouncer offers Alan his choice of weapons in *Land's End*. Westminster Theatre, 1938. Angus McBean Photograph. © Harvard Theatre Collection, Houghton Library, Harvard University.

I was the lover in this play; the husband returns from Africa unexpectedly; he challenges me to a duel; I am a man of peace but honor will not let me back away. The old family dueling pistols are brought out; we stand back to back; five paces. As I turn to face certain death my beloved fires the family fowling piece through the window and her husband dies. End of Act II. During the interval we dump the body over those famous Cornish Cliffs. At any moment the children will return. Horror of horrors! A pool of blood in the middle of the floor. We pull a sofa over it.

Well now—that pool of blood. At the dress rehearsal, no blood. "Michael," I say, "how come no blood?"

"It's all right Alan. I can't see from here. Just react as though it was there."

"But the balcony, Michael. They can see from there."

It was not like Michael to have ignored this. What are we to do? I have a very practical side to my nature. I say, "How about cutting out a circle of red cloth, wetting it down and laying it in the exact spot during the interval." Brilliant. I have solved the problem. The rehearsal continues.

Then, one night, the moment comes as usual when Cathleen sees the blood. Sudden intake of breath. "What are we to do?" she says, wringing her hands. "The children will be back at any moment." She's wearing a long red dress that sweeps the floor. She paces up and down, distraught. This particular evening she does not look where she is going. She paces across the pool of blood. Her skirt catches the edge of the red cloth and rolls the pool of blood up into a neat little sausage.

The balcony was delighted—but the groundlings could not make out what we were all laughing at. Well, it was another lesson. Stick to your own job and let the property department do theirs. Only there was not much of a property department at the Westminster—it was "Off Broadway."

The Westminster was becoming my home—the scene of triumph and disaster. It had one more delightful experience for me, even if it never paid a decent salary. It was at the Westminster that I appeared in Dorothy Sayers' splendid play *The Zeal of Thy House*.

I had met Dorothy a year or so before when our mutual friend Muriel St. Claire Byrne, a notable historian of late Tudor times, introduced us. Muriel had collaborated with Dorothy on the dramatization of *Busman's Honeymoon* and thought I would be the answer to Dorothy's prayer for a suitable actor to play Lord Peter Wimsey. I thought so too. So the three of us had a delightful lunch at Chez Victor in Wardour Street, where I got on with Dorothy like a house on fire, though she studiously avoided any reference to Peter Wimsey. Muriel telephoned later to say that Dorothy was terribly sorry but Peter was five foot eight. She could not be shaken. Lord Peter Wimsey, for private reasons, was as real to Dorothy as any living man and it seemed to her just as absurd to cast me for Peter as to cast me for Napoleon.

However I continued to enjoy the friendship of this remarkable woman. By this time she had made all the money she needed to support her invalid husband in the manner to which he was accustomed. This had been the motive that led her to write her famous detective stories—Peter Wimsey being an idealization of her husband. Now she was able to revert to her true interests in life—theology and the classics—and to indulge in a new passion for the theatre.

T.S. Eliot's *Murder in the Cathedral* had inaugurated an annual Canterbury festival in 1935. The next year some enlightened soul induced the organizers to invite Dorothy Sayers to write the next play to be performed in the Chapter House of the Cathedral. The result, *The Zeal of Thy House*, tells the tale of the selection of an architect and the rebuilding of the Cathedral after the disastrous fire of 1174. The theme of the play is that of the artist thrown down at the supreme moment of mastery by the sin of pride. The story is reasonably accurate as far as the human participants are concerned; and to point her moral and dramatize the spiritual conflicts, Miss Sayers introduces four magnificent Archangels who watch the proceedings, comment on them and interpose when necessary to see that God's will is done. *Sayers had obviously not forgotten her luncheon with Alan. On January 18, 1937, she wrote to Margaret Bibington, the organizer of Canterbury Festival, "I had, in a half jesting manner—and explaining of course that casting did not come within my province—mentioned the subject of archangels to Mr. Alan Napier. I have now heard from him and he says that he would seriously be delighted to be Michael if called upon. This is, of course, just a suggestion, but if you did think of strengthening the cast with one or two professionals, I do think we could not possibly find a more suitable leading archangel. He is, as I told you, six foot four, and magnificently built; good-looking in rather a severe way with a very fine voice, and excellent training in the speaking of verse. He is a young man, and has a considerable reputation as a rising actor. I do not think, however, that he would be out of the way as regards fees. A further recommendation, perhaps, is that having been brought up more or less in the bosom of the church and a highly intelligent man, he would act his part with understanding and in the right spirit." Babington responded favorably, to the author's delight. "I am so glad you feel* that it would be a good thing to approach Mr. Alan Napier about being the archangel Michael," she wrote on January 23. "I really think he would be an excellent choice, and in the hope of getting him, I am allowing myself to give some importance to the part."

Dorothy invited me to direct this play, a splendid opportunity I was unable to accept because I was acting in London. (The salary offered, twenty three pounds, hardly warranted my forgoing whatever acting job I was up for at the time.) It was lucky for Dorothy that I was not available, for she secured a far more experienced and able man, Harcourt Williams, who not only directed the play with great imagination but also played the leading role of William of Sens. "Billy" Williams had directed for many seasons in the early days of the Old Vic and was a beautiful actor; but at this time had fallen into one of those inexplicable periods in an aging actor's career when suddenly his services are no longer in demand. Younger men are in the eyes of producers, who, possibly without ever having seen the older man's work, regard him as old-fashioned. Maybe it is because, with all the talent in the world, he does not have a flair for getting on—for promoting a career.

However that may be, Billy's career was in the doldrums and he leapt at the chance of doing Dorothy's play. The production at Canterbury was a big success and Billy was magnificent in the part of William of Sens. When the twelve performances came to an end, Dorothy bid Billy farewell with great emotion and said: "If it should ever happen that anyone wants to do *Zeal* commercially, I want you to direct it, Billy, and you to play William of Sens."

"That's very nice of you, Dorothy. And I do hope you get an offer. It's a great play."

And I'm afraid he went back to London thinking, "I'll believe that when I see it." He had had too many such promises before from enthusiastic authors caught up in the emotion of the moment. And he did not yet know his Dorothy.

That winter Dorothy received a call from the Old Vic management. Would she come over and discuss with them the possibility of doing *The Zeal of Thy House* at the Old Vic as a special Easter attraction?

"You'll be delighted to hear, Miss Sayers, that we have Tyrone Guthrie to direct the play, and Laurence Olivier will play the leading part."

"Oh," said Dorothy, "Well, no."

"What? Did you understand what we said? We are offering you Tyrone Guthrie and Laurence Olivier."

"Very kind of you. Very flattering. But no one could do it better than Billy Williams. Besides, I promised him. If my play is ever done again Billy will direct it and Billy will play the leading part."

They argued with her. They couldn't believe their ears. But she was adamant. So the whole plan was called off. But Dorothy reasoned that if the Old Vic thought the play merited a theatre production, by God it should have a theatre production. So she decided to put it on with her own money—Billy Williams directing and Billy Williams playing the leading part.

This story of unprecedented loyalty has a happy ending. The play ran for five months and toured England for the rest of the year. It even showed a small profit.

* * *

Immersed in his 116 performance run of Judgment Day, *Alan, in addition to not directing, had also been unavailable to play the role of Michael in the Canterbury Festival production of* The Zeal of Thy House. *The part was played by Anthony Quayle, who, along with the rest of the cast, was invited to recreate his role a year later in London. However, as Dorothy Sayers reported to her friend, Maurice Browne, on March 5, 1938, "Tony Quayle, the little beast, backed out at the last moment to go to the Gate, of all places; so Michael is being played by Alan Napier—his robes have had to be let down 8 inches!"*

When it was produced at the Westminster following *Land's End*, I played Michael, the leading Archangel. Dorothy had her own ideas about Archangels. They must be tremendous figures, powerfully masculine and, when occasion demanded, terrible in their might. So the four of us were all over six feet tall, in magnificent yet austere golden robes with our long sleeves lined in red, green, blue, and white silk, and with wings ten feet high springing from our shoulders. In fact these were designed by an aircraft designer and we really looked as if we could take off at any moment. No sentimental wings of the dove for Dorothy. At the dramatic crisis of the play a young boy testifies:

"I saw a great angel stand before heaven and earth—all in gold and scarlet, with a drawn sword. Oh, and he had great wings too. He cut the rope and the cradle fell." (This was the cradle in which William of Sens is raised to supervise the placing of the keystone.)

In fact, the wings weighed a good deal for all their clever design; and supporting them as one stood motionless on narrow ledges built for the occasion in front of the proscenium arches for long periods between our participation in the action, was a considerable physical strain. But that we were tremendously impressive figures, there can be no doubt. Just before the moment described by the small boy, I, as the Archangel Michael, follow William down the center aisle of the auditorium to execute God's will on him for his arrogant declaration that he is God's equal as a creator. Those on the stage view the tragic fall (is it an accident?) as though it happened high up at the back of the auditorium. While this is happening, I wait unseen behind curtains at the back of the last row of seats. At the appropriate moment I return down the aisle, sword drawn, a terrifying instrument of God's vengeance. At one performance a member of the audience (who was probably there because he thought the play would be a murder mystery) chose this moment to try to slip out unobserved. He was in the aisle seat and as he rose and turned to leave, there was I bearing down on him. I shall never forget the look of terror in his eyes as he muttered "Christ Almighty! I beg your pardon" and sat down again.

It was an extraordinary play, much of it in good serviceable verse, rising at times to high poetry. There are many beautiful moments. One in particular has always seemed to me touched with genius. William has been having an affair with a rich lady of Canterbury. He warns her that he is in love with a dream, which only makes her more in love with him. After his fall from the scaffolding, when he is lying on a bed of pain, she visits him, ready to devote her life to caring for him. He will have none of it—she is too young and beautiful to waste her life nursing an impotent old man. In anguish she says, "I have broken what I cannot mend. William, tell me—had I at any time, even for a moment, any part in your dream?" He answers:

"I hardly know. But once, high in a corner of the clerestory, where none but God will look for it, I carved an angel with your face."

The play ends with the Archangel Michael stepping forward to the audience to expound to them the theory of the Holy Trinity in terms of the act of artistic creation, which is described as both one and triune. At one performance the audience went quietly home without any applause. I've always wondered whether I was particularly good that night or particularly bad.

It was an exciting production to be in. Billy Williams' direction was excellent and his performance superb. But it was also, because of the wings, physically exacting. So when the four-week run at the Westminster came to an end, I left the cast before the play reopened at the Duke of York's Theater. The salary had been the standard Westminster fifteen pounds a week and I had been offered a film.

Dorothy's joy at having a success in the theater, at the friendliness and camaraderie of theater people (which blossomed in response to her bubbling appreciation of it) made the production one of the most delightful experiences I have had in the theater despite the physical burden of the wings. How Dorothy, her pince-nez glasses trembling on her nose, loved to greet her four Archangels every evening with fond motherly kisses!

This was the time of the W.P.A. Theater Project in America. Dorothy received an offer to have *Zeal* produced under W.P.A. auspices in five major cities of the U.S.A. But there was a condition—that she rewrite the parts of the Archangels for women. This idea, abhorrent to the author, was presumably intended to give the play more sex appeal. Dorothy turned it down flat. So America has never had a major professional production of this splendid play.

I corresponded with Dorothy until the year of her death. It has always been a grief to me that I missed her great work for the BBC during World War II.

23

Tomorrow to Fresh Woods

From the end of *Zeal* it was really downhill all the way for me until I left England to start a new life in America.

My private life was a shambles. I have never been a club man or a joiner of groups. I am not gregarious and prefer a settled companionship that insulates me from loneliness. The institution of marriage suits me down to the ground; and my marriage was a mockery. I forget just when Nan took off to live with her nice leathery girlfriend who, as I have said, was a very decent chap. (In World War I, serving in the armed forces, she had been assigned to drive the Prime Minister, David Lloyd George, when he quartered the country visiting munitions factories. She said she had no objection to the great man disporting himself with young women on these long journeys; but she did think it was a bit thick that she had to clean up after him and collect the condoms. The vitality of great men!)

I was left in a sort of comfortless limbo, my career getting nowhere and no settled, loving companionship. John Justin had returned from exile and glad I was to see him. There was a strong, indeed a tender, bond between us. But it stopped short of being complete. So I became involved in a series of desultory affairs, in which I seemed quite incapable of any deep commitment. The marriage I had failed to salvage hung on me and constricted me like dead ivy on a tree.

I still found it hard to identify the sexual act with love. Whatever my head might say, to my subconscious mind (conditioned by my upbringing), sex, unsanctified by marriage, remained to some degree a degrading activity. "Next time it may be different if I can find the right person, someone with whom I'm really in love," I would think, unwilling to accept the idea that my own inhibitions were to blame.

After *The Zeal of Thy House* I went into a minor musical, *No Sky So Blue*, in which I played a Russian diplomat. It was a job, but brought me neither acclaim nor much money. And it was during the prior to London tour that I got word from my sister-in-law Elizabeth that my father, who for nine months had been dying of cancer, was near the end. I took the night train from Newcastle-upon-Tyne after the Saturday night performance and spent the Sunday at Rivernook. He died that evening.

We had been very close for the last two years of his life. One of his best jobs of translation had been done on a novel by Hjalmar Bergman called *Granny and Her God* (for some reason the English publisher changed the title to *Thy Rod and Thy Staff*). The book got a first rate review in *The Times Literary Supplement*, the reviewer writing that, amongst other things, he could best describe the remarkable quality of the portrait of Granny by saying that she would provide a splendid part for Edith Evans. When I read this, down at Rivernook, I said to my father, "All right. Let's dramatize it. Let's write the part for Edith Evans."

23. Tomorrow to Fresh Woods

So we became collaborators. The book tells the life story of a masterful peasant girl (who rises roughshod to the top of the pile) from the age of fifteen to eighty. My great contribution was to see that the essence of the story could be compressed into the day of her eightieth birthday. My father supervised the dialogue, the quality of which had been first rate in his translation of the novel. When we sent the finished work to the author's widow for approval she immediately replied that she did not want to change one word, and that she would like to buy the Scandinavian and German performing rights. We settled, rather foolishly, for an outright sale for seventy-five pounds. The play has been successfully performed all over Scandinavia, in Berlin, and in Vienna.

I have never succeeded in getting a production in England or America. Edith Evans was in her period of rejuvenation in England (she played Rosalind in *As You Like It* at the age of forty-two at about this time) and was not interested in playing an ugly old matriarch. Dame May Whitty said she would play the part and then changed her mind. In America, Aline MacMahon has shown interest, but was unable to convince her producers. I have now given up hope. It is a difficult play about old and middle-aged people with no sex in it. But Granny is a great part for a great character actress.

(I have enjoyed writing a number of plays, none of which have been produced. The truth is, once they are written, I lose interest and lack that pertinacity in face of initial rejection which is necessary to secure production. Heaven knows, the world has been denied no masterpiece; but some of them are certainly better than many a venture that reaches the West End or Broadway with disaster written all over it before a line has been rehearsed).

Vera Balser-Eberle, Hedwig Bleibtreu, Maria Mayer and Helmuth Krauss in the world premiere of *Großmutter und der liebe Gott* **at the Burgtheater, Vienna, April 10, 1940. Translation by Heinrich Goebel of the play by Claude and Alan Napier based on the novel** *Farmor och vår Herre* **by Hjalmar Bergman. Courtesy Österreichisches Theatermuseum, Vienna.**

None of Alan's plays survive, unfortunately. I have tried to track down Granny and Her God *without success. The Swedish translation (by Stina Berman, the author's widow and a successful writer herself), can be found at the Götesborgs Stadmuseum in Sweden, but there is no trace of Claude and Alan's original English manuscript.*

The play was actually first performed in German, with its world premiere taking place in Vienna in 1940. This was followed by a Swedish premiere at the Götesborg City Theatre later in the year. It was revived in Götesborg in 1964. Alan doesn't mention it, so he may never have known that in 1956, his play was adapted for Swedish radio by Stina Bergman, in a production overseen by film director Ingmar Bergman.

Rivernook had its own quiet beauty at any time of the year. The great poplars across the backwater, the weeping willow at the water's edge, the majestic swans cruising protectively around their nesting place, the splash of oars and the green sheen of the river were very conducive to relaxed and quiet meditation. I loved working there with my father, earning his pleasure at a good idea, receiving words of wisdom from him about the problems of my life. When I complained bitterly about Nan not living up to her promises at either of the times I took her back into the fold I remember him saying "promises extracted under duress can never be counted on; and certainly not to change anyone's nature." He always liked Nan and could understand why I valued her so much as a companion. Indeed the last time I was ever close to her was on the final Sunday of his life. When we arrived in the morning he greeted her from his bed.

"I'm sorry not to be a better host. This is one of my bad days. But it's nice of you to come down. Betty, give Nan a drink."

I was glad that he was not cooped up in a hospital bed at the end, but looking out on his little garden in full summer bloom, out over the quiet backwater to the tall poplars shimmering in the evening breeze.

For the last two years John Justin had been seriously preparing for a career as an actor at the R.A.D.A. I met him for lunch one Saturday and somehow the conversation turned to Martin Harvey.

"That old ham!" he said.

"Have you ever seen him?"

"Good God, no."

"You're going to see him this afternoon. I happened to notice in the paper this morning that he's at the King's Theatre, Hammersmith, on a farewell tour..."

"Another?"

"Yes, another. He's playing *The Burgomaster of Stilemonde*. And you're coming with me if I have to drag you by the scruff of the neck!"

Many years before, I had seen Martin Harvey in *The Burgomaster of Stilemonde* during one of his infrequent visits to the West End. I left the theatre still dissolved in tears and so profoundly moved that I had difficulty in collecting my faculties. Somehow I got home, knowing that I had seen greatness on the stage and uplifted by the experience.

Some years later, George Thirlwell (an outrageous character but a most entertaining companion), who had been on many tours with Martin Harvey, asked me if I would like to go down to Southend and meet him. George, who was very fond of the old man, wanted to congratulate him on his recently conferred knighthood. He would be playing *The Only Way* that night. (*The Only Way* was an adaptation of Charles Dickens' A Tale of Two Cities *that Harvey had been playing since 1899.)* I was in two minds. *The Only Way* had become such a joke amongst smart young actors—they all did an imitation of Martin Harvey's final speech, "It is a far, far better thing that now I do …"—and I did not want to stain my memory of his performance in *The Burgomaster*. But his career had been so remarkable (encompassing a triumph in New York, in *Oedipus* [in 1923] and, in London, an incomparable *Hamlet* [in 1904] in addition to the staple repertoire he played on tour) that I felt I must seize this chance to meet him. So down to the Theatre Royal at Southend—or was it Hastings?—George and I went.

I need not have feared that seeing *The Only Way* might tarnish my memory of *The Burgomaster*. Martin Harvey's magic was just as powerful in Dickens' melodrama as in Maeterlink's tragedy. The impression of naturalness, the sly touches of comedy, the extraordinary beauty of thought and voice, the magnetism and power to convince—all were at work. When the end came, with the noble face in profile, the guillotine in silhouette behind him, and the matchless voice with its orchestrated rhythms speaking the words "it is a far far better thing …" it took your heart out of your breast.

We went back to his rooms after the show. He was careful with his money and always stayed in the number one theatrical lodgings of the towns in which he played rather than a hotel. It was a very cozy evening. Lady Martin Harvey had at last given up the ingénue roles in his repertoire and was at home in their country mansion. It was his complete loyalty to her that had kept him out of The West End. With a limited power of attraction and a talent in no way matching her husband's, Miss Nina da Silva for thirty years had been his inevitable leading lady.

George and he reminisced about their days on the road together—missed connections in Canada, drunken stage hands at Derby, the landlady's daughter at Halifax—and I listened and watched and loved every minute. It was a world of actors' theatre we shall never see again, warm and secure and old professional. He was small and old and beautiful and the Gods had brushed him with genius.

So when John said "That old ham!" I felt my hackles rising and I thought, "I'll show you."

The *Burgomaster of Stilemonde* is superficially what we call now a corny melodrama. In World War I, the German invaders driving through Belgium station a regiment on Stilemonde. A German soldier is shot. Reparation is demanded—a life for a life. The incident took place near the Burgomaster's garden, in which he grows the finest grapes, and suspicion falls on old Klaus, his gardener. The Burgomaster knows Klaus is incapable of such an act and, rather than see an innocent man perish, he faces the firing squad himself. But Maeterlink was a poet and he was a Belgian so that the bare bones of the plot are covered by the sinew and muscle of personal involvement and the symbolic significance of self-sacrifice in face of barbarism. Self-sacrifice was Sir John Martin Harvey's forte.

When the curtain went up that afternoon at the King's, Hammersmith, I was appalled at the tatty old scenery and the flat mass of the inartistic lighting. The supporting company at the opening of the play did nothing to allay my fears that the production had fallen way behind the times. Had I made a mistake to bring John with me and risk compromising my memory of a supreme theatrical experience?

Then Martin Harvey entered and I forgot everything else. I was even glad of the brilliant light that bathed the stage, for it illumined that beautiful face, and revealed every indication from the luminous dark eyes that could convey such variety of thought and feeling. At first the beautiful voice was only a sound—no words were clear because he was tasting grapes, and you could taste them with him.

It was not until the end of the second act that I became aware that John was, indeed, there. In the scene on the stage the Burgomaster is talking with old Klaus in his garden, talking about grapes and the times they have seen together; and you know he is coming to an inescapable conclusion. It is a very quiet scene and the impression of golden evening sunlight bathes the garden. Deeply moved, I became aware that an irrelevant noise was disturbing me. John was sobbing. At the end of the play when the Burgomaster goes out to face the firing squad, sobbing became general throughout the theatre.

We went round to see Martin Harvey after the play. He was seventy four years old, in long wool combinations and a faded red silk dressing gown. He was very happy to see us and to know that we had enjoyed the play. He told John that he had some influence with the Worthing Repertory Company … but already the Kordas had approached him about a long-term film contract. However, I'm quite sure he never again spoke of Martin Harvey as "that old ham."

The three greatest actors I have seen in the Theatre are Gerald du Maurier, Martin Harvey and Laurence Olivier. Du Maurier excelled in the lightness of touch, magnetism and charm of his work; Martin Harvey in the sheer beauty of his communication of emotion; and Olivier in his moments of imaginative revelation and his compelling power. All had in abundance that unwavering authority that rivets one's attention and fills one's soul with utter and unquestioning devotion. *Alan's admiration for talent was not limited to these star players, however. For example, after seeing Reginald Tate's performance as Stanhope in the 1934 revival of* Journey's End *(a role which had been created by Olivier and popularized by Colin Clive), he made a visit backstage and followed it up with a note the next day: "Dear Reggie Tate. I hope you've forgiven me for coming to see you last night with the tears rolling down my face! I don't know when I have been so moved by a performance as I was by yours. As I said it didn't seem like a performance at all. Yours, Alan Napier."*

* * *

The idea of making a clean break, of starting again in a new country, came gradually. I think the spark that started it was a sudden call I received at the end of the run of *No Sky So Blue*—it was not a very long run—from an agent I had never heard of asking if I would be ready to go to Hollywood for a movie in five days. I had had very little dealing with agents—all my work in the theatre had come to me unsought, direct from the producers—and I imagined that this was a firm offer. I immediately went out and ordered what I imagined to be a Hollywood light-weight suit. (Because of my height my clothes always have to be made to measure.) *Ruggles of Red Gap* was the name of the film in question and I imagine the part I was being considered for was the English aristocrat by whom Ruggles was employed before he took service in America. Roland Young in fact played the part in his own inimitable way. I suppose Charles Laughton must have talked about me to the producer and stimulated enough interest to initiate inquiries as to my availability. The salary quoted by the agent seemed to me astronomical. In any case it came to nothing and I had a new light-weight suit on my hands.

But the idea that I had nearly been on my way to Hollywood made me realize that there was another market for English actors in the land of perpetual sunshine. And I remembered with what enthusiasm Mary Grey had spoken of the climate and her happy time in

Hollywood with Jim. That was a positive inducement. There were also negative inducements. Far from rising on the West End ladder, I was actually going down. The last well-paid job that had come my way was in *Sweet Aloes*, a supporting role of an elderly peer. I knew I could make a living that way as long as elderly peers were in demand, but this did not present a very inspiring future.

I had not seen so much of the Rankines since I had called off my divorce. I was always welcome; but Muriel would no longer accept Nan. By now they had left the Old Rectory (I imagine Ian had sold it in a desperate effort to retrieve his financial position), and one weekend I went down to visit them at the country house, not far from Bletchingly, which they had rented. There I met Auriol Lee again. In her curiously off-hand but kindly way she told me that she had been to a theatrical party recently where I had become the topic of conversation.

"Alan," she said, "you've got to make a new start somehow. You used to be a boy wonder, but people are getting tired of you."

I did not press her, nor did she elaborate. I just let it sink in. It hurt. But I knew Auriol was a wise old bird.

Then I got another job. Nancy Price, who had employed me in *The Witch*, did a production of *The Shoemaker's Holiday* at the Playhouse and asked me to play the King—not a big part but quite showy. One day I ran into Michael MacOwan and he said:

"I saw you in *The Shoemaker* the other evening." He said no more so I observed, for something to say:

"I thought I was very charming in it."

"Yes," said Michael, "I thought you thought you were very charming." We both laughed. Michael was never one to be bitchy so I knew he was giving me a warning message out of friendship. I thought to myself, "I suppose I'm getting superficial and playing on my charm." I realized that I was leading a very superficial life and did not feel deeply about anything. "Yes, I've got to get out of this mess, this slough of despond, and start a new life." And I thought of a movie I had just finished, in which, for the first time I had felt fairly comfortable and given an effective performance. Perhaps I could make a living in Hollywood.

But that was the summer of 1938 and there were two circumstances that made it quite impossible for me to leave England. One was the Czechoslovakian crisis with the imminent threat of war. The issuing of gas masks and the digging of trenches in Hyde Park (a somewhat futile exercise in face of the anticipated mass bombing) left no doubt that the government considered the threat real. The other circumstance was my sister Molly's nervous breakdown.

She had been living alone for some time in a little house on the outskirts of the Sussex village of Henfield. I had no very clear idea of how she occupied her time there. She had always been "the cat that walks by itself" and my own life was so full of unresolved problems that I had little capacity to concern myself with the problems of others.

My aunt Cecily Debenham was driving through Henfield one day and decided to call on her niece. She found Molly in a very weak state physically and behaving in what seemed to be an irrational way. Aunt Cecily prevailed on her, then and there, to come with her to Moor Lane House at Affpuddle in Dorset, which had been the Debenham's country house for many years.

My cousin Gilbert Debenham was a rising young psychiatrist at this time and was therefore in a position to put me on to the best man in the field of psychological disturbances.

It was found that Molly was in a manic-depressive condition. The nursing home for neurasthenics to which she went from Moor Lane House was unwilling to go on treating her since her refusal to eat, and the suicidal intent that it indicated, required stricter supervision than the institution supplied. She was moved to a small, private nursing home (she now refers to this period as "when I was in prison"), under strict supervision, where she could receive such aid as psychotherapy then had to offer. Eventually she made a miraculous recovery.

While I was making these difficult decisions about my sister, the tension over Czechoslovakia was relaxed by Neville Chamberlain's dramatic encounters with Hitler. When he finally returned from Munich with a piece of paper promising peace in our time I, like millions of other Englishmen, believed that promise. Hindsight shows that we were credulous, but at the time, belief in our deliverance from the threat of war was almost universal. Free at last from the patriotic obligation to stand by my country in time of need, I laid my plans to start a new life in America.

While the arrangements for my departure were proceeding I was offered a final engagement to round out my career in the English theatre. I was asked to play Sir Francis Chesney in a special Christmas production of *Charley's Aunt* at the Haymarket Theatre. The production was to be in the classic tradition of farce, with Amy Brandon Thomas, the daughter of the playwright, directing.

Oddly enough I had never seen *Charley's Aunt* and when I read the script I was appalled. How could anyone laugh at such imbecile, old-fashioned nonsense! I was even more appalled when, at an early rehearsal, Miss Brandon Thomas said to me:

"Mr. Napier, on that line you will find that it will augment the laugh if you walk upstage three steps, turn and come down again."

I was staggered. It had not occurred to me that the line would conceivably get a laugh in the first place, and, if it did, why on earth should walking upstage and down again augment it? Solemnly I performed this rite at every rehearsal thinking, "Ah well. It doesn't matter if I make a fool of myself. I shall soon be in America."

The production had been meticulously plotted like a plan of battle rather than rehearsed like a play and I faced the first night with grave misgivings. However as I stood in the wings waiting for my first entrance I was happy to hear gales of laughter coming from the audience. I entered. Gales of laughter were soon coming my way. And when I went through my prescribed routine, my word, how it did augment the laugh!

Charley's Aunt was a glorious farewell to the London theatre. My old friend Richard Goolden was playing the lead and he played her to the hilt. At the breakfast scene the laughter was so overwhelming and continuous that one could carry on long conversations while waiting for it to subside sufficiently for the next sally to be heard. This idiot concoction of genius remains the funniest play ever written.

The secret, of course, lies in the continuous invention of crazy situations. People laugh far more heartily at predicament than at funny lines. *Charley's Aunt* is unsinkable just so long as the actors play together, keep the pace going, and don't try to be funny. The only time the play has really failed was when an all-star cast of stand-up comedians performed it for American television. Each comedian took his time trying to be funnier than the next and the play lay down and died.

24

Filling Quotas

James Bigwood

When Alan looked over the first draft of my *Films in Review* profile, one of his notes picked up on my somewhat glib characterization of his British film career. In the article, I had observed that, aside from his unsuccessful shot at the role of Henry Higgins in *Pygmalion*, "Alan's British movie career consisted of minor roles in minor films...." His margin scribble was emphatic: "They were *not* minor roles!" The published article eliminated the first "minor" and everybody was happy. Until...

Several issues of *FIR* later, there was a letter to the editor from the iconic film historian William K. Everson, which read in part: "I think James Bigwood's dismissal of Alan Napier's entire British film career as consisting of 'minor films most of which were not released outside of Britain' is an unfair generalization which suggests that he has not seen any of them." He was right of course. I hadn't. In those pre–VCR days, even the most avid of 16mm film collectors didn't have Bill Everson's resources when it came to obscure British titles. Alan himself hadn't seen them since they had first been released, if then.

In England, as he has noted, Alan was primarily a stage actor. And with the exception of his struggles with Basil Dean on *Loyalties*, he doesn't have much to say about his British film output, which averaged less than a title a year from 1930 to 1939. Paradoxically, this may well have worked to his advantage.

The 1930s were the heyday of Britain's infamous "Quota Quickies." In an attempt to bolster the anemic local film industry, the Cinematograph Films Act of 1927 had been introduced to insure that an increasing percentage of films shown in English theaters (5 percent in 1928; 20 percent by 1937) were of British origin. The unintended result of this legislation was an endless string of low-end films (often funded by newly created British divisions of the American studios) that were dumped on the market in compliance with the letter of the law. Sometimes deliberately, sometimes not, these films cleared the way for the unfettered release of the glossier, more popular American imports. Not all the Quickies were bad, certainly, but at an average budget of £1 per edited foot of film, and an average length of between 7,000 and 8,000 feet (short enough to comfortably fill out the lower half of a double bill), they definitely started out at a distinct disadvantage.

Alan was smart enough to pick his film roles carefully, although he would certainly have credited his "benevolent deity" for the choices he was offered. The majority of his eight British films were, by strict definition, Quota Quickies, but, as a successful West End actor, he was not forced to accept everything that came his way. As a result, unlike many of his colleagues, who might chalk up as many as six or seven credits a year, he was able to limit his output and was seen in some of the better films to emerge from the quota system (although he did not escape the occasional dud). Several of his films were actually released as first-run features in the UK, although, despite Everson's protestations, most of them did not have significant distribution in the U.S.

Alan made his first film, *Caste*, in 1930. Although he has made much of Carol Reed's involvement in *Loyalties*, still three years in the future, it is interesting that he fails to note the participation of another future great of the British film industry, Michael Powell, in his film debut. Powell, years away from his legendary partnership with producer Emeric Pressberger, is only credited with the script for *Caste*, but he actually co-directed as well. As he describes it in his autobiography, *A Life in Movies*, the film was a textbook Quickie, budgeted at £8,000 (about $40,000 at a time when Hollywood B's were budgeted at four times that) for an 80-minute running time (although it was finally released at 70 minutes). Based on an often-revived 1867 play by J.W. Robertson, the screenplay was updated to the First World War. Alan plays Captain Hawtree, the best friend of an upper-class Army officer who has fallen in love with and eventually marries a dancer. Paradoxically, his often lamented height was actually an asset in the role, for Hawtree is referred to as "a long drink of water" by another character, and Alan is given all sorts of physical business ducking through the doorways of the heroine's tiny home. He is even introduced in evening dress with a top hat that makes him look taller than usual. One might be tempted to assume that these specifics were added to the part to capitalize on his height, but in fact the original play contains multiple references to Hawtree's "longness." J.W. Robertson was actually accommodating the well-documented (and much caricatured) height of S.B. Bancroft—later Sir Squire Bancroft—the actor for whom he originally wrote the part. Alan also plays his own age in his film debut, turning in a charming and amusing performance as a man who starts out as a champion of the British class system, and winds up with a distinctly more egalitarian point of view.

Modern viewers of the film will certainly share Michael Powell's delight in the performance of Hermione Baddeley as Polly Eccles, the heroine's outspoken sister, but will be equally confused by the director's characterization of his Captain Hawtree: "The immensely tall Alan Napier (who played [the] languid friend) strolled through his part, as he was to stroll through his life, with complete detachment." Powell never expands on the comment and Alan never mentions Powell, so this cryptic encapsulation of his life remains a mystery.

Caste was followed in 1931 by *Stamboul*, also based on a play, in this case a 1912 French drama by Pierre Frondaie called *L'Homme Qui Assassina* (The Man Who Murdered). The play had been filmed in Germany the previous year in two versions—German and French—under the direction of Kurt Bernhardt. Paramount-British acquired the rights to adapt and reshoot the original German screenplay in two additional languages: English and Spanish. The production was more lavish than the run of the mill Quota Quickie, perhaps due to the economies of shooting two features simultaneously, although reports that the English version was shot during the day while the Spanish version filmed the same material at night seem unlikely, since Dimitri Buchowetski is credited as director on both versions (with Fernando Gomis as his co-director on the Spanish) and Rosita Moreno plays the female lead in both languages. The story, set in 1912 Constantinople, concerns a sadistic baron who terrorizes his wife in order to force a divorce which will allow him to keep custody of their son. He is thwarted by a French officer, recently arrived in Stamboul, who kills the baron after accidentally witnessing him and his mistress forcing the wife to sign a false admission of adultery. Alan was cast as Bouchier, the French ambassador, and shared most of his scenes with Abraham Sofaer, making his film debut as Mahmed Pasha, the head of the Stamboul police force. Paramount-British executive Reginald Denham, who wrote the English adaptation, offered the script to the recently screen-tested Charles Laughton. The actor was interested in joining the cast until he discovered that he was being considered for the role of the brutal baron rather than the noble murderer. In his autobiography, *Stars in My Hair*, Denham recalls that Laughton "shouted, stormed, and raved at me, screamed abuse at the Almighty and kicked the furniture. Finally, when he had worn himself out, he threw himself across the desk sobbing wildly." The sadistic husband was eventually played by Henry Hewitt. Had Laughton played the part, it would have been his first major screen role, and the fate of the project might well have been different. Denham recalls the finished film as "a disaster," and, since *Stamboul* is the only one of Alan's 86 feature films which appears to be lost, we will probably never be able to confirm or refute his opinion.

Alan has already touched on his next film project, *In a Monastery Garden*, probably the worst of his English films. Reasonably believable as an Italian count and father of the

Abraham Sofaer, Alan Napier and Warwick Ward in *Stamboul* (Paramount British, 1931). Courtesy Jennifer Nichols.

painfully mannered Joan Maude, five years his junior, his relaxed performance stands in direct contrast to the remainder of the cast. The script, an original this time, is contrived beyond belief, pitting two composer brothers against each other for the favors of a girl who is already promised by her father to an Army officer. The officer, in turn, is eventually murdered by his dancer mistress, and one of the brothers is convicted of the crime. Upon his release from prison, he takes monastic orders (hence the title of the film), only to be cleared of the crime when the dancer offers a dying confession after collapsing during a ballet performance. The lofty pretentions of the script are further hampered by severe budget limitations, with the cramped fatal ballet being performed before a stock footage audience (with the same succession of cutaway shots used twice) and a climactic symphonic concert taking place off-screen. And amazingly, in one close-up of the normally smooth-tongued Count, Alan's stammer is quite evident, there apparently having been no time or money for additional takes.

Fortunately, his next project was the 1933 *Loyalties*, with its strong script and the star power of Basil Rathbone. No Quota Quickie, the film had a significant release in the United States a year later, prompting the following from the New York *Times*: "A sensitive and engrossing film transcription of John Galsworthy's play, 'Loyalties,' has come to the screen.... Skillfully directed by Basil Dean and possessed of an exceptionally fine British cast, the drama must be rated one of the best that has come from England's studios."

Also in 1933, Herbert Wilcox's film adaptation of *Bitter Sweet* was released, starring Anna Neagle in the role created on stage by Peggy Wood. While the original musical opens in the present and flashes back to the 1880s with a brief pause in the 1890s before returning to 1929, the movie returns directly to 1933 from 1880 without the stopover, thus completely eliminating both the character of the Marquis of Shayne, and the delightful proposal scene that made the role such a pleasure for Alan to play. In spite of this, a number of internet websites, probably taking their cue from the British Film Institute film database, have listed *Bitter Sweet* among Alan's movie credits. This is improbable, first because Alan doesn't mention filming one of his favorite stage roles, and second, because there is a matched close-up connecting Anna Neagle's youthful face in 1880 to her aged face in 1933 that makes it likely that the plan was always to skip over the intervening years. Alan is certainly not visible in any current prints of *Bitter Sweet*, but the tantalizing possibility presumably exists that the 1890 material was shot and cut, either before the original release of the film or sometime since, and sits in an archive somewhere. What *does* exist, remarkably, is footage of Alan playing Lord Shayne *on stage*. In 1929, British Pathé filmed a significant portion of the show, although without sound. From a single static position at the front of the first balcony of His Majesty's Theatre, the newsreel camera covers the entire width of the proscenium and never moves closer, making the actors' features hard to discern, but allowing Alan's unmistakable height to stand out.

Another dubious credit, also traceable to the BFI, comes from the same year. In the database, Alan is listed as playing an unnamed knight in *The Wandering Jew*, the second filming of E. Temple Thurston's play about a Jew doomed to eternally wander the earth as punishment for a slight to Jesus Christ. Watching this unbearably creaky piece today, it is hard not to hope, for Alan's sake, that the credit is an error. Certainly he is nowhere to be found in currently available prints.

It was three years before Alan would appear on screen again. The film was *Wings over*

Africa, a diamond smuggling yarn which incorporated documentary footage of Africa in a less than successful attempt to disguise its studio-bound origins. Despite this, the film was quite well received and obtained some respectable bookings in the UK (as well as an American release three years later by Merit Pictures). A villain in this one, Alan is Redfern, a disgraced doctor. Playing his own age, he appears quite at home in jungle khaki, a look he would return to more than once in the years to come.

Alan's next film, *For Valour* (1937), starred the British comedy duo of Tom Walls and Ralph Lynn. They were first teamed in the mid-twenties, appearing in a series of West End successes known collectively as the Aldwych Farces, named for the theater where they played to enthusiastic audiences for a year at a time. Written primarily by Ben Travers, the plays featured, in addition to Walls and Lynn, a recurring cast of talented supporting players who would eventually become successful on their own. In 1930, Tom Walls started shooting film adaptations of the plays, which proved so popular that once the backlog was exhausted, Travers had to start writing scripts directly for the screen. Walls was not a naturally cinematic director (his earliest efforts were no more than filmed stageplays, even finishing with a final curtain call from the cast), but by 1937 his technique had matured, no doubt aided by scripts that had never been framed by the Aldwych proscenium. *For Valour*, although written by Travers and directed by Walls, eschewed the familiar supporting cast and replaced the farce with gentler, more sophisticated comedy. Perhaps for this reason, and despite the fact that the team of Walls and Lynn were named among the top ten most popular British performers in England in a 1937 exhibitors' poll, *For Valour* proved to be their final collaboration. They certainly went out with a bang. With the help of some very well-executed process work, both Walls and Lynn play dual roles; Walls as his own father, Lynn as his own grandfather. Alan, however, appears in only one scene in the film. As an unnamed, deskbound, Boer War general, he sets the plot in motion by revealing the Walls character's criminal past and denying him the medal requested by his commanding officer (Lynn), whose life he has just saved. Alan is perfectly believable, but equally unmemorable, in the tiny role.

In *The Wife of General Ling* (1937), his part is much larger. Fourth billed, as the British Governor of Hong Kong, Alan presides over a mind-boggling compendium of Oriental stereotypes in a fevered story of Chinese warlords and gun-smugglers. Amusingly, the film allowed him yet another opportunity to cross paths with a future giant of the British film industry, although it is possible that, given the speed of filming and their positions on the production, they never actually met. The film's editor, David Lean, had been cutting Quota Quickies since 1930 and was only a year away from his big budget editorial breakthrough with *Pygmalion* and five years away from his directorial debut on Noël Coward's *In Which We Serve* when he edited *The Wife of General Ling*.

On *The Four Just Men* (1939), Alan's last British film, he finally collaborated with a British film giant whose career was not in its ascendancy, but emphatically in the present. Michael Balcon, the producer of many of Alfred Hitchcock's greatest British successes, was the man behind this adaptation of Edgar Wallace's 1905 novel, a deeply disturbing book whose titular heroes are a group of private citizens who take the law into their own hands, murdering anybody whose politics or morals they disagree with. The movie mitigates the premise to some extent by updating the novel and making the sole target of these "Just Men" a member of Parliament who is secretly an agent of Hitler, although in the still iso-

Alan as Sir Hamar Ryman in *The Four Just Men* (Ealing, 1939). Collection of James Bigwood.

lationist United States, the 1940 release of the film (under the title *The Secret Four*) earned an admonishment from *New York Times* critic B.R. Crisler: "Like all pictures seeping over from England nowadays, it is more than a little infected with the virus propagandistus." Alan is Sir Hamar Ryman, the villain of the piece, one minute affably eccentric, the next suavely evil. The character in the original novel, written as more misguided than evil, is said to have been based on Joseph Chamberlain so, either by coincidence or by design, Alan Napier found himself playing a fictionalized version of his own great uncle.

The Four Just Men ended Alan's British movie career on a high note. Although not in the same league as Balcon's Hitchcock pictures, it was a prestige project, not a Quota Quickie, and one with significant American input, in the person of the Myron Selznick Agency, whose London office was involved in the casting process. Alan Napier was ready to make his move to Hollywood.

25

Crossing the Pond

In my career as an actor in England I took part in no momentous theatrical revolution because that is not the way things happen in England. Evolution is the English way and that, I think, goes on all the time. What persists is a high regard for professionalism. (Watching a young Hollywood film starlet attempting a role made famous in England years before by Meggie Albanesi, Dame May Whitty turned to Aubrey Smith and said, "My dear, she doesn't even know what she doesn't know!")

I started in London with *The Cherry Orchard*, which introduced a whole new type of theater to the English speaking world and I finished with *Charley's Aunt*, gloriously old-fashioned farce. In between I played Shakespeare, Shaw, Ibsen, Strindberg, operetta, musical comedy, tea-cup comedy, adventure thriller, sentimental sob-stuff, high drama, low comedy, and romance. The general standard of acting and production was superbly polished. The objective was to entertain and to make a profit. Because the London Theatre provided a wide range of entertainment, and still does, London is now the entertainment capital of the world.

I am proud to have been almost continuously employed for ten years in that never-ending source of entertainment, the West End, where plays were put on by professional producers and directed by professional directors with a singular absence of hysteria. Because everyone concerned knew what he was doing, rewriting and recasting at the last minute were practically unheard of. Most of the plays in which I appeared opened cold in London. One did not make a fortune but one made a steady livelihood and one was constantly practicing and polishing one's craft.

So-called "gut acting" had no place in the London theater of that period. Good acting came from imagining the most revealing truth for each moment of your performance. This revelation of truth might come during study of your role or during rehearsal—it could be triggered in reaction to another actor's moment of truth—but when it came, the good actor would, so to speak, photograph it, fix it, and thence forward produce a perfect print of it at every performance. A good performance would be a succession of perfect prints. A great performance would be a succession of perfect prints taken from superior negatives—that is to say negatives of moments imagined with a more arrestingly penetrating vision.

I do not believe that Martin Harvey, who could hold an entire theater in his hand and leave the audience racked with emotion, had to experience any emotion at all during a performance. What he did, for thousands upon thousands of performances, with extreme delicacy and power, supported by perfect control over voice and face, was to reproduce in crystal-clear focus, images long ago composed with the eye of a master. I'm sure he was often able to count the house or plan what he was to have for supper while the attention of the audience was on the supporting players.

I remember going round to see Jean Cadell, after being intensely moved by her performance as an old nanny in some play, and saying, "That moment when you burst into tears…" She cut in, "I put my handkerchief to my nose and you thought I had burst into tears. If I had really been crying you would not have heard what I said."

Gut acting may well have a place before the camera where conditions of work are entirely different. In theater long rehearsal hopefully prepares one, in a cooperative activity, for hundreds of repetitions of performance under identically favorable conditions. In movie acting only one performance need be captured, often under unfavorable conditions—on horseback, in a torrential storm or hanging from a cliff—and the camera pries much closer to your face. In close-up you are not really acting and reacting to another player, you are exhibiting your face for perusal. If tears are required, the make-up man will supply them. If you can supply them yourself, fine—the words can be dubbed in later if they should be inaudible or sound revoltingly sniveling in the take.

In both media the objective is the same, the revelation of truth. In theater you must achieve this on your own to a congregation of people again and again and again. In movies, with the help of the camera, you must achieve this once, and let the film editor select what is best and leave the rest on the cutting-room floor. Some people are good at instant acting—they are naturals for the movies. But instant acting, like instant coffee, often lacks the depth of flavor, the aroma, of the real thing.

* * *

So finally, on April 18, 1939, having sold whatever I possessed that Nan could not use (and that was very little) I set out in my car with a trunk full of clothes and the leather-bound Shakespeare and Milton I had won as prizes at Clifton, heading for the abode in Surrey which Nan was sharing with her lady friend. It was a beautiful spring day with young green leaves bursting forth on the trees, daffodils nodding in the gardens and old dogs lying out in the sun at cottage doorways.

It was not a day that made leaving England easy. Uprootings are always difficult for me and this was total. I had no job to go to, not much money, and no one in particular to welcome me on my arrival. I felt alone and afraid as I faced my new life. Though I was thirty-six years old with a solid reputation as an actor, in my heart I still lacked the confidence of a grown man.

Part Three

America

26

From Sea to Shining Sea

My arrival in New York, on a cold wet morning, was cheered by two unexpected happenings. One was the delightfully human and unstuffy behavior of the customs official who cleared my luggage, when he saw my name on the label.

"Napier, eh? I once had a lotta trouble with a guy called Napier. Invented logarithms, didn't he? Any kin of yours?"

"Yes, actually. He was my great, great, great, great grandfather."

"Well, is that so? Proud to meet you," and he shook my hand. Then, with a kindly twinkle in his eye added, "I certainly don't want any more trouble … so … here you go!" And he stamped all my luggage without more ado.

"Thank you."

"You're welcome and good luck to you."

If this was typical of America, I liked it. Such geniality from an English customs official was unthinkable, let alone such esoteric knowledge.

Very soon after my arrival I re-established contact with Jack Houseman. Our old habit of corresponding had ceased after he became embroiled in the supervision of the W.P.A. theatre project in Harlem with Orson Welles, followed by their Mercury Theatre season. Jack was now involved with Orson (and therefore hectically) on the Campbell's radio program.

"Come to breakfast." Jack said, "Come at once—I'm busy all day."

I had a quick breakfast and took a taxi to his apartment where I found him, surrounded with manuscripts, in bed. We poured out questions and answers. I followed him as he got into his bath. The bell rang.

"That'll be Annie. Let her in."

I opened the door to a tall, slender blonde with the liveliest blue eyes set in a beautifully chiseled little face. She was looking harassed. Before we had time to exchange a word Jack shouted from the bath.

"You're late, Annie! Go get me some breakfast! Coffee and two doughnuts."

"Oh, Houseman!" And with a sigh and a grimace she dropped more manuscripts on his bed and was gone.

The pace of New York was not really congenial to me. Some people it stimulates; me it quells. I began to think of California. I would buy a second-hand car and make a voyage of exploration across the United States.

I had a delightful evening in New York before I set out on my journey, when Jack asked me to dinner to meet Orson Welles. I have no recollection of what we talked about. Orson's mood was gentle, quiet, and full of charm, but the emanation of power and assurance coming from this young man of twenty-three impressed me deeply. The image of a beautiful young bull, a modern Minotaur comes back to me. The day was to come when the bull would shake his horns at me.

I bought a great old Buick Straight 8 convertible for my trip across America. I was enraptured by its size and power, never having owned anything larger than a small Austin in England. I was to discover in time that I had been cheated. For one thing it had been rebuilt and for some mysterious reason the exhaust pipe passed directly under the driver's seat, frying me daily until an ingenious mechanic in Amarillo, Texas devised a remedy. Also, it had a cracked cylinder head; just a teeny-weeny crack, but enough to make frequent stops for oil and water inevitable. But it never failed all the way to Los Angeles—though I suspect there was as much water in the crankcase as oil. Raising the top required immense concentration and energy and, in an adverse wind, herculean strength. It was dark crimson with bright red lines of longitudinal trim. High on my hot-seat I felt king of the road in it, and to me it was worth every penny I paid for it.

I don't remember much of the start of my trip south, except that it was so unendurably hot in Washington that I determined to press on without doing any sight-seeing. I gave a young man a ride down to the outskirts of Richmond where he pressed me to turn off the main road to his home. There he would give me a glass of "the best buttermilk in the U.S.A." He had been anticipating this miraculous thirst-quencher all the way from Washington, so, as an aspect of rural Americana, I went along with him. I had never drunk buttermilk. I hated it. In Richmond I spent the night at a "tourist home," for motels had not yet spread to the East Coast.

In New Orleans I had an interesting evening with a professor of Tulane University, who amazed me with the information that the United States had a very exact class structure based on income. I dined at Antoine's, discovered the Sazarac cocktail, tried to swim in Lake Pontchartrain (only to be devoured by mosquitoes) and went on my way, West by North. At Shreveport I was sold a defective second-hand tire that let me down five miles out of town, and in the dust bowl of Texas I discovered the oddity of local prohibition.

I arrived at a little town after a long, torrid morning, exhausted and dehydrated. I drew up at a hotel. I had discovered bourbon in New Orleans and the idea of a tall highball had become obsessive. In the coffee shop I slumped down at the counter and ordered one. The girl looked at me reprovingly.

"We don't serve liquor here. You'll have to get a prescription."

"A prescription? I'm not ill—I just want a drink."

"I said I can't serve you. The drugstore's across the lobby."

In the drugstore, the clerk asked what he could do for me. I said I wanted a bourbon highball.

"You'll have to get a prescription from the Doc." And he indicated a seedy-looking little man in a bedraggled white coat sitting behind a desk.

"I want a highball."

"Yes. What brand?"

"Oh ... Four Roses."

"A fifth?"

"I just want a drink."

"You'd better take a fifth."

"You mean I have to buy a whole bottle?"

"I don't prescribe for less. What's your name?"

I took a fifth. I think the prescription cost 25¢, the bottle $3.50. Across the lobby in the coffee shop I surreptitiously poured a generous slug into my glass of water.

Pushing on to Amarillo in the afternoon was a nightmare. For some time I had realized that I was being fried by the motor's exhaust but had been told that nothing could be done about it. The wind was whipping the flat, featureless landscape into little miniature tornadoes of whirling red dust. From time to time I would pause to slake my dusty throat with a pull at the bottle of Four Roses. When I reached Amarillo, I was desperate and a trifle drunk. What led me to a laconic little German mechanic on the far side of town, whose shabby shop said "Auto Repairing—Nothing Too Difficult," I don't remember. I explained my predicament. He burrowed under the seats.

"No problem," he said.

"What will you do?"

"Asbestos."

"How much?"

"Nine, ten dollars."

"Can I have the car tomorrow?"

"Vot time?"

"Early as you can make it."

"Nine, ten o'clock."

"Okay."

I took a taxi to a hotel and had a terrible night. My English ignorance led me to open my bedroom window—it simply wasn't done to sleep with the window closed. In those days traffic control at intersections in Amarillo was effected by railroad type signals that popped up and down. As the arm of the signal rose or fell a bell would ring. My hotel overlooked two intersections. Later I wrote a poem, "The Bells of Amarillo"; the last couplet went:

> Sleepless on my burning pillow
> I loathe the bells of Amarillo.

In fact my pillow was covered with a quarter of an inch of red dust when I woke up, somewhat hung over, next morning.

From Amarillo on, shielded by asbestos, my long hours at the wheel were infinitely more enjoyable. I gave an ex-con hitchhiker a ride and was fascinated by him and his conversation, much of which I could not understand. For that matter, he was fascinated by me and similarly baffled by my English accent. We parted affably—it had been a pleasure.

Then, on a long, straight stretch in New Mexico (I guess I was now on the old Route 66), I devised an ingenious way of stretching my long legs. The car—I think its vintage was about 1930—had a hand accelerator on the steering wheel and I found that, by setting the accelerator for a modest 40 miles an hour, I could sit in the back seat and steer with my bare feet. You could see ten miles ahead and nary a car in sight. It's not the sort of thing I'd recommend today—indeed, after one rather anxious pedipulation as a farm truck came towards me (I could see the driver's sudden look of unbelief and terror), I abandoned it.

In Gallup, New Mexico, I had a delightful encounter in a coffee shop at breakfast. I became fascinated by the story of a very lively young woman sitting at the counter. She was apparently "commodore" of a fleet of private cars illegally transporting a group of passengers across America—illegally, because they were not licensed. This was a minor racket of the times. The Greyhound bus people (with whom, of course, they were in competition) had tipped off the Gallup police. The cars had been impounded and the drivers thrown into jail. So this lively lady had taken a case of beer into the jail where she, the cops, and the drivers had made a night of it.

I moved up to the counter as the story developed, entranced by this gloriously un-English happening. When I rose to leave the lively lady came with me.

"Where you going, Slim?"

"Oh, back to my car at the motel."

"Mind if I come with you?"

"No, indeed."

It was Sunday and she made some amusingly irreverent comments on a batch of church-goers. We reached my car.

"Where you going from here?"

"Los Angeles, eventually."

"Mind if I come with you?"

"I'd be delighted."

"You see, my boss is in Hawaii and I'm flat broke. I gotta get back to L.A."

"Fine. Actually, I'd planned to go by way of the Grand Canyon."

"That's okay by me. Crossed the country thirty, forty times but never seen it."

"Well, we must get to know each other. My name's Alan Napier. What's yours?"

"Call me Tex. That's what the boys called me. For me, you're Slim."

I was enraptured. The only thing I did not like about Tex was her voice. She may have been born to command—at any rate, her voice was as strident as a drill sergeant's. And she was a great talker. In time, however, she calmed down and began stroking my arm and making little observations to the effect that she liked my build. We came to an impressive view-point and got out to stretch our legs and, discretely hiding behind rocks, answer the call of nature. When Tex rejoined me by the car she came into my arms automatically and we kissed. As we neared the Grand Canyon all sorts of official signboards began to make one realize that one had to have some sort of plan for the night.

"What are we going to do, Tex? I mean, hotel reservations and all that?"

She left me in no doubt.

"Honey, I'm gonna sleep on your arm tonight."

As soon as we'd had showers it started. Then there was dinner, and back to bed. Finally, we staggered out about lunch time the next day, took one fleeting acrophobic glance at that vast chasm, ate lunch and went on our way. I think we spent the night at Holbrook. We made an early start the next morning with Tex driving. Some minor electrical defect had developed in the car and she had a way of coaxing it along. Somewhere past Needles she knew just the place to have it fixed—she knew every mechanic on the route by name—and for a small charge we were on our way again.

I was immediately enchanted by California. The arid rocky ranges of New Mexico and Arizona left (and still leave) me cold. But here were orange groves scenting the warm air, and bungalows set in neat little gardens ablaze with flowers, instead of the ramshackle two-story frame houses, set in rank grass, that I associated with so much of the country I had passed through.

It was about six o'clock when we got into L.A. By the Union Station, Tex said to pull into the curb.

"This is where I get out."

"It's been awfully nice knowing you."

"We had a great time. Right?"

"I should say so. When shall I see you again?"

"Slim, you're a great guy but, honest, I'm not your sort. You know—you'll be running with all the movie crowd. We've had a party. Let's leave it at that."

She was right. But I did not want to accept the role of superior person. I said,

"Oh, I don't know. Couldn't we…"

"Uh-uh. Tell you what, I'm flat broke till my boss gets back from Hawaii. If you could let me have ten bucks…"

I gave her twenty and we kissed goodbye. She was a good girl. Six weeks later when I was living at the Chateau Marmont, she telephoned me. I had just landed my first movie job and the fact, together with my place of residence, had been announced in a publicity release to the trade papers.

"Tex? Hello! How are you?"

"I'm fine. I just thought I'd say hi and tell you good luck. I'm sure glad you've made it."

"But Tex, where are you? Why don't we meet…"

"I can't hear you. I'm in a bar." There was a kind of scuffling noise and Tex's voice at full strength "Aw, can it, Chuck." Then to me, "So long, Slim. Take it easy."

Before departing, Tex had told me how to get onto Santa Monica Boulevard. I drove on and on, past endless used car lots until at last I saw the Pacific Ocean. Dusk was falling and it seemed to rise, framed by the houses on each side of the street, like a bar of indigo supporting the horizon.

I drove right to the end of the long boulevard, parked on Ocean Avenue, and walked across the narrow green park, shaded by palm and eucalyptus trees, to the cliff's edge. There below me was the pier and the little boat harbor with the rollers breaking in clouds of white spray over the breakwater.

"This is it," I thought, "this is where I want to live." I spent the night in a motel at the corner of Olympic Boulevard and Eighth Street.

27

A Toe in the Door

I had been told, I think by Auriol Lee, that a good place in Hollywood for English actors to stay was the Chateau Marmont; so I soon moved into a small apartment in this noble pile at the east end of the Sunset Strip. But the vision of my first evening in California kept luring me back to the ocean. A mile north of Santa Monica—on the beach halfway between the Coast road and high-water mark—there used to be a ramshackle hot-dog and Coca-Cola stand, with little tables roofed over by a trellis supporting an immense Copa de Oro vine. Its great cups of gold, veined with purple, glowed in the mid-day heat and scented the evening air. Here I would lie, a votive offering to the sun, in a kind of ecstasy until the heat became too much. Then, a quick battle through the raging surf and a lolling rest on the green swelling bosom of the ocean before fighting my way back, tumbled, chilled and breathless, to stretch myself out in ecstasy again.

I grudged the time conscience told me I must devote to the business of trying to get started in movies. While on the beach I felt utterly content; but, back at the Chateau Marmont, I was lonely and a little alarmed at the realization that my small capital was rapidly dwindling.

True, I was lucky in the matter of agents—so indispensable in Hollywood. The last film I had done in England had been cast almost entirely, myself included, through the London office of the great Hollywood Myron Selznick Agency. It was my good fortune that the head of that office, Harry Ham, returned to Hollywood about the time I arrived there. An English actor with a solid reputation held some promise of success, so he took me under his wing and introduced me to his numerous associates in what was then the pre-eminent agency. But the weeks went by and nothing developed. At the time when I arrived in Hollywood no one I knew well was living there; my friends in England had been theater people. True, there was Basil Rathbone. After the filming of *Loyalties*, and especially when he and Ouida, his famous party-giving wife, saw me in *The Lake*, he urged me to look him up if ever I came out to the coast. So I telephoned and was told by the butler that Mr. Rathbone was not at home. I left my number. Nothing happened. I telephoned again. Mr. Rathbone was at dinner and could not be disturbed. I left my number. Again nothing happened.

Then I remembered that some years before I had met Brian Aherne in connection with the founding of British Actors' Equity Association. I did not know him well, but had liked him enormously. Now, I hate to force myself on people, but I was lonely and a little desperate. So, one morning, about eleven o'clock I called him up.

"Hello!" a friendly voice answered. "What are *you* doing here?" I told him.

"Why don't you come to lunch? I think there's a cold lamb or something."

I went, was treated like an old friend, and the cold lamb and mint sauce were delicious.

Brian is one of the kindest, most generous men in the world. Suddenly I was in the Hollywood swim, meeting interesting people, going to parties, enjoying something of the *dolce vita* of Hollywood's golden era.

Brian took me to the Hollywood Bowl. Afterwards, at a party for Pierre Monteux, the conductor, we met Joan Fontaine who Brian soon after married. *(Indeed, according to Fontaine, Alan was actually best man at their wedding.)* He gave a cocktail party for me to meet useful people. As a result of this, Edmund Goulding gave me my first Hollywood job in *We Are Not Alone* starring Paul Muni. It was the name Gerald du Maurier that did the trick. Years before, Eddie had understudied Gerald and when he heard I had played with him, the brotherhood of du Maurier worshippers brought us together. True, I had to go through the formality of doing a test for the part (and my competition was formidable) but I think the result was a foregone conclusion.

At this time Hollywood was divided into a high society of the Right and a high society of the Left. I blew my chances with the Right very early on. Through an encounter at Brian's, I was invited to dinner with the Robert Montgomerys. Now, I had not become adjusted—I never have—to the long cocktail hour (or hours) that precedes the evening meal at Hollywood social functions. One martini so easily leads to another and, if one is not careful, one loses too many inhibitions. When I went to the Montgomerys, I had just been reading Hewlett Johnson's (known as the "Red Dean of Canterbury") book about Russia. I had been very much impressed, for he had added a preface at the crucial moment when Hitler attacked Russia. All other pundits had predicted that the incompetent Russians, under the yoke of their bloody dictator, would collapse in six weeks. The Red Dean predicted otherwise and proved to be right.

So I gave the Montgomerys and their guests a spirited defense of the Red Dean and all those aspects of the Soviet regime he praised. There was no ugly scene chez Montgomery—just an appalled silence followed by small talk. I was not invited again.

As for the Left, I was not in an income bracket to interest them. They wanted your money. George Coulouris had an amusing experience at this period. George, whom I later came to know intimately, was doing very well in Hollywood and had a great talent for picturesque vituperation of the American plutocracy. Intoxicated by the exuberance of his own verbosity he would lambaste one American sacred cow after another, while enjoying to the hilt the material comforts of his sudden affluence. At a party of the Left one evening his host patted him on the back and took him into his den.

"How about joining The Party, George?"

"What do I get out of it?" asked canny George. His host looked pained.

"You don't get anything. You work for the Party by giving. Five percent of your salary. Ten if you like."

That was it. Give away his not so hard-earned money? George never became a member of The Party—though his pungently expressed leftward views, which were quite genuine, were to haunt him when the war was over and Russia again became America's Public Enemy Number One.

Then there was the English Colony. Its days of glory were coming to an end. However, I would meet Aubrey Smith on the cricket field which now bears his name and where, later on, George Colouris, John Buckmaster, Jack Merrivale and I rather shocked the stolid British players with our frivolity. (George would go in to bat singing "Forty Years On" at the top of his voice.) By this time, I had two daughters, both Jennifers (one a step-daughter) who scored inaccurately in the intervals of flirting with John and Jack. Old Aubrey would bear down on them waving his ear trumpet and peer over a Jennifer's shoulder.

"You've got it wrong!" he'd shout. "Partridge was out L.B.W.!" *(L.B.W. stands for "legs before wicket" and is a complicated rule in cricket designed to keep a batter from using his body rather than his bat to prevent the bowler from hitting the wicket.)*

In my early days I saw quite a lot of the Ronald Colmans. Mrs. Colman, one of the loveliest of women, I had known at the R.A.D.A. as Benita Hume. She roped me in to work on Bundles for Britain at their house on Summit Drive. I remember Ronnie being very endearing about the embarrassment of introducing an elderly relative from England—a Miss Balls. "If only she was in the singular, it wouldn't be so bad. But Balls…"

I even attended Ouida Rathbone's celebrated Christmas party for British charities at the Beverly Hills Hotel. Tons of artificial snow were imported and laid down on the slope behind the hotel; a sparkling Christmas scene in the subtropics. We were to drive down to the hotel in sleighs. Jingle-bells, jingle-bells. And then it started raining in the afternoon and all the snow disappeared. I remember poor Basil arriving late and going from table to table saying that Ouida was simply prostrated with grief. There were a lot of mean people simply prostrated with laughter.

The part I played in *We Are Not Alone* for Eddie Goulding was quite small, but the character, a prison chaplain, appeared in various scenes so that it carried a three-week guarantee, and the Myron Selznick Agency was in a position to get me a good salary. For three weeks "work," in which I only went to the studio for five days and spent the rest of the time lying on the beach at Santa Monica, I was paid the equivalent of six month's real work at the Westminster, rehearsing and playing six days a week!

"This is the place for me," I thought as I went straight out and bought an eight cylinder Hudson convertible, sky blue with red leather upholstery. They even gave me $100 trade-in on my old crack-headed Buick.

The only shadow over my happiness came from the fact that the very day we were making a street scene in *We Are Not Alone* depicting the outbreak of World War I, news came over the air of the invasion of Poland by Hitler. In fact, the difficult decision for English actors in Hollywood as to what they should do was soon taken out of their hands. The British Military Attaché in Washington (who happened to be an acquaintance of Brian's, so that I heard it straight from the horse's mouth) flew out to the Coast to tell us that it was the policy of the British Government that the colony of English actors in Hollywood should stay put, since they would be far more valuable to England making pictures for which they were trained, than making war for which they were ill-equipped. And so it proved. Such pictures as *Mrs. Miniver*, *The White Cliffs of Dover*, *Waterloo Bridge* and many more were of tremendous value in helping to swing the isolationist masses of America to support lend-lease and the war against Hitler.

The outbreak of war, however, produced some very strange shenanigans amongst the English colony and its anglophile hangers-on. There were the Hollywood Rough Riders, for instance. I don't know who was responsible for organizing this equestrian unit or of what value their proposed maneuvers in the Hollywood Hills were expected to be. But at a meeting of the equestrian cream of the colony where the project was being debated, George Sanders had his finest hour. On being asked what he thought of the idea, he rose slowly to his feet, tweaked the end of his nose twice and said with measured deliberation,

"The purpose of all this, it seems to me, is to enable a lot of silly shits to whitewash themselves."

To quiet my conscience I took the physical for the U.S. Army and was told that, with my degree of myopia, no army in the world would accept me. Thus, doubly fortified, I rather shamelessly gave myself up to the pleasures of being a bachelor in a town with the most wonderful climate in the world, where money fell from Heaven into the pockets of actors who were "in." For, once the ice was broken, the Myron Selznick office took more interest in me and things began to happen.

John Houseman arrived on the Coast soon after my first movie and with him I met again the "Annie" who had been his secretary. She was now working for Howard Koch at Warners. We became great friends, saw a great deal of each other in the evenings for dinner and on the beach at weekends, where we were often guests at Harry Ham's house at Malibu. I was enchanted by her delicate golden tan and her tremendous commitment to what she believed in. There were certainly no half measures about her liberalism.

Now, during my last years in England G.B.S. had, to say the least, tempered my belief in the efficiency and morality of capitalism as an economic system; but I had been loath to embrace Socialism—all those labor people had such terrible accents! So I settled for the Douglas Social Credit System; I, Ezra Pound and the inhabitants of Alberta, Canada. The last picture I did in England, *Four Just Men*, had a big scene in the House of Commons and Aneurin Bevan was present (at a handsome fee, I'm sure) as technical expert on procedure. *Bevan was a longtime Labour Party Member of Parliament, famous for Winston Churchill's remark during debate on whether to recognize the Communist takeover of China in the person of Mao Zedong: "Just because you recognize somebody does not mean you like him. We all, for example, recognize the Right Honourable Member from Ebbw Vale."* As always in moviemaking there was a lot of boring hanging around so, when I saw Mr. Bevan yawning his head off, I thought I'd get his reaction to Douglas Social Credit.

"It's a juggler's trick with figures. It has nothing to do with flesh and blood," was about all I could get out of him.

I was still trying to avoid taking sides between the Right and the Left, saying that the important thing now was to defeat Nazi dictatorship. But the U.S. was not yet at war and Annie took a dim view of my Cousin Neville's "sell-out" of Czechoslovakia. I remember one night at a well-known Italian restaurant on the Strip, after a couple of martinis, finding myself completely opposed to an ideological position Annie was advocating. Our minestrone was cooling before us and, in the best English-gentlemen tradition, I terminated, as I thought, an awkward conversation by saying, "I'm afraid, Annie, we must agree to differ." Thumping the table, with eyes flashing, Annie screamed,

"I will not agree to differ!"

I was thunder-struck. But Annie liked me, thought I was intelligent but mistaken due to an unfortunately conservative background, and was damn well going to convince me of the rightness of her stand to the Left! I guess she did. After thirty years we are the best of friends and now see eye to eye on everything important.

28

Old Friends and New Experiences

One of the great pleasures of this period was renewing a friendship with John van Druten started many years before at the Old Rectory, Bletchingley. It saddens and amazes me how quickly Johnny seems to have been forgotten, how small his imprint on the theater; for he was tremendously successful in his day, and the author of a considerable volume of distinguished work. From *Young Woodley* in 1928, which started a vogue in plays dealing with school-boy romances, to *The Voice of the Turtle*, which ran three seasons in New York, he produced his own individual brand of comedy-drama; low in key, ironic and completely realistic.

Theater was his passion in life and he disciplined himself to become a superb technician, so that his plays were always beautifully constructed. Perhaps that is why he is, for the time at least, unfashionable and forgotten. Mastery of a difficult craft does not seem to play a part in the making of many of our modern playwrights. Indeed, to call them playwrights is to flatter them—contrivers of stage-happenings would be nearer the mark.

Johnny was also responsible for many skillful and tremendously successful adaptations of other peoples work, dramatizing Isherwood's *Berlin Diary* as *I Am A Camera* [later the basis for the musical *Cabaret*], and Kathryn Forbes' *Mama's Bank Account* as *I Remember Mama*.

When I first came to know him, soon after the successful launching of *Young Woodley*, he asked me to lunch one day at the newly opened Arts Theater Club in London. I think I must have felt very much in the swing sitting at this chic bohemian meeting place with one of the up and coming young dramatists of the day. I remember while I was looking round the room to see, as one does, if anyone "important" was there, Johnny tapped me on the arm and said,

"Do you see that young man standing in the doorway—the one with the bar of black eyebrows across the top of his nose?"

"Yes," I said. "What about him?"

"His name is Laurence Olivier. He has been with the Birmingham Rep. He's going to be important."

I was not impressed; I had been brought up on the Birmingham Rep. "Indeed?" I said and resumed my search for someone really important.

One of Johnny's endearing characteristics was his astonishing memory for all things theatrical. Twenty years later, I remember strolling down a row of grapes at Brian Aherne's ranch near Indio—Johnny had come over from his place in the Coachella Valley—and hearing him spout my lines as Professor Bolland in *Storm*—lines which I had long since forgotten—in an attempt to recall the name of the obscure actress who, twenty-five years before, had played Mrs. Bolland! I really believe he knew the cast and the date of every successful play produced in London between 1922 and the day of his death. And evidently whole sections of dialogue. C.K. Munro, who wrote *At Mrs. Beam's* and *Storm,* had been in many ways his model and his favorite dramatist, for Munro had a unique capacity for finding humor, pathos, and drama in the apparently placid lives of totally unimportant people. What storms their imaginations could brew up in their chipped boarding-house tea cups!

We had many delightful dinners either at Brian's or Johnny's, vehemently discussing the merits of this actor and that play. I remember Brian, as we drove back from Johnny's one night, laughingly commenting on the absurdity of three middle-aged Englishmen, in the midst of a world war of unprecedented magnitude, arguing passionately in the California desert as to whether or not Cecil Parker was a male Marie Tempest! As I happen to be a great admirer of both I evoked the contemptuous scorn of Johnny who had a prejudice of monumental proportions against my adored Marie. He felt that her comedy and Cecil's was too obviously calculated.

* * *

It was also at this period that I began to be an intimate of the very select group of "Poor Little" cognoscenti. The Poor Little, invented by Johnny, was a variant of the improper limerick. The rhythm and rhyme pattern was different and the objective was to achieve an amusing verse less gross than the average dirty limerick. Indeed, ugly words had no part in a proper Poor Little. The impropriety must be decorously implied. The whole thing started one day when Johnny was walking up Finchley Road in the St. John's Wood area of London. He saw on the opposite side of the road an actor with a rather improbable name, Romilly Lunge. For no apparent reason the following verse sprang to life in Johnny's mind.

> Poor Little Romilly Lunge—
> His penis is made out of sponge.
> Just put it in water and watch it expand,
> But it's nothing to do with the pineal gland.
> Poor Little Romilly Lunge....

And more was coming when Romilly ran across the road and said, "Hello, van Druten! I thought you were in America. How are you?" "Very well," said Johnny and nearly added, "How's your penis?"

Now it will be observed that much of the charm of this verse form lies in its lilting rhythm—two dactyls and a monosyllable (Poor Little Somerset Maugham) or a disyllable (Poor Little Selma Vas Dias). This strictly limits the available victims who, to add spice to the pillory, should be public figures of some renown, or at least well known in one's own set.

Poor Little Alan Napier, for example, simply doesn't work unless one turns Napier into Napeer. On the other hand,

> Poor Little Brian Aherne
> Thought it better to marry than burn:
> And misunderstanding these words of St. Paul's
> Set a light....

works splendidly. I forget, alas, how it concluded.

28. Old Friends and New Experiences

In the great canon of Poor Littles—that is, the ones I can remember—it is not always possible to attribute total authorship. Many were the result of collaboration. For instance, Johnny left me a first verse (on a virginal Catholic actress of our acquaintance) to work on in Hollywood while he went down to his ranch for a few days' serious writing on a play.

> Poor Little Una O'Connor
> Will refer to her parts as her Honor.
> Imagine the pain and the shame she can't tell
> When she found that her Honor was burning like Hell!
> Poor Little Una O'Connor.

"It's a splendid opening," I said.

"Yes," he replied, adding, with that touch of the acid school-master he never quite lost, "and don't you muck it up! Remember—I've given you the exposition; it's up to you to pursue the plot line to a proper, or improper, conclusion."

On the stroke of noon the next day I was visited by the Muse. Beside myself with pride and delight I could not wait to communicate my second verse to the Master. It seemed to me that it would be amusing to have it delivered by telegram. I imagined the Western Union boy peddling bravely through the shimmering desert heat, past bosky groves of date palms, down the long drive to the ranch house in its oasis of green. He beats dramatically on the door. Out comes Johnny, annoyed at being interrupted, yet titivated and apprehensive as one always is in face of telegrams in wartime. He tears open the envelope while the boy waits for an answer. Johnny reads:

> Poor Little Una O'Connor
> Thought the judgment of God was upon her;
> For once, oh the thing was a sin of a scandal,
> She dishonored herself with an outsize church candle,
>   Love,
>   Alan.

In fact, that was not how it worked out at all. Because of a war shortage of boypower, Western Union had taken to delivering messages to remote areas by telephone. And Johnny was on a party line. He was rather sour about it all when we next met.

"The Western Union dispatcher, my dear Alan, was from the deep South and by the time she'd spelled out Una's shame, letter by letter, it seemed about as funny as a lynching. Besides, everyone listens to everyone else on my party line."

About the time Johnny was listening to my *jeu d'esprit* in the desert, I received a call from Dame May Whitty, another friend from Bletchingley days, "Alan, would you like to come to tea this afternoon? I know it's rather short notice, but..."

"I'd love to, May. What time?"

"Oh, four o'clock. Just a few old friends. Una's coming—she was saying how fond of you she is."

I felt like a traitor at the party and could hardly look Una in the eye. Poor Little's were definitely not her cup of tea.

A classic I always enjoy for its extravagant gusto:

> Poor Little Hedy Lamarr
> Knows all the perversions there are.
> She does it with chains and she does it with whips

> And with long rubber boots that come up to her hips ...
> Poor Little Hedy Lamarr.
> We fear that she once went too far,
> When a gentleman died of the passion he felt
> While picking the lock of her chastity belt.
> Poor Little Hedy Lamarr.

After Johnny's accident—he fell from a horse he should never have mounted—he became less indulgent of frivolity. Failure of the arm to mend at the hands of conventional medicine drew him more and more towards Christian Science. Indeed, he was quite annoyed when I reminded him of a story he once told me of May Whitty, also a Christian Scientist. She was explaining to him how Christian Science had saved her from that common English complaint, constipation. It was the power of thought that did it.

"Oh," said Johnny, "I see. One just sits and thinks things out." But he never lost his light touch. Speaking the eulogy at May's funeral he said, "I think, to May, Heaven would be an everlasting cocktail party where she could meet the great company of her dear friends." It was very moving, because it spoke of May's gossipy but never malicious love of her fellow men. May, by the way, was an early feminist, though she was not so foolish as to object to "mankind" or "fellow men" as general terms.

Shortly before Johnny's death, when I think he knew that neither Christian Science nor any other humorless discipline could save him, he blossomed out again into his old ribald self. Because he could not manage the steps up to our house, my second wife and I went over one evening to dinner with him at a beach house he was renting for the summer. We had a hilarious time remembering old Poor Littles and planning new victims for the future. A few weeks later he died of a stroke.

I have cherished these offspring of your lighter moments, dear Johnny, for many years. And, now that the liberation of the written word from the Puritan humbug that was ever the target of your scorn make it possible for them to be more widely enjoyed, I do not think you would feel that they can detract in any way from your reputation as a brilliant dramatist.

* * *

Soon after *We Are Not Alone* I got a very good part in *The Invisible Man Returns* as the foreman in a Lancashire coal mine. The fact that coal miners are short and stocky to a man apparently did not occur to the producers. As for me, I was delighted to be playing a character part again far removed from the aristocrats I had been typed for in England. In fact, this performance typed me in Hollywood as a "heavy." I had to ask what a "heavy" was and, when it was explained to me that guys in movies were either good guys or bad guys, I was puzzled. I had always thought of the characters I'd played as people, not as types. In any case, I was not the possessor of a bad guy personality—I was not tough enough. But owing to my size, Hollywood could not see me as, literally, a gentle man. For that you had to be a Donald Meek type. Anyhow, Hollywood preferred to see the English upper classes as fat and pompous like Nigel Bruce, or thin and silly-ass like Claude Alister. Oh, there was always Aubrey Smith—but he played all the Aubrey Smith parts.

I was so ignorant of motion picture values, so conditioned to the theater, that I did not realize what a good part I had. At one point in the story I had half a dozen pages of script alone with the camera; but because there was no dialogue I hardly gave them a thought. When we came to shoot them I was the victim of one of our sudden California viruses and felt like death, with a fever of well over one hundred degrees. It was a hot November day at Universal and one of the things I had to do was to run in terror through a wood, supposedly in the English winter. I wore a heavy overcoat with a wool scarf around my neck. Because of my blindness without glasses, my route had to be marked with a trail of chalk running parallel to the smooth track laid down for the camera. We shot it once and I lost my way. We shot it again and I tripped at the wrong moment. The director, a tiny German called Joe May shouted some insult at me. I came up to him and shouted back. Delighted, he climbed on an apple box, reached up and pinched my cheek.

"Ach! It is goot! Ve haf temperament, you and I!" And I found I had made a friend.

Incidentally, all that running (kill or cure) sweated the fever out of me and I ended the day feeling fine.

The shooting of this film also produced a classic remark from Cedric Hardwicke, who also kindly pointed out to me what a very good part I had. Many of the scenes in *The Invisible Man Returns* were shot in my "cottage." Now, we all know that a miner's house in 1940, foreman or no foreman, would be one of 50 identical hovels in a squalid street. But not at Universal. There, it was set in a wood, half-timbered, with a large open fireplace and a cop-

Alan, as mine foreman Willie Spears, with Louise Brien in a scene omitted from the final cut of *The Invisible Man Returns* (Universal, 1940). Margaret Herrick Library, Academy of Motion Picture Arts and Sciences. Core Collection.

per kettle hanging over massive logs. The living room was about 30 feet by 20 with a spinning wheel in one corner and a Welsh dresser filled with Wedgewood china against the wall. When Cedric walked in for the first time he raised one eyebrow and said, "Of course, in England, this would be a national monument."

Alan, in costume, poses in front of his sky-blue eight-cylinder Hudson convertible (with red leather upholstery) on the Universal backlot during the filming of *House of the Seven Gables* **(Universal, 1940). Collection of James Bigwood.**

Joe May's appreciation of my temperament led to his finding me a job in his next picture, *The House of the Seven Gables*. I was to be a New England mailman. When I was being interviewed, Joe pointed out to the producer that with a little beard and my tall spare figure I would look splendidly Uncle Samish. As an afterthought the producer threw out: "Of course, you can drive a horse?"

"Oh, yes." I answered.

I had not been near a horse since my traumatic experience when I was little more than a baby. And there was no time for me to do anything about it—my casting for the part had come up at the last moment.

The next day, there I was on the back lot at Universal looking remarkably like Uncle Sam, being given instructions by the dialogue director on how to turn my British English into New England English and wondering what the hell I was going to do when I mounted the seat of that mail cart.

I found a friend in the wrangler. I have never met one yet who was not a friend to anxious actors. He showed me how to hold the reins. But how to stop the animal? How to turn right or left? How to get it to start?

I need not have worried. The horse had been in pictures longer than I. When the director called "Action!" the horse trotted forward; when he called "Cut!" the horse stopped. The only trouble I had was to prevent him from trying to steal the scene by leering at the camera as he passed it. The wrangler told me what to do and we got the shot at the third take. I've always said that I could do anything a part required and I've never failed to find a way to do it.

However, I began to realize that horses and I must come to terms if I was to make a living in Hollywood. I took riding lessons and, though I never feel at ease on a horse, I learned to sit a horse well and look at ease provided I was not expected to do more than break into a gentle trot or modest canter, on horses trained to movies. At one point when a lot of equestrian roles came my way I used to ask for a big bay horse called Banjo. I would come to the day's shooting with a pocket full of apples and lumps of sugar and he became my friend. He saw me up precipices, through sand storms, and once he even galloped me safely down a rocky trail. I think I owe him my life.

In *The House of the Seven Gables*, in addition to coming to terms with horses, I came to terms with George Sanders. I introduced Annie to George and his attractive girlfriend, "Su-su." It was not a very good idea; George did not care for people who held strong views, contradicted him, and beat him at parlor games. He called her "Screaming Annie." He also persuaded me to buy a boat, a beautiful little sixteen foot Bermuda cutter, but I did not have much time to enjoy it; all sorts of things were coming to a head.

29

Broadway

In my early, solitary days in Hollywood I asked the lady at the desk at the Chateau Marmont if there was any place of particular interest in the neighborhood that I should visit. Without hesitation she replied, "Why yes! There's the Farmer's Market." I expected, if not a genuine scene of antiquity, at least an MGM replica with cobbled streets, horse-troughs, and a central fountain. Instead I found a ramshackle huddle of rather expensive little shops housed in a low hanger-like building of no architectural interest. However, there were little patio areas with tables where one could bring one's choice of food from any one of a dozen adjacent cook-shops. It was a pleasant place to have lunch.

Lunching at the next table to me one day I became aware of an unpretentiously distinguished-looking grey-haired man with the accent of a cultivated English gentlemen. Because of my solitary existence I had a powerful urge to strike up an acquaintance; he appeared to be a man of charm and humor and very much at ease. Also, I was aware that he had been eyeing me, although he was too well-bred to allow his curiosity to become intrusive. Eventually I turned to him.

"Forgive me for asking but… You are English, aren't you?"

"Of course. And forgive me for the way I've been staring at you. But you are Alan Napier, aren't you?"

"Yes, I am. How on earth did you know?"

"*Bitter Sweet*. How could one forget you? But the extraordinary thing is, I was talking to Brock Pemberton about you last week. I had no idea you were out here."

"Yes, I … rather think I'm here to stay. But what … why would you be talking to Brock Pemberton about me?"

"Brock's an old friend and he's planning to produce an adaptation of *The Nutmeg Tree*. I told him that you simply have to play Sir William."

"How awfully kind of you."

"No, no. It's just so obviously right."

We had a pleasant lunch together, and while I cannot remember my benefactor's name, I found out later from Brock Pemberton that he was a secret service man. He told me he was flying east the next day and would give Brock Pemberton my address. In due course I received a letter from Mr. Pemberton. He had never seen me in his life but he was impressed by what Colonel X had told him. What did I feel about doing a play in New York?

An interesting correspondence ensued, ending in my engagement. Brock told me afterwards that he took a chance on me because my letters made him laugh. He knew I'd look right and would be suitably aristocratic from what he'd heard—but would I be one of those damned stuffed-shirt English actors without a sense of humor? I think I had been funny in my letters about Hollywood—just the right touch for a New York producer whose last big success was *Personal Appearance*, a satire on Hollywood which took New York by storm and made Gladys George one of the hottest stars on Broadway.

Gladys was to star in *Lady in Waiting*, as the adaptation of *The Nutmeg Tree* was called. The original version submitted to her elicited from Gladys, with some outrage, "What's in this for me? It's all about a guy called William!" So it was rewritten and the heart was taken out of my part. But it still could be a prestigious introduction to Broadway. (I hate the word prestigious—to me it has the smell of publicity rather than the fragrance of merit. That is why I use it here.) The great Myron Selznick Agency got me a very handsome salary.

In the sunshine of a February heat-wave I basked on the beach at Santa Monica until the last moment and very nearly missed my plane to New York, where the airport was deep in graying snow. I felt terribly important when a New York representative of the Myron Selznick Agency met the plane and drove me to my hotel.

The rehearsals of *Lady in Waiting* provided a classic case of the success of a play being jeopardized by the director becoming bored with the opening scene of exposition. The cards were stacked against the scene being comprehensible in any case. It was played in a moonlit garden in France by the youngest and least experienced members of the cast, who were both English. They could not be brightly lit and their accents made them difficult to understand by an American audience. The next scene, which featured Miss George in the bathtub of a sleazy London flat coping with bailiff's officers, should have been hilarious, but was meaningless unless her relationship to the young lovers in the south of France had been made clear.

I got on splendidly with the director, Antoinette Perry, who was delighted with everything I did until we came to the dress rehearsal, at which I appeared in my expert make-up as an elderly gentlemen. "Oh, no," Miss Perry cried. "How could I think of disguising my handsome self?" They wanted me just as I was—their charming young leading man. I thought of Marie Tempest ("Whatever you play you must always look your best."), but I was not happy. In Miss Sharpe's novel the whole point was that an elderly retired diplomat with a slightly dickey heart and an aging lady of doubtful virtue but a heart of gold, miraculously find in each other what they need to make them happy. True, Gladys was not playing the broad a day older than she had to, nor was she showing that awestruck adoration for Sir William's status that was a charming feature of the cockney lady in the book. So Miss Perry was probably right; but my belief in the truth of my performance was badly shaken.

When we tried the play out at Princeton, the bathtub scene fell flat and the play never quite recovered. Brock Pemberton left a sick-bed to hurry to Washington—our next stop—to preside at revisions. I forget what they were but the Washington opening was successful. For me there were reviews in the newspapers that said Hollywood would soon be welcoming another fascinating English leading man, and revived, briefly alas, my dreams of stardom.

Briefly, because at our first night in New York, perhaps because they were nervous, the young lovers failed to win the attention of the audience, and the bathtub scene again fell flat. Poor Gladys, who had problems of insecurity for all her recent success, began fortifying herself with brandy. In the second act her effervescence won the audience over; but by the third act she was so effervescent that the text as rehearsed, the moves, the timing, all went by the board. The third act, in which we shyly discovered our mutual love, provided

Alan with Gladys George in *Lady in Waiting*. Martin Beck Theater, 1940. Photograph by Vandamm Studio © Billy Rose Division, The New York Public Library for the Performing Arts.

my big scene and I am not good at improvisation, particularly on a first night. I grasped at straws and only just managed to keep my head above water.

The New York reviews were enthusiastic about Gladys, and, though kind enough to me, failed to see me as a new threat to Hollywood. The unworthy thought did occur to me that Gladys might have felt that "that guy William" had rather stolen the show in Washington and she would darn well see that it was her show in New York. But I'm sure what happened was in fact due to her sudden craving for alcoholic support. I was amazed that not one of the critics detected her condition. But then they expected her to give a dizzy performance, and the play, as a vehicle for her, was kindly received. Everyone said we would run for a year. At all subsequent performances Gladys played the third act beautifully and my performance was much admired. But in New York it is what the critics say on the first night that counts.

We did not run for a year because the fall of France, the evacuation of Dunkirk, the expected collapse of England all took place about the time we opened. Suddenly the dizzy gyrations of a golden-hearted broad caught up in maternal responsibilities and a rather improbable romance seemed unimportant with a catastrophe in Europe actually threatening to engulf the United States. We only lasted until late July.

29. Broadway

Americans had little faith, at this moment in history, in England's ability to resist invasion. Conquest by Hitler's armies would be only a matter of time. Various friends urged me to get Nan and Jennifer out of the country. They were in the south of England, right in the path of the invading hoards to come—a defenseless woman and her child. In fact, I could not believe that England would be invaded; but since I only had blind faith, I allowed myself to be persuaded. I arranged for Nan and Jennifer to secure passage on a boat to Canada where I met them in Toronto at my brother Mark's apartment.

When the play settled into what at first promised to be a long run, I decided to take a cottage in the country rather than endure the fierce heat of New York City's summer. In the New York *Times*, I saw an advertisement for just what I wanted—a cottage on a doctor's estate at Sands Point, within comfortable driving distance of New York. (A friend of John Houseman's had driven my car over from the coast.) I telephoned and was asked to call at the doctor's house on East 53rd Street. I found myself being interviewed by the doctor's wife to establish my suitability as a tenant. Actors might mean noisy parties and heaven knew what else! But Mrs. Hawkes and I got on tremendously well right away—indeed it was the beginning of a friendship of many years.

The cottage was a delightful little modern house within a few hundred yards of a private beach on the Sound. There was tennis at the Hawkes's, sailing at a boat harbor nearby, and sun-bathing on the flat roof of the house. Ten almost flawless weeks. The only flaw was when, not being used to an electric stove, I put my hand down on a burner which, though gray to the eye, was still red hot.

The drive into New York in my beautiful blue Hudson was a breeze. Breezing a little too exuberantly I was eventually given a ticket for speeding. At the crowded traffic court when my case came up I was horrified to hear the judge call out, when I pleaded guilty, "Twenty-five dollars." I had not expected it to be anything like this much. I said:

"I haven't got twenty-five dollars on me, your Honor."

"How much have you got?"

"Um ... about seventeen fifty."

"Okay! I'll take it. Cut rates today!"

30

Down to Earth

When the run of *Lady in Waiting* finished, I went to meet Nan and Jennifer in Canada. We drove down from Canada to Westport, Connecticut, where Nan had old associations and old friends. We found a suitable house immediately but by the time I had installed them there and paid two months' rent in advance, what with the expenses of the trip to Canada and the cottage at Sands Point my savings from the run of *Lady in Waiting* were seriously depleted. In addition, far from getting the summons to star in Hollywood predicted by the Washington press, the only communication I received from my agents in Hollywood were bills for the upkeep and state tax on my boat, and the suggestion that, if I planned to remain in the East, I might be well-advised to sell it. I sold it.

When Brock Pemberton told me he was lining up a tour of *Lady in Waiting* I was only too delighted to let him know I was available. I rejoined the company and was on the road until early in 1941. When the tour was over, I set out by car for Hollywood.

For the next six months the only work that came my way was in radio. (On a *DeMille Playhouse* I remember May Whitty exclaiming with wicked innocence as she gazed at Mr. DeMille's beautiful director's riding britches, "Oh, but don't you come to work on horseback?" when C. B. explained that car trouble had delayed him.) Though I was in funds again from the tour of *Lady in Waiting*, the failure of the studios to employ me was very disturbing. The justification for my easy life in Hollywood while England was at war was that I should be making pictures *about* England. I tested for the Vicar in *Mrs. Miniver* and did not get the part. If I was not needed here, should I not go home?

Two small parts finally came along, in one of which, *Eagle Squadron* at Universal, I played an air-raid warden in a scene depicting the bombing of London, thus justifying my presence in Hollywood. But it was so long since I had worked that I was extremely nervous and not very good. *(He only had one line as well: "Are there any expectant mothers down there?")* The other *(the role of "Updike" in* Confirm or Deny, *20th Century–Fox, 1942)* was ultimately left, in toto, on the cutting room floor. I had had a beautiful suit of midnight blue evening-dress tails made for it, which I have worn only once since. If the moths have not got it, it must be hopelessly out of fashion by now.

Funds were running low and when Joan Fontaine used her influence to get me a job as dialogue director and English expert on a film she was about to star in with Tyrone Power, I gratefully accepted although secretly I felt it was a sad come-down. *(Fontaine does not remember going to bat for Alan, but acknowledges that it was jolly nice of her.)* A lesson I was not to forget concerned the attitude of the producing side of the business towards actors. In the pre-production period, during which I was to advise on all sorts of things (the picture, *This Above All*, was an English war-time story), the second assistant director,

Jennifer and Nan at the time of their arrival in the United States, 1940. Courtesy Christie Nichols.

now a big producer *(Aaron Rosenberg, Oscar-nominated in 1962 for* Mutiny on the Bounty*)* said to me, "Look, you're one of us now, not one of them," meaning the actors, who were to be regarded as cattle—pampered if necessary to bring them to market in good shape but only in proportion to their contribution to the film. The same man later said of Gladys

Cooper, who played a not very large part in the film, "Aw, she used to be someone in London, but nobody gives a shit for her out here," because she complained of unnecessarily early calls in the morning. I gritted my teeth and knew on whose side my true loyalty would always lie. It was lovely meeting Gladys again. We remained close friends for the rest of her life.

During the making of *This Above All* the Japanese bombed Pearl Harbor and the United States finally came into World War II.

Shortly afterwards, I met Gip.

31

Meeting Gip

There are two quotations about enduring love which have always seemed to me to be poetically beautiful and illuminating. In *Wind Sand and Stars*, Antoine de Saint Exupery wrote: "Love does not consist in gazing into each other's eyes, but in looking outward together in the same direction."

Evan John, an English actor, playwright and novelist, wrote in a book, the title of which I forget: "To see, in another's eye, the light of an abiding home."

The first would seem to be at war with the second, but this is not so. First you must find your abiding home; then, from its security, you may look outward together in the same direction.

My life with Gip came to an agonizing end. I shall not harrow the reader with a description of a brave woman dying from cancer. I will tell, however, quite unsentimentally, of the strange way we came together and how we found in each other the qualities that made our marriage beautiful. I have always known that she was "too good for me." The surprising thing is that she sometimes thought I was too good for her. The great thing was that we were good for each other.

Born on February 17, 1907, she was christened Aileen Dickens Hawksley, the "Dickens" being a remembrance of her great-grandfather Charles. She was called Gipsy, Gip or Gippy throughout a well-lived life, which came to an end on the eve of her fifty-fourth birthday.

Just as some people have the gift in music of perfect pitch, so Gip possessed another kind of perfect pitch. Every day, confronted with issues great and small, we have to make decisions. What is the good, the right thing to do? Unerringly Gip knew. And with the imaginative flexibility that also knows that what may be right for me on Monday may not be right for you on Tuesday. This gift was based on the rock of a pure morality, interpreted by an intuitive psychological insight. It is not always a comfortable thing to live with; often enough I've stubbed my toe against that rock. Yet what a comfort it has been, when torn apart by the question, "Should I do this or that?" to know that Gip would have the right answer. Her morality had nothing to do with convention; it was a matter of love and respect for the life force.

We met on the beach at Laguna. Gip was staying for the weekend at a house overlooking the beach which her old friend George (Melville) Cooper had taken for the summer. I was staying next door at a house my new friend, George Sanders, had taken for his parents. On my way up from an early morning swim a pretty little girl with thin legs came up to me.

"I say, have you seen a white dog anywhere?"

"No. Wait a minute, yes! A white dog with a tail curling over his back?"

"That's him. That's Terry."

"He was wandering around behind the house and then headed off over there." I pointed to the low cliff overlooking the beach.

"Thanks awfully. You're English, aren't you? My father's English. He's called Terry, too. I'll tell Gip."

Before I could sort out this family information—in fact, I was not very interested and wanted to get back to my breakfast—the white dog cantered up to us and was led off with admonitions for disappearing and praise for reappearing.

At mid-morning, there on the beach was the little girl, the white dog, and a small-to-medium young woman in sweat shirt and jeans. With her springy, dark chestnut hair, somewhere between curly and wavy and worn pretty short, her slim, upright figure, freckles and tip-tilted nose, she might, at a distance, have been a boy. The little girl introduced us.

"This is the man I met when I was looking for Terry."

"I'm Alan Napier," I said, holding out my hand.

"I know." She had the levelest gaze and looked me straight in the eye. I think then and there, I saw the light of an abiding home.

We walked up the beach together to where George Sanders, his girlfriend, and his old mother were lying out on blankets. I introduced them.

"Hello," said George, hardly opening his eyes and certainly not getting up. Gip sat down near to me and conversation flagged. After a little while George said, "I want a drink. Water." His girl got up at once and made her way over the belt of rounded rocks and pebbles that separated us from the house. Rising on his elbow George pulled out a cigarette.

"Anyone got a match?" A bleary look in my direction. Gip and I shook our heads. George collapsed back. "I want a match."

His old mother struggled to her feet and started for the house. I saw Gip's hazel eyes widen.

"D'you mean you're going to let her…" No response from George. With an edge to her voice, Gip continued, "Why do they do it?"

George opened his eyes, looked with aversion at the tiresome female Nape had picked up on the beach then, smiling to himself, conceded, "Because they're damn fools, I suppose." It was a year before Gip, who was prepared to make no compromises, was accepted into the Sanders fold. She had implied that George's comfort did not have to be the first consideration of his family.

George was a strange character. A born amateur, for he was never prepared to work hard enough at anything to become a professional, and a self-indulgent egoist—this was his proclaimed philosophy—he attracted people by his lively intelligence and his wry sense of humor. He liked to be surrounded by uncritical admirers: George's henchmen. For a time I was a sort of super-henchman; that is to say he would ask me to do things instead of telling me.

At this period I was working with him on his current craze: aerodynamics. His nimble, lazy brain rambling afield, he would come on some aspect of science that intrigued him, sure that he could become a master of it without all that boring groundwork. Because he lacked manual dexterity and patience, someone else had to do, so to speak, the lab-work for him. In aerodynamics, this is where I came in.

Later, when he imported his brother Tom to be an actor ("Nape, I'm bringing Tom

31. Meeting Gip

out to Hollywood." "Can he act?" "Who cares? He's the right shape."), George took up optics and with Tom as his mechanic, designed a telescope. It looked beautiful but when you put your eye to the lens you could not see anything. Then it was mathematics. George calculated the diameter a toilet roll would have to be to satisfy the needs of an average man for a lifetime. Nine feet, eight inches. Later still it was high finance and, still an amateur, he lost a million dollars in making sausages.

I worked with him on balsa-wood models of gliders because I was at a loose end at that time and I loved to see them, lifted by an up-draft from the beach, gliding high out over the ocean and, if the rudder had been rightly set, veering off-wind and swooping back to land safely on the sand. (My gliders, incidentally, had little to do with George's theories—but they did fly.) At such times George would lose his habitual lethargy and suddenly become an excited and endearing little boy. He never, of course, really grew up. His charm for women lay in the fact that they sensed, beneath the blasé, cynical man-of-the-world exterior, a little boy to be mothered. All little boys are selfish and demanding; this little boy could be cruelly cold.

But his mind was ingenious and, so long as he was fun to be with, I did not feel any need to make moral judgments. When I first met him, he was under contract to Twentieth Century-Fox and Darryl Zanuck was his boss. It did not sit well with George that anyone should be his boss. One night at twelve-thirty, with typical lack of consideration for someone else's sleeping habits, he called me on the telephone.

"Nape. It's just occurred to me that Darryl Zanuck is worth his weight in balsa." To me this conceit was deeply and satisfyingly amusing; and it was this kind of thing, I later explained to Gippy, that drew me to George. "I know," she'd say, "But does it make up for his being such a shit?" Eventually she accepted him because, I think, she too was conscious of the little boy in him, and knew in her bones that the little boy would one day be in need of help.

The Coopers asked me over for a drink that evening and Gip and I got on very well together. I learned that she was separated from her husband, who had rejoined the British Army, and that she worked in Westwood as a dental assistant. I asked for her telephone number and said we must see more of each other. When I called her a day or so later I very nearly blew the relationship. I started telling her how beautiful she was—the conventional romancing routine.

"Nonsense. I'm not beautiful at all. If you've nothing more interesting than that to say I must get back to my washing."

She did not regard herself as beautiful and any falseness she detected immediately. She was quite right. Though I liked the way she looked, I had not thought her beautiful and I called her up because I was attracted to her as a person. The conventional techniques of making out with a woman simply did not wash with Gip and I should have known it. However, she relented and ten days later sent me a little note saying she was sorry she had been so abrupt and that she would very much like to see me again.

A strange courtship followed. I was quite ready to start on a new love, but Gip was actually deeply in love at the time with another man. In addition, she had a child to look after and her work was extremely exacting. Her dentist (the best I have ever known), though charmingly easy-going in manner, was a demanding employer. All his lab work was done in his office and he had taught Gip to cast the inlays. She also was responsible for all office work, accounts, income tax returns, everything. And she had had a major operation, a hysterectomy, not long before I met her. Consequently by the time she had fed her daughter, read to her perhaps, and prepared her for bed, Gip had not a great deal to give to a new suitor.

The days of her love affair with the other man were numbered. He was an Englishman, on Air Force service in the United States, and his wife and child had just come out to join him in America. He had to make an agonizing decision. In fact he put it largely up to Gip. When I helped her to decide to give him up she knew very well that this was at least partly self-interested just as she had known my first approach was phony. We agreed that he was the sort of man who would never forgive himself for abandoning wife and child—indeed this quality of integrity was a part of his attraction for her. I even drove her to a final meeting with him at the motel where they had first made love.

But I had something going for me. She had been an actress in England *(her professional name was Gypsy Raine)* and had known and admired me as an actor. She recalled passing me at the stage door of the Little Theatre in London and that it had been a moment of great excitement for her. Two or three evenings a week, I would take her out to dinner and entertain her with stories of my family. Or so I thought at the time. Years later she confessed that she was often too tired to concentrate on what I was saying or would find herself

Face to face with Mickey Rooney in *A Yank at Eton* (MGM, 1942). Margaret Herrick Library, Academy of Motion Picture Arts and Sciences. Core Collection.

dreaming of the other man. But gradually we became very fond of each other. I got on well with her daughter, who, like mine, was called Jennifer. Sometimes in the afternoons I would take Jennifer down to the beach. And there was one splendiferous evening we all three used to laugh about.

I had gotten a job at MGM, in *A Yank at Eton*. I had come down in the world to the point of being paid by the day, instead of the week. (My part was optimistically scheduled for three days, but the kids playing the Eton boys caught chicken pox and the job stretched to five weeks.) No one had told me that, in those days, day players were expected to pick up their wages, paid in cash by the studio cashier, at the end of each day. On my third day I learned of this, presented myself at the cashier's window, and was handed the biggest pile of paper money I had ever seen.

I went straight to Gip's little apartment and said, "Tonight we celebrate! Champagne! Anything you like." And threw the whole bundle of bills in the air. Jennifer screamed with delight as the shower descended on our heads and all over the apartment and Gip took me in her arms and hugged me—not because I'd promised her champagne but because she was so happy at my lightheartedness.

One of the joys of being an only spasmodically successful movie actor is that you feel really rich two or three times a year. Your bank balance has been dwindling, the gas and telephone and electricity bills are overdue, and then, suddenly, you get a fabulously paid job. A three week guarantee perhaps—thousands of dollars! You are rich in a way a man earning a steady salary never feels rich, not even if he's a millionaire.

It was at this point that the Myron Selznick Agency asked me to leave them; they did not handle day players. Twenty-five years later another agency which, having asked to represent me, subsequently became very grand, suggested I should leave soon after I had earned them ten thousand dollars in two years! They said they did not expect me to maintain that average. How right they were!

32

Take One

JAMES BIGWOOD

The Selznick Agency's lack of confidence notwithstanding, Alan's tentative steps forward in his personal life were being matched by equally encouraging professional momentum. His unbilled stint in *A Yank at Eton* (1942) had proved to be an entrée to the prestigious MGM studios and it was quickly followed by an equally small—but billed—part in the Oscar-nominated *Random Harvest* (1942) and another in the lesser known *Assignment in Brittany* (1942). The three roles could hardly have been more different. In the first he is a Cockney restaurateur, pitted against the 5'2" Mickey Rooney in a wildly mismatched comic battle in which most of his punches clear the top of his opponent's head by a good six inches. It is only when he is finally brought to his knees that he is able to face his adversary eye to eye. In his single scene in *Random Harvest* he is firmly ensconced in the British upper class, dryly welcoming Ronald Colman back from "three years in darkest Amnesia" as one of several relatives less than pleased by the unexpected return of the missing heir to the family estate. In *Assignment in Brittany*, he is a Scot—nicknamed "Tiny" of course—one of a pair of escaped POWs in occupied France. In this one the fistfights are real, as the two escapees, along with star Jean-Pierre Aumont (making his American film debut), take on the Nazis. Though his sub-plot is a minor one, consisting of only two extended scenes, Alan receives screen credit (albeit in thirteenth position), while tellingly, Donald Stuart, playing his fellow POW—a part equal in size and importance—does not.

However, Alan's first substantial American role came not at MGM, but at Columbia. In *Appointment in Berlin* (1943), he is Col. Patterson of the British Secret Service, recruiting disgraced Airman Keith Wilson (George Sanders) to pose as a defector to the Nazis. This was his second of nine films with Sanders, who certainly must have appreciated working opposite somebody who kept his own 6' 3½" height from calling attention to itself (they had both appeared in 1940's *House of the Seven Gables*, but hadn't shared any scenes). Patterson is present throughout the film, monitoring Wilson's "Lord Haw Haw" style propaganda broadcasts from Germany and decoding the secret messages they contain. There is nothing out of the ordinary about him (Wilson: "So you're Secret Service. I never suspected." Patterson: "That's the whole point of Secret Service, to prevent people suspecting.") but Alan invests the character with a quiet, comforting authority and he and Sanders are a pleasure to watch together.

The movie starts with a strange scene, however, that appears to have been tacked on after the fact. In it, Patterson, Wilson, and Wilson's father (played by H.P. Sanders, George's

Alan as "Tiny" with Jean-Pierre Aumont and Donald Stuart in *Assignment in Brittany* (MGM, 1943). Collection of James Bigwood.

actual father, in his only movie role) listen to the 1938 radio broadcast of Neville Chamberlain's "Peace for our Time" speech—which can't have been very pleasant for Alan. It is the other two men's relief at Chamberlain's announcement that sets Wilson off on the bender that eventually causes his downfall, but Sanders' anger as he exits doesn't match his calmer demeanor as he walks down the street in the scene that immediately follows (in what one feels must have been the original first scene of the film). Somebody must have felt it necessary to firmly anchor the opening of the story in 1938 and emphasize the context, but the scene actually starts an entertaining and well-made piece of propaganda off on an awkward note. Additionally, Patterson's satisfied reaction to Chamberlain's speech is 180 degrees removed from his passionate championing of British military preparedness only a few scenes later. Perhaps this is just another way of preventing people from suspecting…

More small roles at MGM followed in quick succession. Although his "Dr. Bladh" in *Madame Curie* (1943) was cut from the finished film, in *Lassie Come Home* (1943), Alan has a nice scene as a Scottish bounty hunter on the lookout for stray dogs that have been attacking the local sheep. Like all of us, he is won over by Lassie and deliberately misses his clear shot at her, thus allowing her to continue on her homeward trek. In *Lost Angel* (1943) he is Dr. Woodring, one of a team of professors who have raised six-year-old "Alpha" (Margaret O'Brien) according to strict scientific principles. This ethically dubious premise

As Col. Patterson of the British Secret Service with Leonard Mudie in *Appointment in Berlin* (Columbia, 1943). Collection of James Bigwood.

is actually played for gentle humor and Alan has several amusing scenes, not to mention a chance to show off his physique (starkly juxtaposed with his academic demeanor) while overseeing his young charge's exercise period.

Alan played another doctor—although a much more serious one—in 20th Century–Fox's *The Song of Bernadette* (1943). As the unctuous psychiatrist Debeau, he conspires with Vincent Price to institutionalize Jennifer Jones' Bernadette ("After all, a psychiatrist is not an orthopedic surgeon who can set a broken bone on the spot."), dismissing her visions of the Blessed Virgin as paranoia.

RKO's *Mademoiselle Fifi* (1944) came next, marking producer Val Lewton's non-horror film debut, as well as Robert Wise's first film as a director after years in the editing room. Taking its title from one of the two Guy de Maupassant short stories on which it is based (the other being "Boule de Suif"), the movie clearly has ambitions beyond mere storytelling, drawing a parallel between the Prussian occupation of France in the 1870 Franco-Prussian War and Hitler's invasion of the country in 1940. A character actor's dream, the first half of the film concerns a collection of French stagecoach passengers making their way from to Rouen to Cleresville. The group is a none-too-subtle microcosm of French society: a nobleman and his wife, a manufacturer and his wife, a merchant and his wife, a left-wing politician, a priest and a laundress. Alan, who had already worked for Lewton in a small role in the horror classic *Cat People* (RKO, 1942), was cast as the representative of the aristocracy, with Helen Freeman (17 years his senior) as his wife. His Count de Breville is hardly the most vocal of the travelers (that honor certainly belongs to Jason Robards, Sr. as the wine merchant) but his facial expressions speak volumes, especially during the initial carriage ride, a delightful eleven minute sequence in which the upper class passengers snub Simone Simon's laundress until they realize that she is the only person who has thought to bring anything to eat. At the first overnight stop, the group is prevented from leaving by a sadistic Prussian lieutenant who demands as the price of their departure that the patriotic laundress "dine" with him. This she refuses to do. Her fellow passengers support her until it becomes inconvenient, at which point they encourage her to make the sacrifice for the common good. The next morning the carriage continues on and all but the priest and the politician revert to their previous snobbery. Simon and her two allies disembark in Cleresville but their fellow passengers continue on to Dieppe, and unfortunately we never see them again. Still, the ensemble nature of the first half of *Mademoiselle Fifi* makes it one of Alan's (and his co-snobs') best showcases.

33

Marrying Gip

After the other man in Gip's life returned to England, our relationship became more easy. I never had any doubt as to where I wanted it to go, but I did not force the pace. I learned a great deal about Gip's family and about her first husband. Little Jennifer had made a success in a film in England and Terence Downing had persuaded Gip that there was a bright future for all three of them in Hollywood. Her desire to escape from the tentacles of a somewhat overpowering family had induced her to go along with the idea. Her husband was an actor and might do quite well. But when they arrived, she found that Terry, who had a pathological capacity for antagonizing employers anyhow, had really come to Hollywood with the idea of selling their daughter to the movies as a second Shirley Temple. When this scheme failed to mature he made no attempt whatever to get work himself. He drank a great deal and borrowed money from those of their friends with whom he had not quarreled. To a person of Gip's integrity this was an intolerable situation, and their marriage went to pieces. In fact, the only time that Terry's life had made any real sense was when he was in the Army in World War I. So, when World War II broke out and he talked of rejoining his regiment, Gip took him at his word, borrowed the money, bought his passage to England and firmly put him on a train East.

Gip had never been trained to work and she had not been happy as an actress. She got herself a job in a department store at $22 a week. Sooner or later she was determined to pay off Terry's debts.

February 26, 1942: The evening came when a tender longing for each other, for the joy and reassurance and closeness of physical love kept her at my apartment. Hardly had we got into bed than a tremendous-barrage of gunfire burst over Los Angeles. What was it? Gang warfare? We rushed to the window. The night sky was pierced and criss-crossed by searchlights. We turned on the radio. An enemy plane was raiding Los Angeles! (The West Coast had been very nervous ever since a Japanese submarine had come in close, near Santa Barbara and shelled an oil refinery.) We got back into bed; but every time the mood for love was reborn, a fresh burst of gunfire shattered the night. Finally the radio revealed that the great Los Angeles air raider was in fact nothing but a private plane that had lost its way coming back from San Diego. We laughed so much that I really don't remember whether our coming together was consummated that night or not. But we found that we could laugh in bed together; it was a good beginning.

Summer was coming on and Nan wrote suggesting that I might like to have Jennifer for the long vacation. She must have had some fish to fry for which she preferred to be unencumbered by a child. So Gip and I determined to take a house together so that the two Jennifers might enjoy a family holiday by the seaside. For a week we looked at houses advertised in the Santa Monica *Outlook* but none of them were quite what we wanted.

Then, one day, I went to a house agent in Santa Monica and described what I was looking for. They suggested houses that were too expensive, houses that were not by the sea. No. That was not what I wanted. Well, there was a sort of studio place in the Palisades, but I would not want that. Why? Well, it wasn't very desirable. "I'll look at it," I said. So they gave me a key and told me where it was.

Four miles north of Santa Monica on the coast road to Malibu, just past the point where Sunset Boulevard runs into the sea, I found a little road running up into the hills. Porto Marina Way. One house I passed, then another, and a third. The road wound on with brush on each side till a sharp curve led back towards the sea. Round the corner stood a little house, stuccoed, with a Mexican tile roof, cut into the side of the cliff, looking clear out over the Pacific Ocean. It had a rounded turret at one corner which I found housed a circular staircase leading up from the large, high-ceilinged living room to the bedrooms above. Almost opposite the house, a flight of concrete steps led down to a subway under the coast highway right onto a beautiful, empty beach. It was perfect.

That evening I called Gip at her dentist's office. "I've found it! I found the perfect place." Rather put out, she said, "Really? Well, I found something pretty good myself in my lunch hour." Rather put out, I answered, "Oh, all right. Ladies first. But wait till you see mine!"

An hour after I had left it, we discovered that Gip had found the same house—17919 Porto Marina Way. We moved in a week later and I have lived there ever since. Thirty years. I rented it at first and then Gip told me I should buy it.

"I can't. I haven't got any money."

"You don't have to have money in America. You put down a small lump sum and raise a mortgage." I did not like the idea. "How do I know I want to live here? How can I be sure I can make the payments? I'm an actor. My work may take me anywhere."

"It's an investment," she said, and she prevailed.

It was the best investment I ever made. I bought it for a song. I used to think the reason for the small price ($6,750 furnished) was because there was a war on and Californians were afraid the Japanese would land or at least bombard the coast. Only later, when we had tremendous rains one winter and many cliff slides in the neighborhood, did I realize why the agent had called it "not very desirable." The owner, a city engineer, had been privy to information that the house was situated in a designated slide area. He cannily thought, "I'll unload on some stupid sap from the mid-west or Europe." I was that stupid sap. However, he liked to live overlooking the sea and eventually built himself a handsome house at a new development called Portuguese Bend. Five years later the whole community slid into the ocean.

Not only am I still here, but the City of Los Angeles, in order to maintain the road leading to a five hundred home development inland, lately spent many hundred thousand dollars pinning up Porto Marina Way at the corner just below my house, which is thereby secured against landslides from any cause except a major earthquake. Where ignorance is bliss…

Over the years I have built onto the house, carved a small terraced garden out of the cliff side and surrounded it with wild Californian acacia latifolia so that it is protected from the wind and completely private. Whenever Brian Aherne comes to visit me, he stands on my patio and says, "This is the best thing you ever did, old man. There is not a better site anywhere in the world."

Looking due south over the bay of Santa Monica it is a house for a year-long summer holiday. Two hundred feet above sea level, the sound of the sea is always with us, yet far enough below not to threaten or deafen when a winter storm blows up. The cliff falls away in front of me so steeply that I neither see nor hear the traffic on the crowded ocean highway. Smog never blows my way; yet I am within forty minutes driving time of any movie studio. From my windows I can see the sun rising to my left (or did in the days of early calls to the studios) and the right, the fabulous winter sunsets that blaze across the western skies—gold and crimson, fading to rose and palest lemon.

In the last cliff slide I lost my stairway to the beach, but it is still a mere five-minute walk away. My battle to preserve my precariously perched garden—three times the winter rains have swept sections of it into the road—has kept my spare time healthfully employed. At the time of the last, and worst, collapse I asked a landscape gardening firm for an estimate to rebuild the garden to the status quo ante and was quoted more than the house and garden originally cost me! I did the job myself—with the help of my son-in-law, Bob—over the course of a year, for one hundred and fifty dollars in concrete block, and redwood. The cost in blood, sweat and tears is non-computable. It is deeply satisfying to be an old cock crowing on his dunghill. I owe it all to Gip.

17919 Porto Marina Way. Courtesy Tom Boyd.

33. Marrying Gip

As a child, Gip had been delicate and backward at school. An extreme modesty, a hatred of any kind of showing off, paralyzed her faculties. (This weakness caused her to abandon her career as an actress—rehearsing was for her a torment.) In an uninhibitedly self-confident family she came to be regarded as the stupid one and withdrew into her shell. To the family's surprise, however, she quietly developed an astonishing tenacity in sticking to her guns when it came to resisting certain family accommodations which she regarded as not strictly ethical. The time came when her brothers, seeking to bail out their mother in one of her not very creditable bankruptcies, required Gip's signature to help them circumvent the intention of a family trust fund. Gip refused. They said they would go along without her. She consulted a solicitor (by an odd chance mine too—he happened to be my cousin, Roger Slade) who gave her his unconditional support. Her brothers climbed down.

Gip's mother, a Dickens granddaughter, was a lady of remarkable charm and vivacity, but it was certainly not from her that Gip inherited her ethical sensibilities. She drank a great deal, gambled and was extremely extravagant. Her husband was a solicitor in what had been one of the leading firms in London until his father made an unfortunate gaffe. One of his clients bequeathed a large sum of money to the Royal Family. In elegant top hat and morning coat Mr. Hawksley went to Buckingham Palace to solicit His Majesty's gracious acceptance. It was in all the papers. Then it turned out that the estate of the deceased was so riddled with debts that there would be no money for the King or anyone else. The consequent decline in the firm's fortunes did nothing, however, to check the extravagance of Gip's mother.

Gip was devoted to her father and always felt that the strain of trying to keep pace with his wife's extravagance drove him to drink, a morbid sense of failure and an untimely death.

Suddenly the whole fabric of their lives, a glittering cloth of wealth and privilege and Dickens-worship, fell apart. Only the Dickens-worship remained, to be milked for all it was worth. Their dauntless mother opened a little hat shop in Kensington, charged exorbitant prices, and went bankrupt. Other similar ventures ended the same way.

Gip had had enough. She took a job in a tea-room, acted on tour with Mrs. Patrick Campbell and Martin Harvey, both friends of her family, and finally married Terence Downing. Anything, I think, to get away from her family; to stand on her own two feet and live an honest life that did not cling onto the ways of dissipated wealth or to a famous forebear.

She had received no instruction whatever to prepare her for the realities of married life. But a healthily inquiring mind, her love of dogs, and observation of their act of procreation enabled her to take to sex (it was Terry's outstanding talent) with ease and profound enjoyment. In due course, nine months to be exact, a daughter was born to her and her whole family came back into her life to tell her how a child should be reared. Judging by their own results, she could not put any great confidence in what they said. It is not surprising that when Terry had a dream of gold to be mined in the Hollywood Hills, she went along with him.

* * *

The problem of differentiating the two Jennifers was soon solved. Gip's Jennifer had always been called Poppet by her parents and my Jennifer became Jenny. They got on pretty well together, but there was always a rivalry. Both of them had been only children but, since Poppet's performance in that role had been more rewarding, she naturally associated the importation of this other girl with a loss of her own unique status.

In fact, Gip had felt guilty because her long working hours had prevented her being "a good mother," and Poppet had instinctively developed a bag of tricks to increase this feeling and make herself important. She would not eat. She would have headaches, and so on. In helping Gip to understand this—to realize that Terry had pampered Poppet while vacillating in disciplining her, I became someone quite different in Gip's eyes. Instead of being just a nice man she was living with, I became a beloved teacher.

I never had any doubt that I wanted to share the rest of my life with this woman—so gay and warm and honest, if sometimes rather uncomfortably prickly. For she could not easily bring herself to accept what she felt to be avoidable weakness in the man to whom she wanted to give her whole heart. In fact she soon cured me of my lifelong disease of unpunctuality. One day I left her standing on a corner in Santa Monica for half an hour. I had arranged to pick her up and had no valid excuse for being late. She was desperately hurt that I could be so inconsiderate. There was no need to reproach me for in a sudden rush of grief and love, I realized that it was only a matter of self-discipline never to fail her again in this respect. Nor did I; that weakness was eradicated.

Marriage was desirable for social reasons; the law did not even permit cohabitation, let alone contributing to the delinquency of minors by having two young girls living in a house of sin. Gip, who had a legalistic mind, inherited perhaps from her father, was very much aware of this. But I had great difficulty in persuading her that it was not convenience, or even a chivalrous desire to care for her and Poppet, that prompted me to ask her to marry me. She wanted to be quite sure of my enduring love and, even more, to know that I needed her. Over my years of bachelor living and failed first marriage I had developed a shell of cool self-sufficiency that she found disturbing.

I did not realize until long after, that it was for my sake far more than for her own that she had to be quite sure that I did love and need her. Her innate modesty made her feel that she had so little to offer in comparison with what I could give her; and she was afraid, if someone more glamorous were to come along, that I might find that, out of a sort of high-mindedness, I had entangled myself in something I did not really want. "Oh dear, you're so bloody Christ-like," she'd say, fearing that I was being Christ-like from the head instead of from the heart.

It took a lot of persistence for us to gain our freedom to marry, since our respective spouses were not very cooperative. I was finally divorced for desertion in the state of Connecticut. The alimony awarded Nan was not excessive, but I paid it for thirty long years. For Gip there was a real problem. By British law, the wife of a man in the armed services was not divorceable. In desperation she obtained a mail order divorce from Chihuahua, Mexico. My lawyer here said, "Any divorce is legal unless it's challenged, which is usually only done for financial reasons." It was never challenged.

We were married by a judge in Ventura, California, at a ceremony high on good intentions but short on romance. His Honor was old-fashioned and had a spittoon by his desk. Very thoughtfully he expectorated before the ceremony, but we could hear his throat gagging up during a quite unnecessary lecture on the significance of the state of matrimony and felt we were lucky to get away before the next ejaculation. It was a formality to legalize our union. But the thin band of chased white gold I gave to Gip never left her finger, and it is on mine today.

Gip had great natural feeling for physical love: men who were responsive to sex sensed it a mile off. However, since it was not in her nature ever to play at being seductive, other women were not jealous of her and professional womanizers and charm boys tended to think her dull.

After Terry the sex expert left her, for a time she played the field; consequently was not one of those women who are haunted by the fear that they have missed out. She had had all that, enjoyed it, and valued it for what it was. She was able to settle for me and what I had to offer with no encumbrance of unfulfilled yearning.

She had an amusing list of reasons why a woman might sleep with a man, such as:

- Because his conversation bored her and it was the only way to keep him quiet.
- Because he bet her that (to coin something really horrific) orgasm-wise he could outlast her.
- Because one had to call the bluff of someone who hinted at esoteric aids to excitation.
- To stop the poor little chap from crying.

I was never jealous of her past; only grateful that her curiosity had been satisfied and her attractiveness as a woman vindicated. When a former lover, her "old cowboy" as she called him, turned up at the house I felt no qualms; and he, for his part, saw at once that she had quit playing around and had, found her man. "You're a lucky fellow," he said, "and not like one of them two-bit actors." He took my hand in his horny palm for a real powerful shake when he bid us goodbye.

It turned out that he was the one who bet Gip he could outlast her. She said it had been a dead heat.

So, if I seem to have shown Gip in a somewhat moralistic light, picking on George Sanders for bad manners, and on me for evasiveness and unpunctuality, it is only because this was a side of her nature that earned one's respect. What earned one's love was the joy of life in her which made every day an exciting adventure and, if there was anything creative about them, things one had always thought of as dull or grim, fascinating.

Dentistry, for instance. Most of us put it out of our minds until an aching tooth fills us with gloomy foreboding. When Gip and I were first together, I was often the one at home and she the worker. It is the prerogative of the worker to tell the story of his day at the office, which is often listened to with not very convincing simulated interest. But when Gip came home I was always agog to hear how, for instance, Mrs. Wannamaker's bridge-work had gone; she made the whole field of dentistry interesting and her experiences with patients entertaining. Her dentist was creative, always seeking to save a tooth and rebuild a mouth and Gip's tales of how this was done I came to find engrossing. There has to be something exceptional about a woman who could make other people's teeth a fascinating dinner table topic.

And then she was so sweet in her appreciation of my aspirations to build a garden and so generous in praise of my achievements. At the side of the house there had undoubtedly once been a cliff fall. It was as though a giant cheese-scoop had forced out a section of the cliff leaving a concave broken gully about forty-five feet wide, from cliff top to road. Here I determined to make a garden, cutting and filling, devising run-off channels for the winter rains, building retaining walls with stones brought up from the beach—everything done with hand and pick and spade. There is nothing very remarkable about it except that it is there, where no professional gardener would dream of landscaping. The main patio is at bedroom level and it is an abiding joy to step out of one's room in the morning and see, surrounded by evergreen acacias (a brief glory of blossom in the spring covers them like yellow snow), daffodils, pansies, ranunculi, sweet peas, roses from April to January, gladioli, zinnias, dahlias and chrysanthemums as the year goes by. Most of all I enjoy lying in the sun as near naked as I please, looking up at the bowl above me, once broken earth and scabby brush, now covered with tree and shrub and ground cover of varying shades of green—silver green mimosa, dark shiny green Cape plum, feathery pampas grass, bright green arbor vitae, grey-green ice plants that burst into carpets of purple and yellow in the hot sun, and African daisies, white in the shadow of the surrounding acacias. I feel like God on the seventh day. It is my little world.

When Gip and I first started living together I was not really house-broken. Certain specific activities such as house repairs, window cleaning, even a little cooking I could contemplate as falling into the male field; but tidying up after, dishwashing, bed-making, general house cleaning or removing that odious ring round the bathtub really went against the grain. Like Gip, I had been brought up in a world where these menial activities were performed by servants. At Porto Marina Way, we could at first afford no such luxury, though we soon found a wonderful woman, Margaret, who came in once a week for basic cleaning.

Gip worked from nine till five-thirty every day and cheerfully took on most of the marketing and cooking of dinner; but there were occasional blow-ups when she would come home and find the house in a mess because, engaged in some garden project that seemed to me of paramount importance, my lunch things were scattered over the kitchen, the bed was unmade, the bath dirty and muddy footsteps defiled the tile floor of the living room. Then I would make a great gesture. "All right! Tomorrow I'll wash the damn floor!" And I would—a major project taking the whole day. Every stick of furniture taken outside, I would go down on my knees and scrub our L-shaped room from end to end and corner to corner. Then back, swooshing with ample fresh water, that perhaps left splash-marks on the walls. Once again, feeling excruciatingly virtuous I'd cover every inch with clean dry cloths—left in a pile for somebody else to cope with. And then wax. No one was allowed in; when Poppet returned from school she must find her way to her room some other way if she could not manage to clamber over the piled up furniture on the front porch. Everything would be back and in place by the time Gip arrived home. I would be sitting, surveying my noble work, waiting for Gip to hang a halo on my head; and woe betide anyone who dropped so much as a crumb on my clean floor!

Well, slowly I learned. But I think now with regret of how much drudgery I left to Gip. I didn't mind at all doing any special job she might request, like grinding up the remains of the cold meat for a cottage pie; but the business of putting things back in place, of mopping up a spill, of making a bed, of cleaning a bath—that came hard, hard. My final solution of the ultimate humiliation of the bathtub ring is to take a shower instead of a bath.

But our capacity to cooperate in all fields applied also in the kitchen. To Gip it was not "my kitchen" in which I was an interloper. Indeed, certain dishes were my prerogative and I was happy to turn cook and prepare them. Curry for instance, learned from my father under canvass in North Wales, was my specialty. (His basic precept had been: "Begin the day before yesterday and put in twice as many onions as you originally intended to.") Omelets also fell into my field and, always, coffee. I added Lancashire hot-pot—a delicious way of dealing with leftover meats.

Above all, breakfast has been my great positive contribution. I am a day person rather than a night person. "Hail shining morn!" comes easily to me and breakfast is my favorite meal. For thirty years I have cooked breakfast in my house for anyone who cares to join me. Everything is timed to arrive on a table perfectly laid, piping hot and beautifully cooked to the strains of classical music. This is what I deeply enjoy—starting the day with Haydn, Mozart or Beethoven. I find the familiar breakfast routine helps me listen to the music and I go about my business in a kind of ecstatic trance. More and more, as the years go by, it is Beethoven who stirs me. As the great works—particularly the trios, the piano and 'cello sonatas and the quartets—grow familiar with repetition they probe deeper and deeper, and I await some transcendent moment with exquisite anticipation. Gip would come down as the music finished.

"Oh, the Leonore Overture. You've been crying into the scrambled eggs!"

"It's that trumpet call. Yes. Yes, I have. That's why the eggs are so good."

Over money Gip and I never had one moment of friction. As soon as we were married, because she had a better business head than I, she would usually pay the bills and do our income tax returns. We always lived thriftily through necessity and had to push each other into buying new clothes. In fact, Gip made most of hers and I remember having quite a time persuading her to buy that essential little black dress from a very good shop. "Well," she said, "at eighty-five dollars it'll bloody well have to last forever!" And, the hem going up or down to suit the fashion of the moment, it bloody well did.

My career began to look up. A very good part in *The Uninvited* (perhaps the best ghost story ever filmed because it was done perfectly straight) led to fairly constant employment and, in the course of time, Gip was able to retire from dentistry. However, towards the end of her career in that field, after her original employer had been drafted into the U.S. Navy, George Sanders became a patient of her new dentist in order to have his bite adjusted. For those not familiar with this problem let me say that, with certain people, a settling of the jaw structure causes the teeth not to meet properly. In addition to making chewing, and eventually speaking, difficult, it also tends to impair the appearance. It can be corrected by a tedious procedure involving the grinding down of some teeth and the lengthening of others by attaching high crowns to them, After much discussion with Gip, who was in a position to explain the mechanism of this physiologically and, for an actor, esthetically essential procedure, George grudgingly agreed to have it done by Gip's dentist, so that there would be someone he knew to make special arrangements for him and see that it was performed with a minimum of discomfort.

We were very close to George at this time, largely because Gip had become fond (as I had been from the moment I first met her) of the lovely, warm-hearted, earthy girl with whom George had been living for some years and whom we had encouraged him to marry. This was probably a mistake; he began to feel trapped by someone he chose to think below the social level of a rising film star. However that may be, Gip's busy dentist set aside special hours to suit the convenience of Mr. Sanders, the movie star, and Gip held his hand, often literally, through the long sessions of meticulously calculated work.

With Ruth Hussey, Ray Milland and Cornelia Otis Skinner in *The Uninvited* (Paramount, 1944). Collection of James Bigwood.

Finally it was completed successfully and, since George was a man whose face was his fortune, the dentist suggested that he should really have his front teeth, which were a little irregular and not a very good color, capped. Nobody pressured him. It was a reasonable suggestion. George agreed.

The dentist recommended the new plastic caps since, unlike the old porcelain caps, they were not liable to break. Again George agreed and his front teeth were ground down (precious fragments of George removed) to accommodate the caps. Now, although theoretically entirely satisfactory, in the case of one person in fifty, plastic caps can cause the patient some pain for the first few weeks after they have been fitted. George was such a person. His teeth hurt! Gip and her lousy dentist had committed an outrage! In dudgeon he went to another dentist, who removed the plastic caps and installed porcelain. George never forgot. "When I think of Gippy it makes my teeth hurt."

34

Take Two

James Bigwood

Alan has pinpointed *The Uninvited* (Paramount, 1944) as the turning point in his American film career. In conversation he took it a step further, calling it "my first really good part, in fact the only good part I've ever had in movies." What he fails to mention, or may not even have noticed, is that it is also the first movie in his entire career which treats him as a sexual being. Yes, he has a daughter in *In a Monastery Garden* and a wife in *Mademoiselle Fifi*, but these are not flesh and blood relationships; they are plot points. More often he is "the Count," "the ambassador," "the POW," "the postman," "the General"— roles that do not require the audience to define him by anything other than his profession. But in the closing minutes of *The Uninvited*, when it is suddenly revealed that the handsome Dr. Scott, who has been helping Ray Milland sort out the secrets of his recently purchased haunted house, is going to wind up with the second-billed Ruth Hussey (playing Milland's sister), it makes perfect sense. Yet it is still a surprise. We don't expect "the doctor" to be somebody's love interest, no matter how handsome he is. Character men are supposed to be character men. Leads are supposed to be leads. It is rare for somebody to cross the line. No wonder Alan identified *The Uninvited* as a career highlight. It was. Yet it would be another two years before it would happen again.

In the meantime, it was back to business as usual. First up was *Action in Arabia* (RKO, 1944), set in Damascus and obviously designed to cash in on the popularity of the previous year's Best Picture Oscar winner, *Casablanca*—even going so far as to use the same narrator to open the film over almost identical map graphics. Alan is cast as Eric Latimer, a Nazi sympathizer pitted against an American journalist played by George Sanders (who incongruously keeps his English accent). Introduced in a magnificent boom/dolly shot which carries him along an interior balcony, down a flight of stairs and into the spacious lobby of his hotel, Alan makes good use of his height to project menace and evil. Unfortunately, the script is confusing and ultimately unsatisfying.

This was followed by the role of the Chief Engineer in what was touted as "Eugene O'Neill's *The Hairy Ape*" (United Artists, 1944), despite the fact that it had very little in common with the 1922 expressionist play on which it was purportedly based. Getting past the fact that the words are not O'Neill's, but rather Decla Dunning's, it becomes possible to enjoy the film for what it is: a gritty low-budget class-warfare melodrama. Alan—a Scot again—is given more dialogue than usual and he makes the best of it. His berating of William Bendix and John Loder, for example, becomes almost poetic:

With John Loder (standing) in *The Hairy Ape* **(United Artists, 1944). Wisconsin Center for Film and Theatre Research.**

> I've been at sea for forty years. I've known fools and I've known wild men, but you're in a class by yourselves. It's my plain duty to see to it that you're not left at liberty to put this ship and what she carries in any more danger; to hand you over for trial ashore so that you'll sail on no other ship for the rest of your lives. That's my duty! But I can't do it. I've got to put up with you because there's no one to take your places. Because of some personal feud between you, you forget there's a job to be done. It does nae matter to either of you that we're short-handed at best and that we've lost the convoy. Aye, and we might have kept up with it. But we didn't. Remember that now, in case the worst happens and men that have called you their friends have to pay with their lives for your folly. I'll not ask you to shake hands and forget it. You haven't the sense. But I tell you once and for all, if I have to blow the whistle and feed the furnaces myself, one more word of complaint against either or both of you and so help me I'll have you chained to the wall of the brig. And there you'll stay. Now get back to your work!

Ministry of Fear (Paramount, 1944), based on a novel by Graham Greene, is director Fritz Lang in full Hitchcock mode. Alan's role is quite small. Again a Nazi, part of a spy ring that Ray Milland accidentally stumbles upon, he is actually a stronger presence in the story than his screen time would suggest. More discussed than seen, he pops up menacingly from time to time before being killed in a final shootout. For Alan, the film was memorable, but not for his role. "This was my first encounter with the Germanic type of direction," he recalled thirty years later. "In my first scene, I remember I had to go down a corridor, turn, and go into an elevator. In order to show Mr. Lang that I was sincerely interested in the proceedings, I said, 'What am I feeling at this moment?' He said, 'It does not matter vat you feel! You just valk into ze lift! That is all I ask!'"

Back at MGM for *Thirty Seconds over Tokyo* (1944), the story of the famous 1942 Doolittle Raid on Japan, Alan joined Anne Shoemaker as a pair of gentle British missionaries in China who help the American flyers evade the Japanese after successfully completing their mission. Although still only forty-one, Alan was a believable husband for a fifty-three-year-old actress (who was made up and coiffed to look even older).

Alan's scenes in *Dark Waters* (United Artists, 1944) finish four minutes into the movie. As a New Orleans doctor (he does not attempt a Southern accent), he encourages the newly orphaned Merle Oberon to contact her only living relatives and accept their invitation to stay with them at their decaying bayou mansion. When they turn out to be imposters who are trying to drive her mad, it is tempting to think he might return as one of the plotters, but, complicated as their scheme is, he is not a part of it.

Alan's seven 1944 releases were followed by only two in 1945: RKO's *Isle of the Dead* (which he discusses elsewhere) and 20th Century–Fox's *Hangover Square*, best known today for its incomparable Bernard Herrmann score as well as for containing Laird Cregar's final

With Van Johnson and Anne Shoemaker in *Thirty Seconds Over Tokyo* (MGM, 1944). Collection of James Bigwood.

(and some say greatest) performance: the tortured, murderous composer, George Harvey Bone. Alan's part (Sir Henry Chapman, the father of the girl in love with the pianist) is more run of the mill ... but only until the climax of the film, when he conducts Bone's concerto (Herrmann's *Concerto Macabre*). Many observers of this remarkable eleven-minute sequence have commented on how uncommonly well Laird Cregar matches Ignace Hilsberg's pre-recorded piano performance without having to resort to the use of a hand double. Similarly, unlike so many actors who have played conductors over the years, Alan Napier is completely believable wielding a baton. All the classical music at breakfast must have had an effect.

Three Strangers (Warner Bros., 1946) provided Alan with the most complex character he ever played in movies. Director Jean Negulesco (working from a John Huston script) presided over some truly imaginative casting in this neglected gem, including, in addition to his unexpected use of Alan Napier, an even more unexpected romantic role for Peter Lorre.

The script is smart and adult. Alan, as David Shackleford, gets to play scenes totally unlike any he has played before (or since, for that matter). First with Geraldine Fitzgerald as his manipulating estranged wife Crystal, who is refusing to give him a divorce:

With Faye Marlowe in *Hangover Square* (20th Century–Fox, 1945). Collection of James Bigwood.

DAVID: Why did you ask me to come here tonight? What good can possibly come of it?
CRYSTAL: Must a wife have a reason for wanting to see her own husband? After all, you *are* still my husband.
DAVID: Is it necessary to keep reminding me of that?
CRYSTAL: I thought there were some things you wouldn't want to forget. Do you remember when we were in China? All the strange places we visited and how everything we shared was so new and exciting?
DAVID: 'Til the excitement wore off. That didn't take very long as I remember. And then you began to concoct your own forms of excitement.
CRYSTAL: I told you I was sorry.
DAVID: Oh, I don't suppose you can help it. Emotions as violent as yours aren't apt to be very stable. No one man could hold your interest for long.
CRYSTAL: Except you, David. In spite of the way I've acted, you still belong to me. You're the only one I ever really wanted.
DAVID: Perhaps that's the way it seems to you now, but I don't think you really know yourself. You only want what you can't have for as long as you can't have it.

Then, later, with Marjorie Riordan as Janet Elliott, the girl he loves:

JANET: The worst that can happen is we go on as we are now. Oh, that isn't so bad is it David?
DAVID: Darling. You know how wonderful it's been.
JANET: Been? You're putting it in the past.
DAVID: Janet, I'm thinking of you. Sometimes I feel that the only decent thing would be for me to ... to get out of your life and stay out.
JANET: David, you've no right to speak for me.
DAVID: Then there's your family. We'll be going back to Canada still unmarried. What'll *they* say?
JANET: They're *my* family. Suppose you leave them to me.
DAVID: But Janet darling. Much as I love you, we can't go on like this forever, neither married nor unmarried. It's bound to end badly.

And indeed it does. Crystal reveals David's affair to his superior in the Dominions Office and then pretends to be pregnant to induce Janet to return to Canada alone. David comes to her apartment quite prepared to kill her and is only saved from committing murder by Sydney Greenstreet beating him to it.

And these are only a few of the twists in this amazing tale.

Thanks to *Three Strangers*, Alan was able to show himself as a credible love interest for not one, but two beautiful women, one ten years younger than he, the other eighteen years younger. It would never happen again.

35

Dogs

It was Terry who originally brought Gip and me together—Terry, the white dog. He had the finest spirit of any dog that I have known. He was like a knight of the Round Table—loving and gentle, except in defense of the Right. That meant that no act of hostility or aggression should go unpunished within his Lord's domain. Terry was not a big dog. I doubt if he stood twenty inches high, and he never carried much weight; but his strength was as the strength of ten because his heart was pure. His ancestry was said to have been Spitz and Greyhound with a touch, perhaps, of indomitable Airedale. He was pure white and carried his feathery tail—his panache—curled back over his rump. He had melting, light brown eyes and the tip of his nose was marbled pink and brown. His small ears fell softly to his face.

He was Poppet's dog and she had disciplined him with a firmness and patience quite remarkable for a child of eight. She also had a white cat called Chili whose brood of kittens Terry had once saved from death when he found them cavorting in the gutter of busy Montana Avenue. He carried them one by one to a safe hide-out he had dug in a corner of the vacant lot next to Gip's apartment. Many were the tales of his protective sagacity that he brought with him to Porto Marina Way.

Castellamare was the name of the aborted housing development in which our new home was situated. Aborted because it had been laid out in the wildly inflated housing boom preceding the great American Depression. Because of the war its development remained in abeyance until a new surge of expansion on the West Coast set the builders to work again in the fifties. Until then the area was a paradise for dogs. They could roam the hills above and, by way of the subway under the ocean highway, patrol the beach in safety. Rabbits, raccoons, deer, coyotes, and foxes left delicious scents for them to follow. When we moved in, there were other dogs in the neighborhood, each with a set of territorial rights and it took Terry some time to establish our domain. There was Chang, for instance, a massive chow, who lived at the Mediterranean-style palace just up the road. Terry was unable to exact total submission from Chang, but at least they arrived at a gentlemen's agreement. A boundary line was established across the road exactly where my property ended and the garden of the big house began. So long as Chang did not cross this line Terry left him in peace and vice-versa. If either absentmindedly crossed the boundary, the other would rush out and make a diplomatic démarche with a good deal of growling and show of teeth. The offender would diplomatically withdraw, suddenly turning with an impressive show of force at the borderline. With hackles raised they would snarl savagely at each other as a matter of form, then quietly withdraw. At least Chang kept himself to himself and was not a neighborhood bully.

Puppy, down the hill, was another matter. He thought he owned the bottom end of the hill and the entire beach and he was a bully. Heaven knows what his ancestry was but he was heavyset with a thick, brown coat and weighed at least half as much again as Terry. They had many savage encounters and it was a stand-off for nearly a year until the day when Puppy went too far.

Soon after Gip and I settled into Porto Marina Way we decided to get Terry a wife. We had been on a trip up to the San Bernardino mountain lakes and on the way back had the notion to stop at the Pasadena dog pound. Terry had come from the Santa Monica pound; we thought we would give him a wife with a little more class. But the object who attached herself to me, saying in no uncertain fashion "I'm yours. I love you. Take me. Take me!" had a very plebeian appearance. Smallish, mousy grey, with a little inch-long stump of tail, she hardly looked like a dog at all. But she had dark brown eyes brimming with impish vivacity one moment and slavish adoration the next. She was a personality and would not be denied. We could but love her; Terry thought her absolutely smashing. Indeed, a month or so after her arrival he gave our girls a fine lesson in copulation while we were having dinner one evening.

Six weeks later, Paula, as we had christened her, gave birth to a litter of seven in my bedroom during a thunderstorm. From the litter I chose the one who seemed to me to have the finest coat—a strong, bright tan—and I named him Kentigern. He was my first very own dog.

To return to Puppy. Two months later, I had Kentigern on the beach with me. Terry and Paula had departed on a wild sea-bird chase when Puppy suddenly appeared on the brow of the bank above the beach. He sauntered down with his stiff-legged aggressive walk to investigate this new small dog. Little Kentigern, with a puppy's fearless curiosity, waddled over towards him, tail wagging madly. Puppy growled and made a sudden onslaught, knocking him over. I was just able to pick Kentigern up before Puppy's jaws closed; whereat he jumped up and bit my wrist. I was raising my arms higher and kicking out to keep the brute away when a white arrow of righteous wrath struck. Terry, out of nowhere, had him by the throat.

It was a battle royal. Though neither dog was seriously injured, from that moment Puppy was cowed. If he showed his face on the beach, Terry would only have to take off in his direction and Puppy disappeared. Going down the road from our house Terry would jauntily chase him right up his own front steps and into his house. Then, standing triumphant on the doorstep, noble Terry would, so to speak, wave us on, saying, "Okay, all safe! I've got him cornered." Terry, Paula and Kentigern became the ruling family on the hill.

36

Take Three

JAMES BIGWOOD

Three Strangers was followed by *House of Horrors* (Universal, 1946) which featured the unlikely star Rondo Hatton, an utterly ordinary man whose features, deformed by acromegaly, doomed him to a career as a screen monster. Alan is F. Holmes Harmon, an effete, not quite effeminate art critic who makes the mistake of panning the work of sculptor Marcel De Lange. ("I call it tripe. Pure unadulterated tripe. With an overtone of sheer lunacy.") De Lange befriends "The Creeper," a spine-snapping brute first introduced in the Sherlock Holmes film *The Pearl of Death*, and makes use of him to settle scores with his enemies. Harmon is the first to go, murdered at his typewriter.

Martin Kosleck, Byron Foulger and Alan Napier in *House of Horrors* (Universal, 1946).

Next came Douglas Sirk's *A Scandal in Paris* (United Artists, 1946), based on the memoirs of Eugéne François Vidocq, the 18th century French thief who used his knowledge of crime to become Paris' Chief of Police. Teamed again with his friend George Sanders, Alan gives a delicious performance as the slightly addled Police Minister, who "convinces" Vidocq to accept the position of Chief after watching him "solve" a robbery that Vidocq himself has committed. Watching these two pros making a meal of an uncommonly literate period script is a joy.

The two appear again in Alan's next film, *The Strange Woman* (United Artists, 1946), although Sanders makes his entrance just in time for the funeral of Alan's character, Judge Henry Saladine. The film follows the life of Jenny Hager (Hedy Lamarr) as she makes her way from man to man in 1820s Bangor, Maine. We first encounter her at the age of six, when she refuses the Judge's offer of shelter from her abusive father (Saladine: "You could come and live at the house and earn your keep, I guess. Help in the kitchen and run errands for Mrs. Saladine." Jenny: "No! If I can't go to boarding school with [your daughter], I'll stay with my father!"). We next meet her as a young woman (with a mysterious Viennese accent that she didn't have as a child) worming her way into society. Alan gives a serviceable performance in an unremarkable role but certainly does better than Sanders, who is very hard to take seriously in the role of a lumberjack.

With Signe Hasso and Alma Kruger in *A Scandal in Paris* (United Artists, 1946). Wisconsin Center for Film and Theatre Research.

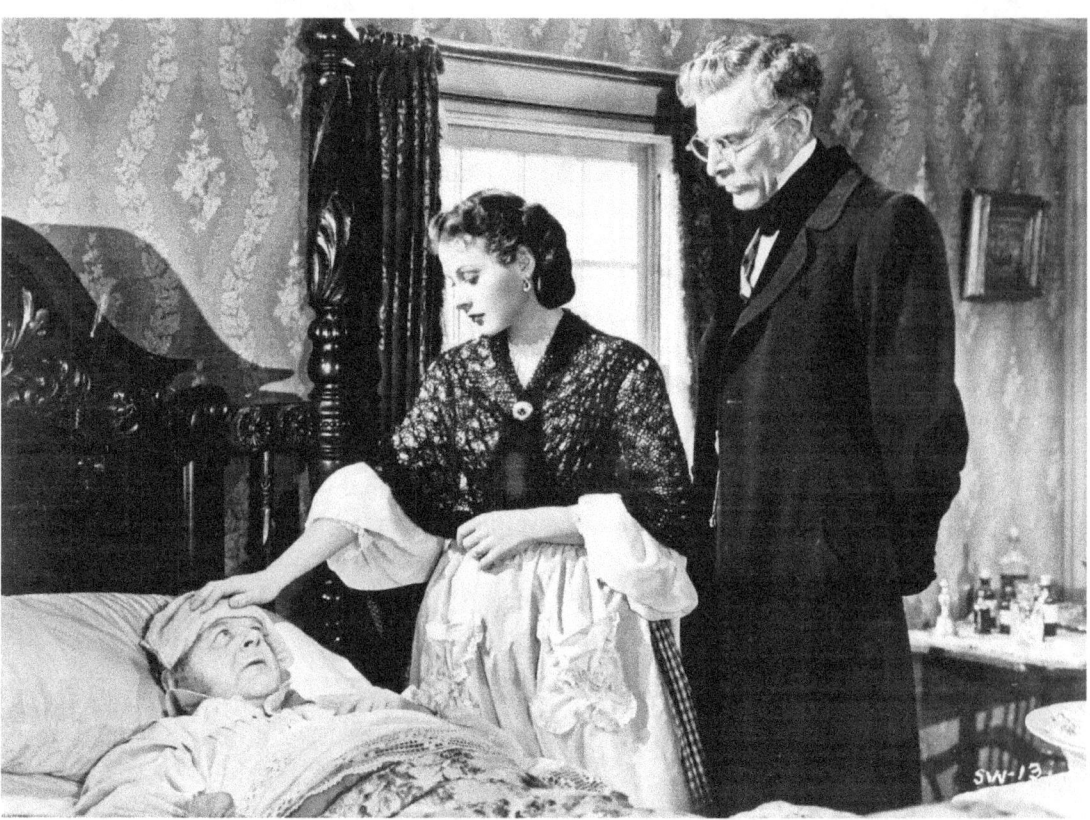

Gene Lockhart, Hedy Lamarr and Alan Napier in *The Strange Woman* (United Artists, 1946). Wisconsin Center for Film and Theatre Research.

Sinbad the Sailor (1947), a lush Technicolor extravaganza from RKO, featured Douglas Fairbanks, Jr., in a role reminiscent of his father's great silent triumphs. Unfortunately, he seems to have taken the assignment literally, waving his arms about like a windmill as if there were no words to help him. But words there are. Lots of them. Florid, flamboyant and self-consciously "Arabian."

Slathered in brown makeup, Alan is the ancient Aga of Deryabar, guarding the riches of Alexander the Great from those who do not comprehend that "all treasure lies here [indicating his heart] or here [indicating his head]. Or in the blue sea. Or in the green land. Or in a pair of bright eyes." His mellifluous voice, so much a part of his success on the stage, goes a long way toward actually making his lines palatable.

In *Fiesta* (MGM, 1947), Esther Williams abandons the swimming pool for the bullring. Playing the twin sister of Ricardo Montalban (!), she secretly takes his place in the ring so that he can pursue his love of music. Alan has a tiny part as a tourist who listens to Montalban play his "Fantasia Mexicana" (actually Aaron Copland's "El Salon Mexico") on the piano while their bus makes a short layover at a café.

Going from the Tiffany of the studios to "Poverty Row," Alan next appeared in his first picture for Monogram. *High Conquest* (1947) tells the story of rival mountain climbers (Warren Douglas and Gilbert Roland) vying for the love of Anna Lee. Alan is an artist

As the Aga of Deryabar with Maureen O'Hara in *Sinbad the Sailor* (RKO, 1947). Margaret Herrick Library, Academy of Motion Picture Arts and Sciences. RKO Radio Pictures Collection.

sharing Lee's train compartment, whose innocent sketch of her with Douglas causes Roland to attempt his rival's murder during a rescue climb up the Matterhorn. Throughout the movie, Alan's character is pursued by Beulah Bondi, despite subtle hints that he actually has little interest in the ladies.

In *Ivy* (Universal, 1947), Alan is barrister Sir Jonathan Wright, interrogating his old friend Joan Fontaine in a brief courtroom scene.

His next film—*Adventure Island* (1947), produced by the low budget Pine-Thomas unit at Paramount—gave Alan a rare opportunity for some real scenery chewing. As Attwater, the self-appointed ruler of a remote island, he befriends Herrick (Rory Calhoun), a crew member of a boat that has landed in search of provisions. (Attwater: "I was sent here to give these

Standing: Rory Calhoun, John Abbott, Alan Napier and Paul Kelly in *Adventure Island* (Paramount, 1947). The two kneeling men are unidentified. Collection of James Bigwood.

islanders what they need, the bearer of the sword of the scourge. From groveling heathen, I have given them something to believe in!" Herrick: "God?" Attwater: "Me.") The madman finally meets his fate in the snake-filled pit he uses as a punishment for disobedient subjects.

Adventure Island was shot in the down-market Cinecolor process and existing color prints are badly washed out with some night scenes almost impossible to make out. In black and white prints, struck before color disintegration set in, the problem is mitigated, although picture sharpness suffers. Despite these barriers, it is worth making an effort to experience Alan's delightfully over-the-top take on the "Dr. Moreau" tradition of island tyrants. It makes an otherwise forgettable sixty-five minute film worth watching.

Lured (United Artists, 1947) was a return to a more conventional role. As Detective Gordon of Scotland Yard (complete with Scottish accent), Alan oversees the investigation of a series of disappearances of young women. He supervises visiting American sixpence-a-dance girl Lucille Ball when she goes undercover and has a nice scene interrogating his friend George Sanders, a suspect who eventually turns out to be a red herring. Beyond that, the role is unremarkable.

Driftwood (Republic, 1947) stars the nine-year-old Natalie Wood, and features a number of great character actors as eccentric citizens of Panbucket, Nevada—Walter Brennan,

Alan Napier, Charlotte Greenwood, Walter Brennan and James Kirkwood in *Driftwood* (Republic, 1947). Collection of James Bigwood.

Charlotte Greenwood, and Margaret Hamilton among them. Alan is Dr. Nicholas Adams, consulted towards the end of the picture when an experimental serum appears to be the only possible cure for Wood's Spotted Fever. Dignified and reassuring, he is perfectly satisfactory in a role which demands no more.

A half an hour into Cecil B. DeMille's *Unconquered* (Paramount 1947), set in pre–Revolutionary War America, Alan appears in a single extended sequence as Sir William Johnson, the British Superintendent of Indian Affairs. Johnson, along with Colonel George Washington and surveyors Mason and Dixon, makes no other appearance in the film, existing only to deliver the exposition establishing the historical background to the story. ("For years, gentlemen, I've had the Indians' friendship. I sometimes think that only an Irishman can really understand the red man. Now, maybe I'm getting old, but I still know the signs. There's a cloud of trouble coming down over the Ohio. With the sound of war drums in it. I've heard 'em before, and I know that closing your ears to 'em can cost you your scalp... When old enemies like the Ottowas, the Shawnees and the Senecas meet together in council, the thread's off the bobbin.") It is left to Gary Cooper to try to keep the thread from unspooling.

As for his relationship with the film's mercurial director, Alan recalls, "I got along very well with Mr. DeMille. You know, he had this reputation, but he knew a pro when he saw

John Mylong, Frank Wilcox (standing), Richard Gaines, Ward Bond, Alan Napier, Griff Barnett, Davison Clark and Gary Cooper in Cecil B. DeMille's *Unconquered* (Paramount, 1947). Collection of James Bigwood.

one and if you knew your job he was extremely agreeable. While we were waiting for an upcoming scene, there was a table laden with the most gorgeous fruit and there we are, out of boredom, eating the fruit and Mr. DeMille comes by and says, 'Ahhhh. I like seeing the actors eating the props. I know they're real actors then!'"

Otto Preminger, another director with a reputation for being tough, hired Alan as a dialogue coach on *Forever Amber* (20th Century–Fox, 1947) "to teach 'instant English' to the entire American cast. An impossible task. There are certain sounds that it is almost impossible to get Americans to speak. Cornel Wilde played the lead in it, and in his first speech in the entire picture (he's landed in England and he's riding through the English countryside—which of course had to have fog in it), he says to a yokel there, 'Tell me, my man. How many miles to Lawndon? I said, 'No, Cornel. Not Lawndon. Lundon.' He said, 'Oh, I see. Luhndon.' That short 'ah' is very difficult for Americans to get."

Alan also wound up acting in the movie, teamed with Norma Varden as a pair of swindlers who cause Linda Darnell to be thrown into debtors' prison. "Otto had this aggravating thing of saying, if you dried on your lines, he'd say 'Alan! Vy don't you conzentrate?! It's quite easy, you do not conzentrate!' Years pass. I'm doing *Batman*. And I see a very *little* man walking about (I'd always thought of Otto as *enormous* on *Forever Amber*) and he's playing one of the guest villains, Mr. Freeze. And it comes time to do a series of different lines—his close-ups—and here's Otto fluffing and drying on every god damn one of them and the temptation to say 'Vy don't you conzentrate, Otto?!' was almost irresistible, but because I'm an actor and I know the strains, the things that can dissipate your concentration, the thousand little things that the cameraman says before you start, all these distracting things, I didn't have it in my heart to say it."

The Lone Wolf in London (Columbia, 1947) was the next-to-last entry in a long-running series of films about a reformed jewel thief turned amateur detective. Alan's Monty Beresford is paired with Evelyn Ankers' Iris Chatham, the brains behind the theft of the "Eyes of the Nile," a perfectly matched pair of diamonds. In a substantially more physical role than usual, he is knocked out by a punch in the jaw in one scene and subdued by police and dragged off struggling in another. On the plus side, he has two quite torrid embraces with his accomplice, before she inevitably double-crosses him. By this point, the plot has gotten so convoluted that his ridiculously detailed confession is the only thing that saves the hero from arrest: "I'll kill you before I let you run away with Lanyard! And you won't either of you live to see those two diamonds again! And you won't get the chance to do to me what you did to Henry Robards! Yes. She killed him. And that's the gun she used. She got Robards to take the stones away from Sir John Kelmscott and then she killed him! … She planned the thing in the first place! It was her idea to take him the stones, offer them at a low price and then demand £10,000 more!"

Helping to offset this hokum was the minor role of Jane Wyman's defense attorney in *Johnny Belinda* (Warner Bros., 1948). This unusually frank tale of rape and murder in a remote Nova Scotia fishing village was nominated for twelve Academy Awards, winning one for Wyman's performance as the young deaf-mute whose story it tells. Alan is one of many in a distinguished cast.

Orson Welles' *Macbeth* and Victor Fleming's *Joan of Arc*, both of which Alan covers later, were next, followed by another Lassie picture, *Hills of Home* (MGM, 1948). A tale of rural Victorian Scotland, it features Alan as an expert London physician brought in at great expense by the local doctor (Edmund Gwenn) to perform a brand new medical procedure on one of his patients. Alan's Sir George is initially cranky ("Turn back at once! Turn back, I say! I'll be utterly and eternally damned if I allow myself to be drowned for anyone!") but by the time of his departure, his attitude has been softened by Gwenn's obvious dedication to his charge. "After my screams at the river last night, you have some right to call me a coward. But I'll never let you think me a mean, miserly rascal." Tearing up his check, he boards the carriage to leave. "My only regret is that I cannot spend more time with you." It is a charming cameo.

Stuffy Melvyn Douglas courts freewheeling Phyllis Calvert in post-war London in *My Own True Love* (Paramount, 1949)—Val Lewton in non–horror mode again. Alan is Douglas' boss in the Army film corps. Although current prints of the film limit his role to a single awkward dinner where Calvert's boisterous friends embarrass Douglas (and Alan barely speaks), production stills indicate that there was once much more to the part.

Tarzan's Magic Fountain (RKO, 1949) is really only fit for younger viewers. The movie's plot is nonsensical, with endless treks through the jungle attempting to pass for action. Alan is in it, and the Magic Fountain of the title is the Fountain of Youth. Nuff said.

In *A Connecticut Yankee in King Arthur's Court,* Paramount's 1949 musical version of Mark Twain's time-travel novel, Alan is imposing in black (with black mustache and hair to match) as King Arthur's High Executioner. Unfortunately, most of the short scene where he condemns Bing Crosby to death is played on his back. He does get a nice reaction close

Alan Napier as Alton Bennett, whose recurring dream of murdering his wife (Irene Hervey)… Collection of James Bigwood.

...makes him the logical suspect when she is actually killed in *Manhandled* (Paramount, 1949). Margaret Herrick Library, Academy of Motion Picture Arts and Sciences. Core Collection.

up though, when, thanks to some effective use of 20th century technology, Crosby turns the tables, and, with an imperious snap of his fingers, barks out, "Slim! Release me here! C'mon! Quickly!"

Manhandled (1949), from Paramount's Pine-Thomas unit, opens on a shot of a rainy night through an open window. A clock ticks. A fire burns in the fireplace. A man, whose face we cannot see, waits up in pajamas and a patterned robe. The apartment door opens, revealing two pairs of legs: an elegantly gowned woman and her formally dressed escort. They embrace in the doorway. She eagerly promises to see him again and he leaves, closing the door behind him. The camera follows her gowned legs up the stairs. The robed man follows her, his face still not visible. When the woman sits to admire herself in her bedroom mirror, her face is finally revealed. She's a stunner. Slippered feet enter from the doorway and cross the room. The distinctive robe appears behind her, reflected in the mirror. She speaks. "Oh, did I waken you darling? I meant to be *very* quiet." The unmistakable voice of Alan Napier answers her. "*Too* quiet my dear. Such overplaying of wifely solicitude might easily be misunderstood." She is offended by his tone. "If you're hinting that I was *sneaking* in..." He is regretful, almost resigned. "Doesn't matter. Nothing matters anymore. The time has come when words fail to have meaning, when only what one *feels* is important. I'm going to kill you, Ruth. I have to." Snatching a large perfume bottle from the vanity, he batters his wife to death. His face is finally visible, eyes wide with horror at the crime he has just committed.

The most dramatic entrance of Alan's career is quickly revealed to be a recurring dream that he, as writer Alton Bennet, is recounting to his psychiatrist. When Bennet's wife is actually murdered, his snide, cynical attitude makes him a prime suspect, although he has what appears to be a solid alibi. His usefulness as a red herring is short-lived though. The real murderer is revealed early in the proceedings, and unfortunately Alan quickly disappears from the movie.

In *Criss Cross* (Universal, 1949), starring Burt Lancaster, Yvonne DeCarlo and Dan Duryea, Alan has a scene-stealing cameo as Finchley, a reluctant, alcoholic, criminal mastermind. Introduced playing chess with himself in a dingy boarding room, he is enticed by the promise of "a month's credit for you at Conrad's Liquor Store on Hill Street" to lend his expertise to an armored car robbery. Seedy and down-at-heels, but with the integrity to wait until his plan has been completely worked out before taking his first drink, Finchley is one of Alan's finest creations.

The change of pace of back-to-back excursions into *film noir* did not radically alter the course of Alan's career. His next film found him back at MGM as "The General"

John "Skins" Miller, Dan Duryea, James O'Rear (on bed), Alan Napier, Tom Pedi and Burt Lancaster in *Criss Cross* (Universal, 1949). Wisconsin Center for Film and Theatre Research.

Robert Coote, Alan Napier and Walter Pidgeon in *The Red Danube* **(MGM, 1949). Collection of James Bigwood.**

(unnamed) in *The Red Danube* (1949), set in the British sector of post–War Vienna. At issue is the forced repatriation of refugees of Allied nations (specifically those of the Soviet Union). Playing the superficially stuffy General with a twinkle in his eye, Alan embodies the shifting military attitude of the time, moving from by-the-book in his opening scenes to reformer by the end of the movie. "We're converting the army, reforming it, getting rid of a lot of old customs, red tape and all that rot… We're reforming the army. Humanizing the army. And I've decided to put you in charge of the operation." This was Alan's first film with the young Angela Lansbury, with whom he had been acquainted socially since her arrival in Hollywood with her twin brothers and her mother, actress Moyna MacGill. "I was a kid when I knew him," she recalls today. "I remember him as being an extremely nice, generous man in his dealings—certainly with me as a young person—but he was not my generation of course and was really more of a friend of my mother's. I do think he helped my mother a great deal when we first arrived here and we really had nothing at all monetarily. We were very, very hard up; had no income other than what we were given by our sponsor."

Alan and Gip would organize play readings at Porto Marina Way in which both Moyna and Angela would participate, and it may be entirely coincidental, but Moyna MacGill did receive an uncredited role in Alan's film *The Uninvited*. By the time of *Red Danube*, of course, Angela Lansbury was a much bigger star than her former benefactor, having been Oscar nominated for her screen debut in *Gaslight*. She laughs now, remembering the cast "all tarted up in our uniforms" and, while she and Alan didn't share many scenes, recalling him as "a very striking figure because he was so tall. He was basketball player height!"

Still at MGM for *Challenge to Lassie* (1949), Alan—in Scottish mode now—plays the Lord Provost of Edinburgh, overseeing a trial which, under an ancient ordinance designed to keep ownerless dogs from roaming the streets, threatens to put the beloved collie to death. His frustrated attempts to explain to the children of the town that he does not make the laws, but simply carries them out as they are written, inject some humor into an essentially bloodthirsty sequence. By the fadeout, though, he redeems himself by coming up with the solution that allows Lassie to live: "By the authority in me vested as Lord Provost, I give ye the freedom of the city of Edinburgh. And a free citizen of Edinburgh needs no license!"

The Bowery Boys comedy *Master Minds* (Monogram, 1949), undoubtedly inspired by the success of the previous year's *Abbott and Costello Meet Frankenstein*, was Alan's final release of the decade. As the mad scientist Dr. Druzik, he successfully (although not permanently) transfers the mind of Huntz Hall's Sach into the body of Glenn Strange's Atlas

Alan as the Lord Provost of Edinburgh, shaking hands with the title character in *Challenge to Lassie* (MGM, 1949). Collection of James Bigwood.

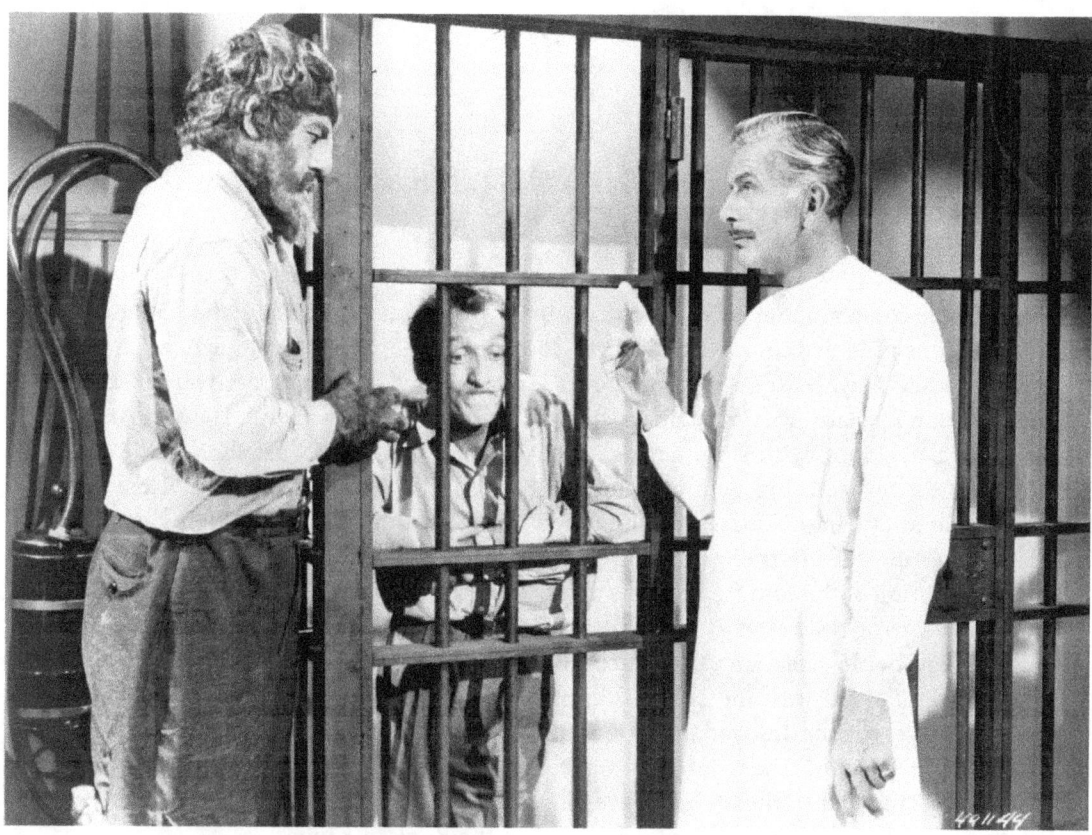

With Glenn Strange and Huntz Hall in *Master Minds* (Allied Artists, 1949). For once, Alan is not the tallest actor in the scene. Collection of James Bigwood.

the Monster (and vice versa, of course). Alan is a surprisingly calm madman here, especially when contrasted with all the lunacy that surrounds him. That may have been his intention, of course, but seems an odd choice to have made.

The best moments in the film actually belong to Glenn Strange in the scenes where Atlas has Sach's mind. Although Strange's voice is dubbed by Huntz Hall, he expertly mimics Sach's unmistakable body movements. Incidentally, in what must have been a unique experience for Alan, Atlas towers over him by a good six inches.

37

Mountains

People complain that there is no real winter in Southern California; that the joy of the four seasons is denied to us who live here. It is true that I have seen 80 degrees registered on Christmas Day. But a mere three hours' drive from Pacific Palisades will take you up into the San Bernardino Mountains, rising to 7,500 feet above sea level. Here, surrounded by pine-clad slopes, with shimmering aspens at the water's edge, are man-made lakes—Gregory, Arrowhead, Big Bear and, loftiest of all, little Green Valley Lake. Here, in the high, clear air, spring sparkles, autumn follows a hot summer with brisk nights and golden days, and snow falls in the winter. Gip and I were drawn to these majestic mountains, to the stimulation of the cold fresh nights and the sparkling waters of the mountain lakes. We went up to Arrowhead after we were married and it was Gip's story that on our honeymoon night I read her to sleep with the Gideon Bible provided in our hotel bedroom.

Reading aloud was one of the things I did well (a gift inherited from my mother) which Gip very much enjoyed; and found that, having been raised a Catholic, she had not been taught "scripture" at school and was totally ignorant of the whole fascinating field of literature contained in the St. James' version of the Old Testament. So I read her to sleep at Arrowhead while "Agag walked delicately" in the Book of Kings.

A few years later (was it for the dogs' sake?) we bought a cabin by the lakeside at Green Valley. We had many fine times there. We trolled for trout from my little sailing dinghy with Gladys Cooper ecstatically reeling in the smallest trout you ever saw. We brought Jack Houseman back to it after marrying him to Joan in Yuma, Arizona. We gambled there all night at canasta with Brian and Eleanor Aherne and we opened the fishing season in swirls of icy mist and brilliant sunshine one year with Val and Ruth Lewton.

In the winter we both skied there till poor Gip, so resolute to keep up with me, broke her leg. That must have been in 1947, because that was the year we made our trip together to England and, when we went to the Department of Internal Revenue to clear our income tax before leaving the country, I remember the tax man, charmed by Gippy's warmth and humor stamped "Paid in Full" in purple all over the cast she still had on her leg.

During the war years we played a good deal of tennis with our wonderful neighbors up the hill, Tommy and Bea Armstrong. The most modest of men, Tommy is a cartoonist of great talent, subtle and gently humorous. He had had a job at Disney's and, at the time of the great strike for better wages and working conditions, he and Bea brought a soup kitchen to the picket line—an act of positive love for his fellow man that lost him his job.

Up the hill, there was a big house, built by the architect of many of the super movie theaters of the West Coast and furnished in the finest late MGM style, with a tennis court cantilevered out over the one rocky spine of our unstable earthen cliffs. On the outbreak of war the owner retired inland and rented it for a small sum to a studio set-designer, a charming man who put the tennis court at our disposal. It was a lovely place to play, perched high above the far-sounding Pacific.

As the war drew to a close, the house passed into other hands, and, with an easily accessible court no longer available, I discovered in the place of tennis, beach volleyball. For this splendid game my height was an advantage and, though I discovered it too late in life ever to become really good, of all athletic sports it has been my favorite. Indeed Gip used to say, "Volleyball is Alan's life; he acts for money when he has to." For nearly 20 years I played it till, in my middle sixties, I noticed that the young players' faces fell when I asked one of them to be my partner. But my interest continues since my grandson, David, inspired at first by his grandfather, is now one of the outstanding young players in America. *(David Nichols actually made a career of volleyball, becoming a successful head coach at Florida Gulf Coast University.)*

The group with whom I played I only knew on the beach—in swimming trunks. I would hardly be able to recognize them in street clothes. They came from all walks of life. We played together and aged together and saw our children (grandchildren in my case) rising from toddlers to formidable players. And they had nothing to do with movies. I think perhaps they tolerated my waning powers because I did.

There was a rather touching moment one Sunday, the Sunday after Gip died. I forced myself to go down to the beach as usual. The news had gone around amongst most of the players and a wonderful camaraderie enveloped me. Hardly a word was spoken but a silent pressure of a hand on my shoulder would express sympathy with an understanding that I wanted everything to go on the same as usual. However, one habitually tactless and rather loud-mouthed player had not heard what had happened and, as I was leaving, called after me, "Hey! How's your wife?" I had to call back, "She died, Bob."

"Too bad," he said, "I tell you what—when you go, Al, we'll plant you right here. Here in the middle of this court!"

And there was the time we went down to La Jolla, where I was starred in a summer production of *Dial "M" for Murder*. The play presented no difficulty for me since I had played the part with some success for many months in Chicago, so the moment rehearsals were over and the play running, I sought out a beach where volleyball was played. The local boys were no theater-goers, had no idea who I was despite the fact that my name was in large letters on posters all over the town and were at first unwilling to let this grey-haired man into their game. But I persevered. Gip's story is that when we were back at Pacific Palisades, some friend was asking about our time in La Jolla and that all I would talk about was volleyball. Finally, the friend said, "But what about the play?"

"To hell with the play," I answered. "That was easy. But for a stranger to be accepted on the volleyball court and introduced with awe as 'Big Al from Santa Monica'—that was something."

Poor Gip was no luckier in volleyball than in skiing. In the first few minutes of her first game the ball struck the end of her little finger. Without leaving the court she called to me and said, "I think I've broken my little finger."

"Oh. No," I answered. "We all do that to begin with. It hurts at the time but you'll be all right."

She played to the end of the game and showed me her finger. It was turning blue.

"Maybe you should see a doctor. Shall I…"

"No, no. You're up to play. Don't worry, I'll take care of it." And she drove into her dentist's office, took an x-ray of her finger on the dental machine, saw that it was in fact fractured, put it in a splint and came home to cook dinner.

The summer vacation had been a very happy one for both girls, and the high point of the week was the gathering of the clan for cricket. With the girls in tow I would pick up John Buckmaster and Jack Merrivale at Gladys Cooper's lovely house on Napoli Drive overlooking the Riviera Country Club golf course. We would go on into Beverly Hills to George Coulouris's where, after a brief halt for sherry we would all proceed to Griffith Park, where the cricket ground, encircled by an equestrian riding track, was located. The girls had invented romantic crushes on John and Jack and there were plenty of other young people for them to play around with at the cricket field.

The standard of playing there was not very high but there were some remarkable characters. There was tiny Doc Severn, a South African, very loyal to the crown, who sired more child actors than one would have thought possible and taught them all a decent game of cricket. I think he ended up fielding an entire eleven of his sons—all of whom had at one time been in movies. *Indeed, not only had they all been in the movies, one of them was in the movies with Alan. Christopher Severn appears in* The Strange Woman *as a schoolmate of the girl who grows up to be Hedy Lamarr. (He grows up to be Louis Hayward.) This evil little girl actually attempts to drown him for a lark but is prevented from doing so by the arrival of Alan's Judge Saladine. Chris recalls being very happy to see his cricket acquaintance on the set. "I actually could not swim at the time! And I thought I was going to drown. I was afraid to say anything to the director, so I was actually scared when that scene was going on. I was glad to see Alan, because it meant that it was time for me to be rescued!"*

We all had fun those Sundays one way or another. On the way home we would stop at George Coulouris's and carouse. "Horses' necks" he called the drinks—vodka and tonic with great spirals of lemon peel from top to bottom of the tall glasses. With luck, John would do bits from his nightclub act that included a fabulous burlesque of one of the Shakespeare historical dramas. A little drunk, I would arrive home with two giggling girls to encounter Gip's wrath for being late for dinner.

On Jenny's last Sunday she was very quiet in the car going home. She went straight into the kitchen where Gip was cooking and burst into tears. Then it came pouring forth. She could not bear it—going back to "Maimie" in Connecticut. And the whole story of her miserable life there came out. Gip heard her out and then said, "Cheer up, darling, you're not going back. We'll see to that."

38

Take Four

James Bigwood

A new decade began with the release of *Tripoli* (Paramount, 1950), not an auspicious start for Alan. The Pine-Thomas production was a colorful enough project, dramatizing the story of the 1805 assault on Tripoli by a small group of early U.S. Marines, but his role was minimal. As Khalil, the primary aide to Hamet Karamanly, a duplicitous Arab ally of the Americans, he spends most of his time sitting silently next to his master, speaking occasionally, but essentially a glorified extra. He did have one piece of action, though. "We were

Phillip Reed, Alan Napier and Alberto Morin in *Tripoli* (Paramount, 1950). Margaret Herrick Library, Academy of Motion Picture Arts and Sciences. Core Collection.

shooting above Palm Springs where there's an Indian reservation. I was lying in the trailer trying to keep cool and suddenly they called and said, 'Alan! Quick! We want to get a last shot before the sun goes behind that rock! It's perfectly simple. Phil Reed comes out of the tent, you mount your horse and follow him.' They didn't tell me that Phil Reed was going to come out of the tent and *gallop* down the hillside with boulders on each side and so on. So Banjo, my darling horse that I always asked for because he was so kind to me, started galloping too. I thought, 'This is the end. This is the end.' However, by hook or by crook I stayed on that fucking horse and I looked forward to the preview with enormous excitement to see how I looked galloping. The scene was cut. My life had been risked for nothing!"

His role is no larger in *Double Crossbones* (Universal, 1951), a lighthearted pirate tale that, had it been made at Goldwyn, would certainly have starred Danny Kaye. As it wasn't, it is Donald O'Connor who periodically breaks into song and dance as the accidentally dubbed "Bloodthirsty Dave." Alan, wonderfully costumed and made up for the role of Captain Kidd, is practically ignored as one of the six pirates who make up the "Brethren of the Coast," a fraternal group of the world's fiercest buccaneers, who accept the unlikely Dave into their ranks.

Better treated in *Tarzan's Peril* (RKO, 1951), he dominates the first third of the film, before being killed by villainous gunrunners who are trying to arm African tribes for their own ends. As Commissioner Peters, due to retire after thirty years representing British interests in the jungle, Alan is a kindly, comforting presence—although an undeniably paternalistic and condescending one—and shares a nice scene with Dorothy Dandridge, three years away from her breakthrough role in *Carmen Jones*.

In *The Great Caruso* (MGM, 1951), Alan has a one-scene cameo as the great Polish tenor Jean de Reszke, whose enthusias-

Alan as Captain Kidd in *Double Crossbones* (Universal, 1951). Unfortunately, the role does not live up to the promise of the publicity still. Collection of James Bigwood.

tic ovation for Caruso's Metropolitan Opera debut in *La Bohème* forces the stuffy New York opera establishment (who are constantly comparing the "peasant" Caruso to the "noble" de Reszke) to take the upstart seriously. The movie is less a biography than it is "Caruso's greatest hits," and the scene has absolutely no basis in truth, but it does make for good cinematic shorthand, metaphorically passing the torch from one generation to the next.

The Highwayman (Allied Artists, 1951) offers Alan a more complex role. His Lord Barton initially appears quite harmless, introduced in an amusing scene where he describes to Norma Varden just what he would do were he to come face to face with the notorious Robin Hood–like criminal known as the Highwayman, blissfully unaware that the mysterious Quaker who has just joined their conversation is the man himself. Later, thanks to revelations by the Highwayman in his true identity as Lord Northwood, he unexpectedly finds himself one of a band of progressive noblemen allied against the villainous Victor Jory. In a final twist, he betrays his friends and their cause and is conveniently killed in the film's confusing climax. Alan deftly balances fatuousness and cravenness in the few scenes allowed him, although in one shot, undoubtedly betrayed by the film's budget, he briefly loses track of his lines: "I take my leave. I must hasten to Walters and waste no time [awkward pause] returning lest they become suspicious of my absence."

39

Don't Talk Politics to Adolphe Menjou

All this time my career in movies had been building, if not sensationally, at least quite comfortably. I knew I would never be a great movie actor; indeed I had no ambition to become a star—the exacting nature of that classification would have cut too deeply into the fascinating occupation of living a full married life, which I was now enjoying. I was content to try to turn in good technically adroit performances.

The eyes are the dominant means of expression before a camera. In my early days in movies in England I remember a Hungarian director, Lotzi Vajda, saying to me, "I do not want you to act; I want the camera to photograph your thoughts and emotions in your eyes." Good advice, but unfortunately, my extremely myopic eyes are not reliable mirrors. And my natural gift for projection in the theater (where make-up can disguise ocular deficiency) was no asset in front of a camera.

In a film I made at Universal with Burt Lancaster, called *Criss Cross*, I received a useful, though at the time embarrassing, rap on the knuckles from the director, Robert Siodmak. At the end of an early scene he said, "No. No, it vill not do. Alan, vy you make devil's eyes?"

"I don't know what you mean, devil's eyes."

"Yes, devil's eyes. It is bad." And he widened his eyes showing too much of the whites.

It dawned on me that in order to give my myopic eyes intensity of gaze this was precisely what I had been doing. So I have been careful ever since to think intensity and hope for the best. An amusing sequel to this event occurred the other day, also at Universal. In the television series *Night Gallery*, I was cast to play one who had risen from the grave. For the first time in my career I was subjected in make-up to the full rubber mask facial treatment. My entire face, eyelids and all, was covered with latex rubber, with hateful lumps imposed here and loose streamers of flesh hanging down there. At the crucial moment of horror the director said, "Alan, I want you to give me more! I want to see the whites of your eyes."

"I can't," I said. "My eyes are stuck together with the damn rubber!"

When I was cast as Alfred, the butler, in the TV series, *Batman*, the producer, Bill Dozier, told me he wanted me to be "just myself."

"You mean I can wear my glasses?"

"Certainly. Why not?"

Until then cameramen had always complained of the high refraction caused by my prescription, and for most of the roles I had played, glasses had not been compatible. But in *Batman*, I felt really comfortable in front of the camera. I did not have to worry about what I was doing with my eyes.

39. Don't Talk Politics to Adolphe Menjou

I suppose I reached the top of my lucrative career in movies in *Across the Wide Missouri* [1951], an MGM super production starring Clark Gable. The most exciting thing in movies for me, far more so than playing a part, was getting it. The interview with producer and director—that was the moment of truth. You had to imagine what they were looking for, yet not insult their intelligences by appearing to put on an act if they felt themselves to be gentlemen of high perception. Then you had to discern whether they were in accord and, if they were not, guess which would have the last word. Quite a game. The story of how I got my part (a Scottish gentleman, bored with civilian life after the excitement of defeating Napolean at Waterloo, seeks adventure with a band of beaver-trappers on the American frontier) is an amusing example.

The author, Talbot Jennings, an old friend, had me in mind when he was writing the part, but knew from experience that a writer's recommendation is often the kiss of death. Producers, directors, even the casting office, all want to claim the credit for inspired casting. So he tactfully fumbled out an idea to the producer, Robert Sisk. "That tall fellow, who played in a Lassie picture for you … what's his name?" Bob Sisk was delighted—this made it his idea. "Alan Napier? Yes, he was very good. And he can do a Scotch accent."

But both knew that the decision would lie with William Wellman, the director. Somehow, I had to be his discovery. So one afternoon, when I was laying new carpet on the bedroom floor at home, the telephone rang. It was Bob Sisk and his tone was conspiratorial.

"Look, I want you to come over to MGM right away."

"Oh … well, I'm kind of dirty and unshaven. I'll be as quick as I can."

"No! Don't shave! Come as you are—I want you to look rugged. And, by the way, don't go through Casting. Come straight to the new office building as quick as you can."

The moment he had rung off I remembered that Gip's car was out of order and she'd taken mine. I called a taxi, put on an old rough Harris Tweed suit and stood on my doorstep waiting impatiently and wondering what all the secrecy was about. In fact, Bob had determined to spring a surprise on Mr. Wellman, and see what shock tactics would do—for, as producer and director, he and Mr. Wellman were not in accord—Mr. Wellman liked to be his own producer. On the way to MGM a sickening thought came to me. Before leaving, Gip had said, "I haven't got any money." Deep in carpet laying, I had replied, "Look in my wallet, take what you want." I now looked in my wallet. It was empty. I made a quick decision to play this disaster for what it was worth. When we arrived at the studio I told the driver to wait a moment—I had to get some money. I went up in the elevator, found the office, went into the reception room, and was almost immediately ushered into a large, luxuriously furnished office. Talbot, tall and rangy, was in the background. Little Bob Sisk was looking anxious, and Mr. Wellman was sitting back, Olympian, at a great desk. Bob came forward to shake hands.

"Ah, Mr. Napier. This is…"

I cut in affably.

"Can any of you guys lend me five bucks? I'm flat broke and the taxi's waiting."

They all looked amazed and then roared with laughter. An actor up for an important part admitting that he was flat broke?! When I came back, Wellman was extremely cordial. I looked rough rather than polished and I had carried off a difficult situation with an air. Just the qualities he wanted in his Scottish captain. I was in—indeed, I was his discovery. As I was leaving, Bob said to me, "You've got the part—but don't say anything about it.

Officially, it'll have to go through Casting." As soon as I got home I called my agent. We were in a strong position; he could make a good deal for me. Looking back, I can't think why he didn't make a better one.

So I had been cast as a Scottish Captain. Later, when I asked Wellman about the accent, he said, "I don't want you to put on any accent. I want you just as you are."

How often have I heard this—the deep fear in movie directors that actors will act. In his film of *Joan of Arc*, in which I played the Earl of Warwick, the only direction Victor Fleming, the director of *Gone with the Wind*, ever gave me was, "Take it easy. Don't do anything!" Maybe they are right. When I used to tell this story, as a joke Gip would add, "And it was the best thing you ever did." *It isn't as though Fleming hadn't been warned… In 1979, Alan recalled his audition: "I was up first of all to play a priest that went through the film very much with Ingrid Bergman and I went to see Victor Fleming. And he took me to Bergman's trailer and stood us up together and did all this stuff and turned me down. Then about four weeks later, I received a call; this time to see him about playing the Earl of Warwick. (I think they were running short of English actors and they thought, 'Well we'll have to use Napier, dammit!') So I come to Mr. Fleming again and he says, 'Hey. Haven't I seen you before?' And I said, 'Yes. I came to see you about that priest.' And he turned to the casting man in great rage and said, 'What is this? First you bring me this guy to play a priest and now you bring him to play a soldier! Which is he? Is he a priest or is he a soldier?' And I, wanting to reassure him, I said, 'Actually, Mr. Fleming, I'm neither. I'm an actor.'"*

As the Earl of Warwick in Victor Fleming's *Joan of Arc* (RKO, 1948). Collection of James Bigwood.

Across the Wide Missouri was made just after the furor over the Hollywood Ten had broken. The Hollywood Ten were ten eminent writers and directors who, under investigation by the House Un-American Activities Committee of the Congress of the U.S.A., had refused on constitutional grounds to answer the question, "Are you or have you ever been a member of the Communist Party?" The McCarthy era witch-hunt was on and Adolphe Menjou, a supporting star in the picture, was an enthusiastic hunter. The last thing Gip said to me before I departed for Durango, Colorado was, "Don't get into a political argument with Adolphe Menjou."

Wellman had warned us before we left, in a Caesarian oration to the troops, "It's going to be tough! You'll be out there in the wilderness for seven weeks with Wild Bill Wellman.

If you don't think you can take it, now's the time to quit!" In fact, though we lived under canvas, eight men to a large tent, six thousand feet up in the mountains, we were tolerably comfortable and well fed.

The toughest thing to take was Adolphe Menjou. In huge black Cadillac limousines the principals were whisked up from our base camp to Mowlas Lake, eleven thousand feet high, where the main action of the film was shot. It was my fate to sit next to Adolphe and, day after day, hear him spouting off about the Red Menace and the iniquities of the Hollywood Ten. He had read 143 books about Russia, he said, and no one could tell him anything. On the fourth morning, his neck swelling and his eyes popping, he declared that the Hollywood Ten should be put up against a wall and shot. Now, one of the Ten, Eddie Dmytryk, had been a dental patient of Gip's, and we had had many pleasant dinners at his house and he at ours. Another, Alvah Bessie, had been an old friend of Nan's and I had gotten to know him quite well at Warners—a gentle, charming, humble man. So when Adolphe advocated a firing squad without trial, I said, "Isn't that rather un-American, Adolphe?"

From that moment I was in trouble! I had come out on the side of the Reds. Adolphe would regretfully report it to those who had influence when we returned to Los Angeles. I say regretfully because, apart from ideological differences, we quite liked each other. Indeed, when someone jokingly remarked—joking yet perhaps seeking to curry favor with Adolphe—"Everyone knows Alan's a Red," Adolphe generously cut in, "No, he's not actually Red; he's just very confused." But then he needed me to help him with his cross-

John Hodiak and Alan Napier perform the Highland Sword Dance accompanied by George Chandler on bagpipes, while Clark Gable, Adolph Menjou (hidden behind Hodiak) and Henri Letondal look on in *Across the Wide Missouri* (MGM, 1951). Wisconsin Center for Film and Theatre Research.

word puzzle. Though most of the company could read, we were not a very literate assemblage.

The importance of my role in the picture was brought home to me when the head of the Property Department asked me, a week before the picture started if I had any preference in the matter of horses. "Yes, I want Banjo." "Banjo? What stable does he come from?" I did not know but they found him and he was passed by the director. For a double I had a wonderful man, Slim Talbot, who had been Gary Cooper's double, friend and stand-in for many years. He had wonderful stories of Gary, with whom I had played in a deMille epic, *The Unconquered*, and he was a magnificent horseman and a perfect double for me—slim, only an inch shorter, with a high cheek-boned Scottish face. It broke my heart to see him losing everything he earned every night at poker. But then I'm not a gambler. Money cannot mean very much to gamblers or they could not lose it with such equanimity. Another wonderful double and stunt man we had was old Frankie McGrath. He was sixty, lived on a bottle of gin a day (his old mother lived on a bottle of bourbon) and, doubling for Jack Holt, took a fall from a horse at full gallop within a foot of the optimum spot for the camera.

It was Jack Holt's last picture. He was dying of emphysema and they brought him up to our base a few days before his scene—one important scene as an old Indian chief—with the idea, perhaps, of letting him adjust to the altitude. Instead, it nearly killed him. He was in the next bed to me and after listening to him struggling for breath for two long nights I went to Wellman. Jack did not want anyone to know, but I was deeply worried. Wellman changed his schedule so as to take Jack's scene right away.

Not expecting to work so soon, Jack did not know his few lines. To tell the truth, I think he had difficulty in concentrating and would never have known them, but it gave him an excuse. It also inspired Wellman with a wonderful idea. He had the old chief painting, painting a little something (I forget what, but it was authentically Indian) in the palm of his hand. There Jack had his lines written out. The effect was wonderful. The old chief's concentration was on his painting. He never looked up as he spoke, but now and then met the white man's eye with a steady gaze while the white man was speaking, to see if he was telling the truth.

When the picture was over, Jack asked Gip and me to dinner—he had judged Poppet in many a Gymkhana at the Riviera Polo Field—and thanked me for getting him down from that mountain. A few weeks later he died.

The great trial of fortitude I was put to by Bill Wellman—and he liked to try his actors—was dancing the Highland Sword Dance, sixteen figures of it, at an altitude of 11,000 feet. In the story I meet a Scotsman, played by John Hodiak, who has gone Indian. We celebrate the land of our fathers by dancing to the accompaniment of the bagpipes, played by my batman and faithful servant. I said to Wellman before we started on the take,

"D'you want us to go on into the dialogue?"

"Sure. If you can." And he grinned sardonically. The first four tries were ruined by mistiming of the background action. Then we had a clear take. We went on into the dialogue. The whole scene could easily have been shot in the studio at sea level but this kind of testing of a man's toughness was very much a part of the great Hollywood Western mystique. Actors were not required to act—they were to be themselves, and tough.

By a stroke of luck I got another fine location job, *Big Jim McClain* [Warner Bros.,

1951] before Adolphe's axe fell. And oddly enough it was with John Wayne—another Red hater but, unlike Mr. Menjou, no informer. It was his first independent picture and he made it on the island of Oahu in Hawaii. I played the villain—a Communist agitator, ironically enough. *(Alan had two other titles released between* Across the Wide Missouri *and* Big Jim McClain: The Blue Veil *(RKO, 1951), in which he has a brief cameo as a Yale professor raising a toast to Richard Carlson and Jane Wyman, and* The Strange Door *[Universal, 1951], in which he unsuccessfully attempts to rescue Richard Stapley and Sally Forrest from the clutches of the mad Charles Laughton.)*

It must have been after Gip had started collecting birds. How she loved them! Tumbler pigeons, doves, cockatiels, parakeets, canaries. I used to build them ingenious cages and put them on poles in strategic places in the garden. But it was about this time that she fell victim to a craving for Chihuahuas. I could see that they were remarkable little beasts, but I could not think of them as dogs. So I gave her no encouragement; another bird cage by all means, but no, not a Chihuahua.

When I arrived in Hawaii, at my handsome quarters in the luxurious though not pretentious Edgewater Hotel, I discovered that I would be in Hawaii for three weeks and only actually work on three days. I immediately called Gip by trans-ocean telephone. "Darling, this place is heaven—you'll simply adore it. I only have to work three days. Hop on the first plane and come."

"Oh, I can't."

"Why not?"

"I've just bought a Chihuahua. He's called Fernando."

I took a deep breath.

"Fernando be damned. It's him or me."

She farmed Fernando out on Poppet (who already had a Chihuahua) and came. We had a fabulous time. Jim Arness, an unknown then, was in the company. He and his wife were in the next room to mine and the four of us made a happy quartet for dinners and excursions.

Because most of the company were western types, accustomed to one-line speeches like "He went thataway," when one of my scenes came up with a page-long speech, which I managed without fluffing a word, the take was greeted with a round of applause and I was regarded as a great actor. "Duke" spoke of forming a stock company for his future films and there was talk of a Mexican grandee for me in the next one. We had a great farewell party at the home of a Navy Captain who had been talked into playing himself in the film (how amateurs love to get into acting!). My future looked as rosy as could be.

Back on the mainland we had a couple of scenes to do at Republic Studios, to finish the film. When I went to John Wayne's suite to say goodbye I found him closeted with Ward Bond, his old buddy from many a John Ford film. "You know Alan Napier?" said Mr. Wayne cheerily. "I know his name," was the grim answer.

That was it. Ward Bond, in association with representatives of the American Legion, had somehow constituted himself arbiter as to who might work in Hollywood and who might not. There was the black list of those who at one time had belonged to subversive organizations—such as, for instance, one which collected funds for the relief of Spanish Civil War refugees. They did not work at all. And there was the grey list of those against whom nothing could be proved but who, because of what periodicals they read, because of what they said, and because of hearsay accusations, were judged to be fellow-travelers. Studios were not forbidden to hire them; they were advised to find more acceptable substitutes. I was on the grey list. I know the exact moment when I came off it five years later—but by then my vogue had passed.

So, since work in Hollywood became very scarce for the next few years I tended in the fall or early winter to head East for New York.

40

Give My Regards to Broadway

Oh, those adventurous trips to New York!

I traded in my old blue Hudson for a sober six-cylinder sedan in 1946. It proved so reliable that I forgot to check it over and put in fresh oil before we started on a fishing expedition for work in New York. We pushed on merrily, forcing the pace, through Las Vegas and up over the great range of mountains separating the West Coast from the fertile plains of Utah. Without pausing for thought at the summit of the pass, we were careening down the long decline when suddenly a tremendous clinkety-clonk burst from under the hood.

On the outskirts of Beaver, Utah, there was a gas station conveniently located for such fools as I. The proprietor was not at all surprised. The long haul up and carefree dash down had brought about disaster to many before me. Our motor was a total wreck. They would have to order a new one from Salt Lake City. How long? Four days.

So, motorless, we trailed into the little town on foot in the soft evening light, suitcases in hand, our shadows long before us, followed by our dogs and a rabble of local canines (Diana was in heat) in search of a cheap motel. Four days. And the repairs would cost four hundred dollars. We were very short of money. The days of *Across the Wide Missouri*, of sending daughters to expensive boarding schools, were over. In fact, the whole trip was a desperation project made possible only because Jack Houseman was lending us his beautiful new house at New City near New York. But we had friends. We telephoned Ruth Lewton, Val's widow. Yes—she was happy to send us four hundred dollars.

Little Beaver was a pretty place, clean and tidy like everything in Mormon Utah, but there was only one tolerable restaurant, The Do Drop Inn. Four days of dropping in was more than enough and we went on our way rejoicing—soberly, because the new engine must be carefully run in. There was another crisis in a snowstorm on the Great Divide—the Donner Pass of grisly memory—happily survived. Then across the endless rolling cornbelts of Nebraska and Iowa, the farmlands of Illinois, Indiana, Ohio and Pennsylvania and so into New York State.

Jack's noble mansion, set proudly on a hillside of primeval forest, was to be our home for the next few weeks. I wasted no time visiting agents in New York. Suddenly a job, indeed a very good job, hove into view. Herman Shumlin was putting on a new play, *Gertie*, by Enid Bagnold. One of the major roles was an elderly English scientist, a man of distinction by birth as well as brain, a widower, crotchety, dictatorial and absent-minded, close to his nubile daughters yet out of touch with them. My interview with Mr. Shumlin was memorable.

Mr. Shumlin has remarkable eyes, troubled pools, dark and luminous. After telling me something of the play, of his admiration for Miss Bagnold and that he felt it to be almost a sacred mission to produce and direct this work for her, the dark eyes narrowed and he said,

"I used to hate actors."

Right in the pit of my stomach—a terrible apprehension. How could a man direct a play if he hated actors? Steady, steady—you need the job. He went on to say that he had conquered this aversion, and offered me the part. I was in no position to reflect that hatred is inspired by fear and that fear is not removed by good intentions. Mr. Shumlin is a martyr to good intentions.

At the first reading of the play, I was so delighted to find that Glynis Johns was playing the leading part that my confidence soared and I made the fatal mistake of putting on a performance, while the rest of the cast, either through policy or inability, mumbled their lines. Mr. Shumlin thanked me for my spirited effort; but his fear that I would get out of hand must have been incubating. He would have to master me. Let us think of a play as a coach, the actors as the horses that draw it and the director as the driver. A good driver neither fears nor hates horses. He will have chosen his team with care, his confidence communicates to them and he can afford to give them their heads, because he knows they will respond to the lightest touch of the reins, the gentlest word of encouragement. Even the flimsiest coach may make the run safely with such a driver. A bad driver, afraid of his horses, will hold them in fear that they will get away from him. Then, when no progress is made he will yell at them and flog them. The coach takes off. Too fast, too fast! He's terrified and yanks back the horse's heads. They rear up and stumble. In no time the flimsy coach starts to disintegrate.

Such a man has no place in the driving seat, even though he may, from time to time, have success with a well-built coach and a team of horses so experienced and willing that they can take his mishandling in their stride and finally set their own pace.

"What a good driver he must be," the ignorant observer may exclaim.

"Yes," says the incompetent Jehu. "It is lucky I showed them who was master." For he does not understand that a light hand and understanding guidance will achieve far more than mastery. *Gertie* was not a very well-made coach and fell to pieces. My experience in the shafts with Mr. Shumlin nagging at the reins was the most disagreeable occurrence of my entire career. At the very first rehearsal, as soon as I stepped on the stage, he took my book out of my hand and started showing me how to play my part. To begin with, his accents are hardly those of an English country gentlemen. Also, he is a small man and, with tiny steps, gave me innumerable meaningless moves around the stage.

"Mr. Shumlin—I'm rather a tall man and a lot of little moves don't work out very well for me."

He paid no attention and in embarrassment I looked away.

"You're not watching me, Mr. Napier! How can you know how to play the part if you don't watch me?"

To that I had no polite answer.

In the evening of the fourth day, he took me into a corner, and, with eyes smoldering, said,

"I feel there's something in you that I have to break!"

Me? Such a willing actor, I had always thought. My sin consisted in having my own creative ideas about the part.

Gip and I had moved into an apartment hotel in New York by this time. When I went home that night I said, "Thank God I have a run-of-the-play contract. The man's impossible! What does he want to break?"

The next night he fired me. I was delighted. "Hurrah, hurrah!" I said to Gip. "I've been fired! We can go back to lovely California, with two weeks' money plus five days for rehearsal. At midnight, as I was cleaning my teeth, the telephone rang. It was Herman asking me to come back. With your mouth full of toothpaste, it's difficult to argue so I said "yes." We arranged to meet for lunch the next day.

George Coulouris has lately suggested to me that Herman's reason for asking me to come back was simply that he suddenly found I had a run-of-the-play contract and he would have to pay me two weeks salary if I left! However that may be, things got worse rather than better. He gave the entire cast New Year's Day off with the exception of myself. Me, he called for a solo rehearsal at four o'clock. I was so frustrated and furious at what I considered an insulting act that I decided on desperate measures. Since I could not afford to walk out, somehow I had to get fired again in order to collect my two weeks' guarantee. So I spent the day composing a most insulting address, outlining my resentment at Herman's behavior and my contempt for his direction of the play, as a result of which he would, I imagined, lose his temper and fire me.

Deliberately, I arrived at the theatre half an hour late. No one was there but the stage doorman, the stage manager, and Herman. I took a good position, sitting on the corner of a high table, looking down at Herman in a low chair, and I delivered my speech. It was shameless. It referred to his family, his entry into the theatre world as a box-office manager rather than an artist, and I finished as follows, "I have been directed in comedy by Gerald du Maurier, Bernard Shaw, Tyrone Guthrie and Noël Coward, beside whom you seem to me an insignificant pygmy!"

According to my script Herman was supposed to break in here and fire me. He did nothing of the kind. He stared at me, his dark eyes opaque. "Is that all?" Unfortunately, it was—I had not had time to memorize any more. After a pause he continued, "The words you say, Alan, are full of anger and hatred. But I do not feel anger or hatred in your heart."

He was perfectly right. So we had a dear little rehearsal together that achieved nothing. However, after this episode I only had to growl, "Herman!" at him and he would stop nagging me.

Throughout these trying days, Glynis had been my friend and strong supporter; and, by an ingenious ruse, she very nearly saved the play. During rehearsals, she steadfastly refused to give a performance so that Herman could not spoil it by trying to alter it. "If you don't show me what you're going to do," he would complain despairingly, "How can I direct the play?" Glynis, like Brer Rabbit, lay low and said nothin'. So Herman turned his destructive energies towards other members of the team, gaining mastery where he could.

On the first night in New Haven, Glynis came up with a smashing performance, turning the second act, which Herman had directed for drama, into hilarious comedy. I shall never forget him as he came round and rather sheepishly declared, "So it seems we have a comedy on our hands,"—something obvious to the cast from the beginning. The play was written in that very English idiom that deals with serious matters in terms of comedy. This

With Glynis Johns, Anita Cooper and Patricia Wheel in *Gertie*. Plymouth Theatre, 1952. Billy Rose Theatre Division, The New York Public Library for the Performing Arts. Astor, Lenox and Tilden Foundations.

is not easily understood in the American theater, where the borderline tends to be clearly defined. Drama is serious with its set of rules (vide Gilbert Miller) and comedy is frivolous with no serious intent at all. (It is not surprising that the inextricable intertwining of comedy and drama in Chekhov so often eludes American performers.)

Gertie was a failure in New York, running only two weeks after a two-week tryout in Boston. But I had maintained the handsome salary established for me in *Lady in Waiting* so that Gip and I were able to face West with all debts paid and money in the bank. The wintery trip home had us snowed up twice. Once on the Pennsylvania Turnpike, passing the scene of an accident, I remember Gip saying, in a rather small voice, "There's blood on the snow. Don't you think we should stop for the night?" At Gallup, New Mexico, the snow froze solid onto the windshield, so we turned south towards Phoenix, Arizona, and were soon back in the glorious sunshine of the Southwest.

At six o'clock one morning in December 1952, Maurice Evans called me from New York. He was preparing a production of his success *Dial "M" for Murder* for an extended run in Chicago. He had hoped, by employing the services of a movie name, to be able to economize with the rest of the cast, but the minor star secured was not able to duplicate Maurice's brilliant performance and greater strength was needed in the supporting cast.

With Richard Greene and Faith Brook in *Dial "M" for Murder*. Harris Theater, Chicago, 1953. Billy Rose Theatre Division, The New York Public Library for the Performing Arts. Astor, Lenox and Tilden Foundations. © Eileen Darby Images, Inc.

Richard Greene, the minor star in question, had yet to achieve his great success as television's Robin Hood (1955–1960). He and Alan had already worked together on Forever Amber, *probably the best known of Greene's film appearances.* Would I fly East at once and replace the actor he had engaged to play the inspector? In spite of being half asleep I realized I was in a very strong position and extracted a handsome contract.

Gip drove across the country to join me later. For the fun of it we had traded up to a second-hand Cadillac convertible, and I must say I enjoyed driving this enormous car, with its power-operated windows, from New York to Boston where our production opened. It was bitter cold in Boston and Gip and I discovered, at the old Touraine Hotel, an ingenious and childish economy. For some reason it galled us, if we wanted ice for a cocktail in the evening, to have to pay a 50¢ tip to the boy who brought it. So we would retain the little plastic cups in which, on our breakfast tray, jelly or marmalade arrived, fill them with water and set them on the wide snow-covered sill outside the window. By the evening we had free ice cubes! The sill also served as a larder for Fernando's dinner—often the leftovers from the enormous hunks of meat served in restaurants famous for their roast beef. Gip had a tiny appetite.

After two successful weeks in Boston, where I gave a party to celebrate my fiftieth birthday, we moved on to Detroit and Chicago, where the play ran on into the early summer. My performance as the inspector was much admired and we made many friends in Chicago. We found it a very attractive city. Because the central hotels had a policy of not admitting dogs, even Chihuahuas, we lived in a southern suburb overlooking Lake Michigan. There was good rapid transport to the center and during the snowy months, we did not use the car. With its sprawl into agreeable suburbs, a pretty, informal park at our door, and little local shops to market at, Chicago, with its feel of being a capital city, seemed to us to be more like London than any other American city we knew. The people we met from the nearby university were cultivated and less frenetic than New Yorkers. The only thing that marred our enjoyment of this profitable run was the fact that one had to play every night in the week, Sundays included. Why the Actors' Equity gave Chicago this dispensation I shall never understand.

Not to have one night in the week to relax became a claustrophobic nightmare and towards the end of the run I had recurrent visitations, at certain hurdles, of my old difficulty in uttering. These were always surmounted—but the anxiety took the pleasure out of playing this excellent part. In May, with the icy lake thawed out at last and pleasant bathing beaches at our front door, we headed west by way of Wyoming. The Cadillac was not a great success; it demanded one costly repair or replacement after another. Waiting in a General Motors Agency (in Utah, again, I think) for a new fuel pump to be installed, Gip fell in love with a two-tone Pontiac Straight-8. On our return to Los Angeles, our bank account swelled comfortably by the run of Dial "M," we bought one.

Next winter it was *Coriolanus* at the Phoenix Theater on Twelfth Street in New York. This was like going back to the Westminster in Lon-

Alan, Gip and Fernando the chihuahua pose with a copy of Gip's grandfather's 1928 memoir of his father, Charles Dickens. While Alan always maintained that he had no talent for self-promotion, he was certainly not above using Gip's Dickens connection and the imminent arrival in Chicago of Emlyn Williams' one-man Charles Dickens show to publicize his own ongoing appearance in Dial "M" for Murder. Collection of James Bigwood.

don—Off Broadway with an Off Broadway salary. However, Menenius Agrippa is a splendid part and Jack Houseman was directing. I looked forward to the production with great excitement.

Not long before, looking down the table of contents in my Clifton school prize Shakespeare for something to read aloud after dinner, I had said to Gip "How about *Coriolanus*? I've never read it and nobody ever acts it. I wonder why?"

There have been quite a spate of productions recently, but the reason why the play was almost totally neglected for 300 years is obvious. Coriolanus is an anti-hero and great actors liked their heroes to be heroes. Any attempt to ennoble Coriolanus makes nonsense of the play, which is a sardonic drama, very modern in mood, rather than a tragedy. Coming to it with a completely open mind, as I did when I read it to Gip, it was fascinating, simply by following faithfully the clues dropped by Shakespeare, to discover this truth. On the very first page the citizens of Rome are complaining what a son-of-a-bitch Coriolanus is and proposing to kill him. A second citizen says, "Wait a moment, fellows," and describes some benefits brought to them by Coriolanus. At this, the first citizen comes back with, "And why? He did it for his mother!" What a Freudian lead! And lo and behold, three pages later his mother, Volumnia, is doing her best, in a scene with his wife, Virgilia, to bitch up the marriage. "If my son were my husband...," she says. Interestingly enough Shakespeare does not give Volumnia's opening speech, complaining of Virgilia's failure to understand her boy, the dignity of blank verse. It is written in prose; a sure sign that he regarded Volumnia as an old bitch and the "noble Roman mother" concept with little enthusiasm. I began to feel the play to be very modern American, with Coriolanus as Mom's spoilt athlete bully-boy and with the tribunes of the people (like trade union potentates such as old John Lewis and George Meany) showing a secret contempt for the masses they can so easily sway with heady rhetoric in order to maintain their own power and privilege. And then there is Aufidius, the crafty manager of the rival football team, who woos Coriolanus by buttering up his auto-erotic ego to play ball on his side.

With Will Geer in *Coriolanus*. Phoenix Theater, 1954. Courtesy Gary Butcher.

Well, it did not quite work out that way at the Phoenix, although Jack went some way in agreeing with my concept of the play. Nor were he and I very comfortable as director and actor. In *Run Through*, Jack suggests a certain lack of comfort, perhaps of assurance, in face of polished, technically assured London actors. And I have indicated distrust for directors who come into the theater without experience as actors. So we had our bad moments. I remember Jack shouting at me, "Don't be so goddamn old-fashioned! You don't have to face the audience all the time." And I thinking, "When I have something as important as this to say I goddamn do!" The last week of rehearsals was largely taken up with Jack working on a large Wellesian crowd who were put through their paces à la Orson. A few discreet readjustments of position went unchallenged—particularly after the producer complained that he could not hear the text. As I pointed out, it is difficult to be understood with one's back to the audience and a rambunctious crowd between it and you.

Jack received fine reviews for his solid direction and one paper became positively lyrical about my magnificent speaking of Shakespeare's verse. (*This was Robert Coleman in the* Daily Mirror, *who wrote, "The honors of the evening go to Alan Napier as the patrician Menenius Agrippa. His beautiful speech and commanding stage presence are thrilling."*) It is amusing to think that, while Jack was worrying about my acting being too old-fashioned, I was worrying about his conception being not modern enough. The play was well attended for its limited run. In subsequent encounters as director and actor, Jack and I reached a comfortable accommodation. Each had mellowed and, while Jack had gained in confidence, I had gained in patience. I was prepared for scenes to be blocked and re-blocked, on a trial and error principle, ten to a dozen times. For Jack's excellent taste would recognize proper dispositions of his troops when they were finally arrived at.

Gip and I had been living as cheaply as possible in an apartment room with kitchen in the poor polyglot neighborhood of the theatre. I grew a beard for Menenius and it and my hair had been fashioned into Roman curls. It was very cold at the turn of the year and one day, crossing Second Avenue in a heavy dark blue overcoat and Homberg hat, a small boy ran up to me, seized me by the hand, and asked, "Are you the new Rabbi?"

On the trip out (Car, Pontiac. Dog, Fernando), we had an amusing run-in, early one morning, with the police in Virginia. Gip was driving and, in the outskirts of a little town, we hear a siren and a cop car, with red lights flashing comes alongside. Fifty-five miles per hour in a forty-five mile zone. We are to follow him to the Justice of the Peace. We follow to a newish development of rather shabby looking middle class dwellings. The cop turns up the brief driveway of a one story house and parks outside the garage. We park beside him. He goes to the back door, fishes for the key under the mat, pulls open the screen door and beckons for us to follow. He lets us into a kitchen, tells us to wait there, and goes on into the house. In a moment he returns.

"His Honor ain't home."

"What ... what do we do?"

"Wait, I guess. Cup of coffee?" And he turns to a pot on the gas stove. Coffee happily perking, he becomes less laconic.

"Can't make out where he'd be. Bed ain't been slept in. Sugar ma'am?" Gip and the cop have been eyeing each other and like what they see.

"Yes, please. You don't suppose, do you, that he's been making a night of it?" A slow grin breaks up the lines of the cop's lean face and he pushes his cap back from his forehead.

"Could be," he says. Encouraged by this crumbling of officialdom into humanity, I ask. "What's this ticket going to cost us?"

"Twenty-five, thirty bucks. If he was here."

"And as he isn't?" asked Gip. The cop downs his coffee and pulls back his cap.

"As he isn't, I guess it's your lucky day, ma'am." He gets up and adjusts his revolver in his belt. "I'll show you back to the highway, folks."

Our next trip was a very speculative venture made possible by an offer from the husband of a cousin of Gip's who happened to be the Rolls Royce representative (a sort of diplomatic post) to the West Coast. A client wanted his three-year-old Bentley driven to New York. Would we like to make the trip? All oil and gas paid. It was irresistible. I had no promise of work in New York, but then I had no promise of anything in Hollywood either. We left in early October 1955.

Choosing the fast central Route 66 we made a rather regal crossing of the continent. Rolls Royces and Bentleys were not so common then, particularly in the middle states, and it was a very handsome car. Also we had a new Chihuahua. Our beloved Fernando had hit his head on the brick curb of our fireplace in a rough and tumble with Kento a year before. Chihuahuas have a soft spot on the top of the cranium like a baby's. It swelled enormously at the time and had to have an icepack on it. I made him a small one and he would lie in his basket balancing it on his head as good as gold, only his dark, shining eyes following us as we moved about the room. He recovered only to have a relapse and die many months later. He had been a dear, cocky little fellow.

Miranda, who succeeded him, was also chocolate and the runt of her litter. She was tiny, with a little turned-up nose like Gip's and a tremendous personality. One of her characteristics was to go wild in a car the moment one exceeded sixty miles an hour—seventy in the Bentley. This suited Gip very well; she always thought I drove too fast. *(Alan's granddaughter, Christie, is quick to second the opinion. "Alan was a wild driver, who always drove fast and aggressively and wove through traffic as though he was the king of the world and other people didn't realize that they were in the way. My foster cousins opine that this attitude of entitlement was an unconscious class thing, as Molly and Alan were in the peerage, if in very small print in DeBret and Burke's.")*

On this trip to New York the back of the car was piled with our belongings and there, on a sort of throne, Miranda would regally survey the gas station attendants when we stopped for service. If they failed to notice her she would utter a single sharp yelp as much as to say "Pay attention to me." Some paid more attention to the car, some to Miranda. The combination was irresistible.

We were by now highly proficient motel users. In those days, before the great new freeways had slashed across the country, the main cross-country highways tended to follow the railroad lines and, if you got into an unknown little town after dark, the chances were that the cheaper motels would back onto the railroad. Just as you were going to sleep after a long day's driving, Whoosh!—that wonderful melancholy warning bellow of American engines—and a whole mile-long goods train would plow through your bedroom. We learned to start early and always settle for the night before it was dark so that a motel could be selected as far as possible from the railroad. We would cruise up and down the little town (always staying in a little town, rather than the outskirts of a big one—it's quieter and cheaper) noting the distance from a potentially noisy corner, the closeness to a decent looking restaurant. Then, having chosen, we would leave the Bentley round the corner and approach on foot, asking first for the lowest prices. If the better rooms were empty and the manageress a dog lover (Miranda was a great charmer) one got better value for one's money. One look at the Bentley and prices would have escalated.

For these economy visits to New York we had learned to go well-equipped to ameliorate the conditions of the house-keeping apartments we were likely to settle into. Stowed in the trunk of the car were extra cooking utensils, a pop-up toaster, and, above all, Gip's sewing machine. It had an interesting history. Made by Willcox and Gibbs, it had come to England from America nearly a hundred years before, had belonged to Gip's Dickens grandmother and now, back in America, modernized with an electric motor, accompanied Gip (who was an accomplished dressmaker) wherever she went.

We had gleaned information from a New York paper as to promising apartment hotels in the district we favored: the West Side round about the sixties and as near the Hudson as possible for we both liked to live near open water. So, with a clear plan of campaign and loaded with our cherished possessions, early one morning we entered New York.

I had studied the map and had no difficulty in finding the first hotel we had planned to investigate. Everything seemed to be going my way for I sailed into a parking space almost at the door. I carefully locked up the car and, with Miranda trotting chipperly at our sides, we entered the hotel. Yes, they had an apartment to rent. For one reason or another it was not quite what we wanted, but the lady who showed it to us was a Chihuahua fancier and in no time she and Gip were on the fascinating topic of Chihuahua breeders in New York and the possibility of tracking down a silver-blue Chihuahua. What the white whale was to Captain Ahab a silver-blue Chihuahua was to Gip; she was prepared to search the whole wide world for one. It was a good half hour before we emerged into the street again.

There was not a single car to be seen on the side of the street! The Bentley, with all our clothes and possessions, was gone. It was a bad moment. We were three thousand miles from home with nothing but what we stood up in, and the car we had lost—was it stolen?—was not even ours.

Beating back panic, I made my way to a cop on traffic duty on Broadway who directed me to a nearby precinct station. There I learned that, if I had only looked, I would have seen a notice on the street prohibiting parking between 8:00 and 10:00 a.m. on Thursdays. The car had probably been removed by the Department of Sanitation. Where would it be? They gave us the address, a huge warehouse down by the river on 12th Street. It was not far, and as we needed to stretch our legs and were in no mood to waste money, we walked. Miranda enjoyed the walk enormously, anointing with her calling card every patch of weed in the cracked sidewalk.

At the desk in the warehouse were two enormous garbage men and one small clerk. The garbage men were jolly fellows and enormously enjoyed our predicament. Yes, the Department would have cleared the street that morning. Could they have a description of the car? At this point I experienced a sinking feeling in the pit of my stomach. I had no proof of ownership of the car. I put Miranda on the desk to create a diversion and she undoubtedly saved our bacon. For the enormous garbage men immediately fell in love with her. When the question of credentials arose, the little clerk quite properly objected that we had produced no proof of ownership and that the Department could not possibly release the car. But by now Gip and Miranda were going great guns with the garbage men.

40. Give My Regards to Broadway

"Aw, c'mon! We can't keep these ladies waiting all day on a technicality. Didn't you hear the man give the right name on the car license?"

So the clerk was overruled. What fascinated me was how the car had been removed.

"Did you tow it away?"

"Tow it? Heck, no. We drove it."

"How on earth did you get in?"

"Picked the lock. Easy!"

"Picked the lock? But it's an English car."

"So what? See here—some of us was pickin' locks before we ever joined the Department. There's not a car I can't get into in thirty seconds flat."

So, for a small fee, we were reunited with the Bentley and all our possessions. The little clerk shook his head disapprovingly. I hope he didn't get into trouble.

We paid our way on this visit and that was about all. Gip went back into dentistry for a time and she and her employer were a mutual admiration society—and I got work in some early television shows. In one, I played a distinguished Jewish merchant, of all things. I also starred in a winter-stock production for the Theater Guild at Nassau in the Bahamas and in one of their great radio shows, *Oliver Twist*. For some reason we went to Washington for the performance. I played Mr. Brownlow, who also narrated the story. It was amazingly well paid.

I don't remember our return. I guess we flew. *The reason that Alan does not remember his return to Los Angeles from this engagement is that both* Oliver Twist *(starring Basil Rathbone and Boris Karloff), which was broadcast on February 24, 1952, and* Libel, *which Alan played for a week at the Bahama Playhouse in Nassau immediately thereafter, actually took place not long after the closing of the brief New York run of* Gertie. *He probably made the roundtrip to Nassau from New York, rather than LA, and then returned home as described earlier.*

Our most rewarding trip to New York was, in many ways, the last. A dramatization of Alan Paton's novel, *Too Late the Phalarope* was planned for the Fall of 1956. In the summer the director, John Stix, came out to the Coast to interview actors for the leading roles. I was chosen to play the Police Captain—a splendid part. It was nearly a very good play and it was nearly a success. In fact it only ran six weeks, from my point of view an ideal length of time. Add two weeks in Boston and four weeks rehearsal. Three months away from my lovely house overlooking the Pacific was all I wanted. But the reward of the play, over and above a very welcome financial reward, was in the friends we made. The author, Robert Yale Libott, the producer, Mary Frank, that wonderful old pro, Finlay Currie and, above all, the leading man, Barry Sullivan, an actor's actor and a warm and wonderful man. Rehearsals—as always in my New York experience—were difficult. There was a moment at early rehearsal when Barry and I were being given some very subtle direction and I suddenly said, "Yes, but what do I do with my hat?"

"Your hat!" said little John Stix, very much put out, "What hat?"

Well, I had studied my part very carefully and knew that at that moment the Captain would have to be holding his hat. The director was only interested in my finding the truth in myself. I was not worried about that—I knew it would be there when I wanted it, but I also knew that there would be one way to communicate that truth if I had a hat in my hand and another way if I did not. John Stix told the producer that he was worried about Alan

Napier—he seemed to be a technical actor. However all was well; he was not a strong enough personality to "bug" me and soon learned that I was not superficial for all my concern with externals. He had much more trouble with a somewhat undisciplined method actor and, after the first night in Boston, very graciously said to me, "I have to admit that you technical actors saved the day."

Too Late the Phalarope was the last play in which I appeared in New York. It was a happy experience. Now that little is seen on Broadway other than musicals, Neil Simon and an occasional Pinter import, I doubt if I shall ever play there again—a probability I can contemplate with equanimity since the pressure of first nights is almost unendurable. In addition to the normal fear of failure, for me there is also a terrible fear that success might condemn one to two years of life in New York.

During all these years of theater work in the East, I also worked quite a bit in Hollywood. I did four pictures for a splendidly efficient producing company, Pine-Thomas Productions, which paid well, shot fast and did not worry about grey lists. Indeed I did not really know I was on a grey list till Jack Houseman requested my services for his movie production at MGM of *Julius Caesar* [1953] with Marlon Brando playing Mark Antony. He

Alan (seated) with Ralph Sumpter, Barry Sullivan and Ellen Holly in *Too Late the Phalarope*. Belasco Theater, 1956. Billy Rose Theatre Division, The New York Public Library for the Performing Arts. Astor, Lenox and Tilden Foundations. © Eileen Darby Images, Inc.

wanted to hire me for the worst part Shakespeare ever wrote: Cicero. A very curious and illuminating ritual had to be performed before I was cleared for the picture.

I was told that I would have to see Mr. Marvin Schenck—a nephew, doubtless, of Mr. Nicholas Schenck, head of Loew's Incorporated, the holding company for MGM. Marvin was a mild little Schenck.

"Sit down, Mr. Napeer," he said. "There is nothing to be alarmed at but … we have here (and he extracted a newspaper clipping from his desk) a notation in the Hollywood Citizen News of October 16, 1948, that 'One Alan Napeer contributed funds to the promotion of disturbances in Chicago, Washington and other cities.' Can you explain this?"

It was such complete nonsense that I was inclined to pooh-pooh the whole thing. Then I remembered.

"Well, I can give a guess," I said. "There was that big open forum at the Shrine Auditorium—it was advertised in the Los Angeles *Times* and Gene Kelly was chairman—in connection with the Hollywood Ten. My wife and I thought it would be a good idea to go, so as to find out what all the fuss was about. There were a lot of interesting speakers in addition to Gene Kelly—that Republican attorney, what's-his-name and so on. Well, in the interval, there was a collection for the legal defense of these people up before the House Un-American Activities Committee. That seemed reasonable to me and, as I hadn't much folding money on me I stood up to get a checkbook out of my overcoat pocket and wrote out a small check. Ten bucks, I think. I suppose, because of my height, some wretched little journalist recognized me and wrote that lie."

But Mr. Schenck would not let it go at that. Could I remember who was there? "Oh, so it's the names game, is it?" I thought.

"Yes," I said, "Your star—Gene Kelly."

"You said him. Anyone else?"

"That Republican attorney."

"You said him, too. There must have been other people there you recognized."

"There probably were, but I don't remember. I'm very bad at names. It's a Freudian thing that means you don't…"

"But why would you remember Gene Kelly?"

"Because he's a dancer and had his leg in a cast."

I had more than one meeting with Marvin, the lesser Schenck, and the upshot was that I was required to write a letter to Uncle Nicholas saying that I was not and never had been a member of the Communist Party (which I was happy to do) and that I "regretted the error of my ways" (which I damned well would not do!). "What ways?" I asked. "Why?" And then it came out.

The American Legion had threatened to picket every movie theater in the United States which showed a picture employing any actor on their subversive list. MGM, in the person of the big boss, wished to have a letter to show the Legion that the suspect was not really a bad boy.

"You people shouldn't get into politics," said Marvin. "It's bad for business. And that goes for the top people too. Why, here at MGM we have Dory Schary for Stevenson and at Fox they have Darryl Zanuck for Eisenhower. Now, if Stevenson wins—it's bad for Fox. And if Eisenhower wins—it's bad for MGM! You people oughter keep your noses clean."

Finally I went to a higher-up—a big shot then, but I don't suppose anyone remembers his name today any more than I do. He said,

"Why would you want to go to such a meeting?"

"My wife and I had applied for citizenship and thought we should take an intelligent interest in the workings of American democracy."

"Do you go to a lot of public meetings?"

"No."

"Ever been to an All-American Rally?"

"No."

"That doesn't sit very well, Mr. Napier."

More inquisitions about names. It infuriated them that I could only remember their star, Gene Kelly. Indeed, remembering him was the only fun I got out of these degrading sessions. But I realized that my livelihood was at stake and produced a semantic compromise over "regretting the error of my ways" that satisfied them and permitted me to go to work.

Gradually the grey list was suspended and I got back into movies. But my day was really over. More and more pictures with English backgrounds were being made in England; or, if they were made in Hollywood, transatlantic air service made the importation of fashionable English actors easy. However, television was coming into its own and with it commercials, opening up a new field of income for actors.

41

Take Five

James Bigwood

Finally back on track in Hollywood, Alan appeared—barely—in *Young Bess* (1953), MGM's highly fictionalized story of the early years of Queen Elizabeth I, shot after *Julius Caesar* had freed him from the grey-list, but released first. As Robert Tyrwhitt, a member of the King's Council, he is visible—but silent—in several scenes. Towards the end of the film, he finally speaks. The Council accuses Elizabeth of treachery against her half-brother Edward VI. After being glimpsed briefly in the master shot, Alan delivers his only line in the movie with the camera on his back.

He was seen to much better advantage in *Désirée* (20th Century–Fox, 1954). As Monsieur Despreaux, organizing and rehearsing the coronation ceremony of Marlon Brando's Napoleon, Alan flutters and fusses, clearly enjoying himself in a scene-stealing part. The sequence is marred by the flat, wooden delivery of the three women playing Napoleon's sisters (only one of whom has any other acting credits), but when Alan is center stage, which he is for a good part of the four-and-a-half minute scene, it is a pleasure to watch him at work.

Thanks to John Houseman, another MGM project soon followed: Fritz Lang's *Moonfleet* (1955). As Parson Glennie, Alan delivers a fiery sermon (filled with convenient plot exposition), and then befriends John Mohune, an orphan played by the nine-year-old Jon Whiteley. Recalling Alan as "the most genial and agreeable of companions," Whiteley notes that "the sermon originally lasted longer than it does now and concluded with the sound of loud bangs from the crypt at which the congregation fled in terror. Perhaps this has been restored? It is necessary to make complete sense of Parson Glennie's anger at the end." Unfortunately, the parson's sermon remains truncated (it just fades out) and his rage unmotivated, especially when contrasted with his gentleness upon meeting Mohune in the scene that immediately follows.

It had been almost a decade since Alan had worked with the mercurial Fritz Lang, who had not mellowed in the intervening years. In fact, he was so universally disliked by the cast and crew of *Moonfleet* that Jon Whiteley remembers "a move at one point to petition for his removal from the film." Alan chose to confront Lang more directly: "I'm up in the pulpit and we're doing a little rehearsal and Fritz starts some of his nonsense. I looked down at him and I said 'Don't try that stuff on me, Fritz! You know your job and I know mine!' He said, 'That iz right Alan, that iz right.' There was no trouble at all. But he took it out on a beautiful old English character actress instead [the 84-year-old Elspeth Dudgeon, who plays a vocal member of Glennie's congregation]. He seemed to have a *compulsion* to bully somebody. I knew him, I had met him socially and he is a very great director, a great man of movies—but it's the same as with Preminger; he *has* to bully! And to me that's absolutely hateful."

Glennie makes a second unexpected appearance in the final fadeout of the movie, helping Mohune un-padlock the gates to his ancestral home for the first time in a dozen years. "This was not originally in my script," recalls Whiteley. "It ended with Stewart Granger disappearing into a grey long shot of the sea. I thought then and think now that this would have been the perfect ending, balancing the cinemascopic view of the sea at the beginning with a darker panorama at the end, but the studio didn't like it and the producer insisted on adding the final scene to give the film a happy but out-of-character ending. Lang was furious. He shot the scene himself but without good grace."

In May 1955, Alan started work on MGM's historical drama *Diane*, although, since he is not in the finished film, it is not clear what part he was filming. *Variety* lists him among the cast in its "Film Production Chart" through July and there are sketches of him by the production's makeup artist, William Tuttle, in the role of "Ruggieri," a character based on Nostradamos. However, *Diane* started production with Walter Hampden playing Ruggieri and when Hampden suffered a major stroke on his way to the studio on June 9, he was replaced within a day by Sir Cedric Hardwicke. Whether Alan was ever seriously considered for the role (it is significantly bigger than the parts he was playing at the time) or whether he simply posed for Tuttle for convenience while playing a role that was later cut, there can be no doubt that Hardwicke's look was based on the sketches that Tuttle drew of Alan Napier.

At the end of the year, Alan was heard, but not seen, as the narrator of *The Queen's Guard*, a 17-minute Cinemascope travelogue released by 20th Century–Fox. He speaks almost continuously throughout the short, describing the duties and privileges of membership in the elite corps that guards the British monarch ("Training makes the soldier, but only spirit can produce a guardsman."), and finishes with a (slightly truncated) quote from Shakespeare's *Richard II*. It is certainly his longest continuous "role" on screen.

In *The Court Jester* (Paramount, 1956), with flowing chestnut brown wig and beard, Alan plays Sir Brockhurst, one of several courtiers surrounding Cecil Parker's King Roderick. Aside from a brief bout of fencing with Basil Rathbone, his part is unmemorable, and, quickly poisoned by Mildred Natwick, he is soon gone. In fact, Angela Lansbury could barely remember his presence in the picture when discussing the film. "We were all so entranced by Danny Kaye and Cecil Parker, who had such funny, funny roles and Alan, I think, had a rather thankless part."

Next came *Miami Exposé* (Columbia, 1956), the first of several low-budget films that would dominate Alan's feature output for the remainder of the decade. In it he plays Raymond Sheriden, a shady attorney who uses sleazy lobbyist Edward Arnold to buy influence in support of legalized gambling in Florida. When money doesn't do the job, Sheriden willingly resorts to blackmail and murder. The tired script is full of holes which erratic bursts of narration cannot disguise, and Alan's accent, which he makes no attempt to modify, is completely at odds with the tough guy dialogue he is given to speak. While not his finest hour, on the plus side, he did get the opportunity to shoot on location in Miami.

This was followed by a role in *The Mole People*, Universal's 1956 minor-league camp

Alan and Edward Arnold in *Miami Exposé* (Columbia, 1956). In Florida, shady attorneys and sleazy lobbyists apparently share similar tastes in shoes. Collection of James Bigwood.

classic. "Oh, *The Mole People*! Yes. I was a High Priest and—who knows how exactly the Mole People articulated or why they spoke English, but anyhow—with the precision with which a High Priest speaks, I remember saying 'evil' and the sound man saying to me afterwards, 'What's this "ee-ville"? I don't recognize it. It's "evul."' This curious idea that the High Priest of the Mole People should speak grip's American. Yes, *The Mole People*. That was what we call a 'B' picture."

Briefly back in an MGM "A," Alan's tiny role as a courtroom prosecutor in *Until They Sail* (1957) is perhaps only notable for being the first time he appeared onscreen in his "Alfred" glasses which, since the movie takes place during the Second World War, are actually anachronistic. The film starred his old friend Joan Fontaine, but they did not share any scenes.

Alan as Elinu, the High Priest of *The Mole People* (Universal, 1956).

In *Island of Lost Women* (Warner Bros. 1959), Alan is Dr. Paul Lujan, a nuclear scientist who, dismayed at the state of the world, has exiled himself and his three nubile daughters to a remote Pacific island. When his idyll is discovered by a reporter whose pilot is forced to make an emergency landing, he panics at the possibility that his location may be revealed to the world. More misguided than mad, he first destroys the plane and then threatens to kill the pair to prevent their leaving. Meanwhile the visitors have fallen for his two eldest daughters, much to the chagrin of the youngest, who has her own designs on them.

What makes all this silliness even harder to take is that the filmmakers seem to think they are making a comment on the evils of nuclear war. Lujan never seriously threatens anyone (except by accident) and everybody survives at the end of the picture. This was the largest film role Alan had had in years, but unfortunately it doesn't even hold up as good camp.

Journey to the Center of the Earth (20th Century–Fox, 1959) unabashedly piggybacked on the success of two other Jules Verne adaptations: Mike Todd's *Around the World in 80 Days* (1956) and Walt Disney's *20,000 Leagues Under the Sea* (1954). Although a lavish production (and nominated for three Oscars), the story has an unmistakably low-budget feel when watched today. Alan's character, the Dean of Edinburgh University, bookends the film, presiding over a small ceremony honoring James Mason's recent knighthood at the start, and gracing a larger gathering at the end, welcoming him back from his journey to the earth's center, where, despite encounters with underwater oceans and giant reptiles, his intrepid group somehow manages to miss meeting up with the Mole People...

Alan with John Smith in *Island of Lost Women* (Warner Bros., 1959). Collection of James Bigwood.

Alan shares a nice scene with Elvis Presley and Hope Lange in *Wild in the Country* (20th Century–Fox, 1961). The Clifford Odets script, which actually allows Presley the opportunity to demonstrate his acting ability, concerns a hot-headed boy whose writing talent is recognized by a sympathetic parole officer. Alan is a college professor who encourages her enthusiasm: "You've got some sort of real natural on your hands, Irene... Give him time and seasoning and anything might happen. His contact with the paper is immediate and instant. He writes exactly as he feels and thinks. I'll try and write a scholarship for him."

Tender Is the Night (20th Century–Fox, 1962) has not aged well, and, in fact, was none too healthy when originally released. An overblown adaptation of F. Scott Fitzgerald's last completed novel, it features Jason Robards, Jr., as 1920s psychiatrist Dick Diver. Alan has a cameo as Señor Pardo, the father of one of Diver's patients. Despite the elliptical dialogue, there is no difficulty guessing what his slight, turquoise-sweatered son's "problem" is.

> DIVER: Señor Pardo is a sophisticated man. He can understand that the boy's impotence might have been caused by an excessive dependency upon his mother.
> PARDO: I desire one quality in a son. Manhood!
> DIVER: Did you think you'd make a man of him when you stripped him to the waist and horsewhipped him until he had to be sent to a hospital?
> PARDO: I hope any gentleman, who was not degenerate, would have the fortitude to do the same!

Roger Corman's *The Premature Burial* (American International, 1962), loosely based—as were so many AIP films of the early sixties—on an Edgar Allan Poe short story, reteamed Alan with his *Univited* co-star Ray Milland. Although they had played contemporaries in the 1944 film (which indeed they were, being only two years apart in age), now

Alan with Ray Milland in *The Premature Burial* (American International, 1962). Collection of James Bigwood.

Alan was playing Milland's father-in-law, adding a decade to his fifty-nine years while Milland tried (less successfully) to shave fifteen years from his fifty-seven.

Alan's unmistakably British voice was also put to use in the mid-sixties to help establish the bona fides of two of Walt Disney's English-themed features. In *The Sword in the Stone* (1963), Alan voices Sir Pelinore and in *Mary Poppins* (1964), he covers several characters in the animated "Jolly Holiday" sequence.

He was next seen in Alfred Hitchcock's *Marnie* (Universal, 1964). "I was hired for *Marnie* to be sort of a piece of walking scenery to give Sean Connery a very aristocratic background. It wasn't much of a part."

Alan's next role came completely by accident. George Cukor was filming the long-awaited musical *My Fair Lady* (Warner Bros., 1964) and in the scene at the Embassy Ball where Henry Higgins passes off the flower-girl Eliza Doolittle as an upper-class lady, he cast Henry Daniell and Lillian Kemble-Cooper as the Ambassador and his wife. Cukor had shot Eliza's arrival at the ball and established all the principals in the receiving line (including the Ambassador) when Daniell died suddenly of a heart attack. Left uncompleted was the Ambassador's presentation of Eliza to the visiting Queen of Transylvania. Rather than recasting the role and reshooting all the existing footage, Cukor created a new character

Hellene Hill, Alan Napier and Joanne Woodward in *Signpost to Murder* (MGM, 1964). Collection of James Bigwood.

to discreetly approach Eliza on the Ambassador's behalf and request her to accompany him to meet the Queen. Although the Gentleman is never heard (his conversation with Eliza is whispered), Alan's aristocratic bearing effortlessly carries the scene. He and Audrey Hepburn make a handsome couple as they make their stately way across the ballroom.

In *Signpost to Murder* (MGM, 1964), Alan, although billed fourth, appears in only one scene. He plays a dithering, but well-intentioned vicar ("Dear Mrs. Thomas. I'd have come the moment I heard. But there was a little confusion in the alto section of the choir practice.") who calls on the distraught Joanne Woodward after her husband has been murdered, bringing along an elderly parishioner to look after her. ("Her name is Mrs. Broom. And I've known her ever since I was a boy. This dear soul has weathered the storms of years, and when I'm troubled I turn to her.") Although the scene ends very abruptly (the vicar and Mrs. Broom simply leave without a goodbye while the camera holds on an extended close-up of Woodward in tears on the floor, a strong indication that the sequence was truncated in the editing room), it still provides Alan a charming little cameo.

MGM's *36 Hours* (1965) is set in 1944 and stars James Garner as an American major who, while in neutral Portugal, is kidnapped and tricked by the Nazis into believing that the war has been over for five years, so that he will innocently divulge the Allied plans for

Front row: Noel Drayton, Robert Morley, Robert Morse, Alan Napier and Christopher Isherwood in *The Loved One* (MGM, 1965). Collection of James Bigwood.

the invasion of Europe. As a British colonel, Alan opens the film and sets the story in motion, making sure that the audience realizes that the Germans believe that the Allies intend to land at Calais, rather than at Normandy, and that they must continue to believe this so that the actual invasion will take them by surprise. Once this is established his job is done and he disappears from the film.

Also in 1965, thanks to John Houseman (credited on screen with "Advice and Counsel"), Alan was one of three actors hired to recreate the early history of the Smithsonian Institution in a twenty minute short sponsored by IBM. The film consists primarily of documentary and archival footage, but one short scripted scene—in which Alan plays Davies Gilbert, president of the Royal Society—dramatizes the story behind James Lewis Smithson's £120,000 legacy to the United States to found "an Establishment for the increase & diffusion of knowledge among men."

Forty years after the start of his professional career, Alan was reunited with fellow Oxford Players John Gielgud and Robert Morley in Tony Richardson's *The Loved One* (MGM/Filmways, 1965). Playing members of the Hollywood British ex-pat community, they must have collectively winced at the woeful miscasting of the lead: the oh-so-American Robert Morse as Gielgud's visiting nephew. Alan, cheekily patterning the delivery of his few lines on Sir C. Aubrey Smith, spends most of his screen time peering out aristocratically from behind Morley's Sir Ambrose Ambercrombie, although they do have an amusing exchange as they sweat in adjoining steam cabinets: Morley: "So I told Her Majesty I said 'Ma'am,' I said, 'you've done us a very great honor.' 'Not at all,' she said, 'Not at all, Sir Ambrose. I enjoyed the picture.' Course Edinburgh was with her you know. She takes him along everywhere these days, I don't know why." Alan: "Well he *is* her husband y'know." Morley: "Yes I suppose that would account for it. So I said, 'Ma'am I...' Do you know I think this damn thing's on fire?" Alan: "Oh? And what did she say?"

42

Family Affairs

The girls, meanwhile, were getting married. Jenny did it first—a splendid piece of one-upmanship in her perennial rivalry with Poppet. I recall the wonderful day when she brought Robert to the house. I can see his round, wholesome face beautiful with the light of love shining from his blue eyes, as he came up the steps onto the patio.

"I'm in love with your daughter and I'd like your permission to marry her."

Bob and Jenny have lived as happily as anyone has a right to expect to live, ever since. A marriage that has endured over 20 years *(over 60 eventually)*, and produced two children who have grown into highly intelligent, well-adjusted, loving and utterly delightful young people must be accounted a huge success.

For Poppet, success in marriage has been a longer haul. Her career as an actress, which started with some promise, since she was pretty and talented, somehow failed to develop. *(Alan actually appeared on stage with his stepdaughter, in the 1955 world premiere of* Please Communicate *at the Pasadena Playhouse.)* Perhaps she wanted to be a success more than she wanted to act. It is a mysterious thing, the authentic need to act that drives the devoted professional on and on past seemingly insurmountable obstacles. Living in Hollywood can sap the springs of this drive; there are too many stories of pretty girls being seen in drugstores and being made into stars overnight. Perhaps her father's dream of turning her into

In *Please Communicate* with Antony Eustrel and Jennifer Raine (Poppet). Pasadena Playhouse, 1955. Courtesy Gary Butcher.

a child star gave Poppet a secret feeling that she only had to wait for this to happen to her. However that may be, she seemed to be waiting for something wonderful to happen to instead of going out into the mainstream of life to look for it.

A first marriage never caught fire; a second marriage was a disaster in everything but the production of a beautiful, talented and enchanting little boy who arrived just in time for Gip to know that she had a grandchild of her own blood. *(This grandchild was Brian Forster, who eventually played Chris Partridge from 1971 to 1974 on* The Partridge Family.*)* Poppet's third marriage to one of the nicest men in the world *(actor Whit Bissell)*, is, I'm sure, making up for all the years of waiting for a way of life which fulfills her and which she can pursue in happiness. *It did indeed. The marriage lasted more than 29 years, until Poppet's death in 1993.*

In the middle of World War II, I had received a letter from my cousin and solicitor, Roger Slade, saying that the doctors taking care of my sister, Molly, had come to the conclusion that the only hope of restoring her mental health might lie in the new electric shock treatment. The result was unpredictable and, in blunt layman's language, kill or cure. They needed my permission before going ahead. I had no doubt as to my answer. That she should drag out an existence in the condition in which I had last seen her, rendered more pitiful by two suicide attempts that had crippled an ankle and a wrist, was unthinkable. I wrote that they should go ahead.

The result was miraculously successful. Often the benefit of this treatment is only temporary because the patient has a subconscious need to relapse into psychosis. With Molly this was not so. She had never been a weak character and, finding England at war and in dire straits, she had an objective in life—to participate in her country's struggle to survive. She became a farm worker, one of an army who raised Britain's home grown food supply to an unprecedented level. And then, even more important for her total recovery, Colin came into her life. Colin was a four-year-old orphan from the bombing of London. That she was permitted to adopt him will be regarded as remarkable in the United States; the result was a life-saver for both of them. Molly found a child to love, an outlet for her generous and courageous nature; and Colin the safety of an abiding home.

When Gip and I went to England in August 1947 to meet each other's relatives for the first time, the most wonderful experience for me, and I think also for Gip—who took to Molly instantly—was our visit to Sixpenny Handley, near Salisbury, where Molly had a little cottage. There she was—crisp, strong, confident, ascetic, with a sense of humor about her asceticism. She had never craved creature comforts for herself but was prepared to laugh with, rather than at, our soft American shrinking from the outside toilet in the coal shed. Colin was then a stalwart little boy with bright brown eyes, red hair and an endearing smile and lisp. They had a beautiful black cat. "What's her name, Colin?" "Thilky."

We went for a picnic high up on a hill overlooking the rolling farmland of that Hampshire, Wiltshire, Dorset border country—the ripening corn interspersed with spinneys and chalky gullies. Bees hummed in a clump of gorse and, lying in the sun as the drowsy afternoon wore on, Molly and I reminisced and laughed about picnics with Cousin Bertha, our favorite Moor Green Chamberlain, and all the lovely places we had enjoyed together on holidays in our childhood.

Molly was soon to rediscover her old and dear woman friend, Jetty van Voorhout, who had spent the war in a Japanese concentration camp in Indonesia. Together they took an old farmhouse near Handley (Sixpenny, because the village had been fined six pence for poaching one of the King's deer in 1087 or thereabouts) and became foster parents to a family of four and, later, favorite relatives to Bob and Jenny and my grandchildren during their sojourn in England in the sixties.

When we planned this visit to England Gip and I, as usual, found ourselves short of money. However, my minute private income, still locked up in the sterling area by wartime edict, had collected a little fat. So we flew to British Jamaica on dollars, transferred to sterling, spent a delightful, luxurious week there, and proceeded to England on a British South American airplane. This was a converted bomber with limited range and island-hopped across the Atlantic—Eleuthera, Burmuda, the Azores, Lisbon. Though less convenient than a jet liner, there was a casual charm about this journey. We had a nice chat with some happy-go-lucky malefactors who were being returned from the Bahamas to Burmuda for bicycle-stealing. On the Azores the Portuguese authorities would not allow us, though manifestly man and wife, to share a room. One never knew what would happen next. Coming in low over England, its checker-board of little fields and clumps of splendid trees suddenly picked out brilliantly by shafts of evening sunlight, took us by surprise.

"No Gip, I'm not crying. It's just so beautiful."

Gip's mother I already knew. She had come out to spend the winter with us in California two years before. A memorable visit it had been. Gip warned me before Enid arrived that I must lock up the liquor cabinet. I never lock anything.

"I can't do that!"

"You've never really known a compulsive drinker, have you?"

I thought a minute. "No."

"Well, you be a good boy and do what I say."

In fact by various ruses Enid collected considerable supplementary supplies. However, she was an entertaining and considerate guest and a very courageous old lady. She had a chronic bronchial condition and vowed that the visit had saved her life. So we had a pleasant reunion in London.

Gip's brothers were rather surprised, I think, to find little Gippy, the former fool of the family, so good looking and assured. At the end of our visit, when we were saying goodbye to Eric, the eldest, who assumes a P.O.B. (pompous old bastard) manner at times to disguise a heart of gold, he started complaining that England was dreadfully overpopulated.

"They ought to emigrate in droves, all these awful people."

"Really? Well, why don't you emigrate?" said Gip. "California's a wonderful place."

"Oh, no, not me. You see, I don't like the Yanks. Not that I've ever known any."

Yet, when Bob, who is a hundred percent American, went to England with his family, Eric took to him immediately and was kindness itself to the whole family during their five-year stay.

Apart from relatives and friends in London (as I have told, I had a wonderful reunion with Glen Byam Shaw), there were many more scattered all over England with whom we wanted to renew old ties of love and friendship. We hired a car and set forth on a long journey of visits. But first there was the Shakespeare season at Stratford for which I had secured tickets, a commitment Gip viewed with some misgiving—her family had tended to patronize the lighter side of the theater. We stayed four days and saw a play each evening—*The Winter's*

Tale, *The Merchant of Venice*, *Troilus and Cressida* and *Hamlet*, all superbly done. There were old friends in the cast—Diana Wynyard, Tony Quayle, Esmond Knight—and wonderful talents, new to me, like Paul Scofield. It was a lovely time and Gip was as loath as I to move on. "I'd like to do this every night for the rest of my life," she said. From Stratford, we went to Molly, then to Lincoln. Crisscrossing the south of England, we met innumerable relatives, including my dear Aunt Cecily and Uncle Ernest Debenham, now in his eighties and resolutely determined to go on forever.

We had been lucky with the weather but, as October set in, a golden September gave way to cold, incessant rain. We were living in a little private hotel in Ebury Street, with the bathroom three floors down and uncertain hot water. One day as we were coming home, Gip saw, a hundred yards ahead of us, a nondescript figure in an old mackintosh and turned-down felt hat, hurrying along the wet street towards Victoria Station.

"Good God," Gip said, "that's Terry!"

"What are you going to do?"

"Oh, I must try to see him." She put her hand on my arm. "You don't mind, do you?"

"No. Shall I come with you?"

"Better not. I'll not be long."

"Hurry or you'll miss him. Meet you at the hotel."

She ran after him. What surprised me was that he looked so little; she had always spoken of him as a tall man. She was back in fifteen minutes. "I lost him in Victoria Station. I had to try ... he looked so old and shabby. Just as well, perhaps."

The rain was pouring down outside. She put her arms round me and said, "Why don't we go home, home to our lovely house in sunny California?"

We knew then where our home was and decided to apply for U.S. citizenship.

Alan became a citizen on November 14, 1952. Judging by a letter he wrote to Orson Welles on the occasion of the death of Franklin Roosevelt, it was an evolving decision, but an inevitable event:

Soon after the announcement of the president's death, I was moved to tears by the report of a little old Frenchwoman who, on hearing the news, said "I shall go into mourning. I feel he was my friend." After this, so touching in its simplicity, though the speakers and commentators from Winchell to Mayor Bowron largely rose above themselves in response to the magnitude of the catastrophe, it was not till you gave your tribute that I felt that the true greatness of the man was celebrated, the pity and tenor of this awful tragedy revealed. You opened in our hearts springs of emotion above and beyond tears. I think you were the poet laureate of the occasion and I hope copies of your words, printed or preferably on records, will be available to revive in us those emotions should they ever threaten to run dry. I would like my children to hear you and know what Roosevelt was, what he fought and died for, when they are a little older and can understand the debt that they will surely owe to that great man. Not long ago I was talking with a typical and inveterate hater of the House of Roosevelt. He kept speaking of "Americanism" and "The American Way of Life." I asked him to define for me what he meant. So he trotted out for me that horse and buggy team Isolationism and Rugged Individualism. Though he was apparently quite a nice old man what he was describing was really gangsterism in party dress. As I looked into his kindly but bigoted old face I knew that argument could never shake him and a kind of frustrate rage filled me. Then I realized that he belonged to the lost, and simply didn't matter any more. I thought to myself, "The young people and the poor people know better. They listen to Roosevelt with clear heads and open hearts—they've elected him four times." At the time when I first met you (it was on a sidewalk in New York), I had a large share of alien antipathy for the American scene. I know now that it was that false Americanism of my bigoted old friend that alienated me—just as in

42. Family Affairs

The Fifth War Loan Drive, broadcast live from the Paramount Theater in Texarkana, Texas, on June 12, 1944. Alan is in the sixth seat from the right. Orson Welles, not surprisingly, is center stage. Courtesy Texarkana Museums System Archives.

England, Old School Tie Imperialism would alienate you. The American way of life which I now love and cherish is the Americanism of FDR—the noble thing you celebrated so very beautifully both at Texarkana and last night. Thank you for that. Like the little old Frenchwoman and all decent people the world over, I feel he was my friend.

By "Texarkana," Alan is referring to the radio kickoff of the Fifth War Loan Drive, which aired live from the Paramount Theater in Texarkana, Texas, on June 12, 1944. He was one of several actors who participated in the program written by, directed by, and starring Orson Welles. Also taking part in the broadcast were Secretary of the Treasury Henry Morgenthau and President Roosevelt himself.

If one is a political animal, as I am, and if one cares tremendously about justice and injustice, as Gip did, one must have the right to vote and to express one's opinion on the conditions of life in the country in which one is living. I had once been subjected in a restaurant, where my English accent and clear speech had attracted attention, to the unpleasantness of an aggressive character coming up to me and saying, "If you don't like it here, Mister, you know what you can do. Get out!" The next time this happened to me it was a pleasure to be able to answer, "I do like it here. Very much. As a citizen I shall be voting at the next election. But I doubt if it will be for your candidate."

43

Friends

I had forgotten how much of an indivisible unit Gip and I appeared to be to other people until my grandchildren reminded me the other day that when they were little, they made no division at all. To them we were "Gipanalan." They came over to see Gipanalan; and Gipanalan had a pool for them to splash in—a two-foot high plastic pool for the very hot days.

Indeed we were very close and never bored when we were together. But it was the great company of our friends that enriched our lives. I am not gregarious; Gip was the magnet that attracted people into our lives and kept them close with her tremendous curiosity about life and loving concern for other people. When Brian Aherne married again, Gip and Eleanor became the closest of friends: and when Gip was your friend you could trust her with your life. It was the same when Jack Houseman married Joan—Joan who thinks of Gip with delight most days in the week, though it is twelve years since she died. Then there were the Armstrongs, the Lewtons, the Stegmans, the Lyndons, the Karloffs, and, visiting briefly from England but forming a strong tie, the Parkers. It may be, as more than one friend said, that we were a team; maybe I did help to bring out the best in Gip. I only know that I would have led a lonelier life without her.

Val Lewton I met when, for some strange reason, he cast me for a small part in his great horror movie, *The Cat People*. I have written of an attempt to indoctrinate me with the idea that those on the production side of movie-making think of themselves as "we" and of the actors as performing animals called "they." This was no part of Val's nature. Human beings were human beings to him. This, plus the fact that he hated being slapped on the back and only once slapped anyone back, may account for the fact that, although described by James Agee, the poet-critic, as one of the outstanding talents in the motion picture industry, he never achieved the success or position of power that should have been his. He was the only producer with whom I never felt awkward because I might be beholden to him for a job. We became friends and, in fact, I worked for him in many pictures. I say "we became friends"; our families became close friends.

I think of lovely times with Ruth and Val up at Green Valley Lake trout fishing; and of Val's horror when Gip pulled a wicked joke on him by driving her fishing license pin firmly through a very convincing looking falsie. *Alan's granddaughter remembers this as an on-going joke. "Gippy was quite flat-chested and couldn't find bathing suits for her figure that didn't have padding in the bust. She was always sewing and used the padding as a pincushion, much to the horror of uninformed guests."*

Best, I think of many evenings at their house when Val would unwind and tell, so vividly and with such humor and beauty, the story of a film he wanted to make if only the god-damned studio bosses were not so unimaginative and cowardly. And there was a great evening when, having ordered a barrel of oysters from the East, he brought them over to our house for a feast.

I must tell the great Lewton-Ginsberg story.

At one time Val was head of the story department for David Selznick. A story department's business was to read all available material for motion pictures, make synopses and classify and file them for possible future development. The department would also deal with questions of availability and copyright. At the end of a morning's work the natural thing for a man to do is to make for the men's room before going out to lunch. On Val's corridor there was a production office in which worked a little man who was an inveterate backslapper, a characteristic which, as I have said, Val utterly detested. It got so that Val would peek out of his door before venturing forth, to make sure that little Henry Ginsberg was not on his way to the men's room. One Friday, just as Val had started a dreamy, contented pee, someone slapped him on the back. It was Ginsberg.

"Hiya, Val. How's everything?"

"Fine. At least it was." And Val hurriedly zipped and went to wash his hands.

"Good, good." And Ginsberg came up behind him. Val's flesh crept. Ginsberg took his elbow conspiratorially and continued in a whisper, "Would you do me a favor, Val? See, I got a promotion. I'm going to Paramount." This was good news indeed. Feeling almost affable, Val said, "What kind of favor?"

"See, I'm going as special assistant to Frank Freeman and I'd like to take something with me."

"Such as?"

"Oh, come now, you've got all those titles on file for Selznick. If you could give me a list of a dozen or so real good ones, I'd have something to show those jerks at Paramount, wouldn't I?" And slyly he dug Val in the ribs.

In a flash, Val saw the possibilities.

"Certainly," he said. "I'll let you have them Monday." And he hurried out of the men's room thinking, "the little son of a bitch! He's taken David's money all these years and now he wants to take his titles. I'll give him some titles to take."

Over the weekend Val had a great time inventing two dozen lurid mythical titles by equally mythical authors. He had a splendid literary background and had been a successful novelist. Any attempt of mine to imitate his list would fall far short of the original; but *The Purple Patch* by Glenda Fasset-Townlee might have found a place on it. In the men's room next Monday, slapping Ginsberg on the back rather harder than necessary, Val handed him a sealed envelope.

At Paramount a sad thing happened. Mr. Ginsberg, from his fine new office, sent out a blue slip to the story department asking for a run-down on *The Purple Patch* by Glenda Fasset-Townlee. A pink slip came back saying that they had no record of *The Purple Patch* by Glenda Fasset-Townlee, whereat Mr. Ginsberg got on the telephone to the head of the department.

"A fine thing," he said. "At Selznick's, with only four men in the story department, I could get a run-down on anything ever written. Here, here at Paramount, with a dozen guys to work for you, you can't even give me information on a well-known book like *The Purple Patch.*"

After a few more tries it slowly dawned on Ginsberg what Val had done to him.

Now this is a cautionary tale. From Selznick, Val went to RKO as a producer of low budget pictures, *The Cat People* for example. Because these were better and more successful than most people's high budget pictures, Buddy DeSilva, head of Paramount, eventually lured Val to his studio, to be his own boss and make whatever kind of picture he might choose. It was a fabulous contract. But, alas, the ink was hardly dry when DeSilva had a severe heart attack and retired. And who was selected to step into Buddy's shoes? Yes, believe it or not, it was Henry Ginsberg. He had manfully worked his way to the top, backslap by backslap. Oddly enough, things did not go too well for Val during his brief stay at Paramount. I asked him if he ever regretted composing that glorious list. He roared with laughter and said, "Never for a moment."

But the hucksters prevailed. Fighting for what he wanted wore Val out, and failure to get it broke his heart. He should have been an independent producer, yet he needed the financial protection of a big studio. He died too young. Ruth asked me to read something from his writings at the funeral; but we could not find anything suitable. Suddenly next morning it came to me, exactly what needed to be said. I wrote it down, Ruth approved and it was my privilege to speak the eulogy. It was short, but I had a great affection for Val and it said things he would have liked to hear.

My agent, who was present, told me, "There wasn't a dry eye in the house, Alan"—which would have made Val laugh. He had always been trying to find a good leading part for me in one of his pictures and here I was successfully playing the lead at his funeral. *Lewton produced fourteen films in his career; Alan appeared in four of them and was in serious contention for the third lead (with Karloff and Lugosi) in* The Body Snatchers, *a role that was eventually played by Henry Daniell.* Ten days later I was at a cocktail party talking to a gossip writer. "Too bad about poor Val Lewton," she said. "I hear that Rabbi Nussbaum spoke a beautiful eulogy at the funeral."

"Rabbi Nussbaum, my foot! *I* spoke the eulogy." I was not going to let any Rabbi steal my credit for Val's funeral.

I met Boris Karloff on one of Val's movies, *Isle of the Dead*. He made a very Karloffian first entrance—pushing a creaking door open and saying in sepulchral tones, "Where are the bodies?" Then he had trouble with a knee and had to go into hospital for three weeks. It was an ill wind that blew me a lovely extra three weeks' salary. Then I found that Evie, his wife, was a cousin of my cousin Donald Hope (husband of that fondly remembered Moor Green Chamberlain, Cousin Bertha) who was instrumental in returning my errant father from the temptresses of New York.

Boris was such a gentle, humorous, candid man; on the basis of personality one would have said totally unsuitable for "heavies." His story of how he got the part of the Frankenstein monster is charming. He had come to California after playing stock all over America and, waiting for a break in movies, got a job delivering sacks of cement. He had parked his delivery truck one morning at the corner of Hollywood and Vine, the classic spot for breaks. A friend saw him and called out, "Hey! They're looking for a strong actor down at Universal. If you can handle those god-damned sacks maybe you're just the man they want."

"So I went down right away, just as I was and got the job."

Now, the director of *Frankenstein* was my old friend from the Oxford Players, James Whale. Jimmy was no fool and must have been looking for more than strength. He must have recognized in Boris's somber gaze and sepulchral voice just the qualities he needed. But it was Boris's gentle charm that made his monsters and villains so acceptable and kept him a major star for the next forty years.

I think of so many of our friends at our Christmas Day parties. We used to collect people who were in Hollywood without family to celebrate with, from a dozen to twenty, and we always played The Game after dinner. It was so amusing seeing famous actors trying to convey the idea of a word in dumb show. I don't remember any specific attempt by Boris, but none of my family will forget Cecil Parker, crouching on all fours on the floor, earnestly trying to be a frog. Cecil had come over to play in *The Court Jester* with Danny Kaye, a film in which I also appeared. He and his pretty wife, Muriel, added a great deal to the Christmas spirit of our gathering, singing old music hall songs together as well as throwing themselves wholeheartedly into The Game. They soon became close friends and constant companions on their future trips to California.

Of all our friends Gladys Cooper was the most stimulating. Her joy of life and delight in birds and beasts and young people paralleled Gip's. I have to say that they took to each other like ducks to water, because I remember Gladys enjoying our pet duck when we had one and Gip responding to Gladys's when she acquired hers. Gladys loved to be surrounded by her family as well as other animals and there was a time when there were rarely less than four or five of them at Napoli Drive. One had to think twice before asking Gladys to dinner because her answer was liable to be, "I'd love to—there'll be six of us." When her family, for one reason or another, dissipated to the four corners of the earth and Gip and I would say, "Let's have Gladys to dinner—who else shall we ask?" the answer as likely as not would be, "Oh, let's ask her by herself. She's such fun."

She would arrive in her racy open Thunderbird looking wonderful and say, "I hope I'm not late, but I only got back from the studio half an hour ago. Then I had a swim in the pool, fed the animals, telephoned Sally in London and ... well, here I am. Oh, Alan—what a delicious drink. Let me guess. Rum, isn't it? Lime and that touch of mint!" During dinner, there would be all the up-to-the-minute news about her family, her neighbors and the film she was working on—vivid and funny, but never malicious. As the evening wore on it would be stories of the old days when she started her great career—stories of Charles Hawtrey, Seymour Hicks, Dennis Eadie, Mrs. Pat and, of course, Gerald du Maurier. Gip and I were people to whom these great theater personalities were more than names—I had played with du Maurier and Eadie; Gip with Mrs. Pat—and our questions and delighted interest would keep her bubbling on. Unlike the stories of most theatrical raconteurs hers were never in the least self-congratulatory; they were concerned with the brilliance of these men from whom she had learned so much when they were not about her own moments of comic discomfiture. I remember one glorious understatement. The period she was speaking of was perhaps 1914 when many people thought her the most beautiful woman in the world. The point of the story necessitated some reference to this fact. "One happened to be rather good-looking at the time," was how Gladys put it.

To my surprise she rated Charles Hawtrey above du Maurier as a master of comedy. I had only seen him once in a rather silly little play called *Ambrose Applejohn's Adventure*. But I can still see and hear him as he joyfully exclaimed, "Aces! All aces!" Gladys was with him in a play called *The Naughty Wife* and, as an example of his style of acting she told us this story. As the naughty wife of the title, she runs away and leaves him a note on the mantelpiece. The audience is agog to see his reaction. He reads the brief note aloud with absolutely no expression till he comes to the end. Every eye is riveted on him. The note ends—it is his *wife* writing—"Yours sincerely." At this point, he raised one eyebrow and the whole house collapsed into laughter. The lovely economy of it!

About midnight Gladys would suddenly say, "Good heavens! Here I am talking my head off and I have a 6:30 call at the studio. I have enjoyed myself! I must dash." Varoom! Varoom! and the Thunderbird is gone. The particular night I am thinking of was during the brief period of recovery in Gip's illness when Gladys must have been over 70. She was a strength and stay to me towards the end. She would come to tea, brisk and unsentimental, but radiating courage and compassion.

To me the miraculous thing about Gladys was that she never ceased to grow. Every year she became a better actress, a warmer, more generous human being. I was in England in 1965 (after playing Don Quixote in Spain in a disastrously ill-conceived pilot episode for a television series that came to nothing). One Sunday, when Diana Wynyard and I were driving down to Henley to spend the day with Gladys, Diana said a very revealing thing. "Gladys isn't really a woman, you know. She's a little boy." I gasped. "Look at the way she stands when she's not being an actress." At Barn Elms, after lunch, the conversation turned to Peter Pan and the awful clothes he had worn in early productions.

"I put an end to that when I played him," said Gladys. "I wore grey flannel shorts with a scab on one knee and a bandage on the other!" Diana's idea of Gladys as a little boy had been fermenting in my mind and here was Gladys clinching it. Then I remembered that she had once said to Gip, "I wasn't interested in marriage. I just wanted good sires for my children." The fact is, I think, that outstanding figures in the arts are less polarized in the matter of sex than the average person. The men's range of sensitivity is increased by feminine intuition and awareness, and certain masculine attributes add to the stature of great actresses. I think of a great moment in Gladys' career.

It was the year after I had suffered in Enid Bagnold's play *Gertie*. The night before Gip and I arrived in New York for our next year's visit, Gladys had opened in Miss Bagnold's play *The Chalk Garden*. Gladys and Siobban McKenna got rave reviews, perhaps giving an impression that the actresses had saved a good but difficult play. On our first night in New York Gip and I dropped into a

Alan as Don Quixote, 1965. Courtesy Jennifer Nichols.

restaurant we had never heard of before for dinner. At a table not far away I was amazed to see Miss Bagnold. I got up and congratulated her on the success of her play and asked if she was very happy about everything. "Not particularly," she said. "Though, of course one is glad that it seems to be a success."

Gip and I went to the first matinée (the evening performances were sold out solid) and heard the story of the production from Gladys. She had never been more unhappy at rehearsals in her life. The original director [*George Cukor*] had to be removed, a second director was worse, the opening in Boston a disaster, and a third director [*Albert Marre*] appointed. Miss Bagnold never seemed satisfied with anything and the producer (an eminent lady from Hollywood) [*Irene Mayer Selznick*] had failed to show Gladys any consideration or support.

"So when we got back to New York I really didn't give a hoot. I thought, 'One will go through the lines on the first night, the play will fail and then one will return to California.' I was exhausted and ... well, one is only prepared to take so much. And then an extraordinary thing happened. You see, one had not done a play in New York for some years and apparently they were glad to see one again. Anyhow, at my first entrance I received a quite extraordinary ovation. I think they said it went on for two minutes. I was really very touched. And I thought 'By God, I'll give them a performance!'"

And a tremendous performance she gave. I doubt if the dramatist and the producer ever knew that it was the love and the loyalty of the playgoers of New York for a great actress that saved their bacon, rather than any loyalty on Gladys's part to her producer.

Fifteen years later I saw her in *The Chalk Garden* again, in the 1971 revival at the Haymarket Theater in London. As with a great claret which has aged a little beyond its span, I thought some of the body had gone out of her work; but it was lovely still, with an exquisite aroma. Going round to see Gladys after the performance could well have been a sentimental occasion for me. Forty years before I had first seen the brass plate on the Haymarket star dressing room bearing the name Marie Tempest. Now it was Gladys Cooper. However, sentimental it was not, for I had two pretty girls with me who had never heard of Marie Tempest and who Gladys greeted with the greatest kindness and vivacity. And in no time she was putting Marie Tempest in her place by telling the girls my story—"Whatever you play, dear boy, you must always look your best."—a story which had always amused her. I asked if she was still driving herself down to Henley every night in an open Thunderbird.

"No, a variety of extraordinary young men with long hair drive me. Very fast. It's lovely to get back into the country."

I never saw her again. But the week after she died she was on television in America in a series called *The Persuaders*. She gave a glorious performance as an old Russian Grand-Duchess in an intrigue over lost diamond jewelry. At the end, aglitter with ropes of diamonds and wearing a magnificent tiara, she thanks the young men who have come to her aid. They call for a toast. Glasses are filled with champagne. Gladys raises hers high. "To life!" she says, empties the glass and tosses it over her shoulder. It was a magnificent gesture and a perfect epitaph.

Over the years my staunchest friend, of course, has been Brian Aherne. When the going was tough, I could count on him at any time for a loan to tide me over—without question or mutual embarrassment. I was always able to repay him promptly when the next good job came along, as it invariably did. But there was a time when, only thinking of what was best for me, he said: "Alan, don't you think you ought to get a proper job?" This is amusing because he called his admirable book of reminiscences *A Proper Job*, explaining that he never felt that acting was a proper job.

We have always disagreed politically. Indeed, for many years he suspected Gip and me of being Communists. This enraged Gippy because she felt it showed a ridiculous lack of understanding. To me it was another proof of his goodness of heart. Despite this eccentric and socially unacceptable aberration, he was still prepared to embrace us as friends with open arms. Then there was my disregard for convention in the matter of clothes. His brother-in-law, Alfred Deliagre, once called me the only English Primitive he had ever met, when I invited them both to lunch and served it on my patio in ragged swimming shorts. The lunch was excellent with fresh cantaloupe melon from my garden.

When Brian appeared as Higgins in the first American tour of *My Fair Lady*, the opening was in Los Angeles. Gip and I were invited on the first night to join a glamorous party including Merle Oberon. A little anxiously Brian called me up to say: "You know, old man, this is going to be quite a smart event, evening dress clothes and all that."

"All right," I thought, "all right. I'll go the whole hog for him." And I took out the midnight-blue tails I had had made many years before for a picture at MGM. I have written that I only wore them once since; this was the occasion. As it turned out I was the only man in the audience wearing tails.

After the performance we were bidden to a tremendously grand party at a tremendously exclusive club in downtown Los Angeles. When we arrived at the anteroom to the great chamber where the party was being held, Gip said she wanted to go to the ladies' room. "Okay," I said, "I'll wait for you here." In came Merle Oberon, with whom I had appeared in a picture not long before, looking superb in a fabulous creation that no one in Hollywood but her could have carried off. She took one look at me and said, "Alan, you're the only properly dressed man here. You shall take me in." And, imperiously laying her hand on my arm she swept me into the assembled cream of Los Angeles society. Having made our very effective entrance, she graciously relinquished me saying, "I expect your little wife will be looking for you." I was happy to have failed neither Brian nor Miss Oberon.

Another glamorous lady we met at Brian's was Greta Garbo, who was much more interested in Gip, with her boyish figure, than in me. My young friend John Justin—no longer quite so young but still my friend and instantly Gip's too—who was out here making a picture, was also present that evening. He made a very acute observation about Garbo, that most intriguing, exquisitely somber, simple, complex, indefinable of human beings. He said, "You know, she likes her boys to be girls and her girls to be boys."

Brian and Eleanor were with me the day Gip died and I went back to their beautiful house on the beach in Santa Monica that evening. I had no doubt that I wanted Brian to speak of Gip at her memorial service. He is a man who recognizes excellence, a man for all seasons.

To Jack Houseman, my friend from school days, Gip was never able to come very close; but with his wife, Joan, as I have said, an extraordinary affinity existed. To tell the truth, it is difficult to come very close to Jack. I had been on what I felt to be easy terms with him for nearly fifty years when his splendid book *Run Through* came out. And I realized that I had never really known him. We had met as little boys at boarding school, each desperately trying to put up a front to hide the inner fears and inadequacies deriving from our home lives. To me, Jack had a glamorous, man of the world, continental aura and to him, I suppose, I had the immense security of a close-knit family background. So we each put on a carapace to hide our secret hurts so that we could brazen it out in the tough world of our aggressive and competitive boarding school peers. The carapace became the man and, for half a century, we lapsed into a relationship of false joviality and old-schoolboy kidding—neither admitting to painful maladjustments to life.

After reading *Run Through*, I wrote Jack to say how moving I had found it to discover for the first time the agonizingly lonely and frightened little boy he once had been. When I went to stay with him and Joan this Spring I took with me the first draft of this book. Since marriage to Gip had rendered my protective shell more or less obsolete, Jack may not have learned from my book as much as I had learned from his. However that may be, I felt a true and sweet friendship at last come to life.

I can never match the intellectual brilliance or the persistence with which Jack has carved himself out a great career and position in the theater. I used to question this success since I felt myself to be a native of this land of theater and Jack a naturalized citizen—the way an American career diplomat may well question the success of Henry Kissinger. And Jack may have questioned the air of "I know better than you because it's my country," which theatrical old-timers tend to assume in face of brilliant new-comers. These attitudes certainly colored our relationship as actor and director.

Now conflicts are resolved. I can enjoy his brilliance and sympathize with the problems in life which beset him. Last Spring I said to him:

"Jack, you always try to do too much."

"I know, I know—it's killing me."

"Then why don't you lay off and take it easy for a while?"

"I begin to feel ill the moment I'm not working."

Jack, I think, enjoys in me a sort of calm, pedestrian wisdom and practical common sense. Also we have memories of people and happenings which few can share with us.

44

Television

JAMES BIGWOOD

As Alan has noted, television came along at just the right moment to bolster his waning movie career, although his first effort in the new medium turned out to be something of a hybrid.

Your Show Time was a half-hour program which aired on NBC starting in January of 1949, one of the first television series to be shot on film rather than broadcast live. Sponsored by Lucky Strike Cigarettes and hosted (with periodic narration) by Arthur Shields, it dramatized "Masterworks of Famous Authors." Alan, top billed for the first time in his screen career, played Sherlock Holmes in Arthur Conan Doyle's *The Adventure of the Speckled Band*, the tenth episode of the 23 produced. Saddled with a ridiculously large Meerschaum pipe, and an impossibly short shooting schedule, Alan gives it his best, but quite rightly observes, "I expect it was terrible—we did the whole show in one day." Indeed, Basil Rathbone and Jeremy Brett have little to worry about.

In 1949 the number of American households with television sets was still quite small, with many markets actually having no broadcast coverage at all. This, coupled with the fact that the show had been shot on film, made it feasible for the producers to increase their audience by releasing individual episodes of the series as theatrical shorts. As a result, Alan's first television show was also his fiftieth (give or take) theatrical film.

His first unequivocal television role came almost two years later, on NBC, in a live 1951 Christmas night broadcast of Charles Dickens' *A Christmas Carol*. Compressed into half an hour and starring Sir Ralph Richardson as Scrooge, the show opens with Alan, as the story's author, tapping on a hanging shop sign with his cane and welcoming the audience: "Scrooge and Marley. There's a story to tell there. I know. It's *my* story. And I shall tell it to you tonight as I've told it many times before. I call it *A Christmas Carol*. May it haunt your houses pleasantly. Your friend and servant, Charles Dickens."

The special had been pulled together quite quickly, with U.S. Steel making its television advertising debut in the time slot normally occupied by Procter & Gamble's *Fireside Theater*, and the cast had still not been finalized two weeks before the air date, although *Variety* reported on December 12 that Richardson might be flying in from England to play the lead. This he did, arriving in New York on the seventeenth to begin rehearsals, preceded one day earlier by the 7-year-old Robert Hay-Smith, also flown over from the UK, cast as Tiny Tim. Alan was already in New York rehearsing for *Gertie* when the offer came for him to join the cast, and, as it turned out, it proved an opportunity not only for him, but for members of his family as well. *Variety*'s review of the show reported that "in toto the cast did well," singling out "Gypsy Raine as Mrs. Fezziwig" among others. *The TeleVision Guide* (precursor to *TV Guide*) also listed Gip's participation, noting that she was Dickens' great-granddaughter (but not that she was married to Alan). Yet, strangely, Gypsy Raine is not listed in the show's on-screen credits with the rest of the cast, nor does the character of Mrs. Fezziwig have any dialogue. The only reference to her comes when Scrooge visits Christmas Past and witnesses his younger self celebrating the holidays with his employer's family ("Why there's Mrs. Fezziwig! And her daughter the young Miss Fezziwig! Ha-ha!"), but this takes place during a jolly dance in which the faces of the participants (all extras) cannot be made out.

It seems likely that once Alan became involved in the production, he mentioned in passing that he was married to Dickens' great-granddaughter. This undoubtedly prompted an offer for her to join the cast, and, despite the fact that her character actually had no lines, explains her eventual inclusion in the publicity distributed to the press. But it turns out that Gip was not the only Dickens descendant to appear in this version of *A Christmas Carol*. Dickens' great-*great*-granddaughter is also among the extras in the show (likely playing the arbitrarily noted "young Miss Fezziwig"). Thanks to young Robert Hay-Smith's hobby of collecting (and fortunately saving) mementos of his screen career, there is proof in his autograph book that, in addition to Alan ("For Robert, Tiny Tim from Alan Napier, Charles Dickens"), the cast of *A Christmas Carol* included Gip ("We will always remember Tiny Tim. Love from Gypsy Raine") and Poppet ("Best wishes for your continued success in the theatre. Yours, Jennifer Raine").

Leon Morse in *The Billboard* observed that "the pin-point accuracy of casting, authenticity of English settings, unique high level of acting, and of production in all departments created a presentation which had many of the qualities of the best of films and all of the merits of the best TV drama," but the show also contains some of the unintended gaffes so common to live television. While Alan delivers his opening monologue, for example, there is an extra in the background who keeps peeping around a building at a "turn" in the street. His speech finished, he walks away under the opening credits, turns to exit at the same corner, and encounters what appears to be a two-foot-drop just out of camera range, causing his cape to billow out on the ground as he takes a giant step down.

Early television credits can be confusing. Revue Productions (the television arm of Universal Studios) hired Alan for episodes of several of their early filmed anthology series, but the individual shows were often packaged under more than one Revue title. For example, in 1952, he starred in "Playmates," a spooky little story with Natalie Wood making her television debut as an orphaned girl who befriends the ghost children in her uncle's house. After initially airing on *Chevron Theatre* in June, it was rebroadcast ten weeks later as an episode of *Schaefer Century Theatre* and finally, in 1954, was seen as an episode of *Pepsi Cola Playhouse*. Similarly, "The Whistling Room," also a haunted house tale (though one that plays Alan's "ghost catcher" for comedy), aired as an episode of *Chevron Theatre* in 1952 and *Pepsi Cola Playhouse* in 1954. Another of his *Pepsi Cola Playhouse* episodes, "Farewell Performance," was originally broadcast in 1954 and then reused in 1965, more than ten years after its initial airing, as an episode of *Moment of Fear*.

Alan was also part of the television debut of DuPont's *Cavalcade of America*, which had been dramatizing important moments in American history on radio since 1935. The show's well received video incarnation premiered on October 1, 1952, with "Poor Richard," the story of Benjamin Franklin's clever procrastinations while ostensibly negotiating Colonial surrender terms with Alan's Lord Howe. "Poor Richard" had an interesting life after its original airdate, with a ten-minute abridgement of the show being released in 16mm for screening as an educational aid in schools. It is this cut-down version of the show that is currently most readily available, but even truncated, Alan's Lord Howe has some fine moments debating tactics with his more hot-tempered brother (Henry Brandon as General William Howe).

Also in 1952, Alan guest-starred on *Biff Baker USA*, an improbable half-hour spy drama (with purported comic overtones) starring Alan Hale, Jr. "Mona Lisa," the sixth episode of the series, featured Alan (Napier, not Hale) as a visiting art professor in Paris who gets mixed up, along with Baker and his wife, in a very convoluted (and highly unlikely) art theft plot. Fans of Hale's most famous series *Gilligan's Island* (still twelve years in the future), may be amused to watch the young "Skipper" interacting with a man he constantly addresses as "Professor," but that's about it.

In 1953, Alan was the title character in "The Man on the Train," an episode of *Four Star Playhouse*, starring David Niven. This was yet another ghost story, smartly directed by veteran Robert Florey, with Alan playing a man who returns to the land of the living to help solve his own murder. He imbues the mysterious passenger with a weariness and resignation that is perversely compelling.

Alan was directed by Flory again—with less impressive results—in "The Bronte Story," a 1953 episode of *The Loretta Young Show* (early enough in its run that it was still known as *Letter to Loretta*). As writer Charlotte Bronte's domineering father, selfishly determined to prevent her marriage, he has to negotiate the script's multiple unmotivated mood swings, joined in support of Miss Young by only two other actors. Modern viewers will be entertained by the teaming of three television icons, years before their fame: *Leave It to Beaver*'s Ward Cleaver (Hugh Beaumont, who also co-wrote the script), *Gilligan's Island*'s Lovey Howell (Natalie Schafer) and, of course, *Batman*'s Alfred the Butler.

Just prior to this, Alan appeared in full Nigel Bruce mode in "Skylark," an episode of *The Ray Milland Show*. As Dr. Sandine, "one of the more mature members of the faculty" at Lynnhaven College for Women, he intervenes when Ray Milland, as Professor Raymond McNutley, causes campus-wide consternation as he tries to determine which of his students (or fellow faculty members) has been sending him mash notes.

In 1955, Alan appeared in another live broadcast, this time a *Front Row Center* hour-long adaptation of Sutton Vane's 1923 play *Outward Bound*. He seems to have developed an affinity for stories with supernatural themes, for this often revived play concerns seven passengers who mysteriously find themselves alone on a ship, and slowly realize that they are dead and have been gathered to be judged. Alan is "The Examiner," who, in the guise of a clergyman, has been assigned to decide their fates. Playing half of a young couple who turn out to have been prematurely taken (they are dying as a result of a suicide pact but eventually escape the ship to face their families) is Pat Hitchcock, daughter of the famous director, sharing the screen with Alan for the first of three times.

Also in 1955, Alan was seen in "The Lucky Finger," an episode of the one hour *Lux Video Theatre*. In it, Edith Barrett plays an aging spinster whose amazing run of gambling luck turns her wealthy overnight. *Variety* was not impressed: "Into each tv [sic] series some rain must fall, but this was a cloudburst. Only because host Otto Kruger said so did the viewer know it was a comedy. Localed in Ireland, hapless story saddled with pea-soup accents so thick much of the dialog wasn't intelligible... [Y]arn rather resembles one of those old, old British pix. Spinster eventually winds up with the local bigshot, Sir Adrian [Alan], no less, but by that time few care."

This was immediately followed by the first of Alan's six appearances on *Alfred Hitchcock Presents*, again in support of Pat Hitchcock. The episode, "Into Thin Air," aired as the fifth episode of the new series, but was actually the very first to be shot. It is 1899, the year of the Paris World Exhibition. A visiting Englishwoman tries to solve the disappearance of her mother, an event made all the more mysterious when the staff at their hotel not only claims to have no knowledge of the missing mother, but also deny recognizing the daughter. Alan is the British Ambassador, a role that consists of two scenes, the first dismissive, as he turns the girl over to his younger and more romantically interesting assistant ("Of course you were quite right to call me in, Farnham, but I think you can handle the situation yourself. Hmmm? Yes. You're in good hands, Miss Winthrop. Mr. Farnham will assist you in any way possible and ... er ... good day.") and the second reassuring and comforting, as he delivers the solution to the mystery: that the missing woman died of bubonic plague and her death was covered up by the French government to prevent panic amongst the visitors to the crowded city. The explanation, which in lesser hands could easily have quickly strayed into melodrama, is beautifully delivered.

"Whodunit," Alan's second Hitchcock episode, was considerably more whimsical. Clean-shaven and in a tightly curled wig, he is the Archangel Wilfred, bending the rules to allow mystery writer John Williams the opportunity to return to earth to solve his own murder. The two share their delightfully dry dialogue in an appropriately tongue-in-cheek heaven, with Williams' wings and harp particular standouts in their tattiness.

Also in 1956, Alan lent his presence to three episodes of *The 20th Century–Fox Hour*. The first, "Deception," starred Trevor Howard as a World War II soldier who believes himself a traitor because he cracked under Nazi torture, not realizing he was a plant deliberately sent out with false information in order to fool the enemy. Alan is fine, but not memorable, as the Governor of the British island to which Howard has exiled himself. In "The Empty Room," he has a small but amusing role as a guest at an engagement party who mistakenly sweeps the host's estranged wife into the gathering, not realizing that her presence at her daughter's celebration is coincidental and unwelcome.

Finally, in "Operation Cicero," a one-hour condensation of the 1952 feature, *5 Fingers*, his role is significantly more important. We are in neutral Turkey in 1944 and Alan is "Travers," tracking down a Nazi spy who has infiltrated the British Embassy. ("I'm probably just a gossip at heart. Maybe that's why I like my work. Counter-espionage is the highest form of gossip, you know.") Excellent as he is in the role, he was actually hired as much for his height as for his talent. The opening credits of the original theatrical feature had bragged that "all the exterior scenes in this picture were filmed in the locales associated with the story" and in order to add production value to the television adaptation, the location footage was simply reused, making it necessary to cast actors who physically approximated their 1952 counterparts. Alan is a close match for the 6'4" Michael Rennie (or, more accurately, for his second unit photo double) and the four-year-old footage fits seamlessly into the television remake.

Also in 1956, Alan made his first of three appearances on *NBC Matinee Theater*, an ambitious one-hour anthology series broadcast—live and in color—five afternoons a week from 1955 to 1958. In *The Perfect Alibi*, an adaptation of a play by A. A. Milne, he is Arthur Ludgrove, "a justice of the King's Bench." Perhaps the toughest aspect of his role is convincing the audience that he is so thick that he can't recognize amongst his weekend guests two men that he sentenced to prison during his long ago service in Kenya—a mistake he lives (but not long) to regret.

Alan started out 1957 in "The Consort," an episode of the CBS anthology series *Telephone Time*, featured in the role of Lord Melbourne, Prime Minister of England and advisor to the young Queen Victoria. The half-hour drama was, by necessity, an oversimplification of the betrothal and marriage of Victoria to her cousin Prince Albert of Saxe-Coburg-Gotha. Robert Vaughn had the title role, and has fond memories of the shoot—not because of anything that happened on-screen, but for his off-screen romantic relationship with his Victoria, Judi Boutin. Alan had very little to do on the show other than to give the British court a badly needed touch of England.

Following this, "A Gift of Death," an episode of the syndicated series *Soldiers of Fortune*, finds Alan embarrassingly over the top as a "silly ass" game commissioner in Kenya who hires the title characters to trap a lion for him to present to an English zoo, in order to preserve his name for posterity. This turns out to be a plan devised by his secretary to get revenge for his treatment of her brother.

Alan's next show, "I Killed the Count," was a unique entry in the seven-year run of *Alfred Hitchcock Presents*. Airing over three weeks, it was the only multi-part story of the series. More of a jigsaw puzzle than an acting showcase, it features Alan as Lord Sorrington, one of several suspects in the murder of Count Victor Mattoni, all of whom confess to the killing, much to the confusion of John Williams' Inspector Davidson.

In "Reincarnated," an episode of the syndicated show *Panic!*, Alan starred opposite June Havoc (who, although 45 years old, is described by the narrator as playing "June Sullivan, age 31") in a story of a knife thrower who believes that the wife he murdered years before has been reincarnated in the person of a vaudeville dancer. In a part that looks very much as though it was written (and indeed performed) with Boris Karloff in mind, Alan sells his character's madness using all the tricks of melodrama at his disposal, shy of frothing at the mouth. The episode also aired under the title "The Moth and the Flame," referring to the half hour's climax, when Alan forces his victim to perform her specialty: a seductive dance in a flimsy dress around an open flame. ("Liar! Cheat! Jezebel! Always other men! And those fine promises that belong to me, to no one else! Infamy! They must be purged, wiped out. I'll kill you again and again and again! Until there comes an end! You shall dance for me tonight. For the last time. Yes, for me, for me only! With none of those leering covetous eyes out there!") *TV Guide* reported that Havoc performed the dangerous dance herself, in two takes, under the watchful (if not leering and covetous) eyes of three firemen and a doctor.

Alan's television work up to this point had emphasized his upper class persona—even when playing villainous roles—but with "The Vigilantes Begin," the premiere episode of NBC's *The Californians*, set in 1851 San Francisco, he rejoined the lower classes. As Alfred Perkins, leader of the Sidney Cove Gang, made up of "every escaped convict from the British penal colony in Australia," he is the impetus for the forming of the heroic "Vigilance

Committee," comprised of the show's main characters. Captured by the end of the half-hour pilot, he is deported to Australia, proving that vigilantes "can act with justice" and be suitable heroes for a weekly network television show.

Next came an episode of *General Electric Theater* entitled "Mischief at Bandy Leg," with Alan cast as Sean O'Donnell, an irascible yet whimsical Irish playwright who is being pursued for the film rights to one of his plays. The show itself is not particularly remarkable, but Alan's makeup and costume as O'Donnell certainly is. Fully bearded and wearing a tweed suit with plus-fours, he is obviously intended to call to mind George Bernard Shaw. Drawing on his friendship with the playwright, he creates an impressive impersonation. "I can look quite a bit like Shaw," he said in 1975, "and I know how he spoke. And I've always thought I should get some great passages and do a one-man show of Shaw called 'An Evening with Shaw' in which I would be made up like him. I was put off for a long time because I thought sticking on that bloody beard every night would be a bore, but I've got one now, which should make it easy!" Indeed, a sold out 1959 benefit reading of Shaw's *Back to Methuselah* at the 1500-seat Ritz Theater prompted the following from the *L.A. Times*: "The cast cannot be overpraised: Alan Napier is gruff, tart perfection as narrating G.B.S. And in walking tweeds, he resembles him almost eerily." He finally gave up the idea in 1978. "Let who will do a Shaw show. The old boy is always worth listening to. I don't have the talent for promotion, especially self-promotion."

Alan finished 1957 with another live performance on *NBC Matinee Theater*. In J.M. Barrie's *The Little Minister*, he is Tammas Whammond, one of the elders of the Scottish parish to which the title character has been called.

Alan's only 1958 television appearance was also on *NBC Matinee Theater*, supporting Gene Raymond in an adaptation of *Death Takes a Holiday*, but he came back with a vengeance in 1959. "And One Was Loyal" on *GE True Theater* starred Joan Crawford as an abused wife in a jungle outpost in Singapore whose husband is murdered by the strategic introduction of a cobra to his bedroom. Alan is the local police inspector, willing to look the other way due to the unpopularity of the victim. He has no scenes with the leading lady, appearing only with Tom Helmore, whom he suspects (incorrectly) of being her lover and savior.

Alan's friendship with John Houseman helped get his next role, physician Sir Luke Strett in *The Wings of the Dove*, a dramatization of the Henry James novel which Houseman was producing for *Playhouse 90*. Alan found a kindred spirit in Inga Swenson, playing his patient, the terminally ill American heiress Milly Theale, not only because she had just played Ophelia for Houseman and would play Juliet for him the following summer, but because, at 5'10", she had had her share of career disappointments due to her height. "I had always had a problem—because of my height—being cast," she recalls. "Very often I would lose a job because I was too tall for the leading man or whatever. So we discussed that at length and he said, 'Hang in there! You'll make it!'" which, given her seven-year run as Miss Kraus on *Benson* in the eighties, she certainly did!

"Dark Island" was an episode of *The Third Man*, the NBC/BBC series which resurrected Grahame Greene's black marketeer Harry Lime (who had died at the end of Carol Reed's classic film) as a mystery solving art dealer. This episode starts in London, moves to Istanbul, then to "an island in the middle of nowhere" and finally to Paris, all within the confines of the 20th Century–Fox lot. Alan is the mysteriously accented Colonel Andresi, the power behind the deluded General Marius (his *Stamboul* co-star Abraham Sofaer), who plans to ensure his return to power in his (unnamed) country by kidnapping qualified candidates to serve in his eventual cabinet. Harry Lime is duly kidnapped and foils the plot, immediately destroying his opportunity to serve as Marius' Foreign Minister.

Another episode of *Alfred Hitchcock Presents* followed. "The Avon Diamonds" featured Alan and Roger Moore as CID detectives trying to prevent the theft of Lady Avon's valuable jewelry. When the diamonds turn up missing, she is immediately a suspect, not because of any insurance money (she couldn't afford the premiums), but because they were supposed to be held to settle a government tax claim. Now free to spirit them out of the country, she immediately does.

Five Fingers was a one-hour NBC cold war drama, ostensibly based on the similarly titled film that Alan had remade for television in 1956, but in reality completely re-imagined. The new premise was neatly established in opening voiceover by the show's star, David Hedison: "To the entertainment world on two continents, I'm Victor Sebastian, theatrical agent. These are my offices. But the business I'm about to transact can never appear on the company books. Not if I'm to survive. Because as it happens, I'm also another kind of agent. Counter-espionage. My employer—the United States government. Although sometimes I pose as its enemy. My code name—Five Fingers." The theatrical agency offices in question are "Wembley & Sebastian," and—in two different episodes—Alan Napier is Wembley to Hedison's Sebastian. Unfortunately, the series was abruptly cancelled after 16 episodes had been shot, depriving audiences of a smart, well-written show and Alan of an exceptional recurring role. Witty and theatrical, yet still with an eye for the ladies, oblivious to the true identity of his partner, and reveling in the glamour of his profession, he is first introduced in *The Unknown Town* (Episode 4) in a quite remarkable telephone exchange:

> SEBASTIAN: Hello, Wembley! How are you?
> WEMBLEY: Rather flatulent actually. Where are you, Victor?
> SEBASTIAN: In Rome.
> WEMBLEY: But you were in Rome four days ago. How very unlike you to be so stationary.
> SEBASTIAN: I signed up this new Italian tenor. He's going to be the darling of Covent Garden next season. Just wait and see.
> WEMBLEY: Oh, dear boy. D'you think the world can really stand another darling tenor?

This is 1959. Could the NBC censor possibly be unaware of what flatulence is?

Wembley reappears in "Thin Ice" (episode 11), making moves on series co-star Luciana Paluzzi ("That delectable confection next to the piano. Is she one of our clients?"). Alan's pleasure in returning to the part is obvious and David Hedison was equally happy to see him back. "He was a charming gentleman with lots of humor," he recalls today. "I thought that if the series had continued beyond the initial episodes, then perhaps something interesting might have happened with our characters. It was all over much too quickly and a disappointment to all of us."

Alan's two episodes of *Five Fingers* were separated by an appearance on a considerably more successful series, *The Detectives*, or to give it its official title, *The Detectives Starring Robert Taylor*. This, as much as anything, was proof that Alan had finally left the greylist behind him, as Taylor was as rabid a red-baiter as Menjou, a fellow founder of the "Motion Picture Alliance for the Preservation of American Ideals." In "The Bait," the sixth episode of the series, Alan is "The Bishop," a drug pusher who is caught by using low end junkie

Chickie Barnes as bait. Jay Adler, of the famous acting family, is really the focus of the episode as Chickie. Alan is suitably menacing (although inappropriately elegant for a hands-on drug kingpin) when he finally makes his appearance toward the end of the half hour.

Alan's first small screen appearance of the sixties was in "Kim," a one-hour episode of *Shirley Temple Theatre*. Shot in color on videotape, the series was specifically targeted to children, and has not aged well. The Rudyard Kipling tale takes place in India, and Alan's appearance as a British Colonel, along with fellow Brit Clive Halliday and Australian born but British trained Laurie Main as "Charters and Caldicott" type schoolmasters, only serves to show up the unmistakable and inappropriate American accents of the remainder of the cast. Even the English born Michael Rennie sounds American!

Alan's role in "The Purple Room" was the first of three appearances on the NBC one-hour series *Thriller*, hosted by Boris Karloff, a show which has been compared by more than one observer to *Alfred Hitchcock Presents*. "The Purple Room" does little to dispel this comparison, as the exterior of the spooky house which serves as the episode's main location is immediately recognizable as the house that looms over the Bates Motel in *Psycho* (released only five months before "The Purple Room" aired). Opening the show as an attorney reading the will that sets up Rip Torn's overnight stay in the house, Alan plays his part with an American accent, something he did not do particularly often, nor, at least in this case, particularly convincingly.

This was followed by an appearance on a very curiously titled syndicated half-hour series: *The Case of the Dangerous Robin*. The show starred Rick Jason as insurance fraud investigator Robin Scott, an expert in the then barely known discipline of karate. Alan's episode, "The Bard Disappears," features him as an eccentric professor holed up in a book-cluttered office, assisting in the investigation of the theft of a Shakespeare first folio from London University.

Including both film and television, Alan had probably worked less than fifteen days in all of 1960—professional inactivity which, either by design or by coincidence, allowed him to devote his time and energy to more important events taking place at Porto Marina Way.

45

Journey's End

A year or so ago, Brian Aherne asked me if I could recommend him a window cleaner. "Yes, indeed. Thad Kennedy. He's been doing my windows for twenty years. He's excellent and very reasonable." Brian called the number I gave him and Mrs. Kennedy quoted a figure no smaller than that of other window cleaning services. Then Brian happened to see Thad's truck parked on the side of a street and spoke to him, quoting my statement that he was very reasonable.

"Ah, but you see, Mr. Napier's my friend," said Thad.

He comes to the house once a month. At his first visit after Gip died, he said:

"Mrs. Kennedy has a special power of giving comfort—a power of the spirit. She has given it to many. You won't take my saying so amiss. It's all we have to offer."

It was Thad who sparked Gip's longing for a camping trailer. For him, with possible rejection at motels, it was a necessity for vacation trips; but the lure of taking a little home with you, so that you can stop for the night when fancy dictates, was irresistible to Gip. We started looking for one in earnest when a nagging pain in Gip's back refused to go away. We thought an extended trip into the giant redwood country and then on to the High Sierras might be just the thing to help her relax and get rid of it. In a second-hand lot we found just what we were looking for and, the next day, a suitable lug for towing attached to the Pontiac, we drove it home in triumph. Across the road from my house there is a narrow shelf above the cliff which I have leveled off for parking. We would admire our new acquisition from our windows as we planned its decoration and equipment.

Gip's back was getting no better and I suggested that a visit to my chiropractor, a friend of long standing, could do no harm. He took x-rays which revealed a patch on the lung. This was eventually diagnosed as cancer.

After a grievous operation Gip came home to recuperate. It was a slow business but she never gave up hope. From our window she could see our trailer.

"Oh, our lovely trailer. Do you think we'll ever…"

"Of course we will."

"Yes, of course. I was wondering about curtains. Something cottage-chintzy, don't you think? Measure the windows for me and I'll work out how many yards."

We planned a trip the moment she was well enough to travel. The doctors, watching their words, had said that there was no reason to suppose that she might not make a complete recovery. So, eventually, in the late spring of 1959, we set forth.

There was a secret place we had come across some years before on a visit to Lake Isabella. We had pushed our way on, up the River Kern, which pours out of the High Sierras fed by the snows of towering Mt. Whitney, past Road's End and up a rough track that led to a logging camp. Rounding a bend, there, far below us, we could see the shining river, its headlong rush stilled as it broadened into a quiet little lake, with a pile of great flat rocks jutting out into it. We clambered down the cliff-side with Kento and Miranda (I had to carry Miranda; the going was too rough for her) and picnicked. We found a rock from which we could dive into deep water to swim naked, then, lying out like lizards in the sun, look up to snow-capped peaks against an azure sky. It was our special secret place and Gip longed to return to it. We both knew that she could not possibly now make the hard climb down the cliff and up again, nor was there space to park the trailer. But perhaps we could find another sequestered spot quite near.

Getting started had taken longer than we expected, so that it was evening when we got to Kernville. As you go on up the river there are a dozen trailer parks; but we wanted a private place of our own. Road's End we found belied its name now, for since our earlier visit the road to the logging camp had been improved and metaled. On we went, up and up, past our secret place, but finding no spot to pull off the road for the night. It was dusk by now and I was beginning to wonder if we had not been too ambitious in passing those convenient trailer parks, when Gippy touched my arm and said, "Look! To the left there." Sure enough, the pine forest suddenly gave way to a grassy slope which ran steeply down towards a tributary of the Kern. I pulled off the road and saw that a rough track led down to a flat little meadow, bounded on the far side by the river. The light was fading fast so I got out of the car to have a better look. It was a perfect campsite.

"It's a bit steep down," I said, "but I guess we can make it."

It was so much steeper and rougher than I thought that, when we came to rest, we entered the trailer with some anxiety. A few pots and pans had clattered noisily from their shelves but nothing important was broken.

Gip cooked us a wonderful dinner and, sleepy from our long day and the keen mountain air, we slept like logs.

The morning, so quiet but for the gentle song of the stream and the occasional screech of a blue-jay, was exquisite. On the other side of the river there was a spinney of poplar and aspen, to our left the pine forest and to our right the curve of the grassy slope. Indeed a secret place. We found a sandy-bottomed spot in the river a couple of feet deep where we could soap ourselves and bathe. Though Gip looked pitifully thin in the bright morning sunshine, she had stood the journey well and was in tremendous spirits. In no time she had breakfast cooking. In the meantime I had a good look at the rocky track down which we had recklessly descended in the dusk. By daylight it appeared to be a precipice.

"What a darling place we've found," said Gip, bursting with happiness.

"H'm," I said with less enthusiasm. "How long will our supplies last? Because I think we're here for life. Come and look."

"I see what you mean. It is a bit steep, isn't it? And we do really want to settle by the big river."

"Yes."

"Cheer up. You can do it."

I unhitched the car and made a dry run. In the car alone, I had difficulty keeping the wheels from bumping and losing traction. I got a spade from the trailer—we were well equipped—and went to work in the hot sun, digging out a boulder here, filling in a chasm there. Then I tried the car again and made it more easily. But with that great trailer behind—

an unknown quantity? Trying to conceal my fears from Gip, I re-hitched the trailer, circled round the meadow two or three times to plot the best approach (there was no room for a fast run at the hill) and told Gip to get in.

"Oh, hadn't I better wait and see what happens? Besides, my added weight…"

"Your enormous weight will help to hold the car wheels down. It's traction, not power that I'm worried about. If anything happens I want us to die together."

"Don't be silly. Oh, you're joking. Oh, I wish you really were joking. I'm not worried. I know you'll do it."

We did. Just. I don't know how. I have been back since in other cars on sentimental visits and I would not dream of going down that track, even without a trailer. The Pontiac was a good, heavy, old-fashioned car. And there was the power of faith—Gip's faith in me.

We found another nice, fairly private place on the bank of the big river and near to Road's End, so that it was easy to get supplies. We had a lovely time, driving to a favorite sandy bathing beach most mornings, drowsing and reading in the afternoons. My deep regret is that after ten days I began to get bored, for Gip, who may have had an intimation that it was our last holiday together in the mountains, wanted to stay longer. Selfishly, I overruled her. This was the only trip we made in the trailer Gip had so longed for and decorated so lovingly with its pretty cottage-chintzy curtains and Woolworth crockery.

A month or so later a terrible sciatic pain fastened its hold on my poor darling. The cancer had returned and would not be denied.

The day of Gip's second operation I was working on a television film, playing a charlatan magician. That morning, while Gip was in surgery, I was being pelted, in a chaotic nightclub scene, with whatever food or drink the customers could lay their hands on; one of the more detestable experiences to which an actor can be exposed, particularly in repetition as the camera moves closer. But it took my mind off what was happening at the hospital. As I was getting cleaned up, there was a telephone call for me. Gip, back in her room, wanted to let me know that she had come through all right. In fact the incision had not been serious for it had quickly shown that neither surgery nor any other method known to medicine could avail. When I went to the hospital at the end of the day's work, Gip had been given a shot of pain-reliever and was sleeping. On the back of a telegram ("Our hands are holding yours. Brian, Eleanor"), there was a little note for me by her bedside, scribbled the night before: "You have just gone. You were wonderful. If things go wrong (which I am positive they won't) please believe me best husband—couldn't have had better or more loving. No more doped to the eyes—couldn't have wished happier life. You made it that. Love, love, love, Gip."

It was three months before the strong life force in her was vanquished.

46

More Television

James Bigwood

The show Alan was shooting when the return of Gip's cancer was confirmed was "Daughter of Illusion," an episode of the ABC series *Adventures in Paradise* which aired in December 1960. The unhappy news prevented him from enjoying what was easily one of the better roles he had had in a while but, always the professional, he gave it his all. As Alex the Great, a second rate cabaret magician who has managed to steal a necklace worth $200,000, he is the main guest star in a popular show and is as much a presence in the episode as the series' leads. His Alex is a cockney who switches to a pseudo-posh accent (quite unlike Alan's own) when on stage, a subtle detail which was probably lost on many in the audience.

In 1961, it was back to *Thriller* for "Hay-Fork and Bill-Hook." While his role had been small in "The Purple Room," this time Alan was a full-fledged guest star—mentioned by name by Karloff in his introduction to the episode. As Evans, the Constable in a tiny Welsh village dealing with witchcraft, he is appropriately mysterious in his interactions with a visiting Scotland Yard detective and his young wife.

This was followed by an appearance in "Black Saturday," an episode of the ABC series *The Roaring 20's*. Here, Alan simply had to look rich and dignified (which he does impeccably) as the father of a society girl whose engagement to a college football player is jeopardized by a gambler's threats to reveal the boy's birth mother's past.

In "Dark Legacy," Alan's third episode of *Thriller*, he was required to simply read a will again, albeit without the American accent. No longer included in Karloff's introduction, he *is* given special billing in the end-credits ("with Alan Napier as The Attorney" in last position in slightly larger type than the rest of the supporting cast) although the part really doesn't merit it.

Tales of Wells Fargo had been airing on NBC for five years when Alan made his first of two guest appearances on the series in "The Dowry," the final episode to air before the show shifted from a black-and-white half-hour to a one-hour color format for its sixth and final season. Teamed with Wynn Pearce as a pair of unscrupulous Frenchmen, he menaces a young heiress traveling with a fortune in jewels and securities.

The Tehran Conference was an actual summit held between Franklin D. Roosevelt, Winston Churchill and Joseph Stalin at the end of November 1943 in the Soviet Embassy in Tehran, Iran; *Assassination Plot at Teheran* was a television special which aired on ABC in September 1961, detailing a fictional Nazi attempt to assassinate the Big Three leaders

As Constable Evans in "Hay-Fork and Bill-Hook" on *Thriller* (NBC, 1961). Collection of James Bigwood.

during the course of that meeting. Initially planned as a pilot for a weekly series about the U.S. Counter-Intelligence Corps, the movie was shown in two one-hour slots on consecutive Saturdays, pre-empting *The Roaring 20's*. As Wilfred Morely of British Intelligence, Alan is not given top-of-show billing, but since he shares his scenes with John Larch (the show's lead) and guest-star Oskar Homolka, who play his American and Russian counterparts, he seems a bigger presence than he actually is.

Alan Napier, Oskar Homolka and John Larch as the heads of British, Russian and U.S. counterintelligence in *Assassination Plot at Teheran* **(ABC, 1961). Collection of James Bigwood.**

Follow the Sun was a one-hour ABC series about two Honolulu magazine writers who constantly find themselves solving crimes. In the episode titled "Annie Beeler's Place," Alan is "The Major," a member of a criminal gang who intimidates the bartender at the writers' local watering hole into rejoining his gang for the robbery of a local Chinese bank.

Switching to the side of the law, Alan next appeared as "Inspector Templeton of the Hong Kong Police" on *The New Bob Cummings Show*. The episode (optimistically titled "North by Southeast," but hardly a patch on the Hitchcock film whose title it parodied) allowed Alan an opportunity to show off his legs in traditional Hong Kong uniform shorts while trading melodramatic epigrams with the show's globe-trotting star ("They play for keeps here you see. And the name of the game's not cricket actually; its murder.") Fortunately, he is spared some of the show's more excruciating attempts at humor. It is tough to watch Hong Kong tailor Mitch Soong (Harold Fong) cheerfully answering in the affirmative after being asked whether his companion Sam Sing has accompanied him: "Sing along with Mitch!"

"A Chant of Silence" was a 1962 episode of the CBS series *Checkmate*. Created by Eric Ambler in 1960, the show featured Anthony George and Doug McClure as San Francisco detectives and Sebastian Cabot as their friend and advisor, former Oxford professor Carl Hyatt. This particular episode centers mainly around Hyatt who, in pursuit of his hobby of recording Gregorian chants, finds himself in the midst of a hostage situation when a Benedictine monastery is invaded by two escaped convicts (Nick Adams and James Coburn). Alan is the Father Abbott, a man of God whose calm demeanor is greatly tested by the two interlopers. ("There are matters that must be understood between us. The brothers here are men of the strict observance. If there is any humility left in you, be good enough to respect their devotions.") A brief flash of anger when he demands to be allowed to attend to his duties comes as quite a surprise, making his saintly character all the more human and infinitely more interesting.

With "Remember the Yazoo," Alan made his second appearance on *Tales of Wells Fargo*, now nearing the end of its six-year run. As the genial Colonel Decatur (again French-accented), he seems pleasant enough as the father of the fiancé of the local Wells Fargo manager, until he is eventually revealed as the brains behind the planned robbery of a cash delivery of $100,000 intended to stabilize the local New Orleans economy. While his partner in crime is still harboring a grudge against the North for the now six-years-past Civil War, Decatur is a man of less lofty principles: "Only Carondelet was in this to discredit Yankee enterprise. I was in it to recoup... I've always been a speculator. Cotton. Horse races. The tables in Gallatin Street. [With a Gallic shrug:] I was very unlucky."

Alan got his first shot at a continuing role in *Don't Call Me Charlie!*, an NBC sitcom about an Army veterinarian stationed in Paris. The show had the misfortune to premiere in September 1962, just as the Cuban Missile Crisis was starting to percolate, and some episodes were preempted for breaking news. Although a full season was shot, the show was cancelled after only eighteen of the twenty-six episodes had been broadcast, and of these, only three are currently available for reappraisal: the premiere episode, in which Alan does not appear, episode two, "No Vacancy" (the show's original pilot), which introduces his character, General Steele, and the last episode to air, "Lorenzo Johnson, D.V.M., Retired."

The show unfortunately suffered from a severe identity crisis. Originally titled *Vive Judson McKay!* (the lead character's name), its title was changed during production to *Don't Call Me Charlie!*, a catchphrase delivered, not by Josh Peine as the veterinarian, but by his superior officer, Colonel Barker, played by John Hubbard. Further distancing the main character from the show's title was the fact that McKay is actually the only character who *doesn't* address the colonel by his first name. In addition, his warm and fuzzy interactions with the local population and their various pets are written in an entirely different style from the scenes incorporating the rest of the cast, which are more sharply comic, and even slightly absurdist. Arte Johnson, who played the role of Corporal Lefkowitz, reveals the underlying problem: "The young man who had the lead of the show was not liked by the producer at all—he didn't want him—and they made it very uncomfortable for him." Producer/writer Don McGuire began skewing the show further and further away from his lead and more towards the supporting cast, eventually eliminating Judson McKay entirely, with Army Archerd reporting in *Daily Variety* on the day of the show's debut that "Josh Peine ... hasn't appeared in the last coupla segs lensed. And looks like his character is written out of future yarns as well." This mid-course adjustment only succeeded in confusing the audience who, viewing the shows in a different order than they were shot, kept seeing the main character appear and disappear.

It's hard to discern what turned McGuire against Peine in the first place. In the words of *Variety*, he played McKay as "a cross between Gary Cooper and Carleton Carpenter," which was certainly the way he was written. In a follow-up review of Episode 7, "School Days," in which Judson McKay is recruited by the colonel to conduct a history class for the base, the trade paper noted that "the segment deteriorated into a maudlin, cornball conclusion with Peine making with the patriotic speechifying as the background music chimed in with the strains of 'America the Beautiful.'" Was getting rid of McKay an attempt by McGuire to deemphasize the cornier aspects of his scripts in favor of more familiar service comedy? It doesn't appear so. A viewing of Episode 18, with Arte Johnson's Lefkowitz now the on-camera assistant to an off-camera Judson McKay, shows McGuire to be perfectly capable of being mawkish without his lead, as a completely out-of-character Colonel Barker helps get an alcoholic colleague back on his feet. *Don't Call Me Charlie* was never able to balance this uneasy mix of smart comedy and pathos in spite of the talents of a fine cast.

Alan as General Steele in *Don't Call Me Charlie* (NBC, 1962). Collection of James Bigwood.

Despite all the intrigue, Alan was having the time of his life performing with actors known primarily for comedy, and relished the unusual opportunity to exercise his own comic chops. "He loved it," recalls Arte Johnson. "It was marvelous for him. It was a great change of pace and he was working with guys that respected him and who treated him well." Linda Lawson, who was Pat Perry, the General's secretary and McKay's love interest (when he was around!), remembers a perpetually happy set. "The tone of the show was set by Don McGuire's sense of humor. In spite of that, however, he ran a very tight ship. When it came time to do the scenes, fun and games were over. But, when we were doing a scene of the General's birthday, Don learned that the 'Happy Birthday' song was not public domain and too expensive to use. So he took us aside and said when Alan came in instead of saying 'Surprise!' or 'Congratulations!' we were to raise our glasses and yell 'Bullshit!' Alan looked startled and paused and then because he was a total pro, tried to go on with the dialogue. It was a very funny moment. As for Alan, he was a true gentleman that I admired and respected. I'm very happy that I had a chance to work with him." Arte Johnson remembers the craziness as well. "Don McGuire was a very fun guy to be around. He was wacky as hell!" McGuire's sense of humor seems to have extended to his relations with the industry press. In *Variety*'s weekly production chart, starting with the series' first listing in May 1962 under its original title, through the end of shooting in November, the cast of *Don't Call Me Charlie* is headed by "Alexander Nuxhall," an actor who not only doesn't appear in the show but is also missing from all industry reference books. The identity of this mystery man was never revealed, although a hint emerges in Episode 12 ("Play It, Sam") when Don McGuire, who originally began his career as an actor, makes his onscreen series debut—in the role of General Nuxhall.

With *Don't Call Me Charlie!* behind him, Alan returned to drama. "Impact of an Execution" was an episode of the ABC one-hour anthology *Alcoa Premiere*, the Fred Astaire–hosted series noted for tackling important themes. *Impact ...* was no exception. A serious examination of capital punishment, it stars Ralph Bellamy as a doctor whose daughter's murderer is due to die at the same time as he is fighting to convince a young boy's mother to approve a life-saving operation for her son. Alan is a retired jurist ("one of the most enlightened and humane of judges") who tries to convince his friend to intercede with the governor to stop the execution. In a single extended scene, Alan exudes a rumpled gravitas as he and Bellamy spar gently over a game of croquet.

The Lloyd Bridges Show had premiered in the fall of 1962 and, after fourteen episodes, had morphed from an innovative series about a writer who each week literally inhabits the character he is writing about, into a more conventional series of self-contained anthology half-hours. Alan was cast in "The Sheridan Square," a punning title referencing Archie Hammond, a decidedly un-hip writer, played by Bridges, whose actress wife has invited all sorts of denizens of Greenwich Village to their home for an impromptu party. Alan is at his most distinguished as Alan Drobney (although listed in the credits as Kurt Drobney), "one of the top literary agents in the world," who agrees to let Archie pitch him a book during the noisy get-together. This leads to one of the most delicious exchanges in Alan's career, as Archie and Drobney pass a beatnik chick (identified as "Mary" in the credits, but not on screen) on their way upstairs.

> MARY (to Archie): Listen honey. This bash is getting a bit noisy. Let's cut to your pad.
> ARCHIE (dismissively): This *is* my pad.
> DROBNEY (handing her his business card): It's not *my* pad.

Alan's timing is impeccable and the twinkle in his eye as he delivers the line (and the card) saves him from coming off as just a lecherous old man. And, it should be noted, he and Mary leave together at the end of the episode.

Kathy Kersh, who played Mary while still in high school, has no memory of shooting the show, even after screening the episode. Her recollections of Alan Napier come from a few years later when, first as Cornelia, a self-absorbed Joker sidekick, and later as Mrs. Burt Ward, she crossed paths with him again on *Batman*. "He was a doll! The sweetest man who ever lived. I really thought seriously about fixing him up with my mother. I didn't know how old he was and I didn't want to insult him, but he was one of those people that, as soon as you meet them, you just want to hug them. Buddy Ebsen was like that too. And there's not a lot of people like that. They're few and far between."

The Alfred Hitchcock Hour, the expanded follow-up to *Alfred Hitchcock Presents*, provided Alan's next role—a reassuringly obtuse bank manager in "An Out for Oscar," in which Larry Storch plays a meek teller who turns the tables on Henry Silva as a thief who thinks that he has secured Storch's cooperation in a robbery at his window in exchange for the murder of his shrewish wife. As was the case with many of the hour-long Hitchcocks, the episode is padded, but Alan is fine in a part that really only exists to move the plot along.

Much more interesting is his role as Captain Protheroe in "Passage on the Lady Anne," his only appearance on the iconic Rod Serling series, *The Twilight Zone*. This remarkable episode features a host of elderly British character actors (Alan was joined by Wilfred Hyde-White, Gladys Cooper and Cecil Kellaway who, though born in South Africa, received his theater training in England) playing passengers on a mysterious ship that, due to a booking error, has taken on board a young couple who are trying to repair their broken marriage. As they settle in, the two begin to realize that, except for them, nobody on board, including the crew, is younger than seventy. Alan has the smallest role among the old-timers (the captain only appears toward the end of the show to put the now-reconciled couple onto a lifeboat so that the *Lady Anne*'s elderly passengers and crew can continue unimpeded on their final voyage to … the Twilight Zone) but the script is so beautifully written and so delicately played that even in a small dose, it is a treat to see him in such august company.

Joyce Van Patten played the young wife, and remembers the episode fondly. "I was pretty new to Hollywood having spent my early days in NYC doing lots of plays. I followed the money to L.A. Lee Philips who was with me on the show had a similar background but was a bit more world weary than I was. We were both so thrilled to find ourselves in the middle of all those fine actors that we had worshipped from afar so many times. Think of it. Not only the marvelous Alan Napier but Miss Cooper, Wilfred Hyde White, and on and on. I was still too shy with famous people at that time to ask all the questions I should have but it stands out as a true high point in my career out there."

Two of the most successful television series in the early sixties were the NBC medical drama *Dr. Kildare* (190 episodes) and its ABC counterpart, *Ben Casey* (153 episodes). Debuting a week apart in the fall of 1961, each show eventually spun off a (less-successful) psychiatrically themed series: *Breaking Point* from *Casey* and *The Eleventh Hour* from *Kildare*. Alan booked appearances on both spin-offs, in coincidentally similar roles. In *The Eleventh Hour*'s "This Wonderful Madman Calls Me Beauty," he is Arnold Todhunter, the passive-aggressive owner of a research lab whose main scientist is risking death by refusing brain surgery in order to finish his life-extending research; and in "So Many Pretty Girls So Little Time" on *Breaking Point*, he is a bombastic magazine publisher whose star writer is allowing his compulsive womanizing to affect his work. In both cases, though his scenes are short and infrequent, he effectively performs subtle variations on the authority figure behind each episode's main guest star.

Between the two medical shows came an episode of *Bob Hope Presents the Chrysler Theater*. Based on the novel by Edward Preston Young, "The Fifth Passenger" concerns a British naval hero suspected by British Intelligence of leaking secrets to the Soviet Union. Alan is Admiral Sherwood, desperately worried that the investigation he has approved will reveal that a man he knows and respects is in fact a traitor.

The Rogues was an NBC show featuring a family of con artists who use their talents to swindle people less honest than themselves. In "Money Is for Burning," Alan plays Sir

John McKellway, the "almost retired" Chief Constable of Oxfordshire, who oversees the investigation of the theft of £3,000,000 in "used notes destined to be taken out of circulation and destroyed by burning." McKellway is so thick that he not only unwittingly shares all the details of his investigation with the mastermind of the robbery (who is collaborating on his memoirs), but winds up being driven around by the man who is suspected of the crime (series star Gig Young) in the very car that the police are seeking. While the role is substantial, it is nonsensical, and Alan unfortunately can't make it plausible. Incidentally, his subordinate—Superintendent Ames—is played by Peter Forster, still Poppet's husband at this point, though only a year away from their divorce.

Alan next made a second appearance on *The Alfred Hitchcock Hour* in "Thou Still Unravished Bride." In a single scene in a London chemists shop, he and Richard Lupino play the working class owner and his grown son, witnesses being questioned by two police detectives who are searching for the American fiancée of one of the officers, who has disappeared on the day of her wedding. Lupino's childish giggles and inappropriate comments are reminiscent of Anthony Perkins in *Psycho* and, combined with Alan's obvious discomfort at his son's eccentricity ("Yes, his funny little ways, you know."), make them a very effective pair of red herrings. The scene is chilling.

"Cain's Birthday" was a two-part episode of the successful NBC series *Daniel Boone*. Alan—appearing in the second of the two hours only—is Sir Hubert Crater, a foppish British militiaman who arrives at Boonesborough with his orderly, played by Booth Colman, ostensibly to help protect the undermanned fort from an Indian attack. The two Englishmen are written so unbelievably that there is little the actors can do to make their scenes remotely plausible—for example, they don't bring the expected amount of gunpowder because Sir Hubert needs the space to accommodate his tea-making paraphernalia. Presumably intended as some sort of comic relief, they just come off looking silly.

For five years in the mid-sixties, CBS partially recouped the costs of many of its unsold pilots by airing them in the summer under the umbrella title of *Vacation Playhouse*. *The Barbara Rush Show*, a failed sit-com, featured its star as a housewife with three kids who works as a public stenographer to put her husband through medical school. In the only episode shot, Alan is a client, a businessman whose attempts to give her dictation are constantly thwarted by domestic interruptions, making it necessary for her to accompany him on a flight to Canada to finish the job.

Alan plays another tea-drinking Englishman in the American West in "The Land Grabbers," a 1965 episode of the NBC series *Laredo*. As Major Donaldson, ex–Bengal Lancers, he competes in a Texas land rush to stake out a prime riverside claim for his widowed daughter-in-law and grandson. Perhaps because *Laredo* took itself less seriously than did *Daniel Boone*, the "fish out of water" aspects of Alan's character don't seem so obtrusive and, although still improbable, his role is much more heroic and written with considerably more respect than was his turn in "Cain's Birthday."

Continuing his association with the Old West in "Perilous Journey," a second *Daniel Boone* appearance which aired the same week as "The Land Grabbers," Alan plays the evil British Lord Brisbane, who attempts to use Boone's wife as a hostage in order to force him to give up a secret dispatch which, when delivered to Napoleon, will authorize the Louisiana Purchase. Needless to say, the combination of Boone and his feisty wife thwarts the plot. Facing off eye to eye with the 6'5½" Fess Parker was a new experience for Alan, as was his participation in the episode's climactic fistfight, in which he takes a punch in the jaw before his henchmen swarm in to overpower Boone. At nearly sixty-three, although in fine shape, this was certainly not something he was prepared to undergo on a regular basis, and fortunately he was not going to have to. After more than forty years as an actor, Alan's professional life was about to take a major turn.

47

Patriarch

In a healthy body a broken limb will heal; so will a broken heart in a healthy spirit. Gip had made me whole and it would have been a sorry tribute to her if I had not recovered. In the light and warmth of her love I had at last grown up and become a complete human being—not just an actor faking his way through life. I have not married again. Such a total commitment to another human being is hard to repeat; anything less a betrayal of standards. But I hope that I am still growing.

Bob and Jenny had taken themselves and their family to England a couple of years before Gip died. Bob's career as an actor had not fulfilled his ambitions in Hollywood and, since he had trained at the R.A.D.A. and had a passion for the English classics, he thought he would see if he could make a go of things in London. It had seemed a crazy gamble to Gip and me, but it eventually paid off. He is a very American-looking type and has a strong singing voice, invaluable for American musicals in England. He played good roles in *Bye Bye Birdie* and *How to Succeed in Business Without Really Trying*, each of which ran over a year. He was also in demand to play Americans in English movies.

They had left their dear old shaggy dog, Bruin, in our keeping when they left (Kento had gone the way of all flesh) and it was Bruin, rather than the tiny Miranda Gip and I had lavished our affection on, who was my great comforter when moments of unbearable desolation overcame me. He would jump onto the bed and push his great face, the brown eyes brimming with tenderness and compassion, up towards mine.

Television was keeping me pretty busy and my life was not intolerable but neither was it satisfactory. So, finding that Jenny and Bob were ready to return to California, I threw out the idea that they should come to live with me at Porto Marina Way. We discussed it by letter and agreed that it made sense. It would necessitate building on a unit for myself—bed, sitting-room and bath—a difficult proposition on my cliff side. Bob had a brilliant idea how this could be done and, designing every inch of the limited space to suit my habits and physique (the wash basin is a foot higher than standard practice), I got an architect to come up with a plan acceptable to the Department of Building and Safety. Ingeniously, it hardly cuts into my garden and looks as if it had always been part of the house.

Indeed, there is much to be said for three generations living together, if the house belongs to the patriarch, for he will then never be forced to feel dependent or superfluous. Actors' incomes, as I have indicated, come by fits and starts, and it seemed to Bob and me that a household with two potential earners could be more easily maintained. In fact the last ten years have been increasingly hard for run-of-the-mill actors unless one happens to get a job in a successful television series.

48

Batman

A few months after my family returned from England my agent rang me up one day and said:

"Alan, I think you're going to be Batman's butler."

"What are you talking about? And who is Batman?"

"Don't you read the comics?"

"Never."

"Oh. Well, you're going to be Batman's butler all the same. You even get to drive the Batmobile."

"This is crazy," I said, "How do I know I want to ... I mean, is it a good part?"

"It's in every episode. You'll get top feature billing after Batman and Robin. If it's a success it could be worth over a hundred thousand dollars."

I did not argue any more. *Batman* was a success; indeed for the first few months it was the success of the season. No one went out to dinner on *Batman* nights. Alfred, the butler, was unlike any butler I had ever known. So I had to invent him from scratch. The essence of a good servant, it seemed to me, is that he is proud to serve and that his happiness comes from cheerfully giving satisfaction to his master's family. This was my guiding light through all Alfred's unbutlerlike activities at Wayne Manor. Apparently it paid off, for children all over the world developed an affection for kindly Alfred, always ready with a tray of milk and cookies and a cheerful word. From the point of view of popular recognition I have to regard Alfred as the climax of my career. From the beaches of California to the streets of New York and London, yes, even on the Acropolis in Athens, children would suddenly look at me at first with wonder then with affection and say, "Alfred! It's Alfred!"

Of course, I loved this recognition. And the money saved our bacon at Porto Marina Way, and relieves me of financial anxiety for the rest of my life. But playing Batman's butler was hardly the kind of glory I had dreamed of at the start of my career. Just before *Batman* began, I did a "guest star" spot on the series *Daktari* [*in an episode entitled "The Killer Lion"*], during which I wrote to my agent:

"I really cannot do any more of these outdoor epics unless I get more money. Two weeks ago a horse stamped on my foot in *Laredo* and this morning, at six o'clock, I drove a truck down a mountainside with a lioness sitting beside me. Tomorrow we are to lie together in a joyful reunion. Little did I think, my dear Bobbie, when I went to the R.A.D.A. forty-five years ago, that I would end up making love to a lioness in Soledad Canyon, California."

49

Alfred the Butler

JAMES BIGWOOD

But the incongruities of lion wrestling were nothing compared to the myriad duties of Alfred the butler.

Alan was actually the very first member of the *Batman* cast to be hired. In a 1966 episode of the Canadian Broadcasting Corporation series *Telescope*, producer William Dozier described his process. "As you know, when you're working on something, you begin to visualize these characters coming to life, and it was not difficult because, having been in this business as long as I have and seen as many actors—and worked with as many—but seen the ones I haven't worked with, there's certain kinds of standard prototypes that stand out in your memory... Alan Napier, to me, has always been the absolute essence of the perfect English manservant or butler." But, as Alan correctly points out, "I never actually played a butler until *Batman* came along (and he wasn't much of a butler; he was a *factotum*) and I found that this one had no relationship to the real thing. The only prop they gave me that they thought was butlerish was a feather duster. I said 'No, that's a housemaid.' They said, 'Well, you can use it to dust the Bat machinery.'" In fact, as he later related to Joel Eisner, author of *The*

"And in Wayne Manor, stately home of millionaire Bruce Wayne and his youthful ward, Dick Grayson, Alfred the faithful butler responds to the hotline." Collection of James Bigwood.

Official Batman Batbook, it was not Dozier at all who first thought of him as Alfred, but Dozier's assistant Charles Fitzsimons who, earlier in his career, had been associated with Alan's agent. "He, for some reason, envisioned me as Alfred because, after all, what I did as Alfred was quite different from what was written. He sold the idea to Dozier, and I was hired."

As apparently the only servant in all of stately Wayne Manor, Alfred is responsible for everything. He dusts, he cooks, he chauffeurs, he escorts Aunt Harriet to concerts. But most importantly, he supports Batman and Robin as they take on the various dastardly criminals that periodically prey on Gotham City.

In the early episodes of the series, he is primarily a receptionist, or, in the words of William Dozier in his persona as narrator Desmond Doomsday, "And in Wayne Manor, stately home of millionaire Bruce Wayne and his youthful ward, Dick Grayson, Alfred the faithful butler responds to the hotline." At this point, it seems that his hardest task is to figure out new and different ways to ask Commissioner Gordon to hold the line.

Alfred tinkers in the Batcave. Collection of James Bigwood.

"I'll beckon him, sir, immediately."

"I'll solicit his presence, sir."

"I shall secure him without further delay, sir."

"One moment Commissioner. I shall expedite his presence."

But it isn't long before Alfred becomes a more active part of the team. When Batman is pitted against the Archer, for example, he is quick to rely on his butler's unique skills:

> BATMAN: Alfred, in your youth you were familiar with the long, the short, and the cross bow, were you not?
> ALFRED: Yes indeed, sir. I was known as the William Tell of Liverpool.
> BATMAN: You've always been prepared to join us in our crime fighting, have you not?
> ALFRED: To serve you in any capacity, sir, has always been my duty and my pleasure.

Lorenzo Semple, Jr., the script consultant for the series and writer of sixteen of its 120 episodes (as well as the feature film released between seasons one and two), has a very simple explanation for Alan's increased visibility. "He was perfect from the beginning. I don't really recall that there was ever 'let's make Alan Napier more important.' It just happened. He was such a good character. There were never any notes from the network or anybody. Bill Dozier and I just did it. He just sort of evolved because he was a good actor and a great character."

Alfred takes on a number of undercover assignments over the course of three seasons, occasionally in disguise, but often not. Posing as an insurance photographer from "Floyds

Alan as Alfred, disguised as Batman, with Adam West and Burt Ward. Collection of James Bigwood.

of Dublin," he plants a bug in Penguin's umbrella; claiming to be a genealogist, he hides a homing device in a hat targeted by the Mad Hatter; he acts as Batman's trainer for his boxing match with the Riddler ("I trust no one will penetrate my disguise, sir, but I think perhaps you'd better call me 'Gus'"); he takes the place of his lookalike cockney cousin Egbert (night watchman at the Gotham Waterworks) to prevent the Joker from salting the city's water supply with time control pills (allowing Alan to demonstrate his versatility as, with the help of visual effects, the two cousins—one with glasses and the other without—converse with each other). But Alfred's most convincing disguise, and one that he assumes three times over the course of the series, is that of Batman himself—on the occasions when Bruce Wayne and the Caped Crusader need to be at the same place at the same time or, in one case, when Batman needs to be sprung from prison. Adam West, in his memoir *Back to the Batcave*, claims that Alan hated wearing the Batsuit, recalling that "he felt self-conscious and a bit ridiculous." This hardly seems likely, especially as West only remembers the bit occurring once, not three times, after which—he claims—Alan refused to ever do it again. Alan was 63 it's true, but he was still a beach volleyball player who was extremely proud of his physique. Far from being embarrassing, it must have been incredibly flattering to be considered a viable double for a leading man twenty-five years his junior, especially one encased in a skintight suit. Indeed, it can be credibly argued that Alan was better qualified to wear the suit than his slightly paunchy co-star. However much he may have dissembled at the time, he must have been secretly chuffed. While West notes that "[t]hough I ached for Alan and offered to intercede on his behalf, he wouldn't let me," he attributes this to some sort of *noblesse oblige* on Alan's part, rather than accepting it at face value. His assertions are further undermined by the fact that Alan unsuccessfully pitched another costume-related gag to the show's writers. As he recalled to Joel Eisner, "I had an idea, which they wouldn't do, but I think it would have been very funny: that I am cleaning Robin's Bat-Pole and slip, and I come down wearing Robin's costume, which is too small for me."

In the third season, the show's cast was expanded to include the character of Batgirl, who Alfred quickly discovers is the alter ego of Commissioner Gordon's daughter Barbara. The new arrival coincided with the reduction of the show's airings from two episodes a week to one, paradoxically reducing the screen time of the individual characters while at the same time increasing Alfred's importance, as he juggled his knowledge of the identities of all three disguised crimefighters while acting as their unofficial liaison. This resulted in one of Alfred's most bizarre disguises in the entire series. With Batgirl about to be sliced up by Catwoman's steel pattern cutter, Batman is at a loss as to how to rescue her without risking war with Belgravia by missing his scheduled audience with the visiting Queen Bess. He suddenly has a brainstorm and reaches Alfred using Commissioner Gordon's Batphone.

> BATMAN: This is one of your sticky wickets, Alfred.
> ALFRED: Indeed, sir.
> BATMAN: If she recognizes you as Bruce Wayne's butler, she's liable to analyze the connection and learn Robin's and my secret true identities. But we have to take the chance, otherwise Batgirl dies.
> ALFRED: What do you suggest, sir?
> BATMAN: A disguise. Something as alien as possible to your normal self. But speed is of the essence.

Alfred—bearded, sandaled, wearing a poncho and headband and waddling to hide his height—arrives just in time to disable the cutter and un-strap Batgirl from the table.

> BATGIRL: Thank you, whoever you are.
> ALFRED: Think nothin' of it, sweetheart. As a matter o' fact, it was selfish of me.
> BATGIRL: Selfish?
> ALFRED: Yes. I'm the janitor 'ere. If that machine 'ad sliced you to bits, I'd a 'ad to clean up the mess.
> BATGIRL: You look very familiar to me.
> ALFRED: Me? Oh no. No, I'm the oldest living hippie in this country. 'Course, you may have heard about my being the first Boy Scout dropout at the turn of the century. (Handing her a flower) Love. See ya 'round.

Alfred in disguise as "the oldest living hippie in this country." Courtesy Jennifer Nichols.

Alan's suggestion that the writers add a line about his having burned his library card in his Boy Scout days was rejected because it was felt that it might give ideas to impressionable young fans.

Having begun the series making $500 an episode, the second highest salary of the regular cast (second-billed Burt Ward was only making $350), by season three Alan had been outstripped by Neil Hamilton and Stafford Repp ($750 each to Alan's $650) and the newly arrived Yvonne Craig. Still, it was a nice steady income and the show gave him the opportunity to catch up with old friends like his RADA classmate Reginald Gardiner and his West End and Broadway co-star Glynis Johns, with the lack of artistic satisfaction more than compensated for by his sudden celebrity. Alan's granddaughter Christie, thirteen at the time, has fond memories of the *Batman* years:

> The four of us moved in in the late summer of 1964 or 1965. I'm not sure what years—I know we were in England for five years because of school. I skipped a grade when we got back to California and the years get confusing. Alan had just been in "Marnie" and had a new little dog he'd named Tippi, after Tippi Hendren. He got the part of Alfred in "Batman" shortly after. No big deal for me and my brother—we were going to school in Pacific Palisades and Brentwood with the sons and daughters of many very well-known actors, directors, producers and so forth. Alan would zoom off to work in his yellow Barracuda, leaving a wake of honking cars and proudly telling stories of how policemen were so charmed by him being late to the studio for Batman that he never got a ticket. He was always friendly and kind when people recognized him as Alfred. He'd chat and tell stories about his version of Alfred's earlier life. One of the stories was that Alfred was a nobleman with a chequered past who, like Batman, needed to hide his identity.

Alan's final theatrical film was the feature version of *Batman* (1966), shot between the first two seasons of the series. In it, Alfred adds gardening to his list of Wayne Manor duties. With four guest villains taking up screen time, he doesn't have much else to do, although, since Robin doesn't get his driver's license until season three, Alfred *does* get to drive the Batmobile—wearing what appears to be one of the Boy Wonder's spare masks under his glasses to hide his identity. Together he and Robin shadow Batman/Bruce Wayne as he wines and dines visiting Russian journalist Miss Kitka in a misguided attempt to protect her from the threat of foul play from the combined forces of Riddler, Joker, Penguin and Catwoman—misguided because Miss Kitka is, of course, Catwoman in disguise.

In the summer of 1967, while William Dozier was retooling for Season Three, Alan booked a guest shot on *The Beverly Hillbillies* as a London pharmacist who mistakes Granny Clampett's request for a collection of obscure mountain medicines for a reference to Shakespeare, which he is all too happy to quote. (Alan: "Ah, you're one of *those* doctors. Well, now, let me see if I can remember the formula from *Macbeth*. 'Eye of newt and toe of frog. Wool of bat and tongue of dog. Adder's fork…'" Granny: "Now *there's* a druggist!") Confusion mounts as he offers more and more recitations from the Bard, first numbering all of Granny's graces and then comparing her to a summer's day. Next, he begs her to "touch but my lips with those fair lips of thine," and by the time Jed Clampett has loaded his lovestruck mother-in-law over his shoulder and hauled her out of the shop, the pharmacist is well into the balcony scene from *Romeo and Juliet*.

The *Batman* phenomenon ended as abruptly as it had started, but its 120 episodes have been rerun constantly in the ensuing years, guaranteeing the entire cast a place in television history. When it became clear that the series had been well and truly cancelled (there was a brief moment when NBC considered taking it over from ABC), Alan sent a letter to his producer, starting off with one of his favorite theater stories:

Dear Bill,

When I was a young actor in England, there was a column in the classified section of The Daily Telegraph called "theatrical cards," in which actors advertised their availability.

I only used it once. I had done a season of Rep, in the course of which I had played a boy of 19, and Old Blayds, aged 90 in "The Truth About Blayds" by A.A. Milne. So my card read "Alan Napier. At liberty. Anything from 19 to 90." Pretty well covered the field … how could they overlook me? Oddly enough, I did get another rep job pretty soon.

The column was also used by successful actors who wanted to show off. As … "Gerald de Courville. Just completed 42 wonderful weeks with Martin Harvey. What a prince! Thanks again, Sir John. Opening Boxing Day, Panto at Scunthorpe."

If we had such a column in the L.A. Times I would like to submit…

Alan "Alfred" Napier. Just completed over two years with "Batman." Thanks again, Bill Dozier. What a pro! At liberty.

I know you'll understand that "What a pro!" is the highest compliment an actor can pay a producer nowadays, when so many have no idea who can do what, or what makes a production tick.

My gratitude to you for casting me as "Alfred" is deep and lasting.

Cordially,
Alan

50

After Batman

The day after the *Batman* series ended, I had my sixty-fifth birthday and became eligible for various old age pensions—U.S. Social Security and the Screen Actors' Guild being the main sources. This was just as well, for *Batman* seems to have been the kiss of death to my career. Apart from a few commercials I have only worked four days in front of a camera in the past four years. In theater I had the great pleasure of working with Celeste Holm, America's most brilliant light comedienne, in a Chicago run of her play *Affairs of State*. I say her play since it was written for her and, contrary to expectations of the experts in New York, she made it a resounding success. I have also enjoyed a recurrent job playing the narrator and Mr. Jenkins in a brilliant little production of *Under Milk Wood* at a local theater-restaurant. All my childhood knowledge and feeling for Wales went into this and it was a work of love.

I look back and a hundred plays and films come to mind with more interest for me than for the casual reader. However, Orson Welles' film of *Macbeth* will, I hope, justify more than a passing reference. It will also enable me to tie up a loose end. Writing of my first meeting with Orson in New York I likened him to a beautiful young bull and observed, somewhat portentously, that the day would come when he would shake his horns at me.

When Orson determined to make a film of *Macbeth* he invented a new character for the play—to the hidebound, a staggering piece of effrontery. But then, few of the hidebound had Orson's profound knowledge of the play or his empathy with Shakespeare as a practical man of the theater. The new character was called "The Holy Friar." Orson did not take it upon himself to write the Friar's lines. He selected, with extraordinary skill, lines from Ross, Lennox and many other characters. The function of the Friar was to symbolize, in this pervasively superstitious era, the forces of good in the person of an early Celtic Christian to counterpoise the

As the Holy Friar in Orson Welles' *Macbeth* **(Republic, 1948). Collection of James Bigwood.**

314

forces of evil symbolized in The Witches. The Friar, present at the time of Duncan's murder and in no doubt as to the identity of the murderer, carries the news of Lady Macduff's murder to England and finally leads the forces of good (Malcolm and Macduff) in their march to overthrow the tyrant. Orson wanted a commanding figure for this warrior priest and asked me to play the part.

At this time Orson's honeymoon with Hollywood was over. It had been a very expensive honeymoon and its offspring were not making money. The major studios would have nothing to do with his *Macbeth*. And then Republic Studio, hitherto almost exclusively concerned with westerns, capitulated to Orson's powers of persuasion and agreed to let him make the film on condition that he would bring it in in twenty-one shooting days. To save time, Orson decided to pre-record the entire script before shooting began, so that he would never have to wait on favorable conditions for sound—we would mouth our lines to the pre-recording if necessary, just as songs are sung in musicals to pre-recordings. Since the Scottish accents he demanded of the cast were in most cases as incomprehensible as they were unauthentic, most of the film had to be dubbed (post-synced) after it was completed, so that those weeks of pre-recording would have been a total waste were it not for the fact that they gave the actors a chance to rehearse and Orson a chance to permeate the cast with his feelings about the play. I remember those evenings with delight. We were called

With Orson Welles on the set of *Macbeth* (Republic, 1948). Collection of James Bigwood.

at six o'clock but nothing serious was done till after an extended and pleasantly alcoholic dinner at which Orson would regale us with tales of his famous days with the WPA, the Mercury Theater and the Campbell Soup Hour. Then we would return to the studio and, mellowed and uninhibited, record Shakespeare until midnight. The soundmen's overtime must have been prodigious. I was a little unhappy because Orson kept urging me to use a lighter, higher pitched tone than I would myself have chosen; but it was all great fun. (When the picture was finally shown, Gip said to me, "Of course he didn't want you to use your real voice—it would have competed with his!" She was brought up in theater by Martin Harvey and aware of the tricks of leading men.) The horn-shaking episode came when the Holy Friar has led his troops, a forest of Celtic crosses in their hands, to the very walls of Macbeth's castle. Macbeth, from a towering battlement hurls down his spear and pierces the Holy Man's breast. Now, there are ways and ways of doing this kind of shot, and perfect verisimilitude can be achieved with no conceivable danger to anyone. Orson, however, wanted the scene life-like. That is to say he, or to be exact his double, was to hurl the spear so that it would strike the ground just in front of me but look to the camera as if it had hit me. At which I said:

"Wait a minute! Are you asking me to stand there and have a spear thrown at me?"

"It's only balsa wood, man! And my double is an expert."

"Even so..."

"You're afraid, are you? And he shook his horns at me; for, dressed as Macbeth in armor, his Viking helmet sprouted horns on each side.

"Certainly I'm afraid until I see exactly what happens when he throws the bloody spear."

So, with a great show of contempt for my pusillanimity, Orson told the stunt man to throw the spear exactly two feet in front of the camera. He threw it. It hit and broke the camera, sending the camera crew flying in all directions.

When writing of *Coriolanus* I said that my subsequent encounters with Jack Houseman as director were more felicitous. While he was artistic director of the Theater Group, a professional company associated with the University of California at Los Angeles, I played for him in *Murder in the Cathedral*, as the doctor, Chebutykin, in *The Three Sisters* (one of the few really successful productions of Chekhov in the American Theater) and as Escalus in *Measure for Measure*. Now, old Escalus is not, on the face of it, much of a part and I was in some doubt as to whether to accept Jack's offer. So I read the play very carefully and concluded that I could play the part better perhaps than it had ever been played before—an example of the kind of arrogance that keeps actors going. It happened that at one performance of the play a man in the television world, then riding high as author, director and producer, was looking for an actor to play a major role, that of an American Lieutenant-General in his upcoming series. He wanted his General to be a man of quiet authority rather than a Patton blood-and-guts type. When he saw me playing Escalus in *Measure for Measure* he said to himself, "There's my General." One never knows when virtue in the theater will be rewarded.

In fact the series, *Don't Call Me Charlie*, failed to win renewal, but the twenty-six episodes we did make saw me comfortably through a long dry summer. It must have been the autumn after *Don't Call Me Charlie* that I appeared in *Marnie* for Alfred Hitchcock and acquired Tippi. The two events go together because I christened my new puppy after the star of the picture, Tippi Hedren, who told me that, in Swedish, "tippi" was used as an affectionate diminutive, as one might say dear little one. Miranda, the last Chihuahua Gip and I had cherished, died a few days before the assassination of President Kennedy. It was a heart-rending week; I loved them both. Some people were shocked that I could say such a thing; but it was true. I loved Miranda as a man loves his dog and I loved John Kennedy as a man comes to love a public figure whose quality seems to him to be outstanding. I was living alone at the time and I was desolated.

Suddenly I remembered that in a scene in *Don't Call Me Charlie* I had held a funny little dog in my hand and said to the dog handler responsible for the animals in the series "What on earth is this?" "Well," he answered, "it's half Chihuahua and half Poodle and it's one of the cleverest little dogs I have." So, in my grief and loneliness, I called him up and asked him where I could find such a dog.

"Well," he said, "it's not a breed, you understand—but there are a couple of old ladies in the Valley (the San Fernando Valley section of Los Angeles) who have a lot of Poodles and a lot of Chihuahuas and they're not very careful. Why don't you go out there and see what you can find."

I found the old ladies living in a quiet dead-end street. At first I was shown a lot of rather unattractive dogs. There was a little girl with dark, somber eyes watching me with disapproval as I turned down one puppy after another. No, I said, I really wanted something smaller and well, more attractive. The old lady turned to the little girl:

"You'd better go across to your Aunt Emmy and get Squeaky, love."

"Aw, Mom!" And she glowered at me.

"Go on. Do as I say."

In a few minutes the little girl returned with an immense old lady who held something small and white to her bosom. As she put it on the floor I went down on my knees. With shrill squeaks of delight this tiny ball of white fluff dashed across the floor, climbed up me and started licking my face with what I later came to describe as the fastest tongue in the west.

"I'll take this," I said. "How much do you want?"

She was six weeks old and perhaps nine inches long and looked exactly like a toy dog designed by the most slavishly sentimental dog-lover. But I very soon found that she herself, Squeaky—renamed Tippi—was not sentimental in the least. She was amazingly self-possessed and confident, with a strong will of her own and no fear of man or beast. She also originated the slogan "Make Love Not War" long before the hippies thought of it. I have never been able to make her come when I call unless she wants to—a humiliating failure. But then how can one chastise something nine inches long with a fluffy white coat over a black undercoat, soft black ears set off with a touch of fawn, a little cheeky black button nose, the brightest black eyes and a perky white plume of tail rising from a circle of black? One can't. So one lavishes affection on her instead and she thinks, "Very nice man. I shall come to him when it suits me."

Her greatest joy is a visit to the beach where there are dozens of groups of people to say hello to and conquer with her charm, some of whom will, with a little bit of luck, be eating sandwiches. I would take her with me when I played volleyball. At first, saying hello to my fellow players would keep her near me; then, as I started to play, she would trot off in search of fresh conquests. When it was time to go she would be nowhere to be seen and the search would begin.

"Excuse me, have you seen a little white dog anywhere?"

"Oh, yes. She was hungry, the poor little thing. We gave her a bit of chicken. She was cute. She went that way."

And so proceeding from group to group I would eventually track her down. Her taste was impeccable; she would usually finish up with the prettiest girl on the beach.

"I do hope my little dog hasn't been bothering you."

"Oh no, she's just darling! What kind of dog is she?"

"She's the one and only Poohuahua."

"She's just adorable."

With regret at parting on all sides I would pick Tippi up and carry her away, for she would not willingly follow me. As time went on she began to get wise. When she saw me approaching she would take off in the opposite direction.

"Tippi! Come here! Time to go home."

"I didn't hear you."

As I increase my pace she would increase hers.

"Tippi! Come!"

"Not bloody likely."

And she would really start running.

One day my humiliation was complete. She led me a good half mile towards Santa Monica, a tiny white dog fleeing from her master. I suppose I could have outrun her but there is something ludicrously humiliating about having to run down one's own dog, particularly if one happens to be a tremendously tall, white-haired old man in swimming shorts.

I retrieve her by cunning. Cupping my hands to my mouth I call to a couple on a blanket some 40 yards ahead of me:

"When my little dog comes to your blanket" (I knew she'd have to stop to say hello) "will you hold onto her, please?" I pick her up and try desperately to be furious. "Bad dog," I say, looking her in the eye. She licks my nose. I have to laugh. With great difficulty I have at last taught her to stop dead in her

Alan, almost unrecognizable without glasses and mustache, holding Tippi during a publicity shoot for *Marnie* (Universal, 1964). Collection of James Bigwood.

tracks when I shout, "Stay!" It's the best I can do. With the years she has grown a bit. Eighteen inches now and we have to watch her weight. But just as endearing—just as sure that if you are pretty and approach people with love you will be loved in return. Never jealous of new arrivals—puppies, kittens, children, she loves them all—she is a small compendium of the Christian virtues. Until she is given a bone. Then suddenly a wild beast, a dangerous jungle creature springs to life. Sharp little teeth bared, eyes blazing as she snarls and yaps, she defends her prize with terrible ferocity. None of my family would dare to take a bone from Tippi. "Nonsense," I once said and stretched out my hand. She sunk her teeth into my knuckle. I laughed till the tears ran down my face. How could she have the nerve to do it? We have a very close relationship and, except on the beach, we are inseparable.

During the making of the *Batman* series she became the darling of the entire crew. One day an old fellow came up to me and said, "You'd better be careful of that little Tippi. What would you do if anything happened to her?" It turned out that he thought I lived alone and that if Tippi went I would go too. "I've seen it happen before with an old man and his dog." Now, it's true that when Tippi came into my life I did think "I guess she'll see me out." In fact, it would be best if she goes first. I know from experience that a new puppy will fill the place in a man's heart; Tippi would never find a new master to put up with her as I do.

My family tells me that my picture of Tippi is incomplete, that I have failed to mention her positively ear-splitting bark. It is true that she uses it constantly to greet friends and to give warning of strangers. It is music to my ears (less sensitive than my daughter's) and it amuses me to see her put her whole little body, from nose to tail tip, into a really heartfelt protest. Indeed, she is an excellent watchdog, her shrill yap triggering the deep baying of David's big dog, Jason.

It is fitting perhaps that I should end my story with Tippi, a figure of comic enchantment, totally liberated, and barking for sheer *joie de vivre*.

51

The Vortex

JAMES BIGWOOD

Alan finished his autobiography in the early seventies, a time of change at Porto Marina Way. Bob Nichols had been cast as Frank Kennedy in a new musical adaptation of *Gone with the Wind* which, after a run at the Dorothy Chandler Pavilion in Los Angeles, was scheduled to go on a nationwide tour before opening in New York. The show never made it to Broadway, but Bob and Jennifer decided to remain on the East Coast, where both Bob's acting career and Jennifer's career as a movie costumer flourished. Their daughter Christie was by now at UC Santa Cruz, leaving their son David the only member of the family still living with Alan. "Bob got *Gone with the Wind*," Jennifer recalls, "and we were going to be away for a year so we left my father thinking he was taking care of David, who had just started at UCLA, and David thinking he was taking care of Alan. And I left a whole freezerful of food—Alan was a very good cook—to have enough there for both of them, only unfortunately at some point Alan unplugged it to plug something else in and never put it back so the freezerful of food rotted."

As David describes it, Porto Marina Way soon became "a home for itinerant volleyball players."

"I graduated from high school in '72 and in the fall of '72, went to UCLA and my first year there I still lived with Alan—a bit of a commute to UCLA, but not bad. He had this beautiful home, and he loved young people, he loved my friends, so we constantly had dinners over there, constantly had friends over. It wasn't like we would throw *big* parties, but there were constantly five or six people and he very much enjoyed being a part of that. He loved sit-down dinners with conversation. I stayed with him through '73-'74 and then it was always friends of mine living over there.

"It started because all these guys were volleyball players with me at UCLA. They were close friends of mine and volleyball was a theme, only these guys were pretty esoteric and pretty bright. There was a lot more to them than just playing a game. Alan no longer really played at that time, so it was more that he had this beautiful place right on the beach."

The core group, which came to be known as "The Vortex," consisted of David, Sean Myhill, Dane Selznick (who would go on to become a three-time U.S. Olympic Beach Volleyball coach), and Denny Cline, who remembers the first time he met David's grandfather.

"When I was probably twenty, I was playing volleyball at UCLA. We were going from UCLA up to Santa Barbara to play UC-Santa Barbara in a tournament and the way to get

The Vortex: Alan, his grandson David Nichols, Sean Myhill and Denny Cline in the late 1970s. Courtesy Christie Nichols.

there back then was to use 'Uni-Cars.' These were university cars which would be checked out to the team and I was always the guy who would drive, because I was always the guy who was sober. So David (by the way, I call him 'Cisco,' so if I lapse into 'Cisco,' that's who I mean), so Cisco says, 'Hey, can you come by and pick me up at my grandfather's house on the way? We'll go up the coast.' I said 'Perfect. Fine. No problem.' I didn't know where Dave had grown up or anything so I'm following directions, I'm down on the Coast Highway, I'm headed out towards Malibu, come to Porto Marina Way … what the hell? … winding little street up the cliff above the ocean. I pull up before this sort of ramshackle old place that looks out over the Pacific, just this vast view of Santa Monica Bay and Catalina. Wow, this is where Dave grew up? Nice deal! I walk up—I have no idea who his grandfather is—and I knock on the door. Door opens and there's Alfred the Butler, 6'4", white shock of hair, dressed in shorts. He goes, 'Good evening. May I help you?' And I just about fell over. I started laughing. 'Hi. I'm Denny. I'm here to pick up Cisco.' So I come in and we're waiting for Dave to get ready to go and Alan and I sat in his front room for about half an hour or something like that and we started talking Shakespeare. I was the only guy from the volleyball world who was able to talk Shakespeare with Alan, so he always liked me.

"At some point, there were something like four of us living there and one of the things that he used to do for us, was to give readings. Once every couple of months—maybe not even that often—he would prepare a Shakespeare play or a George Bernard Shaw play, or whatever he thought was interesting (he would usually go through and abridge them somewhat) and then play all the parts. He'd just give a reading of the play. We'd do that on a Sunday afternoon and, I gotta tell you, it was brilliant. The guy was unbelievable. Especially with Shakespeare. It was the first time I ever heard Shakespeare actually make sense. He knew all the parts intimately, though he loved some parts more than others because he'd played them, I suppose, and he could make Shakespeare come alive. It was incredible. But not just Shakespeare. One time he read *Under Milk Wood* by Dylan Thomas. That was one of the great days of my life."

Alan made up for no longer being able to play volleyball by giving the Vortex cricket lessons. "I remember one day he took us down and tried to show us how to play cricket on the beach. That was pretty fun," Denny recalls with a hint of sarcasm. "Dave had seen a cricket bat because he'd grown up some in England, but us Americans were like 'What the hell is this game?' and no Englishman can ever explain the game to you anyway. We used to tease Alan that it had no rules." Christie Nichols recalls the lessons well. "I remember visiting when they had a mad cricket game on the beach with Alan teaching the rules and batting with a real cricket bat and the ball going in the ocean and all four boys screaming and crashing into the water to get it."

52

Back to Work

James Bigwood

In January 1969, almost exactly a year after the cancellation of *Batman*, Alan reappeared on the air in "Oh, to Be in England," an episode of the gentle CBS sitcom *Family Affair*. He provided an air of tweedy realism to scenes supposedly set in London in his role as the head of an English-French syndicate trying to organize the building of a tunnel under the English Channel. Unfortunately, it was another year before he would be seen again.

Having somehow managed to miss being cast in *Perry Mason*, one of the best remembered television dramas of the late fifties and early sixties, and seen only once on the equally iconic *Twilight Zone*, Alan made up for it with multiple appearances in their lesser seventies incarnations, *Ironside* and *Night Gallery*. In fact, his next five jobs were on one or the other of these two shows.

Things started well enough with his first *Ironside* appearance in 1970. "Return to Fiji" featured Alan as Walter Branford, a war buddy of Raymond Burr's Chief Ironside. Both of them are kidnapped to force Walter's niece to help in the theft of two million dollars worth of gold. It's a good part, with all of Alan's scenes shared—by phone or in person—with the star of the show, and he does a fine job. Despite a mediocre script, the role gives hope that the ghost of Alfred is behind him and his career is back on track.

Unfortunately, "House with Ghost," his first *Night Gallery*, almost two years later, doesn't live up to the promise. In it he has just one scene, as a doctor confirming that his patient hasn't long to live. He does a perfectly fine job, but the part exists for exposition and nothing more. Twelve episodes of the series later, he has even less to do in "The Sins of the Father." Credited as "The Man," one of a roomful of mourners waiting for the arrival of a "sin-eater," he is fully bearded, barely visible, and has just one line: "There's Dylan Evans. Lives in that hut on the north side of Plynlimon."

In "Fright Night," his final *Night Gallery*, he has a much more important part, though paradoxically no more screen time. He is the dead Zachariah Ogilvy, terrorizing the couple who have inherited his house. The haunting is all done by proxy, however—primarily by a possessed steamer trunk—while Zachariah's presence is felt throughout the show by multiple cutaways to an oil portrait of him on the living room wall. His disintegrating body finally makes an appearance at the very end of the episode at which point Alan delivers his only line ("The trunk. I've come for the trunk!"). The painting actually has more screen time than he does.

Back on *Ironside* for "All About Andrea," Alan has two very pleasant scenes with guest

Alan subjected to "the full rubber mask facial treatment." With Stuart Whitman and Barbara Anderson in the "Fright Night" episode of *Night Gallery* (NBC, 1972). Photofest.

star Myrna Loy but is curiously unbilled in the episode's credits, despite the fact that his character's son turns out to be the criminal that Ironside is seeking. Loy plays a wacky feminist author (the script's heart is in the right place, but is painfully corny) and Alan is Marcus Lowell, her publisher—although his main scene with his client concerns, not publishing, but Andrea's attempt to get him to try out her latest gadget: a bio-feedback machine.

    ANDREA: You will have to stop conceptualizing entirely.
    MARCUS: Stop thinking? I'll turn into a brussel sprout!

For five years after *Batman*, Alan managed to avoid playing another butler, but in *Crime Club*, an unsuccessful 90-minute CBS pilot, he was back in livery, with precious little to do but open the door to Lloyd Bridges and then hover discretely in the background. "People seem to think that I'm typed as a butler," he commented a few years later. "But I find them rather boring and empty roles and, in fact, I really can't think of anything interesting to say about butlers except that they can bring in a little revenue."

It was another year before he appeared again, this time in *QB VII*, the ground-breaking award-winning ABC mini-series based on Leon Uris' best-selling novel. One can only hope that his role was originally larger, for his character, identified by name in the credits ("Semple" rather than the more appropriate "Man at Party") has absolutely nothing to do. Ben Gazzara, having just been introduced to "Margaret Alexander," attempts to recall where he has heard the name "Alexander" before. After "humorously" topping the suggestions "Alexander the Great" and "Alexander Woollcott" with "Alexander's Ragtime Band," Semple abruptly excuses himself and leaves the scene. And that's it.

The Wide World of Mystery was an ABC late night anthology of low-budget 90-minute television films which aired at irregular intervals between 1973 and 1976. They were shot on videotape, which, combined with their limited sets and studio-bound atmosphere, gave them the feeling of soap operas, rather than actual movies. Alan appears in one of these gems, *Come Die with Me,* American-accented, as a lawyer reading a will. Again he only appears in a single scene, and once we get the necessary exposition out of the way, the audio fades, there is a cut, and we move on.

Alan followed this with a role in "The Lost Cotillion," a third episode of *Ironside*, memorable only for his reunion, however brief, with Cesar Romero. Romero, with whom he had memorably fenced (using fireplace pokers) in "Flop Goes the Joker" on *Batman*, is now one of the guests at a gathering which saddles Alan with the immortal cliché, "Madam. Dinner is served."

Finally at the end of 1974, he was seen in a television show worthy of his talents, albeit still in a small role. CBS had commissioned *The Lives of Benjamin Franklin*, a mini-series consisting of four plays by four writers detailing different aspects of Franklin's life. The first episode was "The Whirlwind," with a literate (and Emmy nominated) script by Loring Mandel. Lloyd Bridges was the old Franklin reminiscing while posing for his portrait; his son Beau took on the role in flashback. Alan was cast as the leader of a group anxious that Franklin allow his name to be submitted for the position of Clerk of the Assembly and was even permitted an aphorism worthy of the great man himself: "He who quotes himself too often seems to wear only the medals he's awarded to himself."

Airing after "Whirlwind," but shot before, was an episode of *Kojak* entitled "The Forgotten Room" (the order of shooting can be determined by Alan's facial hair: full beard for the first, cut back to a mustache for the second). "I've just done a Kojak segment," he wrote me, "as an old Greek bum in a sleazy N.Y. rooming house. It was the beard that did it— and an imaginatively cooked-up Greek accent when they asked me to read. They hired me before they had time to realize that I was Alan Napier." In truth, the Greek accent comes and goes, but Alan's scenes, nicely spread throughout the episode, are vital to the solution of the mystery. It was one of his better roles in a long time.

Early in 1977, he was seen in "The Golden Dog," a *Walt Disney's Wonderful World of Color* episode which had actually been shot in April and May of 1974. By late 1975, Alan was already despairing of it. "The Disney film may never see the light of day," he wrote me. "It probably fell between two stools. Traditionally, the Disney Hour has been about an animal with humans, give or take a cute little boy or girl, very much in the background. The technique has been action and narration. In 'The Golden Dog' they tried to make a story about two old men and a dog. But the story is very poorly developed, still held together with narration, and the dog isn't called upon to do anything extraordinarily heroic (bar licking my face in a sandstorm!) or to be in mortal danger. Its true they called me in to do some dubbing the other day, but were quite unwilling to say if or when it would be released."

Alan's co-star in the film (apart from the title character) was Paul Brineger, whose

Paul Brineger, director Fred Krug, and Alan on location for *The Golden Dog* outside Tuscon, Arizona, in 1974. The show would not air on *Walt Disney's Wonderful World of Color* until 1977. Courtesy Fred R. Krug Productions.

career had been primarily in Westerns. He and Alan play prospectors, Jock and Archie, who fall out but are reconciled thanks to their devoted dog. Fred Krug, producer and director of the film, had just finished another Disney hour, "The Secret of Old Glory Mine," and was able to modify his existing sets slightly for the month-long shoot outside Tucson, Arizona. Archie was written as a "limey" and, according to Krug, Alan was "the only person seriously considered" for the role. "It was a given that Alan Napier could play anything you wanted him to. He certainly wasn't limited to being butlers or stuffy aristocrats. I think he liked the idea of doing something different. He and Paul worked together pretty well because they were both very very professional men—Napier especially, but even Paul Brineger had a credit list as long as your arm. Brineger was a little bit envious of Napier's higher status, though. Alan was in a different league of acting from Paul, who kept going around behind Alan's back imitating his British accent—calling him 'the eck-tor Napier'—but we kept them working together nicely."

Fred Krug was as frustrated with Disney's tinkering as Alan was. The original script had been straightforward enough, if trite—a story of friendship tested by greed—but the studio rewrote the narration after the fact to create the character of Henry Thomas, a dead third prospector who was supposedly trying to reconcile his former partners from beyond the grave. The problem was that the two were perfectly friendly at the start of the film and only needed reconciling after Henry started meddling. "These films were never made by the production company alone," recalls Krug. "The studio fooled around with them all the time. They made this very, very boring 'Golden Dog,' which was admittedly based on a very, very boring script, by not using the very best footage. It was just awful. The dubbing! They did that on almost every film I can remember. They didn't like an actor's voice so they hired another actor to dub the whole thing over. They wanted to do that on this one too. They decided Alan was too British and I really had some fights with them. It was just the most awful thought; to have some turkey from Arizona do a Western character voice over Alan's performance!? They finally decided that they would 'let it go' but said we had to take some of the stuff out where he said 'bloody this' or 'bloody that' and that's what he had to go in there for, to cover those deleted 'bloodies' and a few other things. That's another reason the whole thing came out so boring. They took a lot of his dialogue out, leaving us with nothing but the two of them sitting around a dinner table watching the dog eat." Alan thankfully never knew how close he came to having his performance dubbed, but he still had a very strong negative reaction to the finished film. "To try to salvage it with elaborate narration—only faintly connected with the stupid story we attempted to tell—was a mistake. It was a corpse from the word go and should have been decently buried."

On January 3, 1977, not having worked since "The Forgotten Room" a year before, and with the memory of the previous night's broadcast of "The Golden Dog" fresh in his mind, Alan wrote, "My New Year resolution must be to get myself an agent of some distinction." Whether he managed this or wound up sticking with his existing management, it was still another year before he was on screen again, although there were two intriguing near-misses in the interim: First, he lost the role of "The Head" in Buck Henry's science fiction sit-com, *Quark*, to Alan Caillou; and then, chosen by Ralph Bakshi to play Gandalf in *Lord of the Rings*, he was ultimately priced out of that opportunity to return to feature films. "The Lord of the Rings outcome was sad," he wrote me. "Bakshi told me that regretfully he had to abandon the idea of combining live action with animation—his backers wouldn't come up with the money. And they're going to England for the voice over—cheaper and more suitable than American accents. So I'm totally out of it. Altogether this has been a discouraging year."

Quark was ultimately an eight-episode failure (though it has since earned a cult following), and Bakshi's animated *Lord of the Rings* has undeniably been overshadowed by Peter Jackson's overblown trilogy. But being considered by talented artists for quirky, personal projects was immensely flattering, and made it that much more of a letdown to wind up having to settle—yet again—for the run of the mill. "I have recently appeared in a Universal 'movie for television' about which, I feel, the less said the better," he wrote in February 1978. "The script was terrible and the role minimal. I did it for the money, which was good. The sequence I appeared in dealt with the upper reaches of the English aristocracy (period 1770) and I suppose they thought I might add 'an air of verisimilitude to an otherwise bald and unconvincing narrative'—a quotation I have always loved, tho' I cannot now identify it."

"I think the piece is called 'The Bastard.' It is a sort of Little Lord Fauntleroy story with a lot of blood and violence added. The modes of address amongst the aristocracy are

Eleanor Parker and Alan Napier in a publicity photograph from *The Bastard*. Why a shot of Alan wearing his glasses was released to the press is not known. He definitely has them off in the show itself. Collection of James Bigwood.

all wrong (as I told them) and the casting odd to say the least. It was shot 'on location' at a stately Beverly Hills mansion during two days of torrential rain. Everyone was very deferential and all that, but I have come to the conclusion that I don't mind if I never appear before a camera again. I get bored and irritated surrounded by second-rate people engaged in a vast effort to produce trash."

Trash or not, *The Bastard*, based on John Jakes' novel, was successful enough to spawn two sequels (in which Alan did not appear) and was a cornerstone of the *Operation Primetime* syndication experiment that extended into the '80s. For Alan, it would lead to three more jobs in 1978, including the best role he would receive in his entire post-*Batman* career.

First came *Flying High*, a one-hour CBS comedy-drama which tried to piggy-back on the success of ABC's *Charlie's Angels*, but with stewardesses. It lasted less than one season, with four of its eighteen episodes remaining unbroadcast and the remainder shown out of sequence, a sure sign of desperation. Alan's episode, "Beautiful People," did make it to air, but, along with the rest of the series (save the two-hour pilot), is now unavailable for viewing—even in bootleg. One of the episode's sub-plots involves Stewardess Marcy (Pat Klous) dating a Boston millionaire, so it seems likely that Alan (as "Arthur") and Natalie Shafer (as "Woman") were there to provide a wealthy background to Bernie Kopell as the millionaire boyfriend.

Later in the year, Alan shot a small role in "The Crime," an episode of *James A. Michener's Centennial*, to give the NBC mini-series its full title. He had high hopes for this one, but after it aired early in 1979, he wrote, "Centennial has been a disappointment—not vital to the story and therefore cut and what was left played on Lynne Redgrave's lovely face. There's a darling woman and beautiful actress!" He was being unfairly hard on himself. In a nice little scene, his Lord Venneford lies on his death bed, struggling to breathe, as he offers the majority shares in his Colorado ranch to his once-estranged niece … with conditions: "I believe now that your father and I made a mistake in requiring you to return to England. So the … condition is this. That you return at once … to your Red Indians … your wooly cowboys' uncivilized ways. To Colorado. To your home… And I don't want any argument about it."

And he gets plenty of close-ups.

Finally came "The Sorcerer's Apprentice." Alan certainly had John Houseman to thank for his role in this episode of *The Paper Chase*, if only for his having agreed to reprise his Oscar-winning role as law professor Charles Kingsfield in the CBS series. While his long friendship with the show's star certainly had something to do with his being cast in the role of Supreme Court Justice Allen Reynolds, the part still fit Alan like a glove. Houseman may have opened the door, but Alan had every right to be in the room. The top-billed guest star for the first time in a decade, he plays a distinguished alumnus visiting his old friend Kingsfield's campus to commemorate the 25th anniversary of the admission of women to the law school. He gets caught up in a feminist protest when it is revealed that, for all his liberal rhetoric, he has never hired a female clerk in all his years on the Court. It's a great part for Alan, but unfortunately, the script doesn't live up to the role. Reynolds is at odds with series regular Francine Tacker's Elizabeth Logan throughout the episode, as she tries to avoid being co-opted by strident outside agitators in her legitimate quest to point out his unintended hypocrisy, but the resolution to their conflict comes completely out of left field. In a private meeting (so private that even the viewing audience doesn't see it) they conveniently resolve all their differences so that when we next see them, he is waltzing with her at the anniversary reception. Having taken the lion's share of the hour to box their characters into a philosophical corner, the writers leave themselves no time to resolve the conflict properly on camera. This decision to take the lazy way out did not go unnoticed by their guest star. "Paper Chase had good reactions and I looked good in it," he wrote, "tho' to tell the truth, the writers were content just to set Reynolds up as a sort of Aunt Sally for the kids to take pot shots at. He could have been developed more interestingly, for instance if they'd written the obligatory scene with the girl when he convinces her he is OK. There has been no rush for my services as a result [of the show]. As you know, I don't really like acting to a camera, so drop me no tears please."

53

Hitchcock, Hubbard and Hawkins

James Bigwood

"I had known Hitch for years, but we never really hit it off," Alan told me in 1975, while discussing his role in *Marnie*. "When I came out here at first, I was used to playing rather good parts in the theatre. Hitch offered me a small part and I turned it down. He didn't think I should have, and I don't doubt that he was perfectly right."

Unfortunately, I neglected to ask him which Hitchcock movie he was referring to. While it could conceivably have been the thoroughly British *Rebecca*, which started principal photography in the summer of 1939, just after Alan arrived in California, there is no reference to him in the Selznick files for that film. His name *does* come up in the casting suggestions for *The Paradine Case*, however (for a role that does not appear in the final film), and while 1946 hardly qualifies as "when I came out here at first," it seems likely that this was the time that Alan turned Hitch down. And it was the time that another actor—John Williams—most emphatically did *not*.

Williams was almost Alan's exact contemporary (actually three months younger) and, although tall, a manageable 6'1". Yet, when Alan was beginning his career with the Oxford Players in 1924, Williams had already achieved West End success and made his move to Broadway, where he remained a constant presence for the next thirty years (save a stint in the RAF from 1941 to 1945), content to specialize in light comedy and drawing room drama with no ambitions to play the classics. He had appeared in four films in England in the early forties, before beginning his war service, but *The Paradine Case* was his Hollywood feature debut. In the uncredited role of Barrister Collins, he is really no more than an extra; a professional associate of the main character constantly visible beside or behind Gregory Peck throughout the lengthy trial which serves as the film's centerpiece, but never speaking a word. Whether Barrister Collins was the "small part" that Alan turned down or not, Hitchcock certainly "hit it off" with John Williams.

The 1952 Broadway hit *Dial "M" for Murder* provided Williams with his defining role: the sly, wily, yet humorous Chief Inspector Hubbard. He won the 1953 Tony Award for Best Featured Actor in a Play for that part and went on to recreate his performance in 1954 when Hitchcock directed the film version. Hitchcock used him again as Grace Kelly's father in *To Catch a Thief*, and cast him as Audrey Hepburn's father, the title character in *No Bail for the Judge*, before abandoning the project. In addition, he appeared in three episodes of *Alfred Hitchcock Presents* directed by Hitchcock himself (as well as seven more directed by others). His visibility led to major roles in the Billy Wilder films *Sabrina* and *Witness for the Prosecution* as well as sizeable appearances in many other successful (if not particularly memorable) big-budget features throughout the fifties and early sixties.

Obviously, none of this is to say that Alan would have been cast in all these roles if he had only agreed to play "a small part" for Hitchcock in 1946. Among other things, he was fighting his grey-listing at this point. It is fascinating, though, to observe how often he and John Williams managed to cross paths after Williams made his big breakthrough in 1952.

First, as Alan has detailed elsewhere, he played Williams' part in the Chicago company of *Dial "M" for Murder*. Then, in four appearances on the various incarnations of the Hitchcock television show, he acted in support of Williams, who was billed over the title in all ten of his episodes, while Alan was either featured or in the final crawl in his eight. Tellingly, unlike Williams, Alan was never cast in one of Hitchcock's self-directed episodes.

Norman Lloyd, a producer on both *Alfred Hitchcock Presents* and *The Alfred Hitchcock Hour*, as well as the director of Alan's LaJolla Playhouse production of *Dial "M" for Murder*, had the opportunity to observe both men at work and describes John Williams as "the perfect Hitchcock actor." Alfred Hitchcock always liked knowing what to expect from his actors and cast accordingly. If he found somebody whose persona he liked, he would keep using them. Essentially, he preferred to fit the role to the actor rather than the actor to the role, and this is where Williams had the edge. According to Lloyd, "John Williams was a *favorite* actor of Hitchcock's. Absolute favorite. He had the attitude, the speech, the physical

Alan Napier, Charles Davis, and John Williams in "I Killed the Count" on *Alfred Hitchcock Presents* (CBS, 1957). Collection of James Bigwood.

carriage. Alan Napier was a *very* good actor, but there was an overtone to John Williams that was different from Alan's. They were not the same. Particularly, John Williams had a kind of a humor and hidden sort of slyness. I never felt that with Alan. I felt something else in Alan, he was more open.

"John Williams played that one character. He never changed, which by the way is one of the secrets of a very successful acting career. Not only John Williams. Jimmy Cagney, Bogart, all of them. They found that character and they stayed with it and that brought the commercial reward. If you could latch on to a character that the audience identified with and liked, you made a fortune. Alan had a variety to his work which perhaps resulted in his not having great commercial success."

Alan's final interaction with Williams came at a time when both their careers were on the wane. In a 1978 ABC Weekend Special, *The Contest Kid and the Big Prize*, Williams was cast as Hawkins, a butler whose services are won in a contest by the title character, a twelve-year-old boy. When it came time to shoot the sequel, *The Contest Kid Strikes Again*, a year later, Williams was ill and couldn't play the part. Alan was brought in to replace him. "Did I tell you that I did a lead in a childrens afternoon T.V. for ABC?" he wrote me. "5 or 6 weeks ago. In great heat on location in Pasadena—with a lot of little boys and hens, both groups so unpredictable. I didn't enjoy it much and I don't think the producer, Bob Chenault of MGM, enjoyed me. Anyhow not a word of praise (or blame) from him since the last shot was fired. I expect *them* to tell me when it shows and am damned if I'll demean myself by asking. So I may have missed it already, which doesn't really worry me—in no way can it have been a peak in my career (maybe a black hole!). It didn't pay very well either."

Harvey Laidman, who directed both the shows, recalls that no attempt was made to have Alan duplicate Williams' earlier performance. "You just didn't do that kind of thing. They sent the script to the actor and three days later they were there on the soundstage or on the location and two rehearsals and we're shooting. It was that quick." In the first show, Hawkins had been introduced in a shot starting on his highly polished shoes, tilting up his liveried body, and finishing on his face. The shot was simply recreated with Alan and used as the only visual reference to Hawkins in the recap of the previous show that opened the hour. "He came in and put his own spin on it," recalls Laidman. "He was much more energetic and affable. John came off

Alan as Hawkins in *The Contest Kid Strikes Again*, a 1979 *ABC Weekend Special*. Collection of James Bigwood.

much more formal than Alan." Indeed, Hawkins 2.0 *needed* to be more energetic. He had to spend a significant portion of the show chasing chickens.

One trait that Laidman feels the two actors shared was their professionalism. "Both of them had a tendency to go quietly about their work. They just came in, did their work and were very easy. Easier than a lot of them. I'm thinking of an actor who has just died and I remember so much about him because he was so dyspeptic and cranky and difficult to work with. I remember a lot about him where I don't remember much about John or Alan. It was such a good experience that I don't remember it much!"

John Williams kept himself in the public eye for years (well beyond his death) by appearing in a commercial for a multi-disc mail-order collection of classical music that holds the record for the longest-running television ad in history:

> I'm sure you recognize this lovely melody as "Stranger in Paradise." But did you know that the original theme is from the Polovetsian Dance Number 2 by Borodin? So many of the melodies of well known popular songs were actually written by the great masters....

Alan's only known comment on John Williams was his observation one evening as this commercial aired that he wouldn't have minded the money that the job must have brought in.

54

Family and Friends

James Bigwood

Alan took advantage of the various fits and starts in his post-*Batman* professional life to catch up on his travelling. Not long after the series ended production, he went back to England and visited family members he hadn't seen in years, including his brother Mark's children and grandchildren. Julian Mulock remembers his great-uncle Alan's visit to the tiny village of Lower Padworth in Berkshire. "He came and visited our family in England in the '60s, which was great fun because he was Batman's Butler at that point and he was asked if he'd mind if the local village kids met him. He said he'd be delighted, so the little villagers in our very small village got dressed in their Sunday best and stood in a circle 'round him in our sitting room with their mouths hanging open, unable to say a word as this incredibly tall distinguished Batman's Butler stood amongst them. It was lovely."

Alan also reconnected with Gip's family, specifically her niece Sally Boyd. "My mother died when I was a baby. She was Gip's older sister so I had these glamorous American relations that I'd never met. They used to send us Hershey bars during the war and I had hand-downs of Poppet's rather glamorous Californian clothes and things which didn't really suit me in austere England. Anyway, I went out to Montreal and worked my way across to California so I could go visit them. This was in '58. I stayed with them for a while and they got me organized where to live and how to get a job and those sorts of things. I was very fond of them. Gip was like a surrogate mother. When I met my husband Tom and we got married out there, Gip was going to do the wedding for us but she developed cancer and couldn't. Alan did give me away though." In Tom Boyd's memoirs, *A Bowl of Cherries*, he recalls the ceremony. "Sally's family has its own private wedding march. It was written in 1876 by the French composer Charles Gounod, specially for the marriage of Sally's great-grandparents, Marie Roche and Sir Henry Fielding Dickens, son of Charles. Some weeks before our wedding, Sally's uncle (Aunt Gip's brother) sent a photocopy of the original manuscript (which has never been published) over to me and I presented it to the organist at St. Augustine's. In spite of all the time he had to practice the short and not very difficult piece, he made an absolute hash of it on the day, and as Sally and Alan Napier came solemnly down the aisle, I, instead of admiring the beauty of the bride as a waiting groom should do, could only wince at the sour notes and curse the inept organist." Tom and Sally had returned to England two years after their marriage and Alan was happy to reconnect with some of Gip's saner relatives. Tom's father happened to be visiting from the States at the same time and a family outing was arranged. "A.W. was not easy to entertain on his own, but he did like the theatre,"

Alan giving away Gip's niece, Sally, at her wedding to Tom Boyd, 1961. Courtesy Tom Boyd.

Tom writes, "so we took him to see a number of West End plays. During his stay, Sally's uncle, Alan Napier, flew over from Hollywood to see relations of his. He and my father had precious little in common, but it was suggested that we all go and see Alan Bennett's amusing play *Forty Years On*, starring John Gielgud. As it was set in, and much of the humour drawn from an English boys' public school, I can't imagine that my father got a lot out of it, but he laughed a time or two in the right places. When the curtain fell, Alan, who knew several of the actors in the cast, suggested we go backstage with him to say hello. Before we knew it, the four of us were in Sir John's dressing room, being offered drinks by his manservant. Alan, who knew him well, kept the conversational ball rolling and it was all very jolly. But after a few minutes, Alan said to 'Johnny,' 'I must just go down the corridor to say hello to darling Mona Washbourne. I haven't seen her for years,' and with that he left the star's dressing room. There we were, Sally, my father, and I plunked on our own with this famous theatrical legend, who didn't know us from Adam. Furthermore, we were abandoned there for a full twenty minutes, while Alan nattered happily in Mona Washbourne's dressing room down the way. To his ever-lasting credit, Gielgud carried this awkward situation off with the greatest aplomb. He kept the drinks flowing, and asked my father all about his law firm in Indianapolis, as though he cared two pins… After several gin and tonics and a really pleasant chat, Alan returned and rescued us … or rather rescued Sir John from this trio of strangers."

Alan later accompanied the Boyds on an organized tour for an "Anglo-American group of twenty-eight" to the USSR in 1970. Alan, who brought his grandson David along on the trip, was disconcerted to find himself suddenly noticed again only for his height, the Caped Crusader and his faithful butler being completely unknown behind the Iron Curtain.

In the mid '70s, he reunited with his brother Mark, then living in Newmarket, north of Toronto. It was a warm reunion with any childhood grievances long forgotten. Mark's grandson Julian was there for the visit and attests that any distance between the brothers by that time was geographic rather than personal. Alan also took this opportunity to reconnect with his childhood friend Humphrey Carver at the Carver summer home in Port Joli, Nova Scotia. Humphrey's youngest daughter, Jenny, recalls the excitement of welcoming the visitor from Hollywood. "I was one of the lucky Carvers and did meet Mungo (and we called him that, as did my parents). He came to Port Joli for I'd say at least a week, and we had extremely jolly times. He was absolutely gorgeous in every way … quite a perfect specimen of a human being, a work of art. We had wonderful times playing charades, laughing, and talking about when the boys (i.e., Humphrey and Alan) would have played parlour games at Harbonne with the Carver/Napier-Clavering group." Humphrey's grand-daughter Stephanie (daughter of Jenny's much older brother, Peter) was also there. "I remember very, very well the time that Mungo visited Port Joli. When I discovered that my grandfather's best friend from childhood was none other than Batman's butler, and that he was going to be visiting us, I was star-struck!! I can conjure up quite vividly in my mind's eye two photographs that were taken at that time. The first is a picture of Grumpy (the grandchildren's nickname for Humphrey—the Napier family clearly weren't the only ones with quirky nicknames!) and Mungo standing side by side in the living room of the house at Port Joli. I remember we were all chuckling as the picture was being taken, as the two very stately gentlemen were vying like school-boys to see who could be tallest. I can't recall who won out! Together they were a striking pair—tall indeed, still athletic, so, so handsome, both with shocks of gorgeous white hair. A living advertisement for healthy, long-living British men. The second photograph is much less interesting to anyone but me—it was of me standing beside Mungo, gazing up at him quite adoringly."

Alan's next trip was memorable as well, but for other reasons, as Christie Nichols recalls. "In 1981 Alan took me and one of the Vortex guys, Sean, on a tour of Egypt, Istanbul, Yalta, and up the Danube to Vienna. Sean and I took a side trip to Israel to visit my brother's ex-girlfriend, who Sean later married. My brother always adored Alan and gave him unconditional loyalty and support. I was more critical of Alan and we'd argue at times. We stopped near Athens during this trip and had an argument on the way to the Parthenon—I don't remember what about. We were so furious with each other that people in the train station

Alan in his garden with his granddaughter Christie Nichols, 1977. Courtesy Christie Nichols.

just parted like the Red Sea in front of us, the energy was so intense. I felt like Athena, Goddess of War, springing full grown and fully armed from Zeus' head that day. We always made up and were good friends, except for once when Alan made a horrible remark about Molly having been sexually abused by her Uncle Alan when she was a little girl. I didn't speak to him for two years. He could be very cold and insensitive about his sister. And about my mother. And *his* mother, who Molly described very differently."

55

One Role Too Many

James Bigwood

Alan's final screen appearance came in 1981, in *The Monkey Mission*, the second of three "Joe Dancer" television movies which aired on NBC following Robert Blake's Emmy-winning run in *Baretta*. In addition to starring as the titular detective, Blake was credited as creator and executive producer on all three films, as well as on the one-hour series that was intended to follow, but which never materialized. Given the self-conscious—or, better yet, self-indulgent—quality of the three pilot films, in which Blake cannot seem to decide whether he is an eighties private eye or a forties shamus, it is not surprising.

Alan's bizarre cameo in *The Monkey Mission* may have been meant to be whimsically surreal, but it simply comes off as nonsensical. Breaking into a mansion, expecting to find a Medici vase which he has been hired to replace with a copy, Dancer finds a barren room occupied by Briarton, the dwelling's ancient owner, who ignores the ringing alarm and invites the intruder to play gin with him. Shooing away his housekeeper and security guard when they respond to the clanging bell, he and his guest continue their card game until morning. Collecting his $12 winnings, he bids the detective farewell, telling him, "I've a hunch you'll do better next time." "I wouldn't bet my life on it," comes the reply. "Well, I'd only be placing a small bet, wouldn't I? Hmm? Hmm?" The old man's cackle disintegrates into wheezing.

This contrived sequence exists only to reveal that the vase has been donated to a museum, and *that* piece of information comes in Dancer's *film noir*-style narration, not in the written scene. The whole break-in plays like ten minutes of padding, since the movie is actually about the subsequent museum heist. Briarton is never seen or heard of again.

Ironically, given that Alan started his career specializing in playing old men, his performance here is—to be frank—not a good one. Encumbered with a motorized wheelchair and coke bottle glasses, he's a stereotypical old geezer, not a real person, and his coughs and wheezes sound forced. The artificiality of the writing doesn't help, it's true, but Alan had risen above weak scripts before. Perhaps it was simply no longer worth the effort.

56

Writing

JAMES BIGWOOD

"I've been getting together, from dozens of old cartons and envelopes, old photos for a family album and have come on all sorts of forgotten literary and dramatic writings," Alan wrote in 1979. "Some very good. God knows why nobody used them. I probably didn't push hard enough."

Alan has already detailed the story of his collaboration with his father and touched on his collaboration with the Robert Nichols who was not his son-in-law. But his writing continued well beyond his years in England, according to his grand-daughter. "He wrote every day, to my recollection, for a couple of hours in the mid morning, a script or letter or poem. He'd hire a stenographer and dictate when he was really serious about a project, for example his autobiography. He was a wonderful correspondent. We wrote each other frequently for years. He sent me a birthday present when I was nine or ten in England and included a poem that ended 'Lots of love—a gallon—from (something something) Alan.' I wish I could find his letters—I had a couple of boxes of them at one time."

Alan didn't limit his letter-writing to family. Any fan that took the trouble to track down his address and send him a note was sure to get a response, hand-written and often very difficult to decipher.

Gary Butcher was just a high school student in Lincoln, Nebraska, when he first wrote to him. "I've collected autographs since I was ten and I wrote him a fan letter," he recalls. "He's one of the first people who wrote back answers to questions I had about his career. I wrote him back and then when I was a junior or senior in high school I had a column in the high school paper. We were planning to go and see my aunt and uncle in Ojai, California, and we were going to go through L.A. and I wrote to several actors to see if I could interview them for my paper. He was one. Fritz Feld was one. Eddie Quillan. Alan Hale. After I interviewed him, we struck up a correspondence."

Alan was also a valuable resource to film historians. James Curtis interviewed him for his biography of James Whale, Joel Siegel for his Val Lewton career study, Rick Atkins for his book, *Let's Scare 'Em*. Greg Mank approached him in 1979 to inquire about his work with Laird Cregar on *Hangover Square* and they exchanged letters until Alan's death. An added benefit of these epistolary relationships was often an invitation to Porto Marina Way with the host at his entertaining best.

"My wife Barbara and I met him in May of 1983," recalls Mank. "He and I had been corresponding for a while and we were out in LA for a research trip and I called him. We went on a Sunday—one Sunday in May—to that beautiful house up on the cliffs above the ocean. We got to his house and he was up in the garden area. And I remember he came down and was stripped to the waist and barefoot and of course he was bronzed and 6 foot 5 or whatever. He came down like Zeus coming down from Olympus. Very gracious. He eventually went in and put a shirt on which was kind of charming. I guess he felt he was overexposed or something so he went in and put on a shirt that he never got around to buttoning. He made us some broth or soup as I recall and served us some tea and then sat down and told stories all afternoon. He told one story after another—most of which were unprintable!"

Alan enjoyed the company of writers because it gave him the opportunity to talk about his own writing projects and to commiserate about the difficulties of getting books published or screenplays optioned. One of his pet projects (and one of the few that survive him) was *The Great Montrose*, a screenplay about James Graham, the first Marquis of Montrose (1612–1650), the Scottish nobleman, poet and soldier.

"I first met him in Aytoun's 'Lays of the Scottish Cavaliers' when I was 8 years old," he wrote in 1976. "I have loved him ever since. I cannot speak of him without deep emotion. But it was only when I read John Buchan's great biography that I learned how close he had been to my forbear Archie Napier (at the time of the events in my film story Archie was 70 years old. Who do you think will play him if the film is made?). Incidentally I got a copy of the synopsis to Michael York in Japan. He wrote me a charmingly appreciative letter and is looking forward to our meeting and to reading the full script when he returns via California. I *KNOW* it is a great story and that I have been inspired in the telling of it. I am starting a new campaign to get it published. If it were to achieve any sort of acclaim as a book I'm sure the money would be forthcoming for the movie."

On a more frivolous note, "I have a very entertaining story for movies which my agent thinks he can sell," he reported in 1975. "We all know about the Abominable Snowman. Well I suddenly had a thought. They never talk about Abominable Snow*children*. The offspring of all mammals, with the possible exception of humans, are absolutely adorable. Tiger cubs. Lion cubs. No matter what, absolutely adorable. So I thought, supposing you were on some sort of ecology job, high up in the mountains of Northern California— big virgin forests—and you woke up one morning and you opened your front door and there on the porch is this sort of furry fella, with a bullet wound in his neck. And the story goes on from there..." By 1977, with no takers, he was thinking of turning it into a novel as well.

It was hard not to recall this sweet story in 1987, when *Harry and the Hendersons* was released.

In 1982, Alan described another of his projects to Greg Mank. "What really interests me now is the fate of my novel, 'Whom the Gods Love'—contemporary, funny and full of emotion—but short on violence. I have a good agent who thinks it perfectly delicious, so I have hopes. But, as you know, giant publishers, like giant movie makers, are only interested in giant sensational smash hits. There used to be room for the nice little movie and charming little book. No more, it seems."

Ultimately, Alan's writing never reached a wider audience, either on screen or in print, with the exception of "Tolstoy Betrayed," an article in the Spring 1969 issue of *Film Heritage*, in which he took issue with the recently released (and highly praised) Soviet version of *War and Peace*, ending on a typically entertaining note. "A recent news release announces that Sergei Boudarchuck, acclaimed for his production of the Russian-made *War and Peace* will direct the upcoming spectacle *Waterloo*. Can one man have two *Waterloos*?"

57

Last Hurrah

James Bigwood

By 1983, the last of the Vortex had moved on. Porto Marina Way felt quite empty after years of being filled with David and his friends. Alan reached out to Gary Butcher, who was contemplating a move to Los Angeles in hopes of breaking into the movie business.

"I graduated from high school in '82 and worked at a restaurant for a while to earn some money," Gary recalls. "As time grew on, David moved away—I think he got married—and then Sean and Christine moved to Wales, and Alan said 'I will be here by myself and I could use some help' and, unbelievable as it may sound, that's how I wound up living at Alan's."

Although he still preferred to drive his Barracuda, Alan's concession to old age was to allow Gary to chauffeur him to appointments that required his being out after dark. While still being called to audition for the occasional commercial, requests for his services on television—already infrequent—had dried up. Given his low opinion of some of the parts he had played in the 70s, this was probably for the best. On the threshold of his eighth decade, he was no longer interested in performing the work of mediocre writers. It was time to return to his roots.

George Bernard Shaw's *Heartbreak House* was published in 1919 and first performed in 1920. Alan first acted the play's lead role—the eighty-eight-year-old Captain Shotover— in 1927, at the age of twenty-four, with Shaw in the audience. Described by the author as "an ancient but still hardy man with an immense white beard," Shotover was probably the best part Alan played in his Oxford Players career, and he cited it on more than one occasion, along with *Bitter Sweet*'s Lord Shayne, as his favorite role. Now only seven years too young for the part, he was ready to tackle Shotover again.

Actually, he had already had a dry run ten years before. "I have recently done a sort of version of *Heartbreak House* up at San Simeon for Peggy Webber," he told me in 1975. "She played Lady Macduff in Orson's *Macbeth* and has been a friend of mine ever since and is always trying to get a hold of me to do things. She's mad! One of these people who love the theater passionately. For a long time she was married to a gynecologist—they get very rich you know—and she was always putting on plays with the proceeds. I did *Under Milk Wood* for her at a little theater in Santa Monica Canyon—beautiful production. We did *The Hostage*. She gets you to do these things and it's very good for one. Never any money of course. So she calls me up and says, 'Alan, I want you to do *Heartbreak House*. I want you to play Captain Shotover. I suppose you want to direct it too.' I said, 'Yes.' She said,

'Will you do it?' I said, 'Yes, of course I'll do it.' Then it turns out it's a reading with amateurs! So I have a look at them and I think, 'How can I snatch victory from the jaws of defeat?' Well, the important thing is to stop them 'acting' at all costs, just to make them read clearly. As it's a reading, I put them on stools and I keep telling them 'You've got such a wonderful voice; we want to hear what you're saying.' I butter them up to speak loud and clear straight out, and finally they do and the audience hears Mr. Shaw's lines absolutely clearly. I, in the meanwhile, to my amazement, having last played Shotover almost fifty years ago, found that it came back to me so easily that I gave a dazzling virtuoso performance without a book! And I thought the audience had a very good money's worth and I had a very interesting evening." Very good money's worth indeed. Building on the success of Peggy's New Hope Inn in Santa Monica ("Southern California's first and artistically most eminent dinner theater," according to the *L.A. Times*), where Alan had appeared in two acclaimed productions of Dylan Thomas' *Under Milk Wood*, her Jolly Rogue Dinner Theater in San Simeon offered Alan Napier in *Heartbreak House* plus a prime rib dinner for $8.50.

In 1977, hopes for a professional mounting of the play were raised again. "In the spring a new management at the Lobero Theater in Santa Barbara invited me to direct and play the lead in a production of Shaw's 'Heartbreak House'—my favorite play and role. Yesterday I heard that this new management had been fired! However I did go there for a matinee celebrating Shakespeare's birthday, giving a talk on the miracle of the man's achievement, with scenes from the plays."

In 1984, Peggy Webber reached out to Alan once more. Her career had started in radio and they had performed in several broadcasts together before they appeared in *Macbeth*. "I always was so impressed by his virtuosity," she recalls. "He could take a role and find the climax moment and hit it. Hit it with all of his emotional intensity and it always enriched every play that I ever did with him on radio. I worked with a lot of big movie stars and people who *should* have been doing it that way, but he actually *did* it. He would really put his teeth into it and make something great out of a script that sometimes maybe wasn't very well written."

Performing *Under Milk Wood* at the New Hope Inn, 1969. Courtesy Peggy Webber.

Peggy's theater company in the early 60s was the Rustic Canyon Players, which evolved into the Los Angeles Shakespeare Repertory Company as the decade progressed. Alan eventually became a member of its board of directors and, in addition to the productions of Brendan Behan's *Hostage* and Dylan Thomas' *Under Milk Wood* already mentioned, played Malvolio in Shakespeare's *Twelfth Night*. Working with Peggy actually became something of a Napier family affair as Poppet's second husband, Peter Forster, her third husband, Whit Bissell, and Jennifer's husband Bob Nichols all appeared in Webber productions.

Thus, Alan was still on Peggy's go-to list in 1984, when she and her second husband, Sean McClory, started a new theater company. "We leased a building on Magnolia in North Hollywood," she recalls, "and produced a number of shows, and *Heartbreak House* was one of them. It was more than just a reading. It was a 'staged reading' so that people were costumed and they moved around a bit. Shaw lends himself to that type of production."

This time, the play was cast with professionals. Leslie Easterbrook, not yet famous for her *Police Academy* movies, but already recurring weekly on *Laverne & Shirley*, played Shotover's daughter, Hesione Hushabye. "We performed the play as a staged reading, with minimal blocking and our scripts in hand, at the Finnish Center in North Hollywood. We were provided with a tiny playing space, and the audience sat in folding chairs. The set was minimal, with some comfortable furniture, but certainly indicated we were giving a reading, not a production. What happened on that stage was magic, though—certainly for me. Peggy asked Alan to speak to us before we started rehearsing. All I can remember is that we were spellbound by having him in our midst and by what he said. He strongly emphasized that with Shaw, it's all in the dialogue. Use every word and make every thought clear. If you do it well, your heart, and the audience, will be one. Let the passion come on its own—it's all there, but focus on what you are saying/reading/meaning and not what you are feeling. Say the words clearly and make sense of them, and the rest will follow." Alan actually prepared a written essay for his castmates on how to approach the production (see Appendix B), beginning with characteristic humor. "The first order of business will be to ignore totally the author's suggestion that *Heartbreak House* is a play in the Russian manner. Shaw could no more write like Chekhov than Chekhov could write like Shaw."

"When I was young," says Peggy Webber, "I remember being so in awe of Alan that I was afraid to speak to him. I was 16, 17, 18 years of age when I began doing network radio shows and he looked like he would be so imperious that he could knock you down with one word. I was so dumbfounded by him that until I did the Orson Welles picture, I didn't have the courage to talk to him. Afterwards I found that he was delightful and very easy to talk to. And after many years, when we did the last version of *Heartbreak House*, he asked me to be the director. And I was very flattered. *He* was actually the director, but I learned a lot from working with him."

Leslie Easterbrook recalls that it was "a collaboration. In the best sense of the word."

"Peggy did the movement of the play; the blocking entrances and/or exits. She gave it physical shape. Yet she always consulted with Alan about the floor plan, if you will, as she created it. When it came to notes on line delivery, intention, or motivation, she would first discuss them with Alan. She did this with us there, not behind the scenes. It was very much established that Alan was our interior guide to Shaw. His instruction was always spot on, if not always easy to enact. But he was patient with us, and always to a good end. When we had questions, or hit snags in rehearsal, Peggy would always defer to him. In very few words, he could answer our questions, and/or solve our problems. He was the consummate professional. Never would he direct us, or criticize our choices, unless Peggy asked him to. He saw himself as a member of the acting company, not as our director, and kept himself

Rehearsing *Heartbreak House* with Leslie Easterbrook, 1984. Courtesy Peggy Webber.

focused on Shotover. He behaved as if he was learning with us—and I think he was. His performance was astonishing, and I think he helped us all rise to the occasion."

Alan was pleased to discover that the play still had so much to say to a modern audience. As he had noted in 1974, "the interesting thing was to find that this play, written in 1914, is so topical today for America. It's saying (then about England, but it applies anywhere), 'Don't leave your government to disreputable businessmen or you'll get it in the neck!' He talks in nautical terms, Shotover does, and when his son-in-law, Hector says, 'What about things today?' he says, 'The captain's in his bunk drinking bottled ditchwater and the crew are gambling in the fo'castle!' How's that for Watergate? 'The captain's in his bunk drinking bottled ditchwater and the crew are gambling in the fo'castle. She'll strike, she'll sink, she'll split!' It couldn't be more timely for America today. Get into the business of running your country or it'll be run by the crooks! Wonderful play. *Wonderful* play! Terribly funny. Shaw could always say things that were in the most fabulous dramatic prose, blending poetry and humor about serious subjects, and it absolutely works."

Although Alan had always secretly harbored a hope that he might have a shot at King Lear ("Lear, I fear is an ignis fatuus of my wishful thinking. But I keep learning the lines, marvelous, in case…"), *Heartbreak House* turned out to be his professional swansong, a fitting end to a distinguished career. Gratifying, too, to have Shaw, rather than *The Monkey Mission*, as his final credit.

Peggy Webber went on to found the California Artists Radio Theater (CART), which has been responsible for hundreds of hours of radio in its nearly thirty years of existence, including two different versions of *Heartbreak House*. The first featured Kay Kuter as Shotover; the second, in 2014, starred Norman Lloyd in celebration of his 100th birthday. Peggy's attempts to revive radio had begun in the 60s and there are still reels of tape in her archives of Alan and Ford Rainey in *Twelfth Night*, recorded during the heyday of the Los Angeles Shakespeare Repertory Company. Understandably, though justly proud of both her broadcast versions of *Heartbreak House*, she regrets not having been able to record her original star's performance for posterity. "Alan died before we did the radio version. I was very sorry not to have him."

Alan Napier and Betsy Hale in *Heartbreak House*, **Los Angeles, 1984. Courtesy Peggy Webber.**

58

Playing Oneself

James Bigwood

In 1979, Alan, Norma Varden, and Charles Lane agreed to sit down for interviews with me to include in *The Real Stars*, a filmed proposal I was putting together to raise interest in a documentary on Hollywood character actors. Shooting on 16mm black-and-white film, I only had enough stock for ten minutes of camera time with each of the three, so was reduced to asking very specific questions to which I already knew the answers. These were edited together with unauthorized clips duped from rented 16mm prints of their films, including, in Alan and Norma's cases, some of their rare British work. Had there been any interest in the project (which ultimately there wasn't), I would have filmed longer interviews in color and licensed the clips properly, but this was all I could afford at the time. Eventually I had a work print of my film ready to show Alan, who quickly responded to my announcement. "I look forward with some trepidation to your next visit. I'm always embarrassed by myself when *not* acting. But the English clips should be intriguing."

Seven years later, portable video equipment was much more accessible and Jeffrey Vance, the son of one of Alan's frequent bridge partners, Nina Wrangell, decided to attempt a proper full-length interview. Jeff, nine when he first met Alan, was now a student at UC Santa Cruz and, realizing that his mother's occasional escort was about to turn 83, asked her to ask Alan if he would willing to participate. "So the next thing I know, he says yes. He thought it would be interesting, so we were off and running."

"I was staying with the guy who did sound on it, David James, who was also a film student. We were staying at his sister's house in Hollywood and we would drive out to Alan's every day. We shot two sessions a day. We did a morning shoot and let him take a break and have lunch and we'd go play down at the ocean or whatever and then we'd shoot an afternoon sequence.

"If I'd been more ready for the job at hand, or more mature—it was the first thing I'd ever shot in my life on video—and if I had not been as close to Alan as I was, not so impressed with him. If I'd been there more as a journalist—someone who was friendly, but who really wanted to get to the meat of the matter—I think it would have served the film better. At the time it was the best I could do.

"I wasn't really sure what I was getting myself into until we sat down a night or two before the shoot. That's when he asked me, 'Are we going to be doing this like an interview or do you want me to talk about my life, because I've written a book…' I didn't know that he had written a book until he told us, and I just took the easy way out. I would at least be getting material back that had some kind of relevance. I didn't know his whole theater history. I didn't know his early life. So it was, 'Oh, you have a script that you've memorized? Let's use that! You bet!'"

In addition to setting his stories down for his book, Alan had been performing them for years for family, friends, and fans. They had become highly polished party pieces and the shoot for *Through the Mill*, as Jeff's film came to be called, became simply a matter of his going through his well-rehearsed repertoire on camera. This may seem like an exaggeration, but it can be corroborated by watching him in *Through the Mill* as he tells of being hired by Victor Fleming for *Joan of Arc*. He uses almost exactly the same words and hand gestures that he used in telling me the story in *The Real Stars*, seven years previously. It's quite remarkable. As Jeff Vance puts it, "He really spent his life perfecting the performance of Alan Napier."

Alan's birthday came on the fourth day of shooting. A surprise party had been organized by Gary Butcher for that evening with the guest list including most of Alan's bridge cronies and John and Joan Houseman.

"David and I were both pretty excited because we knew that John Houseman was coming," recalls Jeff. "We knew that Alan was Batman's butler, but to have two actors in the same room, especially with one who is as intimidating as John Houseman—at least that's how we perceived him from the movies he'd been in—this was no nonsense. You can get away with being a complete amateur student in front of Alan Napier because you grew up with him and now it's been three days of shooting, but this is a whole nother matter.

Alan in his garden with his daughter Jennifer and his son-in-law, Robert Nichols, 1986. Courtesy Christie Nichols.

"The night went on. John and Alan were just sitting on the couch quietly talking to each other and David and I were sitting nearby thinking, 'God what a treat this is. We're getting to hear these great old stories.' It had just basically started when we stared at each other. 'What are we doing sitting on the couch watching this go on?! We're not here to socialize!' So I went up to John's wife, because I didn't want to just whip out the equipment, but at the same time I knew that if I asked them if I could film it, I'd interrupt them talking and everything would get ruined. So I explained that part of it and said, 'Do you think you can give an OK and if he's annoyed after the evening's over I'll just let you have the tapes.' She said, 'Oh you wouldn't even have to do that,' and she gave us the OK. So we're crawling around like inconspicuous cats in front of these guys trying to cable everything up and they're trying to act as if they're not really watching what we're doing. But they know they're going to be filmed! It's old U-matic days. Just the tripod stand was like opening up a tent in somebody's room! There was no way to be discreet about this stuff. The deck weighed seventy five pounds; we had it on a dolly! It was ridiculous. There was cable for everything! It's not like these days when you can just flip up your iPhone and shoot a couple of old guys talking. So anyway, at the end of the evening, things were wrapping up and we just

Alan with his "bridge ladies" at his surprise birthday party in January 1986. In the back row with Alan are Doe Avedon, Cathy Makoul and Peggy O'Neal. In front are Nina Wrangell (Jeffrey Vance's mother), and Annie Taylor, formerly John Houseman's assistant, and the force behind Alan's political awakening. Courtesy Gary Butcher.

let the camera roll until they were walking away at the door saying goodnight. Alan went off to bed and David went home and I was left alone with the camera and the deck and my Mom, who had come down for the party. I played the tape back and there was just snow. Just completely fresh undisturbed video. No recording. The blood just drained from me."

Alan's 84th birthday celebration with John Houseman and Gary Butcher, January 1987. Courtesy Gary Butcher.

Even without footage of Alan and John, Jeff had five hours of interviews with his subject which, along with stills and VHS recordings of broadcasts of some of Alan's films provided by Gary Butcher, allowed for the creation of an impressive twenty-five minute video profile. And there was an added bonus.

"For a long time Alan and my Mom played bridge at a bridge club together and he would often recite sonnets or different parts of Shakespeare. He loved great theater and great literature and if it was something that was in his vocal range that worked well, he was always delighted to do readings at parties. After we'd finished the end of the shooting we had another two twenty-minute tapes and I asked he if there was anything he wanted to recite."

As a result, there is videotape of Alan performing scenes from *Lear*, *Macbeth*, and *Under Milk Wood* the day after his 83rd birthday.

Not long after taping the interviews for *Through the Mill*, Alan checked into St. John's Hospital in Santa Monica for elective surgery to insert a pacemaker. There were complications after the operation and it took much of 1986 for him to fully recover. His 84th birthday was a much more subdued affair, with the Housemans the only guests.

Six weeks later he had a stroke.

Fortunately, it happened at breakfast with Gary Butcher there to call Poppet and take him to St. John's. The stroke was a mild one and after a few weeks of rehabilitation, he was back at Porto Marina Way. His speech was still clear but, as he wrote to Greg Mank, "As you can see handwriting dreadfully affected. Also physical equilibrium—and memory. But interest and appearance unaffected. Also sense of fun and humor I believe."

Nina Wrangell brought a copy of Jeff's work in progress (then known as *Footsteps in the Sea*—the original title of Alan's autobiography) to Alan's 1987 Christmas celebration. Christie Nichols remembers the occasion. "My sister-in-law and I cooked Alan's last Christmas dinner, a beautiful goose with Yorkshire pudding, served quite formally, of course. Alan's step daughter Poppet and her son Brian came, my second husband, Gary, a sort of girlfriend of Alan's (I discovered some antipathy between her and Poppet as they both strongly objected to each other's presence when they each got me alone in the kitchen) and some members of The Vortex came by later. We drank a lot of champagne and watched a homemade film about Alan called 'Footsteps in the Sea.' He was quite frail by then, and fell asleep in his chair, but still a graceful and beautiful man, with his beautiful voice."

59

Batman *Redux*

James Bigwood

"What I might call the echoes of rumors come to my ears of renewed *Batman* activity," wrote Alan in 1978. "A movie? Yes, I'd do it if they paid me enough—which I doubt. It would probably be a pretty cheap package."

And indeed it was. In January 1979, Adam West and Burt Ward reprised their roles as Batman and Robin in *Legends of the Super Heroes*, two execrable specials shot on video tape by Hanna-Barbera. That Alan was not invited to join the proceedings can only have been a great relief.

In 1983, West and Ward were joined by Yvonne Craig, Lee Merriwether (Catwoman in the *Batman* feature), and Vincent Price (Egghead) as celebrity contestants on *Family Feud*, pitted (for charity) against the casts of *Lost in Space* and *Gilligan's Island*; in 1985, Adam West, Yvonne Craig and Julie Newmar were reunited and interviewed by McLean Stevenson and Sarah Purcell on the syndicated series, *America*. Alan was not asked to participate in any of these shows.

Finally, in February 1988, apologizing for his handwriting—which was still very much affected by his stroke the year before—he wrote to Greg Mank. "Suddenly Batman is all the rage in London again! A Hollywood producer is planning to cash in on this and has asked me to appear in a review of that great work next March 9—I don't know what time or channel. He says 'Alfred' has hitherto been underrated (dam right!) and plans to correct that. I dread the effort but will probably make it. If you have access on the 9th it might amuse you."

Actually, three reunions were scheduled. March 9 was an appearance at the Stock Exchange, a downtown Los Angeles nightclub, which was covered by the press, but not broadcast. This was followed by Fox's *The Late Show* on April 28 and the syndicated *Wil Shriner Show* on May 13. All three gatherings were the brainchild of Hal Lifson, a publicist then working for Tokyo based Dentsu Advertising.

"I was promoting *Batman* in Japan at the time, classic *Batman*. This was more than a year ahead of the Michael Keaton *Batman* movie coming out in June of '89. I was working with a lot of the cast members and reunited most of the cast. They were doing promotional work for 20th Century–Fox Television, because they were going to syndicate the show. This was twenty years after it was cancelled. I knew that Alan was living but I had heard that he was quite old and was living a quiet life in the Palisades. I contacted him and spoke to him on the phone and he was very nice, and he invited me to his house which is actually where I first met him—in his home. I convinced him to do the nightclub event, we sent a car to pick him up and he made it there. It was really something to see Adam West and Alan Napier reunited after so many years. Close to twenty, I'm sure."

"I was really glad to see Alan Napier," recalled Yvonne Craig in James Van Hise's "Batmania II," four years later. "When you're on the set you're so busy working. And we didn't socialize so I was unaware, until I went to the first reunion, of Alan's career. I'd had no idea that he had appeared with John Gielgud and Laurence Olivier on the stage, in London.

"When we went to the Stock Exchange reunion he'd had a minor stroke and was having a problem with balance. He had this cane that they'd had to extend because a normal cane was too short for him.

"There were press from everywhere and people came in and danced and they would flash bits of *Batman* on a screen. Then they introduced us and it was a little frantic. But I guess discos are supposed to be frantic. They took us up on the balcony that runs all around the hall because it's an honest-to-god stock exchange building. So we weren't right down there with the fans, but there were loads of fans. They brought in the Batmobile and took lots of pictures. Oddly enough, I don't know what the fans got out of it. I would not want to have paid to go there and see film that I could have seen at my house. We didn't do or say anything there. We were sort of dragged out like mummies and they whisked us along so that we barely got to sign autographs."

Also taking part in the event was an English producer, John Gore, who was in the

Yvonne Craig and Alan Napier at the Stock Exchange *Batman* Reunion, March 9, 1988. Alan is being interviewed by London producer John Gore. Photograph by Joe Russo © 1988.

process of mounting *Batman and Robin: The Last Re-run* for a two-week run for charity at the Bloomsbury Theater in London.

"I was basically creating a stage show of *Batman* in the UK based on the TV show, which had been a great favorite of mine growing up. It was very fortuitous that at that time they were gathering the cast together—it was literally about three weeks before I started going into rehearsals so it gave me a chance to see all of them. I'd gotten to know Adam West beforehand and Julie Newmar was the first of the gang I'd met because at that time there was a huge revival of the TV show on breakfast television in the UK. So suddenly, to a lot of people, the TV show appeared like a brand new thing—people almost didn't realize it was an old show—especially the kids. So getting to meet them all was pretty crucial. I'd been in touch with Hal Lifson, hoping to have everyone there and I basically got on the next plane to LA to sit down and see them all." The upshot was that John Gore wound up conducting Alan Napier's last interview of any substance, backstage at the Stock Exchange.

"I was talking with him as much about understanding the character creation as anything. I wasn't really interviewing him as a journalist. I interviewed him and various others there that night, but sitting down with Alan was fascinating.

"Donald Brown played Alfred in the show. He wasn't as tall as Alan was, but when Adam West came over and opened a store called Forbidden Planet, Donald accompanied him everywhere. Adam was completely amazed by the fact that he'd been able to nail Alan's whole persona. The seriousness with which he took the character was what made it work because, unlike the rest of them, he wasn't really spoofing it. He played it absolutely straight. I directed the show as well as writing it and that was one of the main things, that we made sure that Don's performance was as true to Alan as it possibly could be."

The Stock Exchange Reunion was a joy. *The Late Show*, a month and a half later, anything but.

The show's host, Ross Shafer, despite announcing at the head of the show that, "We have been working on this show for weeks, and we are pumped!" treated the proceedings with an air of condescension bordering on contempt. After wasting two minutes on an unfunny segment about the Baltimore Orioles' losing streak, he had to cram as much as possible into what remained of the hour (minus commercials). As Yvonne Craig described it to James Van Hise, "*The Late Show* was so overbooked. We had the writer, Alan, Adam, Burt, me, Julie, Eartha Kitt, Frank Gorshin, the Batmobile designer and squibs from Cesar Romero. You can't put that many people on a one-hour show." And indeed, by the time they got to Alan, there was barely a minute left.

Shafer introduces his final guest, who graciously acknowledges the audience's applause. "Alan had a very significant role on the show," continues the host, "but you were standing in one position for most of that series it seems. Is that about right?" Alan's answer is short and to the point. "No. Absolutely not." Yvonne Craig, sitting to his left, bursts into laughter and joins the audience in applause. "I'm sorry to spoil your story but it's not true." Shafer makes a lame ad-lib about how fruitless it is to argue with an English butler. Then, as Alan tries to tell one of his favorite stories (about Alfred's illegitimate origins), Shafer pulls the mike away, effectively cutting him off in mid-sentence. Then it's goodbye to all the guests, a quick reminder not to miss the Playboy Playmate of the Year on tomorrow's show, and the evening is over.

In his autobiography, Adam West, under the impression that Alan's stroke was much more recent than it actually was and concerned that his labored speech gave the impression of drunkenness, calls it "a sad end to his distinguished career."

"I sat there, fuming, as he was asked questions that required lengthy answers, or as the camera would catch this wonderful human being gazing blankly into space." It actually isn't as bad as that. Ross Shafer's inanities simply do not lend themselves to sparkling banter and, as the show was almost over, there wasn't time for meaningful conversation. Alan was not at his best, it is true, but he was too much of a professional to have agreed to appear if he knew he wasn't up to it. One only has to read his interview with John Gore to realize that he was perfectly capable of expressing himself when allowed to. Yvonne Craig's explanation to me in 2012 seems more on the mark: "They kept us there too long. He was elderly and not in good health and they had kept us there so long before they ever got the show started that when they asked him a question, he was just really too tired to answer. He kind of rambled and everybody thought he was losing his mind, but he really wasn't. I mean he *really* wasn't. He was okay; it's just he was exhausted."

On the ride home (Yvonne and Alan lived in the same neighborhood and shared a limo), he was back to his old self. "He and my husband and I were in the limo in the back seat and he said, 'Oh I would so love to have a drink.' There were no bars in sight and my husband said, 'Let's stop at the liquor store and we'll get you something.' So he went in and bought one of those pre-mixed daiquiri things. Anyway, Alan loved it. And then somebody told me at his funeral that that's all he talked about. The fact that we were willing to stop and get him a drink!"

60

The End

JAMES BIGWOOD

Alan was furious at his treatment on *The Late Show* and did not participate in the third *Batman* reunion in May. Never really the same after his pacemaker surgery, he was finding it harder and harder to negotiate the many sets of stairs in his cliffside home. "We talked at the time," Christie Nichols remembers, "about how he felt about dying and he told me that he was curious, not afraid, and didn't want to keep living if he couldn't continue his life at Porto. I came down there several times in the spring and summer of 1988 when Alan was being cared for by a slight but very strong Brazilian man who managed to help him keep his dignity when he started taking bad falls and needed help getting up and down stairs. Alan's legs were so long that he couldn't get himself up again when he fell. So he'd lie down wherever he was and wait for someone to come along and help him. It was heart breaking. He'd be apologetic. He was determined to stay at Porto. He loved that house and he loved his routines and complete freedom."

"What was terrible," recalls Jennifer Nichols, "is that his doctor decided that he should have a pacemaker. They put the pacemaker in, he had complications, he was in intensive care, and then he was put into a home. If the damn doctor hadn't given him a pacemaker he would have died at home in his sleep in the house he loved."

"When Alan went to the nursing home," Christie continues, "it was clear that he couldn't go back to Porto. I think he made up his mind that it was time to leave his body. It took a while, not necessarily because of the pacemaker, but because he was tremendously strong and vital. To my memory he was only in the home (the Berkeley?) for a few weeks or a month at the most. It was a horrible time. I remember an old song by The Band in 'Music from Big Pink' going through my head at the time—'Any day now, any day now, I shall be released.'"

Christie's brother David recalls, "When I knew Alan's health was failing, I used to drive down from the Bay Area every two weeks to be with him and actually was with him just a few hours before he died. It was a fascinating night, because he had been suffering with dementia and when I went to visit him that night all of a sudden he was crystal clear. He spoke about a whole bunch of things. He asked me to send love to people. It was a really wonderful visit. I left and he died later that night."

Christie was the last family member with Alan before he died. "He was singing a hymn from Clifton, the school he attended as a boy. He seemed very young. He called me Jenny and mistook me for my mother and I didn't argue, for a change. He asked me 'Is everybody here?' I told him yes and he said 'That's all right, then.' He fell asleep and died in his sleep a few hours later."

It was the early hours of August 8, 1988. Alan was eighty-five.

"I'm sitting here sobbing," writes Christie. "I still miss him. He was narcissistic and maddening and stubborn and more fun. I have some of Alan's books in my office, old volumes of Freud and Adler and Jung. I have the little wooden bowl he kept his keys in near the front door. I saw Kevin Spacey's 'Richard III' at the Curran Theater a few weeks ago and would have loved to get Alan's opinion. It really throws me to see him on television sometimes! My favorite performance that you can see is as the doctor in 'The Uninvited.' The warmth and humor in that part, playing an attractive man his own age, was my Alan. My two other favorites were his Malvolio in a workshop production of 'Twelfth Night' that my father directed, and a reading he did in a little restaurant at the bottom of Santa Monica Canyon of 'Under Milk Wood.' He did those shows for love and was completely brilliant in completely different ways in both of them. And of course I think of him when I really look at the ocean."

61

Memorial

JAMES BIGWOOD

Alan's memorial service was held on August 13, 1988, at St. Matthew's Church in the Pacific Palisades.

"I don't go to weddings and I don't go to funerals," says Yvonne Craig. "I hate all that ritual, but I went to Alan's funeral, and it was the best funeral I've ever been to. Everybody was telling wonderful stories about Alan. His daughter had said, 'Don't dress in anything dark because Alan was a light person and he would have liked to have had people all dressed up in pretty colors,' and so we did and it was terrific."

"It was actually quite a lovely gathering," says Denny Cline. "There were a lot of people there from old Hollywood. A lot of people that I recognized but didn't really know. Friends of the family. The family. Alan had lived through so many different periods; it was great to see everybody collected there. I got up and gave a talk about The Vortex years and how much Alan had meant to us because of who he was.

"We ended with a line I got from Jennifer's husband, Dave's dad, Bob Nichols. 'There's no more cakes and ale.' That was a line from Shakespeare that Alan would use in sad circumstances, and that was the tone of the whole event.

"There's no more cakes and ale; Alan has passed on."

Alan Napier's ashes were scattered at 17919 Porto Marina Way. The house has since been condemned and demolished due to mudslides and the property is now officially owned by the city, although the concrete foundation still remains. And the memories. "I picked some of his roses, his favorite Mr. Lincoln, and put them in his room the night he died, in case his spirit came by," recalls Christie Nichols. "Which I'm sure it did. Part of him inhabits that place still."

Appendix A

Acting Credits

On the Stage

Listed chronologically, the title of the play is followed by the author, the theatre, and the dates of the run. Alan Napier's role then follows in parentheses. On the occasions when he plays more than one part in the same play, the roles are separated by a "/" to differentiate them from roles which include a comma in their description. In some cases, additional notes follow. London theatres not considered "West End" houses are shown as being in London, whereas West End theatres are identified as WE. Try-out tours of an eventual London or Broadway run are treated as separate entries, but transfers from one London theatre to another during the course of a run are treated as part of the same production. When a specific number of performances are noted, it is to indicate a deliberate short run, rather than the closing of an unsuccessful play.

Dandy Dick, Arthur Wing Pinero. Oxford Playhouse, Oxford. April 28–May 3, 1924 (Noah Topping).
The Lady from the Sea, Henrik Ibsen. Oxford Playhouse, Oxford. May 5–May 10, 1924 (Arnholm).
The School for Scandal, Richard Brinsley Sheridan. Oxford Playhouse, Oxford. May 12–May 17, 1924 (Benjamin Backbite).
A Collection Will Be Made, Arthur Eckersley. Oxford Playhouse, Oxford. May 19–May 24, 1924 (Proprietor of the Hotel).
Crabbed Youth and Age, Lennox Robinson. Oxford Playhouse, Oxford. May 19–May 24, 1924 (Charlie Duncan). This and *A Collection Will Be Made* were part of an "Evening of One-Acts"—AN did not appear in the third play.
Twelfth Night, William Shakespeare. Oxford Playhouse, Oxford. May 26–May 31, 1924 (Antonio).
A Slice of Life, J.M. Barrie. St. Martin's Theatre, WE. July 10, 1924 (1st Footman). Charity matinée for the Maggie Albanesi Scholarship at the R.A.D.A.
Storm, C.K. Munro. Ambassadors Theatre, WE. August 13, 1924–September 13, 1924 (Professor Bolland). Transferred to Royalty Theatre, WE. September 15–November 22, 1924.
Judas Iscariot, E. Temple Thurston. New Scalia Theatre, WE. November 23, 1924 (Listed among "Beggars, Merchants, Pharisees, Citizens, etc."). The Repertory Players—One performance only.
Madame Pepita, G. Martinez Sierra. Oxford Playhouse, Oxford. December 1–December 6, 1924 (Alberto).
The Cherry Orchard, Anton Chekhov. Oxford Playhouse, Oxford. January 26–January 31, 1925 (Leonid Gayef).
The Earth, J.B. Fagan. Oxford Playhouse, Oxford. February 2–February 7, 1925 (Roger Morrish).
Overruled, George Bernard Shaw. Oxford Playhouse, Oxford. February 9–February 14, 1925 (Gregory Lunn). Evening of One-Acts–AN did not appear in the other two plays.
The Admirable Crichton, J.M. Barrie. Oxford Playhouse, Oxford. February 16–February 21, 1925 (Hon. Ernest Woolley).

Getting Married, George Bernard Shaw. Oxford Playhouse, Oxford. February 23–February 28, 1925 (General Bridgenorth).

The First and the Last, John Galsworthy. Oxford Playhouse, Oxford. March 2–March 7, 1925 (Larry Darrant).

Wurzel-Flummery, A.A. Milne. Oxford Playhouse, Oxford. March 2–March 7, 1925 (Richard Meriton, M.P.). This play and *The First and the Last* were part of an "Evening of One-Acts"—AN did not appear in the third play.

A Comedy of Good and Evil, Richard Hughes. Oxford Playhouse, Oxford. March 9–March 14, 1925 (The Rev. John Williams).

A Comedy of Good and Evil, Richard Hughes. Ambassadors Theatre, WE. March 30–April 11, 1925 (The Rev. John Williams).

The Cherry Orchard, Anton Chekhov. Lyric, Hammersmith, London. May 25–June 20, 1925 (Leonid Gayef). Transferred to Royalty Theatre, WE. June 22–September 19, 1924.

A Comedy of Good and Evil, Richard Hughes. Oxford Playhouse, Oxford. August 6, 1925 (The Rev. John Williams). Special Matinée—One performance only.

The Cherry Orchard, Anton Chekhov. Oxford Playhouse, Oxford. August 10, 1925 (Leonid Gayef). Special Matinée—One performance only.

The Circle, W. Somerset Maugham. Oxford Playhouse, Oxford. October 26–October 31, 1925 (Clive Champion-Cheney).

Misalliance, George Bernard Shaw. Oxford Playhouse, Oxford. November 2–November 7, 1925 (Johnny Tarleton).

Ghosts, Henrik Ibsen. Oxford Playhouse, Oxford. November 9–November 14, 1925 (Pastor Manders).

The Marriage of Lucrezia, "Peter Spence." Oxford Playhouse, Oxford. November 16–November 21, 1925 (Alfonso, Duke of Ferrara).

Creditors, August Strindberg. Oxford Playhouse, Oxford. November 16–November 21 (Gustav). This play and *The Marriage of Lucrezia* were part of an "Evening of One-Acts"—AN did not appear in the third play.

Dear Brutus, J.M. Barrie. Oxford Playhouse, Oxford. November 23–November 28, 1925 (Mr. Coade).

Crabbed Youth and Age, Lennox Robinson. Oxford Playhouse, Oxford. November 30–December 5, 1925 (Charlie Duncan). Performed as a curtain raiser before full length Robinson play in which AN did not appear.

The Skin Game, John Galsworthy. Oxford Playhouse, Oxford. January 18–January 23, 1926 (Hillcrist).

The Truth about Blayds, A.A. Milne. Oxford Playhouse, Oxford. January 25–January 30, 1926 (Oliver Blayds).

What the Public Wants, Arnold Bennett. Oxford Playhouse, Oxford. February 1–February 6, 1926 (Saul Kendrick).

Arms and the Man, George Bernard Shaw. Oxford Playhouse, Oxford. February 8–February 13, 1926 (Major Sergius Saranoff).

Magic, G.K. Chesterton. Oxford Playhouse, Oxford. February 15–February 20, 1926 (Dr. Grimthorpe).

Marlborough Goes to War, Marcel Achard. Oxford Playhouse, Oxford. February 22–February 27, 1926 (Marlborough).

The Confederacy, Sir John Vanbrugh. Oxford Playhouse, Oxford. March 1–March 6, 1926 (Moneytrap).

I'll Leave It to You, Noël Coward. Q Theatre, London. June 14–June 20, 1926 (Daniel Davis).

The Seagull, Anton Chekhov. Theatre Royal, Huddersfield. July 19–July 24, 1926 (Constantine).

The Wild Duck, Henrik Ibsen. Theatre Royal, Huddersfield. July 26–July 31, 1926 (Gregers Werle).

The Government Inspector, Nikolai Gogol. Theatre Royal, Huddersfield. August 2–August 7, 1926 (Skvoznik-Dmukhanovsky, the Govorner).

It's the Truth (If You Think It Is), Luigi Pirandello. Theatre Royal, Huddersfield. August 9–August 14, 1926 (Councillor Agazzi).

The Cherry Orchard, Anton Chekhov. Theatre Royal, Huddersfield. August 16–August 21, 1926 (Leonid Gayef).
And So to Bed, J.B. Fagan. Opera House, Manchester. August 30–September 4, 1926 (A Pick-Purse).
And So to Bed, J.B. Fagan. Queen's Theatre, WE. September 6–October 30, 1926 (A Pick-Purse). Transferred to Savoy Theatre, WE. November 1, 1926–April 30, 1927; AN left the run early to return to the Oxford Players.
The Taming of the Shrew, William Shakespeare. Apollo Theatre, WE. September 26 & 27, October 8 & 9 (Vincentio). The Fellowship of Players—Four performances only.
La Gioconda, Gabriele d'Annunzio. R.A.D.A. Theatre, London. January 2, 1927 (Role unknown). The R.A.D.A. Players—One performance only.
Uncle Vanya, Anton Chekhov. Oxford Playhouse, Oxford. January 24–January 29, 1927 (Alexandr Serebryakov).
The Philanderer, George Bernard Shaw. Oxford Playhouse, Oxford. January 31–February 5, 1927 (Joseph Cuthbertson).
Quality Street, J.M. Barrie. Oxford Playhouse, Oxford. February 7–February 12, 1927 (A Waterloo Veteran).
Androcles and the Lion, George Bernard Shaw. Oxford Playhouse, Oxford. February 14–February 26, 1927 (Ferrovius).
Full Moon, Emlyn Williams. Oxford Playhouse, Oxford. February 28–March 5, 1927 (Gordon Brentwood).
Intoxication, August Strindberg. Oxford Playhouse, Oxford. March 7–March 12, 1927 (Adolphe).
Othello, William Shakespeare. Apollo Theatre, WE. April 3–April 4, 1927 (Gratiano). The Lyceum Stage Society—Shakespeare Memorial Theatre Fund Benefit—Two performances only.
Dear Brutus, J.M. Barrie. Theatre Royal, Glasgow. May 2–May 7, 1927 (Mr. Dearth).
Heartbreak House, George Bernard Shaw. Theatre Royal, Glasgow. May 9–May 14, 1927 (Captain Shotover).
Intoxication, August Strindberg. Theatre Royal, Glasgow. May 16–May 18, 1927 (Adolphe).
The Circle, W. Somerset Maugham. Theatre Royal, Glasgow. May 19–May 24, 1927 (Clive Champion-Cheney).
Androcles and the Lion, George Bernard Shaw. Theatre Royal, Glasgow. May 25–May 31, 1927 (Ferrovius).
Uncle Vanya, Anton Chekhov. Theatre Royal, Glasgow. June 1–June 4, 1927 (Alexandr Serebryakov).
The Spook Sonota, August Strindberg. Globe Theatre, WE. June 14–June 16, 1927 (The Colonel). Two performances only.
The Spook Sonota, August Strindberg. Strand Theatre, WE. June 27–July 2, 1927 (The Colonel).
Uncle Vanya, Anton Chekhov. Oxford Playhouse, Oxford. July 30, August 9, August 10, 1927 (Alexandr Serebryakov).
The Circle, W. Somerset Maugham. Oxford Playhouse, Oxford. August 2, August 3, August 11, 1927 (Clive Champion-Cheney).
Twelfth Night. William Shakespeare. Oxford Playhouse, Oxford. August 4–August 6, 1927 (Malvolio).
Heartbreak House, George Bernard Shaw. Oxford Playhouse, Oxford. August 12–August 13, 1927 (Captain Shotover).
Heartbreak House, George Bernard Shaw. Oxford Playhouse, Oxford. October 17–October 22, 1927 (Captain Shotover).
From Morn to Midnight, Georg Kaiser. Oxford Playhouse, Oxford. October 24–October 29, 1927 (Stout Gentleman/Soldier/Waiter).
Easter, August Strindberg. Oxford Playhouse, Oxford. October 31–November 5, 1927 (Lindkvist).
Fantasio, Alfred de Musset. Oxford Playhouse, Oxford. November 7–November 12, 1927 (King of Bavaria).
Dr. Knock, Jules Romains. Oxford Playhouse, Oxford. November 14–November 19, 1927 (Dr. Knock).
The Adding Machine, Elmer Rice. Oxford Playhouse, Oxford. November 21–November 26, 1927 (Lieutenant Charles).

What Every Woman Knows, J.M. Barrie. Oxford Playhouse, Oxford. November 28–December 3, 1927 (John Shand).

The Rivals, Richard Brinsley Sheridan. Oxford Playhouse, Oxford. December 5–December 10, 1927 (Sir Lucius O'Trigger).

The Equator, Cecil Madden (from *L'Ombre du Mal*, H.R. Lenormand). R.A.D.A. Theatre, London. February 26, 1928 (Role unknown). The R.A.D.A. Players—One performance only.

Dr. Knock, Jules Romains. Oxford Playhouse, Oxford. February 27–March 3, 1928 (Dr. Knock).

The House of the Arrow, A.E.W. Mason. Golders Green Hippodrome, London. April 23–April 28, 1928 (Boris Waberski).

The House of the Arrow, A.E.W. Mason. The Empire Theatre, Newcastle. April 30–May 5, 1928 (Boris Waberski).

The House of the Arrow, A.E.W. Mason. The Royal Theatre, Portsmouth. May 7, 1928 (Boris Waberski). Tour cut short due to sudden availability of a London theatre.

The House of the Arrow, A.E.W. Mason. Vaudeville Theatre, WE. May 11–July 28, 1928 (Boris Waberski). Dennis Eadie left the show on June 3 and died on June 10—AN played the lead (Hanaud) until Edmund Gwenn took over on June 14.

The Comic Artist, Susan Glaspell & Norman Matson. Strand Theatre, WE. June 24, 1928 (An Old Coastguard). The Play Actors—One performance only.

Down Wind, C. Dudley Ward. Arts Theatre, London. July 15–July 16, 1928 (Colonel Oliver Tripp). Two performances only.

Ginevra, Giovacchino Forzano. Everyman Theatre, London. September 17–September 29, 1928 (Episcopal Vicar).

England's Elizabeth, Muriel St. Clare Byrne. R.A.D.A. Theatre, London. September 30, 1928 (William Cecil, afterwards Lord Burghley). R.A.D.A. Players—One performance only.

Out of the Sea, Don Marquis. Strand Theatre, London. November 23–December 1(Ernie Dunstan).

Dr. Knock, Jules Romains. Strand Theatre, London. December 6–December 15, 1928 (Dr. Knock).

Loyalties, John Galsworthy. Grand Theatre, Southampton. January 7–January 12, 1929 (General Canynge).

Justice, John Galsworthy. Grand Theatre, Southampton. January 7–January 12, 1929 (Mr. Justice Floyd/Capt. Danson V.C.).

Loyalties and *Justice* also played at:
    Theatre Royal. Bournemouth, January 14–January 19, 1929
    Gaiety Theatre, Hastings. January 21–January 26, 1929.
    Devonshire Park Theatre, Eastbourne. January 28–February 2, 1929.
    Grand Theatre, Croyden. February 4–February 9, 1929.
    Opera House, Harrowgate. February 11–February 16, 1929.
    Prince's Theatre, Manchester. February 18–February 23, 1929.
    King's Theatre, Edinburg. February 25–March 2, 1929.
    King's Theatre, Glasgow. March 4–March 9, 1929.
    Theatre Royal, Newcastle. March 11–March 16, 1929.
    Royal Court Theatre, Liverpool. March 18–March 23, 1929.
    Prince's Theatre, Bradford. March 25–March 30, 1929.
    Grand Theatre, Blackpool. April 1–April 6, 1929.
    Grand Theatre, Leeds. April 8–April 13, 1929.
    Theatre Royal, Huddersfield. April 15–April 20, 1929.
    Prince of Wales Theatre, Birmingham. April 22–April 27, 1929.
    Theatre Royal, Brighton. May 6–May 11, 1929.
    Royal Opera House, Leicester. May 13–May 18, 1929.

Bitter-Sweet, Noël Coward. Palace Theatre, Manchester. July 2–July 13, 1929 (The Marquis of Shayne).

Bitter-Sweet, Noël Coward. His Majesty's Theatre, WE. July 18, 1929–February 28, 1931 (The Marquis of Shayne). Transferred to Palace Theatre, WE. March 2–March 21, 1931. Transferred to the Streatham Hill Theatre, Streatham. March 23–April 4, 1931. Transferred to the Hippodrome, Golders Green. April 6–April 11, 1931. Transferred to the Lyceum Theatre, WE. April 13–May 9, 1931.

This Way to Paradise, Campbell Dixon. Daly's Theatre, WE. January 30–March 1, 1930 (Everard Webley).

Brain, Lionel Britton. Savoy Theatre, WE. April 27, 1930 (Professor). Masses Stage and Film Guild—One performance only.

The Devil and the Lady, Alfred Lord Tennyson. Arts Theatre Club, London. July 16–July 20, 1930 (Pharmaceutus). Five performances only.

Richard III, William Shakespeare. New Theatre, WE. September 1–September 27, 1930 (Edward IV, King of England). Transferred to Prince of Wales Theatre, WE October 6–October 18, 1930.

Chèri, Una, Lady Troubridge (from Colette & Léopold Marchand). Prince of Wales Theatre, WE. October 26–October 27, 1930 (Masseau). Stage Society—Two performances only.

The Borrowed Life, Gladys Parrish. Prince of Wales Theatre, WE. December 14–December 15, 1930 (Ivan Petrovitch Stanin). Stage Society—Two performances only.

Little Lord Fauntleroy, Frances Hodgson Burnett. Gate Theatre Studio, London. January 7–February 22, 1931 (Earl of Dorincourt).

Dark Hester, Walter Ferris. New Theatre, WE. April 27, 1931 (Major Ingpen). Charity Matinée for the Middlesex Hospital.

Marry at Leisure, Frank Vosper. Theatre Royal, Haymarket, WE. June 4–September 12, 1931 (Claude Spencer).

The Immortal Lady, Clifford Bax. Royalty Theatre, WE. October 9–November 14, 1931 (The Venetian Ambassador).

A-Hunting We Will Go, Phyllis Morris. Savoy Theatre, WE. November 8, 1931 (Sir Henry Cosham). Repertory Players—One performance only.

Marion's Crime (Hubert Stewart). Faculty of Arts Theatre, London. November 14, 1931 (Role unknown) Cave of Harmony Cabaret—One performance only.

The Home Front, Diana & Bruce Hamilton. Grafton Theatre, WE. November 29–November 30, 1931 (Nasmyth Sheldon). "G" Theatre Club—Two performances only.

The Traveller in the Dark, Charles Thomas. Savoy Theatre, WE. December 6, 1931 (Dr. Hardy). The Repertory Players—One performance only.

The Green Pack, Edgar Wallace. Wyndham's Theatre, WE. February 9–June 25, 1932 (Mark Elliot).

Security, Esmé Wynne-Tyson. Savoy Theatre, WE. March 13, 1932 (Sir Daniel Marchant). The Repertory Players—One performance only.

Shall We Join the Ladies? J.M. Barrie. Theatre Royal, Drury Lane, London. June 7, 1932 (Officer). Charity Matinée for the Hertford British Hospital in Paris.

Firebird, Lajos Zilahy (adapted by Jeffrey Dell). The Playhouse, WE. August 25–December 31, 1932 (Lovasdy).

Well, Gentlemen...? Gwladys Wheeler & Muriel St. Clare Byrne. Cambridge Theatre, WE. October 9, 1932 (Nevill Farrar). "G" Sunday Club—One performance only.

The Witch, John Masefield (from the Norwegian of Wiers-Jenssen), Little Theatre, WE. February 1–February 18, 1933 (Absalon).

The Lake, Dorothy Massingham with Murray MacDonald. Arts Theatre Club, London. March 1–March 5, 1933 (John Clayne).

The Lake, Dorothy Massingham with Murray MacDonald. Westminster Theatre, WE. March 15, 1933–May 27, 1933 (John Clayne). AN replaced P. Kynaston Reeves after filming *Loyalties*. Transferred to Piccadilly Theatre, WE. May 29–September 16, 1933.

Iron Flowers, Cecil Lewis. Shaftesbury Theatre, WE. November 5, 1933 (Thornton Tabard). The Repertory Players—One performance only.

Hay Fever, Noël Coward. Shaftesbury Theatre, WE. November 17–December 9, 1933 (Richard Greatham).

The Cherry Orchard, Anton Chekhov. Sadlers Wells Theatre, London. December 26–January 7, 1934 (Leonid Gayef). Old Vic Company—Two week revival.

Take Heed! Leslie Reade. Piccadilly Theatre, WE. January 28, 1934 (Professor Opal). The Progressive Players—One performance only.

Private Room, Naomi Royde-Smith. Westminster Theatre, London. February 23–April 28, 1934 (Mr. Wise).

Forsaking All Other, Edward Poor Montgomery. Shilling Theatre, Putney Bridge, London. May 14–May 19, 1934 (Sir John Craig). AN refers to this venue as the Fulham Grand when discussing the play, but the theatre was not given that name until 1937.

The Roof, John Galsworthy. Embassy Repertory Theatre, London. May 28–June 9, 1934 (Mr. Lennox).

Sweet Aloes, Jay Mallory (pseudonym of Joyce Carey). Opera House, Manchester. September 24–September 29, 1934 (Lord Farrington).

Sweet Aloes, Jay Mallory (pseudonym of Joyce Carey). Kings Theater, Edinburgh. October 22–October 29, 1934 (Lord Farrington).

Sweet Aloes, Jay Mallory (pseudonym of Joyce Carey). Wyndham's Theatre, WE. October 31, 1934–March 16, 1935 (Lord Farrington).

Take Heed! Leslie Reade. Arts Theatre Club, London. November 18 & November 25, 1934 (Professor Opal). Two performances only.

A Kiss for Cinderella, J.M. Barrie. His Majesty's Theatre, WE. November 22, 1934 (Footman). Gerald du Maurier Memorial Fund Matinée in aid of the Actors' Benevolent Fund—One performance only.

Fire-Works, Charles Windermere. Fortune Theatre, WE. February 24–February 25, 1935 (Bob Crosby). 1930 Players—Two performances only.

Richard II, William Shakespeare. The Old Vic, London. April 15–April 27, 1935 (John of Gaunt).

Sweet Aloes, Jay Mallory. Wyndham's Theatre, WE. May 4, 1935–February 8, 1936 (Lord Farrington). The play resumed its run after a seven-week hiatus caused by Diana Wynyard's operation for appendicitis.

Romeo and Juliet, William Shakespeare. New Theatre, WE. October 17–March 28, 1936 (Prince of Verona).

King at Arms, Evan John. St. Martins Theatre, WE. October 21, 1935 (Charles Windsor). Transferred to the Arts Theatre Club, London. October 27–October 28, 1935. R.A.D.A. Players—Three performances only.

Little Ol' Boy, Albert Bein. Arts Theatre Club, London. May 9–May 12, 1936 (Chock). Four performances only.

When the Bough Breaks, Henrietta Leslie & Laurier Lister. Arts Theatre Club, London. June 7, June 10–June 11, 1936 (Philip Causton). Three performances only.

Gentle Rain, Denison Clift & Frank Gregory. Vaudeville Theatre, WE. September 1–September 5, 1936 (Gray Blackett).

Time and the Hour, Alan Kennington & William McElwee. Arts Theatre Club, London. October 4–October 5, 1936 (Sir Thomas Vallance). New Shop Window—Two performances only.

The Wild Duck, Henrik Ibsen. Westminster Theatre, London. November 3–November 28, 1936 (Hjalmar Ekdal).

Because We Must, Ingaret Giffard. Wyndham's Theatre, WE. February 5–February 20, 1937 (Sir Basil Graham).

Heartbreak House, George Bernard Shaw. Westminster Theatre, London. March 9–April 3, 1937 (Hector Hushabye).

Crisis, Sydney Horler. 20th Century Theatre, Notting Hill Gate, London. April 8, 1937 (Dr. Richard Wingate). One performance only.

Judgment Day, Elmer Rice. Embassy Theatre, Swiss Cottage, London. May 19–May 31, 1937 (General Michael Rakovski).

Judgment Day, Elmer Rice. Strand Theatre, WE. June 2–July 3, 1937 (General Michael Rakovski). Transferred to Phoenix Theatre, WE. July 5–September 11, 1937.

Code of Honour, Vere Sullivan. King's Theatre Edinburgh. November 1–November 6, 1937 (General Count Armin von Ahlenfeld). The play eventually opened in London in July 1938 under the title *Trumpeter, Play!* with Malcolm Keen in AN's role.

Identity Unknown. Jean Anouilh. Duke of York's Theatre, WE. December 5, December 12, December 19, 1937 (George Fox). London International Theatre Club—Three performances only.

Land's End, F.L. Lucas. Westminster Theatre, London. February 23–March 19, 1938 (Hugh Gifford).

The Zeal of Thy House, Dorothy L. Sayers. Westminster Theatre, London. March 29–April 30, 1938 (Archangel Michael).

No Sky So Blue, Henry C. James & Ian Grant & Edward Horan. Opera House, Manchester. May 23–May 28, 1938 (Boris Rachinoff). Royal Theater, Newcastle. May 30–June 4, 1938.

No Sky So Blue, Henry C. James & Ian Grant & Edward Horan. Savoy Theatre, WE. June 8–July 16, 1938 (Boris Rachinoff).

… And Life Burns On, Virginia Isham & Richard George. Arts Theatre Club, London. July 10–July 11, 1938 (Sir Gilbert Keston). Two performances only.

The Old Master, Henry Bernard. Q Theatre, London. August 29–September 3, 1938 (General Sir John Leslie).

The Shoemaker's Holiday, Thomas Dekker. The Playhouse Theatre, WE. November 4–December 10, 1938 (The King).

Take Heed! Leslie Reade. Arts Theatre Club, London. December 6–December 18, 1938 (Professor Opal).

Charley's Aunt, Brandon Thomas. Theatre Royal, Haymarket, WE. December 24, 1938–January 21, 1939 (Colonel Sir Francis Chesney).

Lady in Waiting, Margery Sharp. McCarter Theater, Princeton. March 16, 1940 (Sir William Warring). National Theater, Washington. March 18–March 23, 1940 (Sir Willaim Warring).

Lady in Waiting, Margery Sharp. Martin Beck Theater, New York. March 27–June 8, 1940 (Sir William Warring).

Lady in Waiting also played at:
    Wilbur Theater, Boston. October 7–October 19, 1940.
    Locust Theater, Philadelphia. October 21–November 2, 1940.
    Cass Theater, Detroit. November 4–November 9, 1940.
    Harris Theater, Chicago. November 11–November 30, 1940.
    American Theater, St. Louis. December 2–December 7, 1940.
    Royal Alexandra Theatre, Toronto. December 9–December 14, 1940.
    Hanna Theater, Cleveland. December 23–December 28, 1940.
    Erlanger Theater, Buffalo. December 30, 1940–January 1, 1941.
    Masonic Auditorium, Rochester. January 2, 1941.
    Erie Theater, Schenectady. January 3, 1941.

Shall We Join the Ladies? J.M. Barrie. Drury Lane Theatre, London. October 26, 1948 (Mr. Gourlay). All-Star R.A.D.A. Matinée for the Rebuilding Fund of the R.A.D.A. Theatre—One performance only.

And So to Bed, J.B. Fagan. The Stage, Los Angeles. December 29, 1948–March 29, 1949 (Charles II). The play was extended past its original closing date and AN left the show on February 9. He was replaced by Dennis Hoey.

Gertie, Enid Bagnold. Shubert Theater, New Haven. January 10–January 12, 1952 (Mr. Ritchie).

Gertie, Enid Bagnold. Plymouth Theater, Boston. January 14–January 26, 1952 (Mr. Ritchie).

Gertie, Enid Bagnold. Plymouth Theater, New York. January 30–February 2, 1952 (Mr. Ritchie).

Libel! Edward Wooll. Bahama Playhouse, Nassau, Bahamas. March 9–March 14, 1952 (Hon. Sir Arthur Tuttington).

Dial "M" For Murder, Frederick Knott. Wilbur Theater, Boston. October 26, 1952–January 17, 1953 (Inspector Hubbard).

Dial "M" For Murder, Frederick Knott. Cass Theater, Detroit. January 19–January 24, 1953 (Inspector Hubbard).

Dial "M" For Murder, Frederick Knott. Harris Theater, Chicago. January 26–May 15, 1953 (Inspector Hubbard).

Dial "M" For Murder, Frederick Knott. La Jolla Playhouse, La Jolla. August 25–August 30, 1953 (Inspector Hubbard).

Coriolanus, William Shakespeare. Phoenix Theater, New York. January 19–February 28, 1954 (Menenius Agrippa).

Please Communicate, Mary Oldfield. Pasadena Playhouse, Pasadena. June 30–July 24, 1955 (Dr. Stevens).

Too Late the Phalarope, Robert Yale Libbott. Belasco Theater, New York. October 11–November 10, 1956 (Captain Massingham).

The Song of Galilee, Joan Wilcoxon. Miles Playhouse, Santa Monica. March 27–April 3, 1958 (Pilate).

The Gioconda Smile, Aldous Huxley. Beverly Hills Playhouse, Los Angeles. June 27–July 27, 1958 (Dr. Libbard). AN also directed.

The Nativity Play, Joan Wilcoxon. Santa Monica Civic Auditorium, Santa Monica. December 19, 20 & 30, 1958 (Archbishop).

The Song of Galilee, Joan Wilcoxon. Salt Lake LDS Tabernacle, Salt Lake City. March 27–March 28, 1959 (Pilate). Three performances only.

Back to Methuselah, George Bernard Shaw. Ritz Theater, Los Angeles. September 20, 1959 (Narrated as George Bernard Shaw). A "concert reading" benefit for the LA Civic Theatre Foundation.

Murder in the Cathedral, T.S. Eliot. Schoenberg Hall, UCLA, Los Angeles. January 19, 1960–January 31, 1960 (Third Knight/Tempter). Theatre Group—Twelve performances only.

The Three Sisters, Anton Chekhov. Schoenberg Hall, UCLA, Los Angeles. August 3, 1960–August 20, 1960 (Tchebutykin). Theatre Group—Eighteen performances only.

Measure for Measure, William Shakespeare. Schoenberg Hall, UCLA, Los Angeles. January 15, 1962–February 7, 1962 (Escalus). Theatre Group—Twenty-four performances only.

Under Milk Wood, Dylan Thomas. Beverly Hills Playhouse, Los Angeles. June 6–July 8, 1961 (Narrator/Captain Cat). AN left the cast on June 27 and was replaced by Dennis King, Jr.

The Hostage, Brendan Behan. Rustic Canyon Theatre, Santa Monica. April 3–April 26, 1964 (Monsewer). Performances Friday, Saturday, Sunday only.

Twelfth Night, William Shakespeare. Rustic Canyon Theatre, Los Angeles. June 12–June 13, 1965 (Malvolio). Two invited performances were given before intermittent performances were booked into various area universities starting on June 14, 1965, at the NPI Auditorium at UCLA's Semel Institute.

The Deputy, Rolf Hochhuth. Schoenberg Hall, UCLA, Los Angeles. August 13–October 9, 1965 (Count Fontana).

Twelfth Night, William Shakespeare. Huntington Hartford Theater, Los Angeles. April 17, 1966 (Malvolio).

A Series of Shakespearean Scenes, William Shakespeare. Rustic Canyon Park, Santa Monica. August 27, 1967 (Various). An entertainment devised by AN in collaboration with the Palisades Symphony.

Affairs of State, Louis Verneuil. Ivanhoe Theater, Chicago. August 13–September 22, 1968 (Philip Russell).

Under Milk Wood, Dylan Thomas. New Hope Inn, Santa Monica. June 6–July 7, 1969 (Narrator/Eli Jenkins).

Under Milk Wood, Dylan Thomas. New Hope Inn, Santa Monica. February 5–March 22, 1970 (Narrator/Eli Jenkins).

Heartbreak House, George Bernard Shaw. Jolly Rogue Restaurant, San Simeon. March 5–March 8, 1975 (Captain Shotover). AN also directed.

Heartbreak House, George Bernard Shaw. L.A. Finnish Center, North Hollywood. February 21–March 3, 1985 (Captain Shotover).

On the Big Screen (Films)

Film are listed in chronological order, and include studio, year of release, director, principal cast and role played by Alan Napier.

Caste. United Artists, 1930. Dir. Campbell Gullan. Principal Cast: Nora Swinburne, Sebastian Shaw. AN Role: Captain Hawtree.

Stamboul. Paramount British, 1931. Dir. Dmitri Buchowetski. Principal Cast: Warwick Ward, Rosita Moreno. AN Role: Bouchier.

In a Monastery Garden. Twickenham, 1932. Dir. Maurice Elvey. Principal Cast: John Stuart, Jean Maude. AN Role: Count Romano.

Loyalties. Associated Talking Pictures, 1933. Dir. Basil Dean. Principal Cast: Basil Rathbone, Heather Thatcher. AN Role: General Canynge.

Wings Over Africa. Premier-Stafford, 1936. Dir. Ladislaus Vajda. Principal Cast: Joan Gardner, Ian Colin. AN Role: Redfern.

For Valour. Capital, 1937. Dir. Tom Walls. Principal Cast: Tom Walls, Ralph Lynn, Veronica Rose. AN Role: General.

The Wife of General Ling. Premier-Stafford, 1937. Dir. Ladislaus Vajda. Principal Cast: Griffith Jones, Valery Inkijinoff. AN Role: Governor.

The Four Just Men (U.S. Title: *The Secret Four*). Ealing, 1939. Dir. Walter Forde. Principal Cast: Hugh Sinclair. AN Role: Sir Hamar Ryman.

We Are Not Alone. Warner Bros., 1939. Dir. Edmund Goulding. Principal Cast: Paul Muni, Jane Bryan, Flora Robson. AN Role: Archdeacon.

The Invisible Man Returns. Universal, 1940. Dir. Joe May. Principal Cast: Cedric Hardwicke, Vincent Price. AN Role: Willie Spears.

The House of the Seven Gables. Universal, 1940. Dir. Joe May. Principal Cast: George Sanders, Margaret Lindsay. AN Role: Fuller.

Eagle Squadron. Universal, 1942. Dir. Arthur Lubin. Principal Cast: Robert Stack, Diane Barrymore. AN Role: Black Watch Officer.

A Yank at Eton. MGM, 1942. Dir. Norman Taurog. Principal Cast: Mickey Rooney, Edmund Gwenn, Ian Hunter. AN Role: Restauranteur.

Random Harvest. MGM, 1942. Dir. Mervin LeRoy. Principal Cast: Ronald Colman, Greer Garson, Philip Dorn. AN Role: Julian.

Cat People. RKO, 1942. Dir. Jacques Tourneur. Principal Cast: Simone Simon, Kent Smith, Tom Conway. AN Role: Doc Carver.

Assignment in Brittany. MGM, 1943. Dir. Jack Conway. Principal Cast: Jean-Pierre Aumont, Susan Peters, Richard Whorf. AN Role: Sam Wells.

Appointment in Berlin. Columbia, 1943. Dir. Alfred E. Green. Principal Cast: George Sanders, Marguerite Chapman. AN Role: Colonel Patterson.

Lassie Come Home. MGM, 1943. Dir. Fred M. Wilcox. Principal Cast: Roddy McDowell, Donald Crisp, Dame May Whitty. AN Role: Jock.

Lost Angel. MGM, 1943. Dir. Roy Rowland. Principal Cast: Margaret O'Brien, James Craig, Marsha Hunt. AN Role: Dr. Woodring.

The Song of Bernadette. 20th Century–Fox, 1943. Dir. Henry King. Principal Cast: Jennifer Jones, Charles Bickford. AN Role: Dr. Debeau.

The Uninvited. Paramount, 1944. Dir. Lewis Allen. Principal Cast: Ray Milland, Ruth Hussey, Donald Crisp. AN Role: Dr. Scott.

Action in Arabia. RKO, 1944. Dir. Leonide Moguy. Principal Cast: George Sanders, Virginia Bruce, Lenore Aubert. AN Role: Eric Latimer.

The Hairy Ape. United Artists, 1944. Dir. Alfred Santell. Principal Cast: William Bendix, Susan Hayward, John Loder. AN Role: Chief Engineer.

Ministry of Fear. Paramount, 1944. Dir. Fritz Lang. Principal Cast: Ray Milland, Marjorie Reynolds, Carl Esmond. AN Role: Dr. Forrester.

Thirty Seconds Over Tokyo. MGM, 1944. Dir. Mervyn LeRoy. Principal Cast: Van Johnson, Robert Walker, Spencer Tracy. AN Role: Mr. Parker.

Dark Waters. United Artists, 1944. Dir. Andre De Toth. Principal Cast: Merle Oberon, Franchot Tone, Thomas Mitchell. AN Role: Doctor.

Mademoiselle Fifi. RKO, 1944. Dir. Robert Wise. Principal Cast: Simone Simon, John Emery, Kurt Kreuger. AN Role: The Count de Breville.

Hangover Square. 20th Century–Fox, 1945. Dir. John Brahm. Principal Cast: Laird Cregar, Linda Darnell. AN Role: Sir Henry Chapman.

Isle of the Dead. RKO, 1945. Dir. Mark Robson. Principal Cast: Boris Karloff, Ellen Drew, Marc Cramer. AN Role: St. Aubyn.

Three Strangers. Warner Bros., 1946. Dir. Jean Negulesco. Principal Cast: Sydney Greenstreet, Peter Lorre. AN Role: David Shackleford.

House of Horrors. Universal, 1946. Dir. Jean Yarbrough. Principal Cast: Bill Goodwin, Robert Lowery. AN Role: F. Holmes Harmon.

A Scandal in Paris. United Artists, 1946. Dir. Douglas Sirk. Principal Cast: George Sanders, Signe Hasso. AN Role: Houdon De Pierremont.

The Strange Woman. United Artists, 1946. Dir. Edgar Ulmer. Principal Cast: Hedy Lamarr, Dennis Hoey. AN Role: Judge Henry Saladine.

Sinbad the Sailor. RKO, 1947. Dir. Richard Wallace. Principal Cast: Douglas Fairbanks, Jr., Maureen O'Hara, Anthony Quinn. AN Role: Aga.

Fiesta. MGM, 1947. Dir. Richard Thorpe. Principal Cast: Esther Williams, Akim Tamiroff, Ricardo Montalban. AN Role: The Tourist.

High Conquest. Monogram, 1947. Dir. Irving Allen. Principal Cast: Anna Lee, Gilbert Roland, Warren Douglas. AN Role: Tommy Donlin.

Ivy. Universal, 1947. Dir. Sam Wood. Principal Cast: Joan Fontaine, Patric Knowles, Herbert Marshall. AN Role: Sir Jonathan Wright.

Adventure Island. Paramount, 1947. Dir. Peter Stewart. Principal Cast: Rory Calhoun, Rhonda Fleming, Paul Kelly. AN Role: Attwater.

Lured. United Artists, 1947. Dir. Douglas Sirk. Principal Cast: George Sanders, Lucille Ball, Boris Karloff. AN Role: Detective Gordon.

Driftwood. Republic, 1947. Dir. Allan Dwan. Principal Cast: Ruth Warrick, Walter Brennan, Dean Jagger. AN Role: Dr. Nicholas Adams.

Unconquered. Paramount, 1947. Dir. Cecil B. DeMille. Principal Cast: Gary Cooper, Paulette Goddard. AN Role: Sir William Johnson.

Forever Amber. 20th Century–Fox, 1947. Dir. Otto Preminger. Principal Cast: Linda Darnell, Cornel Wilde, Richard Greene. AN Role: Landale.

The Lone Wolf in London. Columbia, 1947. Dir. Leslie Goodwins. Principal Cast: Gerald Mohr, Nancy Saunders. AN Role: Monty Beresford.

Johnny Belinda. Warner Bros., 1948. Dir. Jean Negulesco. Principal Cast: Jane Wyman, Lew Ayres. AN Role: Defense Attorney.

Macbeth. Republic, 1948. Dir. Orson Welles. Principal Cast: Orson Welles, Jeannette Nolan, Dan O'Herlihy. AN Role: The Holy Friar.

Joan of Arc. RKO, 1948. Dir. Victor Fleming. Principal Cast: Ingrid Bergman, Jose Ferrer, Francis L. Sullivan. AN Role: Earl of Warwick.

Hills of Home. MGM, 1948. Dir. Fred M. Wilcox. Principal Cast: Edmund Gwenn, Donald Crisp, Tom Drake. AN Role: Sir George.

Criss Cross. Universal, 1949. Dir. Robert Siodmak. Principal Cast: Burt Lancaster, Yvonne De Carlo, Dan Duryea. AN Role: Finchley.

My Own True Love. Paramount, 1949. Dir. Compton Bennett. Principal Cast: Melvyn Douglas, Phyllis Calvert. AN Role: Kittredge.

Tarzan's Magic Fountain. RKO, 1949. Dir. Lee Sholom. Principal Cast: Lex Barker, Brenda Joyce, Evelyn Ankers. AN Role: Douglas Jessup.

A Connecticut Yankee in King Arthur's Court. Paramount, 1949. Dir. Tay Garnett. Principal Cast: Bing Crosby. AN Role: Executioner.

Manhandled. Paramount, 1949. Dir. Lewis R. Foster. Principal Cast: Dan Duryea, Dorothy Lamour, Sterling Hayden. AN Role: Alton Bennet.

The Red Danube. MGM, 1949. Dir. George Sidney. Principal Cast: Walter Pidgeon, Ethel Barrymore, Peter Lawford. AN Role: The General.

Challenge to Lassie. MGM, 1949. Dir. Richard Thorpe. Principal Cast: Edmund Gwenn, Donald McBride. AN Role: Lord Provost.

Master Minds. Monogram, 1949. Dir. Jean Yarbrough. Principal Cast: Leo Gorcey, Huntz Hall, Glenn Strange. AN Role: Dr. Druzik.

Tripoli. Paramount, 1950. Dir. Will Price. Principal Cast: Maureen O'Hara, John Payne, Howard Da Silva, Philip Reed. AN Role: Khalil.

Tarzan's Peril. RKO, 1951. Dir. Byron Haskin. Principal Cast: Lex Barker, Virginia Huston, George Macready. AN Role: Commissioner Peters.

Double Crossbones. Universal, 1951. Dir. Charles T. Barton. Principal Cast: Donald O'Connor, Helena Carter. AN Role: Captain Kidd.

The Great Caruso. MGM, 1951. Dir. Richard Thorpe. Principal Cast: Mario Lanza, Ann Blyth, Jarmila Novotna. AN Role: Jean de Reske.

The Highwayman. Allied Artists, 1951. Dir. Lesley Selander. Principal Cast: Charles Coburn, Wanda Hendrix, Philip Friend. AN Role: Barton.

Across the Wide Missouri. MGM, 1951. Dir. William Wellman. Principal Cast: Clark Gable, Ricardo Montalban. AN Role: Humberstone.

The Blue Veil. RKO, 1951. Dir. Curtis Bernhardt. Principal Cast: Jane Wyman, Charles Laughton. AN Role: Professor George Carter.

The Strange Door. Universal, 1951. Dir. Richard Pevney. Principal Cast: Charles Laughton, Boris Karloff, Sally Forrest. AN Role: Count Grassin.

Big Jim McLain. Warner Bros., 1952. Dir. Edward Ludwig. Principal Cast: John Wayne, Nancy Olson, James Arness. AN Role: Sturak.

Young Bess. MGM, 1953. Dir. George Sidney. Principal Cast: Jean Simmons, Stewart Granger, Deborah Kerr. AN Role: Robert Tyrwhitt.

Julius Caesar. MGM, 1953. Dir. Joseph Mankiewicz. Principal Cast: Marlon Brando, James Mason, John Gielgud. AN Role: Cicero.

Désirée. 20th Century–Fox, 1954. Dir. Henry Koster. Principal Cast: Marlon Brando, Jean Simmons, Merle Oberon. AN Role: Despreaux.

Moonfleet. MGM, 1955. Dir. Fritz Lang. Principal Cast: Stewart Granger, George Sanders, Joan Greenwood. AN Role: Parson Glennie.

The Queen's Guard. 20th Century–Fox, 1955. Dir. Carl Dudley. AN Role: Narrator.

The Court Jester. Paramount, 1955. Dir. Norman Panama & Melvin Frank. Principal Cast: Danny Kaye, Glynis Johns. AN Role: Sir Brockhurst.

Miami Exposé. Columbia, 1956. Dir. Fred F. Sears. Principal Cast: Lee J. Cobb, Patricia Medina, Edward Arnold. AN Role: Raymond Sheriden.

The Mole People. Universal, 1956. Dir. Virgil Vogel. Principal Cast: John Agar, Cynthia Patrick. AN Role: Elinu, the High Priest.

Until They Sail. MGM, 1957. Dir. Robert Wise. Principal Cast: Jean Simmons, Joan Fontaine, Paul Newman. AN Role: Prosecuting Attorney.

Island of Lost Women. Warner Bros., 1959. Dir. Frank W. Tuttle. Principal Cast: Jeff Richards, Venetia Stevenson. AN Role: Dr. Paul Lujan.

Journey to the Center of the Earth. 20th Century–Fox, 1959. Dir. Henry Levin. Principal Cast: Pat Boone. AN Role: Edinburgh University Dean.

Wild in the Country. 20th Century–Fox, 1961. Dir. Philip Dunne. Principal Cast: Elvis Presley, Hope Lange. AN Role: Professor Larson.

Tender is the Night. 20th Century–Fox, 1962. Dir. Henry King. Principal Cast: Jennifer Jones, Jason Robards, Jr. AN Role: Señor Pardo.

Premature Burial. American International, 1962. Dir. Roger Corman. Principal Cast: Ray Milland, Hazel Court. AN Role: Dr. Gideon Gault.

The Sword in the Stone. Buena Vista, 1963. Dir. Wolfgang Reitherman. Principal Cast: Sebastian Cabot, Richie Serenson. AN Role: Sir Pellinore.

Marnie. Universal, 1964. Dir. Alfred Hitchcock. Principal Cast: Tippi Hedren, Sean Connery, Dianne Baker, Martin Gabel. AN Role: Mr. Rutland.
Mary Poppins. Buena Vista, 1964. Dir. Robert Stevenson. Principal Cast: Julie Andrews, Dick Van Dyke. AN Role: Huntsman/Reporter #3/Hound.
My Fair Lady. Warner Bros., 1964. Dir. George Cukor. Principal Cast: Audrey Hepburn, Rex Harrison, Stanley Halloway. AN Role: Eliza's Escort.
36 Hours. MGM, 1964. Dir. George Seaton. Principal Cast: James Garner, Rod Taylor, Eva Marie Saint. AN Role: Colonel Peter MacLean.
Signpost to Murder. MGM, 1964. Dir. George Englund. Principal Cast: Joanne Woodward, Stuart Whitman. AN Role: The Vicar.
The Smithsonian Institution. IBM, 1965. Dir. Charles & Ray Eames. AN Role: Davies Gilbert, President of The Royal Society.
The Loved One. MGM, 1965. Dir. Tony Richardson. Principal Cast: Robert Morse, Jonathan Winters. AN Role: English Club Official.
Batman: The Movie. 20th Century–Fox, 1966. Dir. Leslie H. Martinson. Principal Cast: Adam West, Burt Ward, Cesar Romero. AN Role: Alfred.

On the Small Screen (Television)

Television credits are in chronological order by airdate. Series name is followed by episode title, network, airdate and role played by Alan Napier (in parentheses). In the case of a continuing role in a series, individual episode titles are not listed. TV movies are identified as "MOW" (Movie of the Week).

Your Show Time, "The Adventure of the Speckled Band." NBC. March 25, 1949 (Sherlock Holmes).
A Christmas Carol (Special). NBC. December 25, 1951 (Charles Dickens).
Chevron Theatre, "Playmates." Syndicated. June 6, 1952 (Uncle Steven).
The Schaefer Century Theatre, "Playmates." Syndicated. August 20, 1952 (Uncle Steven).
Chevron Theater, "The Whistling Room." Syndicated. August 22, 1952 (Ghost Catcher).
Cavalcade of America, "Poor Richard." NBC. October 1, 1952 (Lord Howe).
Biff Baker, U.S.A., "Mona Lisa." CBS. December 11, 1952 (Professor Beechem).
Four Star Playhouse, "The Man on the Train." CBS. January 15, 1953 (John Dwerrihouse).
The Ray Milland Show, "Skylark." CBS. November 5, 1953 (Dr. Sandine).
Letter to Loretta, "The Bronte Story." NBC. November 15, 1953 (Mr. Bronte).
The Pepsi-Cola Playhouse, "Farewell Performance." ABC. January 22, 1954 (Inspector).
The Pepsi-Cola Playhouse, "The Whistling Room." ABC. July 18, 1954 (Ghost Catcher).
The Pepsi-Cola Playhouse, "Playmates." ABC. August 29, 1954 (Uncle Steven).
Front Row Center, "Outward Bound." CBS. August 10, 1955 (Reverend Thompson).
Lux Video Theatre, "The Lucky Finger." CBS. September 15, 1955 (Sir Adrian).
Alfred Hitchcock Presents, "Into Thin Air." CBS. October 30, 1955 (Sir Everett).
The 20th Century–Fox Hour, "Deception." CBS. March 7, 1956 (Governor).
Alfred Hitchcock Presents, "Whodunit." CBS. March 25, 1956 (Wilfred).
The 20th Century–Fox Hour, "The Empty Room." CBS. May 30, 1956 (Sir Edward).
NBC Matinee Theater, "Perfect Alibi." NBC. August 10, 1956 (Arthur Ludgrove).
The 20th Century–Fox Hour, "Operation Cicero." CBS. December 26, 1956 (Travers).
Telephone Time, "The Consort." CBS. January 27, 1957 (Lord Melbourne).
Soldiers of Fortune, "A Gift of Death." Syndicated. February 17, 1957 (Commissioner Hartledge).
Alfred Hitchcock Presents, "I Killed the Count Part 1." CBS. March 17, 1957 (Lord Sorrington).
Alfred Hitchcock Presents, "I Killed the Count Part 2." CBS. March 24, 1957 (Lord Sorrington).
Alfred Hitchcock Presents, "I Killed the Count Part 3." CBS. March 31, 1957 (Lord Sorrington).

Panic!, "Reincarnated." NBC. July 2, 1957 (Vincent Hawthorne).
The Californians, "The Vigilantes Begin." NBC. September 24, 1957 (Alfred Perkins).
General Electric Theater, "Mischief at Bandy Leg." CBS. November 3, 1957 (Sean O'Donnell).
NBC Matinee Theater, "The Little Minister." NBC. December 26, 1957 (Tammas Whammond).
NBC Matinee Theater, "Death Takes a Holiday." NBC. April 8, 1958 (Unknown Role).
General Electric Theater, "And One Was Loyal." CBS. January 4, 1959 (Jack Simmons).
Playhouse 90, "The Wings of the Dove." CBS. January 8, 1959 (Sir Luke Strett).
The Third Man, "Dark Island" NBC/BBC. March 10, 1959 (Colonel Andresi).
Alfred Hitchcock Presents, "The Avon Diamonds." CBS. March 22, 1959 (Sir Charles Harrington).
Five Fingers, "The Unknown Town." NBC. October 24, 1959 (Wembley).
The Detectives, "The Bait." ABC. November 20, 1959 (Bishop).
Five Fingers, "Thin Ice." NBC. December 19, 1959 (Wembley).
Shirley Temple Theatre, "Kim." NBC. September 25, 1960 (Colonel Devlin).
Thriller, "The Purple Room." NBC. October 25, 1960 (Lawyer Ridgewater).
The Case of the Dangerous Robin, "The Bard Disappears." Syndicated. November 29, 1960 (Professor).
Adventures in Paradise, "Daughter of Illusion." ABC. December 12, 1960 (Alex).
Thriller, "Hay-Fork and Bill-Hook." NBC. February 7, 1961 (Constable Evans).
The Roaring 20's, "Black Saturday." ABC. February 11, 1961 (Mr. Dunston).
Thriller, "Dark Legacy." NBC. May 30, 1961 (Attorney Pinchot).
Tales of Wells Fargo, "The Dowry." NBC. July 10, 1961 (Bertram La Tour).
Assassination Plot in Teheran (MOW). ABC. September 23 & September 30, 1961 (Wilfred Morely). Two hour pilot aired in two parts as a "special."
Follow the Sun, "Annie Beeler's Place." ABC. February 11, 1962 (Julian "The Major" Mosgrove).
The New Bob Cummings Show, "North by Southeast." February 22, 1962 (Inspector Templeton).
Checkmate, "A Chant of Silence." CBS. March 21, 1962 (Father Dunne).
Tales of Wells Fargo, "Remember the Yazoo." NBC. April 14, 1962 (Colonel Decatur).
Don't Call Me Charlie, 18 Episodes. NBC. September 21, 1962–January 25, 1963 (General Steele).
Aloca Premiere, "Impact of an Execution." ABC. January 3, 1963 (Judge Cameron).
The Lloyd Bridges Show, "The Sheriden Square." CBS. March 19, 1963 (Kurt Drobary).
The Alfred Hitchcock Hour, "An Out for Oscar." CBS. April 5, 1963 (Mr. Hodges).
The Twilight Zone, "Passage on the Lady Anne." CBS. May 9, 1963 (Captain Protheroe).
The Eleventh Hour, "This Wonderful Madman Calls Me Beauty." NBC. November 20, 1963 (Arnold Todhunter).
Bob Hope Presents The Chrysler Theatre, "The Fifth Passenger." NBC. November 29, 1963 (Sherwood).
Breaking Point, "So Many Pretty Girls, So Little Time." ABC. February 17, 1964 (Harold Major).
The Rogues, "Money is for Burning." NBC. January 3, 1965 (John McKellway).
The Alfred Hitchcock Hour, "Thou Still Unravished Bride." NBC. March 22, 1965 (Guerny, Sr.).
Daniel Boone, "Cain's Birthday: Part 2." NBC. April 8, 1965 (Colonel Sir Hubert Crater).
Vacation Playhouse, "The Barbara Rush Show." CBS. July 9, 1965 (Businessman).
Moment of Fear, "Farewell Performance." NBC. July 20, 1965 (Inspector).
Loredo, "The Land Grabbers." NBC. December 9, 1965 (Major Donaldson).
Daniel Boone, "Perilous Journey." NBC. December 16, 1965 (Lord Brisbane).
Daktari, "The Killer Lion." CBS. January 25, 1966 (Roger Ealing).
Batman, 120 episodes. ABC. January 12, 1966–March 14, 1968 (Alfred). AN also played Alfred's cousin, Egbert, in "The Joker's Provokers" airing November 17, 1966.
The Beverly Hillbillies, "The Clampetts in London." CBS. September 13, 1967 (Chemist).
Family Affair, "Oh, to Be in England." CBS. January 27, 1969 (Mr. Wilson).
Ironside, "Return to Fiji." NBC. February 12, 1970 (Walter Branford).
Night Gallery, "House, With Ghost." November 17, 1971 (Doctor).
Night Gallery, "The Sins of the Fathers." February 23, 1972 (The Man).
Night Gallery, "Fright Night." October 15, 1972 (Cousin Zachariah).

Ironside, "All About Andrea." NBC. February 22, 1973 (Marcus Lowell).
Crime Club (MOW). CBS. March 6, 1973 (John, the Butler).
QB VII (Mini-Series). ABC. April 29, 1974 (Semple).
The Wide World of Mystery, "Come Die with Me" (MOW). ABC. May 14, 1974 (Lawyer).
Ironside, "The Lost Cotillion." NBC. October 21, 1974 (John).
The Lives of Benjamin Franklin, "The Whirlwind." CBS. December 17, 1974 (Petitioner).
Kojak, "The Forgotten Room." CBS. January 4, 1976 (Antonakis).
Walt Disney's Wonderful World of Color, "The Golden Dog." NBC. January 2, 1977 (Archie).
The Bastard (MOW). *Operation Primetime*. May 22, 1978 (Dr. Bleeker).
Flying High, "Beautiful People." CBS. November 17, 1978 (Arthur).
The Paper Chase, "The Sorcerer's Apprentice." CBS. December 5, 1978 (Justice Allen Reynolds).
Centennial, "The Crime" (Mini-Series). NBC. January 21, 1979 (Lord Venneford).
ABC Weekend Specials, "The Contest Kid Strikes Again." ABC. September 22, 1979 (Hawkins).
Joe Dancer II: The Monkey Mission (MOW). NBC. March 23, 1981 (Briarton).
The Late Show, "Batman Reunion." Fox. April 28, 1988 (Guest).

Appendix B

How to Approach a Production of Shaw's Heartbreak House

Alan Napier

Alan wrote the following in 1985 for distribution to the cast of the play. The note at the end was included in the program for the benefit of the audience.

As a very young man I appeared in a triumphant production of HEARTBREAK HOUSE with the famous Oxford Players Company directed by James Bernard Fagan, friend of Shaw, and the play's original London director. I played Captain Shotover: my stock in trade was playing extraordinary old men.

A year later the production was revived for a successful six week season in Glasgow. [*Alan has this backward. Fagan's Glasgow production came first, in May 1927, followed by two revivals in Oxford: A two-day special presentation in August, and a full week in October.*]

During the next few years I appeared in many of the plays of GBS, for whose work I had a natural affinity.

In 1937 I was invited to play Hector Hushabye in a London revival at the Westminster Theatre, personally supervised by Shaw himself. He was good enough to say that I was the first actor to play Hector right. Under Shaw's firm but kindly guidance the play was rapturously received.

Since then I have given many readings of the play, and last Spring I directed a production at San Simeon in which I also appeared as Shotover.

I can safely claim that no other actor has ever played Hector and Shotover and been directed in the play by Shaw himself. With these unique qualifications, I submit the following observations.

The first order of business will be to ignore totally the author's suggestion that Heartbreak House is a play in the Russian manner. Shaw could no more write like Chekhov than Chekhov could write like Shaw.

In Chekhov the essence is often implicit—implied between the lines and in pregnant silences. In Shaw all is explicit in the lines and there are no silences. While Chekhov's characters commune with themselves in the soft light of a tender probing spirit, Shaw's battle valiantly in the flashing out and thrust of winged words in the arc light of a vivacious intellect.

The moral for actors desiring to play Shaw is as plain as a pikestaff: Say the lines loud and clear, fully understanding and relishing the muscular prose in which they are written.

There must be more to it than that? No. Not really. Though "that," by the way, is not so easy: it requires proper voice production, clear articulation, and great intellectual energy. However, to satisfy our modern thinking actors, as opposed to the drinking actors of yesteryear (of the thinking Dunns and the drinking Dunns of H.H.), I hasten to supply motivation for my present approach—motivation without which we rightly fear to tread the turbulent waves of dramas nowadays.

First, we must recognize that Shaw is a caricaturist, not a portrait painter. His people are more articulate and vivid than in real life. But this does not mean that they are not real: caricature can etch deeper than surface portraiture and it achieves its effect with clean hard lines. For the actor this means that no "ers" or "ums" or little tricks of decorative naturalism are permitted. Any tampering with the text will only blur Shaw's dashing line.

And now for the admonition: to speak loud and clear. Shaw makes it easy. He supplies the motivation, for he is a master at creating situations of confrontation which demand aggressive speech. Furthermore, most of his characters have robust egos.

Let us examine the play from page one on and see how these assertions work out in practice for the actor.

Ellie is a strong character. Oh yes! Mazzini may have brought her up to be a little lady, but when her heart is broken—and it is: this is very real—though she nearly faints what does she do? Burst into tears? No! She damns herself for being such a fool. So this strong character Ellie opens the play with sixty seconds of "Russian manner" silence. But when she wakes to find Nurse Guinness asking her who she is, she protests her reception and treatment at Heartbreak House loudly and clearly.

As for Guinness, she is accustomed to shouting. She knows Captain Shotover is a bit deaf—or only hears what he wants to—so she has to shout to get through to him. And, as none of the bells work, to save her old legs she shouts upstairs to Hesione and downstairs to the kitchen.

So we have started the play off with reasonable vigor. And then Shaw plays his trick, repeated again and again throughout the play, of railing the energy and vocal level by bringing on Captain Shotover—Shotover, that supernatural old man, father of two demon daughters. At one point he says, "I've stood on the bridge for eighteen hours in a typhoon. Life here is stormier but I can stand it." He strides through the play like a typhoon, sometimes with the awful stillness of the central eye, but mostly in full blast. And at his first entrance he has reason, for he has just tripped over Ellie's tennis racket. There are no half measures about, "There's a hold-all and a handbag on the front steps for everyone to fall over, also a tennis racket! Who the devil left them there?"

Next to come on stage is Lady Utterword, mistress of Government House and used to demanding and receiving unquestioning obedience. She instantly goes into a tirade at her reception. This may end in tears, but they are tears of fury, not weakness.

And then, like the sun rising with warmth enough to melt all clouds, Hesione—Shaw's ideal woman, wife, mother, lover, friend—bursts upon us. "Ellie, my darling!" No weakness here, no apology—just a wave of all encompassing charm with mischief ever bubbling just below the surface.

Mangan, on the other hand, makes a discreet entrance: he is anxious to be mistaken for the gentleman he aims to become. So what does Shaw do? Out of the blue Shotover points an accusing finger at him and thunders, "You're going to marry Dunn's daughter. Don't. You're too old." Mangan's veneer dissolves and the raw tycoon is shouting back. As the play continues hardly a moment passes for Mangan without someone baiting or insulting him, driving him to furious rejoinder or abject tears.

So the play goes, one confrontation after another.

Of course, there are modulations. But even in the descriptive scenes the energy level can and should be sustained. When Ellie tells Hesione of her secret love and Hesione recalls the symptoms with such warmth and understanding sympathy, Ellie cries out, "Hesione, you're a witch!" and pours out the tale of Marcus Darnley with all the unrestrained delight of being able to confide the ecstasy of one's first great love.

Mazzini Dunn is naturally mild and mousy. So Shaw immediately puts him in the position of having to assert with all his energy to an imperious Shotover that he is NOT Billie Dunn but Mazzini Dunn, a very different person.

Nor is Randall a strong character. Until provoked by Lady Utterword, he has all the assurance of a professional, upper-class house guest. But when Hector and Lady Utterword tease and torment hint he screams back like a spoiled child.

And Billie Dunn the burglar lacks nothing in self assurance. It is his stock in trade to make himself heard.

The secret of Hector lies in the fact that, under the clear-cut tones and confident manner of the English officer and gentleman, smolders a fire stoked by unused talents and masculine energies denied. He is a latent volcano. "What were you shouting about?" asks Hesione as she cones in on Hector's great scene with Shotover in which they consider the desirability of exterminating the Mangans of the world. Shouting, she says—not talking be it noted. "Oh, he's madder than ever," Hector replies. But he loves the old man—they talk on the same plane and they have a divine discontent within them. Women who love their fathers will often marry men of the same fibre; yes, and when the daughter turns away from the father as Addie turned from Shotover, her husband is very likely to appear a numbskull to the rejected father.

As a young man I'm sure Hector fought in the Boer War, but found peace-time soldiering and the conversation and interests of his fellow officers intolerably boring. So he embarks on Burton of Arabia free-style adventuring from Cape Town to Damascus, even becoming a Moslem and wearing Arab dress. In Zanzibar he meets Hesione and falls under her spell. At the time of the play he is a handsome man of fifty, dangerously at a loose end. Hardly does the curtain fall (I imagine) but he dashes up to London and offers his services and knowledge of the Near East for the Secret Service. The Dardanelles, Turkey. He is landed by a British submarine at Istanbul, disguised as a Prussian Colonel. He arrives at Deraa just in time to witness Lawrence of Arabia's humiliation. Invited by the lascivious Turkish commander to join in the fun he forgets his cover and exclaims, "Is there no honor among gentlemen? I'd rather die!" So they shoot him—much to the relief of Colonel Lawrence, who is well aware of Hector's reputation as a teller of tall stories.

It was Captain Shotover who invented the tank; and Hesione turned Heartbreak House into a hospital for convalescent officers. Ellie worked there as a nurse, and when a dashing young officer with a striking resemblance to Hector fell in love with her she found that her heart had mended and married him. They were as happy as the fact that he had never been trained to earn a living permitted. Fortunately, Ellie discovered a talent for writing detective stories and was able to keep him in the manner to which his aristocratic background accustomed him.

Program Note

Heartbreak House, written during World War I, is set in England just before that war. However, in the third act, as a symbol of the wrath to come, Shaw introduces the first air raid ever known to man—by German lighter-than-air Zeppelin dirigibles.

The plot of the play is concerned with the question—should beautiful Ellie Dunn marry "the bloated capitalist" Boss Mangan?

While there are few aspects of life illuminated by Shaw's piercing vision and witty pen that are not explored, two main themes emerge.

The first insists that people with the advantages of money, education and lies, instead of leading "foolish lives of romance and sentiment and snobbery," should concern themselves with the governments of their country and not leave it to unscrupulous manipulators.

The second theme declares that the pursuit of money never justifies the loss of integrity. In the words of Captain Shotover, one of Shaw's great character creations, "If you sell yourself, you deal your soul a blow that all the books and pictures and concerts and scenery in the world won't heal."

Index

Numbers in **bold italic** indicate pages with illustrations or photographs.

Across the Wide Missouri (film) 15, 245–247, ***247***, 249, 251, 371
Affairs of State (play) 60, 139, 314, 368
Aherne, Brian 46, 151, 181–183, 185, 186, 209, 238, 278, 283, 284, 294, 296
And So to Bed (play) 92–94, 112, 363, 367
Archibald Kenrick and Sons 13, 26

Barnes, Kenneth 74, 75, 83; *see also* Royal Academy of Dramatic Arts (R.A.D.A.)
Batman (film) 312, 313, 372
Batman (television series) 1, 2, 231, 244, 288, 302, 307–314, ***308***, ***309***, ***310***, ***312***, 319, 323–325, 329, 335, 337, 349, 353–357, ***354***, 373, 374
Bayliss, Lillian 141; *see also* Old Vic
Bevill, Nancy *see* Pethybridge, Emily Nancy Bevill
Big Jim McClain (film) 248, 249, 371
Birmingham Repertory Theatre 71, 185
Birmingham University 66, 68, 70
Bitter Sweet (film) 170
Bitter Sweet (play) 1, 103, 105–112, ***106***, ***108***, 114, 115, 117, 134, 143, 144, 192, 343, 364
Butcher, Gary 340, 343, 349, ***351***, 352

Campbell, Mrs. Patrick 82, 211, 281
Carver, Humphrey 33–35, 43, 337
Chamberlain, Arthur Neville 12, 19, 20, 211, 22, 25, 27, 112, 166, 184, 205
Chamberlain, Joseph Austen 12, 19, 75
Chamberlain, Joseph III 11, 12, 14, 16, 35, 172
The Cherry Orchard (play) 85, 86, 90, 140, 173, 361–363, 365
Clifton College 16, 52, 56–59, 61–66, 68, 70, 74, 81, 83, 84, 97, 174, 257, 357
Colman, Ronald 76, 183, 204, 369
Cooper, Gladys 19, 123, 124, 128–132, ***130***, 197, 198, 238, 240, 281–283, 303
Coriolanus (play) 256–258, ***257***, 316, 367
Coulouris, George 18, 240, 253
Coward, Noël 1, 103–105, 109, 137, 138, 140, 171, 253, 362, 364, 365
Craig, Yvonne 312, 353–356, ***354***, 359
Criss Cross (film) 234, ***234***, 244, 370

De Ledesna, John Justinian *see* Justin, John
Dial "M" for Murder (play) 239, 255, 256, ***255***, ***256***, 331, 332, 367

Dr. Knock (play) 93, 94, 99, 100, ***100***, 363
Don't Call Me Charlie (television series) 300–302, ***301***, 316, 317, 373
Downing, Jennifer Dickens (Poppet) 199, 203, 208, 211, 212, 214, 222, 248, 249, ***273***, 273, 274, 287, 304, 335, 345, 352
Dozier, William 1, 244, 308–310, 313
Draper, Ruth 26
du Maurier, Gerald 60, 61, 76, 77, 95, 120, 121–129, ***125***, 134, 138, 164, 182, 253, 281, 366

Elliott's Metal Works 66, 71

Fagan, James Bernard 82–86, 92–94, 102, 153, 361, 363, 367, 375
Filippi, Rosina 48, 76, 77
Fontaine, Joan 46, 182, 196, 227, 267, 370, 371

Gardiner, Reginald 78, 312
George, Gladys 193, 194, ***194***
Gere, Charles 37, ***37***
Gertie (play) 251–254, ***254***, 261, 282, 286, 367
Gielgud, Sir John 6, 82, 92, 144, 272, 336, 337, 354, 371
Gielgud, Val 142
Gip *see* Hawksley, Aileen Dickens
Goolden, Richard 82, 83, 100, 166
Granny and Her God (play) 160–162, ***161***
The Green Pack (play) 120, 121, 123, 125–128, ***125***
Grey, Mary 82, 85, ***152***, 153, 164
"The Grove" 23, 25, 28, 31–34, 36, 44, 49, 50
Guthrie, Tyrone 6, 82, 92, 144, 272, 336, 337, 354, 371

Harvey, John Martin 102, 162–164, 173, 211, 313, 316
Hawksley, Aileen Dickens (Gip) 90, 198–203, 208–216, 222, 223, 235, 238–240, 245–249, 253–261, ***256***, 274–278, 281–285, 287, 294–297, 306
Heartbreak House (play) 82, 93, 99, 115, 149–153, ***152***, 343–347, ***346***, ***347***, 363, 368, 375–378
Hitchcock, Alfred 122, 123, 124, 129, 171, 270, 288, 299, 316, 331, 332
Houseman, John 61, 97, 125, 176, 184, 195, 238, 251, 257, 262, 265, 272, 278, 284, 285, 291, 316, 329, 349, 350, ***350***, ***351***, 352

The Invisible Man Returns (film) 188, 189, ***189***, 369

Index

Joan of Arc (film) 231, 246, **246**, 349, 370
Justin, John 145–147, 160, 162, 284

Karloff, Boris 278, 280, 281, 290, 293, 297, 370, 371
Kenrick, Sir George 25–27
Kenrick, Millicent Mary (mother) 7, 8, **9**, 10, 12, 13, 14, 16, 17, 19, 20, 25, 29, 30, 33, 36, 39–46, 48–52, 54, 64, 71, 78, 79, 81, 84, 88, 112, 117, 119, 238, 338
Kenrick, William (grandfather) 11, 12, 16, 23, 25
King, John Edward 63, 64

Lady in Waiting (play) 193, 194, 194, 196, 367
The Lake (play) 134, 135, 137, 181, 365
Laughton, Charles 78, 84, 95, 140, 141, 164, 169, 249, 371
Lee, Auriol 109, 129–131, 165, 181
Lewton, Val 205, 207, 232, 238, 251, 278–280. 340
Lion, Leon M. 95, 96, 100, 102, 103, 112, 120, 135
Little Lord Fauntleroy (play) 110, **111**, 113, 144, 365
Loyalties (film) 134–137, **136**, 167, 168, 170, 181, 369
Loyalties (play) 95, 96, 103, 364

Macbeth (film) 231, 314–316, **314**, **315**, 343–345, 370
Macbeth (play) 52–54
Mademoiselle Fifi (film) 2, **2**, 206, 207, 217, 370
Martin-Harvey, Sir John *see* Harvey, John Martin
Mayor, Henry Bickersteth 56, 57, 59, 60, 62, 64, 83
method acting 77, 116, 262, 376
Miller, Gilbert 129–131, 133, 254

Napier, Alan: appendicitis 7, 53, 54; birth 8; breakdown 99; and cricket 50, 52, 54, 55, 182, 183, 240, 322; death 357–358; and dogs 30–33, 32, 35, 40, 57, 110, 140, 199, 200, 222, 223, 238, 249, 251, 255, 256, 256, 258–260, 295, 306, 312, 316–319, 318; height 6, 204, 236, 237, 237, 289, 304, 321, 331; and horses 42, 43, 191, 242, 248; and Maxalding 69, 90, 311; and motorcycles 64, 68–70, 107; nearsightedness 1, 6, 54, 144, 184, 189, 244; personal politics 182, 184, 246, 247, 263, 264, 276, 277, 284, 350; and rugby 70; and sex 66, 68, 69, 77, 89–91, 98, 100, 101, 145, 146, 160, 247, 282; stammer 6, 23, 35, 36, 39, 50, 51, 57, 58, 59, 72, 74, 75, 84, 87, 101, 114, 121, 126, 127, 142, 170, 256; and volleyball 239, 311, 317, 320, 322
Napier, Alan Bertram (uncle) 16, 17, 20, 40, 41, 61, 66, 71, 338
Napier, Arthur Lenox (uncle) 16, 17
Napier, Mark 8, 9, **9**, 23, 30, 31, **32**, 33–36, 40–43, **40**, 45, 48–50, 56, 66, 98, 118, 195, 335, 337
Napier-Clavering, Charles Warren (uncle) 16, 17
Napier-Clavering, Claude Gerald (father) 8, 9, 11, 15, 16, 29, 30, **38**, 39–41, 43–46, 48, 49, 52, 66, 70, 71, 79, 91, 117–119, 160–162, 214
Napier-Clavering, Henry Percy (uncle) 16, 17, 30, 46, 99, 100
Napier-Clavering, Mary Helen (Molly) 8, 9, **9**, 23, 31, **32**, 33–36, 38, 40, **40**, 42–44, 66, 108, 165–166, 259, 274, 276, 338
Nichols, Christie (granddaughter) 259, 273, 312, 320, 322, 337, 338, **338**, 352, 357–359

Nichols, David (grandson) 239, 273, 319–321, **321**, 337, 343, 357
Nichols, Jennifer (daughter) 3, 108, 116, 119, 183, 195, 196, **197**, 203, 208, 211, 240, 273, 275, 306, 320, 345, **349**, 357, 359
Nichols, Robert (son-in-law) 127, 210, 273, 275, 306, 320, 345, **349**, 359

Old Vic 140–142, 153, 157, 365, 366
Olivier, Laurence 76, 143, 144, 153, 157, 164, 185, 354
Oxford Players 82, 84, 88, 93, 94, 99, 100, 102, 144, 153, 272, 280, 331, 343, 363, 375

Packwood Haugh 50–56, **54**
Pennyworth, Alfred (character) 1, 244, 267, 288, 307–313, **308**, **309**, **310**, **312**, 321, 323, 353, 355
Pethybridge, Emily Nancy Bevill 107–110, **108**, 116, 118–120, 126, 144–148, 160, 162, 165, 174, 195, 196, **197**, 208, 212, 240, 247
Porto Marina Way 209, 210, **210**, 213, 214, 222, 223, 235, 293, 306, 307, 320, 321, 340, 341, 343, 352–354, 357, 359

Raine, Gypsy *see* Hawksley, Aileen Dickens
Raine, Jennifer *see* Downing, Jennifer Dickens
Rains, Claude 76, 97
Rankine, Ian 109, 110, 145
Rankine, Muriel 109, 110, 165
Rathbone Basil 137, 170, 181, 183, 261, 266, 286, 369
"Rivernook" 118, 160, 162
Royal Academy of Dramatic Arts (R.A.D.A.) 48, 64, 72, 74–76, 78, 81, 83, 109, 128, 134, 162, 183, 306–307, 361, 363–364, 366–367

Sanders, George 183, 191, 199–201, 204, 205, 215–217, 225, 229, 369–371
Sayers, Dorothy L. 156–159, 367
Shaw, George Bernard 82, 93, 99, 137, 140, 149, 150–153, 173, 253, 291, 322, 343–346, 361–363, 366, 368, 375–378
Shaw, Glen Byam 82, 89, 90, 93, 94, 144, 275
Shumlin, Herman 251–253
Sprigge, Elizabeth 66, 71, 118, 119, 160
Storm (play) 84, 85, 88, 104, 185, 186, 361

Tal-y-bont, Wales 19, 39, **40**, 41
Tempest, Marie 114–117, 137, 186, 193, 283
"Tennal Grange" 7, 17, 29, **32**, 33–35, 41, 44, 49, 53, 70, 83, 118

Under Milk Wood (play) 39, 314, 322, 343, 344, **344**, 352, 358, 368
The Uninvited (film) 215, **216**, 217, 236, 358, 369

Vanburgh, Irene 60, 74
Vance, Jeffrey 348–352, **350**
van Druten, John 109, 185–188
Varden, Norma 1, 2, **2**, 231, 243, 348

Webber, Peggy 343–347
Welles, Orson 98, 142, 143, 176–177, 231, 258, 276, 277, *277*, 314, 315, *315*, 316, 343, 345, 370
West, Adam 1, *310*, 311, 353–356, 372
Whale, James 82, 85, 86, 90, 93, 94, 144, 275

Williams, Emlyn 82, 93, ***256***, 363
Williams, John 289, 290, 331–334, ***332***
Wood, Peggy 103–106, 170

The Zeal of Thy House (play) 156–160, 367

www.ingramcontent.com/pod-product-compliance
Lightning Source LLC
Chambersburg PA
CBHW081534300426
44116CB00015B/2626